THE
SILENCE
AND THE
SCORPION

THE
SILENCE
AND THE
SCORPION

※

*The Coup Against Chávez
and the Making of
Modern Venezuela*

BRIAN A. NELSON

NATION BOOKS
NEW YORK

Copyright © 2009 by Brian A. Nelson

Published by
Nation Books, A Member of the Perseus Books Group
116 East 16th Street, 8th Floor
New York, NY 10003
Nation Books is a co-publishing venture of the Nation Institute and the Perseus
Books Group.

Books published by Nation Books are available at special discounts for bulk
purchases in the United States by corporations, institutions, and other organizations.
For more information, please contact the Special Markets Department at the Perseus
Books Group, 2300 Chestnut Street, Suite 200, Philadelphia, PA 19103, or call
(800) 255-1514, or e-mail special.markets@perseusbooks.com.

All maps courtesy of the author
Designed by Brent Wilcox

Library of Congress Cataloging-in-Publication Data
Nelson, Brian A.
   The silence and the scorpion : the coup against Chávez and the making of
modern Venezuela / Brian A. Nelson.
      p.   cm.
   Includes bibliographical references and index.
   ISBN 978-1-56858-418-8 (alk. paper)
   1. Venezuela—History—Attempted coup, 2002.   2. Chávez Frías, Hugo.
I. Title.
   F2329.N45 2009
   987.06'42—dc22
                                                                    2008049104

10 9 8 7 6 5 4 3 2 1

For Natalia
and for the Rubio family

Sound, sound the clarion, fill the fife!

To all the sensual world proclaim,

One crowded hour of glorious life

Is worth an age without a name.

SIR WALTER SCOTT

CONTENTS

A NOTE TO READERS

This is the story of the three-day coup against Venezuelan president Hugo Chávez in 2002.

The information in this book comes from every available source, but principally from the more than forty protagonists I interviewed, including many victims of the street violence, the leaders of the military uprising, Interim President Pedro Carmona, U.S. Ambassador to Venezuela Charles Shapiro, and President Chávez's closest advisers. Most sources were interviewed multiple times. Almost all of them permitted me to tape-record our interviews which helped me tremendously in capturing the narrative flow of each individual's story in their exact words.

It was my goal to re-create the experience of these three turbulent days through the eyes of those who were involved. The thoughts, feelings, and dialogue that I attribute to the participants come either from the persons themselves, colleagues, or witnesses, or—in the case of many public officials—from the TV and print media. All dialogue has been confirmed with the original speaker, or when this was not possible, it was heard by more than one witness or appears in the written record.

The men and women I interviewed were exceedingly generous with their time and forthright about their experiences. Of course, people's recollections, particularly in times of intense stress, are not perfect and on several occasions I found that two people standing side by side remembered events very differently. To deal with these discrepancies, I have looked for alternative sources, but at times it has been necessary to simply rely on the best memory of those involved. To address the intense polarization that grips Venezuela, I have attempted to balance the chapters so that the reader can see the coup from multiple perspectives simultaneously.

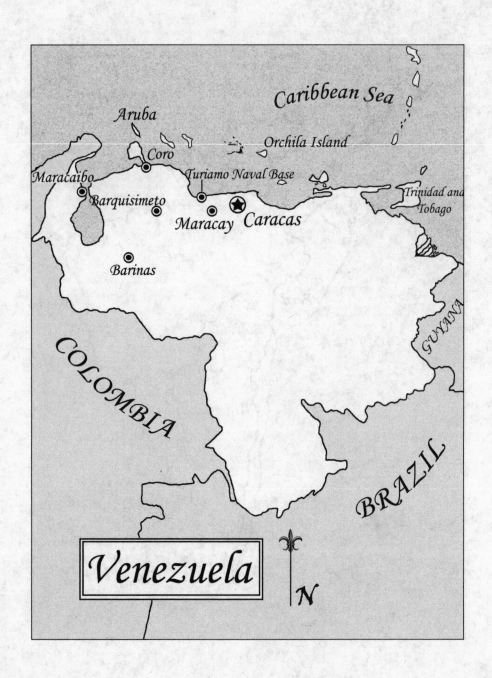

PRINCIPAL CHARACTERS

The Opposition Marchers

Malvina Pesate—A forty-six-year-old architect and member of the Primero Justicia (Justice First) political party. She would be one of the first gunshot victims on Baralt Avenue.

Mohamad "Mike" Merhi—An immigrant from Lebanon. He would lose track of his son, Jesús, in the chaos of the battle.

Carlos Ciordia—The mild-mannered attorney who thought that bringing his sister and parents to the march would make a fun family outing.

Andrés Trujillo—A twenty-eight-year-old graphic designer who was shot on Baralt Avenue and taken to the overwhelmed Vargas Hospital.

The Chávez Loyalists

Douglas Romero—A thirty-eight-year-old grade school teacher and marathon runner who would help the Bolivarian Circles repel the marchers and police.

Dr. Alberto Espidel, MD—A doctor who, with his son, would give first aid to the Chávez supporters wounded in the fighting.

Antonio Návas—A former secret police officer who was shot through the jaw near the palace of Miraflores.

The Journalists

Luis Alfonso Fernández—The only reporter to get his camera crew near the palace before the march arrived. His footage of the pro-Chávez gunmen would tip public opinion against the president.

Francisco Toro—A freelance reporter who was one of the few journalists to venture out during the news blackout on April 13.

Gabriel Osorio—A photographer for an anti-Chávez newspaper *El Nacional* who would break the blackout and try to sneak into Miraflores on April 13.

The Politicians

General Francisco Usón—Chávez's finance minister would feed the president vital information about the conspiring generals.

Dr. Pedro Carmona—The head of Venezuela's huge business guild, Fedecámaras, would become interim president of Venezuela.

Guillermo García Ponce—An old hard-line communist and veteran of the guerrilla wars of the 1960s. He would lead the civilian effort to restore Chávez.

Luis Miquilena—Another veteran communist who had engineered Chávez's election victory in 1998 but would denounce Chávez on national television for causing the bloodshed on April 11.

The Generals

General Lucas Rincón—Inspector general of the armed forces and close aide to Chávez. He would announce the president's resignation on national television.

General Manuel Rosendo—Supreme commander of Venezuela's armed forces. He would refuse the president's orders to use the army against the march.

General Jorge Carneiro—A Chávez loyalist who defied the other generals and tried to send tanks to the palace to help the president.

General Efraín Vásquez Velasco—Head of the Venezuelan army. When the dust cleared he would be the most powerful man in the country.

General Raúl Baduel—A devout Taoist and founding member of Chávez's revolutionary movement. He would lead the rescue mission to save Chávez.

Introduction
The Rise of Hugo Chávez

It was just before dawn on February 4, 1992, when a young thirty-seven-year-old lieutenant colonel named Hugo Chávez attempted to overthrow the Venezuelan government. He was the leader of one of five rogue army units that made simultaneous attacks throughout the country. Three of the units planned to capture key military bases in the cities of Maracaibo, Valencia, and Maracay, while another unit seized the military airport in the heart of Caracas. Hugo Chávez's mission was to capture President Carlos Andrés Pérez. Chávez knew that Pérez was returning from a state visit abroad and hoped to capture him at the Maiquetía airport, an hour north of the capital, but when that portion of the plan failed—because Pérez had been tipped off to the conspiracy—it fell on Chávez to capture him at the presidential palace. However, heavy machine-gun fire soon stopped the assault in its tracks, and as Chávez's soldiers and tanks engaged in a bloody firefight with troops loyal to Pérez, the president slipped unnoticed out the back of the palace. Fleeing to a local TV station, Pérez quickly rallied the rest of the military. Chávez, pinned down and realizing that it was useless to keep fighting, surrendered.

Even though the coup had failed, the other rogue commanders still controlled the military bases and the airport they had assaulted. Some made it clear that they were ready to fight to the last man. In an attempt to avoid further loss of life, Chávez was permitted to make a nationally televised plea to his co-conspirators. He appeared before the nation in his green fatigues and his red paratrooper beret, exhausted but remarkably poised:

> Comrades, regrettably, *for now*, the objectives that we had set were un-
> obtainable in the capital. That is to say, we here in Caracas could not take
> power. You have done well where you are, but now it is time to avoid
> more bloodshed. . . . So listen to my words. Listen to Commander
> Chávez who is sending this message so that you may reflect and put
> down your arms because, now, in all honesty, the plans we had at the na-
> tional level will be impossible to reach. . . . I thank you for your loyalty,
> I thank you for your valor, your self-sacrifice, and I, before the country
> and you, assume responsibility for this Bolivarian military movement.
> Thank you.

It became known as the "for now" speech. *Por ahora.* Chávez spoke for less than two minutes. His words were rushed, and he was not the confi-dent orator he would later become, but in those few seconds the little-known lieutenant colonel was catapulted into the political spotlight. However, instead of his being widely ostracized, many Venezuelans stood up and cheered. By the time of the annual Mardi Gras festival, the mas-querade costume of choice for little boys was the green fatigues and red beret of Hugo Chávez.

Why would people rally around a renegade army officer who had just trampled the constitution and tried to install himself as a dictator? To un-derstand that, one must first understand the intense frustration that a vast majority of Venezuelans felt toward their elected leaders, and to appreciate *that*, one needs to be familiar with the lifeblood of Venezuela: oil.

Venezuela occupies a special place in Latin America because, unlike its neighbors, it once knew (or almost knew) great wealth and prosperity. What much of the world considered its oil "crisis" of the 1970s was a decade of unparalleled affluence and modernization in Venezuela—the world's fifth largest oil producer. This was the time of the *Little Saudi* Venezuela. GDP per capita was the highest in history and the exchange rate was four bolivares to the U.S. dollar (in 2001 it was over seven hun-dred). In fact, the government coffers were so bulging with oil revenue and the exchange rate was so favorable that workers down to taxi drivers could take the morning flight to Miami, spend the day shopping or playing on the beach, then grab the evening flight back to Caracas. In the shops of Florida they were known as the *dáme-dos*, or "give-me-twos." They would look at the price of an item and invariably cry, "Wow, it's cheap! Give me two." Their neighbors in Colombia often commented, "The Venezuelans fell out of the trees and into Cadillacs." And the gains of the 1970s were not limited to consumption: Literacy rose from 77 percent to 93 percent in the course of the decade, and fertility rates fell—an indicator of both better education and increasing gender equality.

But from the early 1980s, Venezuelans watched their country—which had seemed so close to first-world prosperity—sink deeper and deeper into recession. Poverty, inflation, and unemployment skyrocketed, while per capita income plummeted. The oil bonanza had been illusory and fleeting. Not only had the government spent lavishly on wasteful projects, but corruption and pilfering were rampant. Capital flight soared, the high oil prices didn't last, and the debts piled up. By the end of the 1970s, Venezuela had the highest per capita debt in Latin America and had fallen into the same debt trap that plagues so much of the developing world—exporting its natural resources to finance its debt instead of developing social programs. But perhaps the most revealing indicator of the collapse was the increase in violent crime. It seemed that everyone had at least one family member who had been mugged, carjacked, or killed.

Year after year the situation deteriorated, and year after year the collective sense of outrage at the government grew stronger. People knew that this was a nation of extreme wealth and promise—it still sat atop the largest oil deposits outside the Middle East—but those resources were being squandered by corrupt and incompetent politicians who neglected the 60 percent of Venezuelans who remained poor.

When Hugo Chávez exploded onto the scene in 1992, many people applauded. In Chávez they saw someone taking a stand against the corrupt system; someone brave enough to risk his life to change Venezuela. Viewed as an outsider, Chávez, with his coffee-and-cream skin and humble background, seemed more in tune with the needs of the poor and disenfranchised than the light-skinned leaders who dominated politics. And even though Chávez was put in jail after the coup attempt, his popularity grew, until, in March 1994, he was given a presidential pardon by newly elected

President Rafael Caldera. Upon his release, Chávez immediately began building his political machine: the Movement of the Fifth Republic (MVR).

By the 1998 election, Venezuela's economic collapse had become so devastating that voters were ready for radical change. During the administration of outgoing President Caldera, two-thirds of the country's banks had collapsed and inflation had eroded the currency by 345 percent in just five years. So disenchanted was the electorate that neither of the two traditional parties could launch a successful campaign. The election came down to two outsiders: Henrique Salas Römer and Hugo Chávez.

Disgusted by politics, barely half the electorate bothered to vote—the lowest turnout in Venezuelan history and down from 81 percent a decade earlier. Hugo Chávez won with 56 percent of those votes. And while the details of the promised "Bolivarian Revolution" remained nebulous, people were ready to take a chance on a charismatic unknown in order to turn the country around. A brilliant orator, Chávez would flow effortlessly from Marx, to the Bible, to Pablo Neruda. He had run on a platform that called for an end to corruption and promised that the oil wealth would be enjoyed by everyone. For many Venezuelans, Chávez's promised Bolivarian Revolution eponymously tapped into a notion of renewal and rebirth. Once in office, Chávez set out to make sweeping changes, beginning with the constitution. In 1999, a very pro-Chávez Constitutional Assembly (his alliance had cleverly gained control of 122 of its 131 seats) created a new 350-article constitution. With some creative interpretation of the law, the assembly also dissolved the Supreme Court and appointed new judges (all loyal to Chávez) as well as many other public officials. In the "megaelections" required by the new constitution in 2000, Chávez was reelected to a six-year term. He also went from having only a third of the seats in the legislature to having a two-thirds majority. Only a year and a half in office and Chávez had already gained unprecedented control over the three branches of government.

But Chávez soon ran into trouble. Acrimonious clashes with the church, the media, and business and labor groups drove down his approval ratings. He alienated the United States and many Venezuelans by forging close ties with Iraq, Iran, and Libya. Then he openly criticized the U.S. invasion of Afghanistan. The economy, meanwhile, was still in shambles. In 1999, his first year in office, the economy contracted by 10 percent while unemployment rose to 20 percent—its highest level in fifteen years. Investors, too, were pulling their money out of Venezuela at an alarming rate. Capital flight, $4 billion in 1999, would reach $9 billion by 2002. All this, it should be noted, occurred during a tripling of oil prices; the first time in Venezuelan history that the economy had contracted during an oil boom.

Yet most detrimental to Chávez's popularity was his relationship with Fidel Castro. The extent of the close friendship between Chávez and the Cuban dictator came to light in the fall of 1999 when the newly elected Chávez went to Havana on a state visit and was seen playing baseball and warmly embracing Castro. Trade agreements and more state visits quickly followed. Venezuela "is going in the same direction, toward the same sea where the Cuban nation is going, the sea of happiness," Chávez said famously, encapsulating his desire to remake Venezuela in Cuba's image. By 2000, Venezuela had become Cuba's biggest trading partner, selling oil to the island at rock-bottom prices in exchange for legions of Cuban physicians, health care workers, agricultural advisers, sports trainers, and—critics claimed—paramilitaries and intelligence officers. Following Castro's example, Chávez consolidated the bicameral legislature into one National Assembly and started local community groups of loyal party members, which some claimed were being trained as paramilitaries. Many Venezuelans were mortified; they felt they had been tricked and were afraid that Chávez, too, had dictatorial aims.

It was in response to this "cubanization" that the opposition movement against Chávez was born: A group of mothers realized that their children's new textbooks were really Cuban schoolbooks, heavily infused with revolutionary propaganda, with new covers. They organized in protest.

By the summer of 2001 a movement that had begun as a few concerned mothers had ballooned into a massive amalgamation of labor unions, business interests, church groups, and a hodgepodge of both right- and left-wing political parties with only one goal: getting rid of Chávez. What's more, the private TV stations and newspapers, many of which had initially supported Chávez, turned fiercely against him, accelerating the pendulum swing in his popularity.

But at the same time, Chávez's own supporters had coalesced into a well-organized and loyal group. Their passion for their president bordered on idolatry, especially among the poor because, even though the economy was still deteriorating, Chávez was giving them something that no president had given them before: hope. He started progressive social programs that provided health care and education to many who had long been neglected under the old two-party system. The president's program of participatory democracy—everything from popular referendums to town hall meetings to the building of community groups—also gave people a sense of self-worth; they felt that through Chávez they could make a difference.

Two important events set the stage for the inevitable showdown between Chávez and the opposition. The first was in November 2001, when Chávez exercised the Enabling Law (*ley habilitante*) and enacted forty-nine laws in one night without approval from the National Assembly. The new laws included dramatic changes to the government, the oil industry, and land usage and were enacted on the very last day that Chávez had the decree privilege. To the opposition, this was proof that Chávez was a dictator-in-training. In response, they organized the first nationwide strike that paralyzed the country. With the success of the strike the opposition movement gathered new strength and in January held another strike. By now, huge anti-Chávez marches, numbering in the hundreds of thousands, had become regular events.

The opposing factions were set on a collision course: On one side was the opposition, which had control of the business and labor sectors. On the other was President Chávez, who had control of the government and, albeit tenuously, the military. In the middle lay PDVSA (Petroleos de Venezuela)—the state-owned oil company. Although officially owned by the government, PDVSA operated much like a private company and was, without a doubt, the lifeblood of the economy, accounting for 70 percent of the nation's export revenue. It was the jewel in the crown: Whoever controlled PDVSA controlled Venezuela.

At the end of March came the second event that precipitated the coup. Alarmed by the opposition's ability to shut down the economy (and oil production with it), Chávez decided to take tighter control of PDVSA. First, he replaced the board of directors with his political allies; then he began moving down the chain of command and firing all who opposed him. If anything was going to rile up the electorate of this oil-dependent nation it was a change to PDVSA; the opposition took it as a declaration of war. They quickly called for a general strike, which was extended one day and then another. The country ground to a halt and Chávez's fall appeared imminent. Never before had the people put such incredible pressure on a Venezuelan head of state. His 80 percent approval rating had fallen to 30 percent. Sensing disaster, Chávez's allies in government, industry, and the military began abandoning him at an alarming rate. On the third day of the strike, April 11, 2002, a huge anti-Chávez rally, numbering close to a million people, marched on the presidential palace to demand his resignation. Yet, despite the incredible pressure, Chávez was not to go quietly.

This is the story of what came next, during the three days when South America's oldest democracy would be put to its greatest test. On the first day of the crisis alone, 19 people would be killed and over 150 wounded outside Chávez's palace in an afternoon of confusion and bloodshed. The violence would spark a military revolt and the ousting of President Chávez, which, in turn, would precipitate looting, political witch hunts, and more violence. In a crisis that lasted only seventy-two hours, Venezuela would go through three presidents. In the wake of the crisis, fingers would be pointed everywhere—at President Chávez, the military, the opposition leaders, the news media, and the United States. There would be so much political posturing that few knew the truth about what had happened. What's more, the changing of regimes would destroy any chance of an impartial investigation. In the wake of the coup both sides would fund TV specials, books, and documentary films to spin the event for political ends, depicting themselves as the true victims of what they claimed had been a conspiracy. As a result, the coup would become one of the most important, yet most misunderstood, events in recent history.

PART ONE
THE MARCH
April 11, 2002

A Confrontation between Brothers.
> —Government title given to the events of April 11

The Massacre of the Silence.
> —Opposition title given to the events of April 11

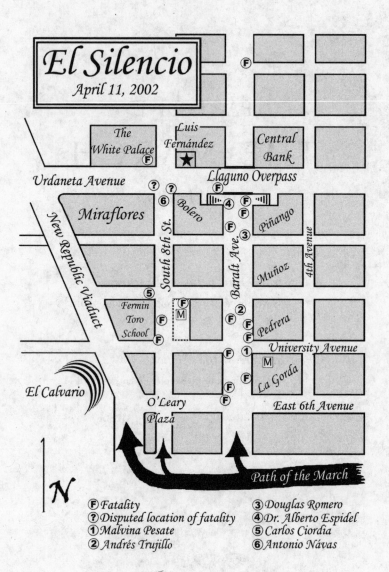

El Silencio

April 11, 2002

Urdaneta Avenue

The White Palace Ⓕ

Luis Fernández ★

Central Bank

Llaguno Overpass

Ⓕ

Miraflores

South 8th St.

Bolero

Baralt Ave.

Piñango

Muñoz

4th Avenue

Fermín Toro School

M

Pedrera

University Avenue

La Gorda

M

East 6th Avenue

O'Leary Plaza

El Calvario

New Republic Viaduct

N

Path of the March

Ⓕ Fatality
❓ Disputed location of fatality
① Malvina Pesate
② Andrés Trujillo
③ Douglas Romero
④ Dr. Alberto Espidel
⑤ Carlos Ciordia
⑥ Antonio Návas

1 | The Call to Miraflores

10:00 A.M.

Emocionada. Malvina Pesate was very excited. How could she not be? If there was a place to be in Venezuela today—in all of Latin America, for that matter—then it was here. Right here. In this march. Never had she seen so many people, and scarcely could she have imagined so many if she'd tried. There had been big marches before, plenty in the past year, but nothing like this. An awesome river of people, filling both directions of a four-lane highway and stretching for kilometers. People with portable radios were saying that it was more than a million people—almost a third of the population of Metro Caracas. She believed it. And this was no somber procession, it was a huge rolling party, Venezuelan style. People were blowing whistles, playing guitars, beating drums, chanting political songs, and, of course, doing *cacerolazos. Cacerolazos,* or casserole strikes, were the popular form of protest where people banged their biggest ladle against their noisiest pot like a drum. In recent months, at a predetermined time—usually in the evening—everyone opposed to Chávez would come out of their homes and do a *cacerolazo,* and the sound could be heard all over the city, echoing into the hills. As the march moved through the street, people in the high-rise apartments were cheering them on with *cacerolazos,* making an incessant, unremitting *clang-clang-clang-clang-clang-clang-clang.* Malvina looked up and saw one apartment where the residents had dispensed with the laborious task of actually hitting their pots and pans together, had placed loudspeakers on their patio, and were blasting the *cacerolazo* CD at airport decibels. Malvina loved it. All

11

that noise. It reminded her of being a kid again. Here you were supposed to make as much noise as you could. It was allowed.

Around her people were chanting:

Esta es la ruta,
esta es la ruta,
esta es la ruta
pa' sacar este hijo de puta.

(This is the route,
this is the route,
this is the route
to kick this son of a bitch out.)

Undulating above this sea of bodies, bobbing like buoys, were thousands upon thousands of homemade signs and banners. Up ahead Malvina saw one with a picture of a toilet with President Chávez and Fidel Castro sticking their heads out. It read, "Same shit." Another read, "Long live Chávez!!! . . . in Cuba." And then there were all the political parties with their banners and matching T-shirts—big clumps of red, green, yellow, and white. There was Bandera Roja, one of the communist parties; MAS (Movement to Socialism), a socialist party; Acción Democrática and Copei, the two parties that had shared power before Chávez; and Malvina's party, Primero Justicia, or Justice First. Of course, Malvina had diligently donned her bright yellow Primero Justicia T-shirt for the rally.

Today, Thursday, was the third day of a nationwide strike that had paralyzed Venezuela, and Malvina was in the midst of the largest civic protest in the history of the country. Around her were Venezuelans of every shade, make, and model. There were old people being pushed in wheelchairs, toddlers in strollers, teenagers with Limp Bizkit T-shirts, middle-aged couples with matching fanny packs, fat people, skinny people, light-skinned people, dark-skinned people, rich *sifrinos* (snobs) from neighborhoods like Chula Vista and Country Club, and poor *caimánes* (rednecks) from the shantytowns of Petare and Bolívar. People whose lives would normally never intersect were talking, singing, and playing music together; political rivals who just three years ago would have spit at each other now laughed and chatted. They had all been brought together by their venom for one man: Hugo Chávez. They had put aside their ordinary lives in order to get rid of him, to exorcise him, to purge him from Venezuela.

Malvina, forty-six, a very tall architect with short blond hair, came to all the marches because she felt the country had made a terrible mistake in electing Chávez. Malvina was Jewish, the daughter of Romanian immigrants. In fact, her father had survived the German concentration camps before coming to Venezuela after World War II.

Marching beside her was Gorka, her boyfriend of seventeen years. Gorka Lacasa was a stout, barrel-chested man with light skin and a kind face. His parents were originally from Guernica in the Basque country of Spain and had come to Venezuela after Franco bombed their home in 1937 (inspiring Picasso's famous painting). Gorka was also, like most Venezuelans, Catholic, which is why he and Malvina had never married . . . not officially anyway. It wasn't because they didn't want to, but because whenever the subject came up both their families erupted in protest over the proposed Catholic-Semitic union.

"Miraflores! Miraflores! Miraflores!" people chanted. All morning pockets of the crowd had been taking up this chant—the call to take the march to Chávez's doorstep, the presidential palace of Miraflores. Opposition marches were not allowed near Miraflores, and Chávez often deployed the National Guard around it on days like today in order to emphasize his point.

Malvina and Gorka soon came into Chuao, where the march was scheduled to end—at the headquarters of the national oil company PDVSA (Petroleos de Venezuela S.A.; the *S.A.* is the equivalent of *incorporated* in English). In this wide-open plaza Malvina got a better sense of how immense the march was. She was looking at a square kilometer of people. A high stage had been erected in front of PDVSA with enormous speakers, and from here the leaders of the opposition were rallying the crowd. And when they did, when the crowd really let loose, the noise reached such a crescendo that Malvina had to cover her ears. All those pots and pans and whistles and drums and shouting, it overwhelmed the senses.

In recent weeks, the battle between PDVSA and Chávez had become the focal point of the public outrage against the president. For Malvina, it was not simply that Chávez was firing PDVSA officials and handpicking their replacements, it was how he was doing it. The president was making it into a spectacle. Just four days ago, on Sunday, April 7, Chávez had fired seven more PDVSA officials during his weekly TV show, *Aló Presidente*.

"Eddy Ramírez, General Director, until today, of the Palmaven division. You're out!" Chávez had cried. "You had been given the responsibility of leading a very important business, Palmaven, a subsidiary of PDVSA. This Palmaven belongs to all Venezuelans. Anyway, Señor Eddy Ramírez, *muchas gracias*. You, sir, are dismissed." The firings had been done in front of a studio audience who cheered wildly as Chávez announced each dismissal. "In third place, the Manager of Strategic Negotiations. I will repeat the title." Here the president paused. "Do you see the title this person had, 'Manager of Strategic Negotiations'? Well, that would be like a member of the military high command." Then with a doubtful look the president asked, "This is a member of the high command?" Then with a thrust of his hand he cried, "You're out! Horacio Medina, you were, Mister Medina, until today, Manager of Strategic Negotiations. *Muchas gracias* for your services, Señor Medina." Again the audience had cheered, and on it went through the list of names. "In seventh place is an analyst, a lady. *Muchas gracias,* señora. Analyst for PDVSA Gas Projects, Carmen Elisa Hernández. Thank you very *very* much, Señora Hernández, for your work and for your service. These seven people have been dismissed from Petroleos de Venezuela, and this is going to continue." Chavez went on to explain that he would not tolerate saboteurs in the ranks of PDVSA blocking the advance of the revolution. He then picked up a whistle from his desk and, in a nod to the upcoming soccer World Cup, blew the whistle and shouted, "Offsides!"

Malvina had been angered by the firings, which she felt were illegal: The president had no right to fire anyone within PDVSA save the company's president. But she was also embarrassed that this man, this *buffoon*, was her president. Chávez was right on one count, Malvina thought, PDVSA did belong to all Venezuelans, which meant that the people had a right to defend it. She felt that Chávez had deceived them in so many ways with his "revolution." She was not going to let Chávez take control of PDVSA, then raid its coffers to finance his Cuban-style reforms.

The energy of the crowd kept building as more and more and still more people joined them. Increasingly persistent now was the chant, "Miraflores! Miraflores!" Before long, the two leaders of the opposition took to the stage. The first was Dr. Pedro Carmona, the head of Fedecámaras, the national federation of private businesses. Malvina was a fan of Carmona. He was a short, balding, grandfatherly old man who knew how to channel the energy of the people and to get them into the streets. She felt that Carmona had made this march happen.

When Carmona finished, it was Carlos Ortega's turn to speak. Ortega was the head of Venezuela's massive labor union, the CTV, which represented over 1.2 million workers and was one of the strongest political bodies in the country. As Ortega addressed the endless crowd, he told them he had a list of demands for Chávez and he was going to be certain that the president complied with every one of them. "No! No! No!" the crowd booed. Not because they didn't want the demands met, but because it seemed that negotiating with him would only prolong his rule. Ultimately, Ortega, heeding the supplications of the crowd, dramatically ripped the list into pieces. The crowd went crazy: "Let's go to Miraflores! Let's go to Miraflores!" Finally, whether by acquiescence or design, Ortega announced, "And I say that this march, that this river of humanity, goes . . . goes to Miraflores! . . . You have squandered the state's resources and now this river of humanity is going to Miraflores to get your resignation!"

The crowd roared, Malvina and Gorka along with them. This was an energy like nothing she had ever felt before, a euphoria. She laughed out loud. They would go to Miraflores and President Chávez would hear them. She would tell Chávez—to his face, if she could—that she wanted him out.

2 | Preparing for a Fight

11:30 A.M.

News that the march was going to Miraflores spread quickly over the airwaves. Every TV station in the country, except the official government channel, VTV, was covering the march live.

Surrounding Miraflores was a contingent of National Guard troops as well as several hundred loyal Chávez supporters. Many of these supporters were members of the local community groups known as Circulos Bolivarianos, or Bolivarian Circles. Circle members had been on permanent guard duty around the palace since Sunday and had set up a stage in the middle of the street for speeches and music. The creation of the Bolivarian Circles was one of the most controversial aspects of the Chávez regime. The opposition claimed they were paramilitary units that Chávez used to do his dirty work, while the government claimed they were harmless community groups. The truth was somewhere in between. While most of the Bolivarian Circles were exactly what they said they were—groups of party members organizing to better their community and spread the word of the revolution—there were other Circles that were modeled after the Dignity Battalions—the local militias used by General Omar Torríjos and Manuel Noriega in Panama—that had impressed Chávez when he was a military attaché there. Many Bolivarian Circles received military training and arms, and some of their leaders were sent to Cuba for training. Some of these Circles were now congregated around the palace too.

It would take several hours for the march to travel the five miles from Chuao to the palace, and the loyalists were using the time to get ready. Rallying the supporters with a megaphone was National Assembly Deputy Juan Barreto, a member of Chávez's party and a close ally of the president. When interviewed by a news crew about the approaching march, Barreto made this appeal: "The call is to Miraflores! Everyone to Miraflores to defend your revolution! Don't let them through!"

On the government channel VTV, Freddy Bernal, mayor of the Caracas municipality El Libertador and part of Chávez's inner circle, denounced the opposition: "There is a conspiracy at work here. You know there are people there," he said, referring to the Chávez loyalists around Miraflores. "You are provoking us."

⁂

Doctor Alicia Valdez, fifty-two, a small, raven-haired accountant, was in her office near Miraflores when she began to see groups of people moving down the street toward the palace. Having heard that the march had illegally changed its scheduled route, she knew that these were loyalists going to defend the president.

Both Alicia and her sister, Florangel, worked for the Chávez administration, her sister as a counselor in Miraflores and Alicia as a notary—an important political position in Venezuela because all official documents had to be authenticated by a certified government officer. Neither Alicia nor Florangel had been involved in politics before Chávez because they had become disenchanted with the corrupt two-party system. But the more Alicia learned about Chávez, the more she liked what he was offering, especially his recognition of the poor. Eventually she and her sister became staunch believers in the movement.

As Alicia sat at her desk and tried to focus on her pile of papers, she found herself looking out the window over and over again to see what was going on. Finally, she gave up. She couldn't concentrate. When someone in the office said that the people in the street were armed, she and her friend Mariela decided to go investigate. What they found was that some people *were* armed, but with umbrellas and sticks, and they told Alicia and Mariela that, all the same, if the march tried to get to Chávez, they would defend him with whatever they had.

Now that Alicia was down in the street, it seemed as if everybody was going to the palace. She and Mariela knew they couldn't miss this, and, besides, how were they supposed to get any work done with all this going on? They started toward Miraflores.

3 | General Usón

12:00 NOON

On the eleventh floor of the Venezuelan Central Bank, two blocks east of Miraflores, Finance Minister General Francisco Usón was starting to worry. From his window he could see Chávez supporters converging on the palace.

He thought back to the meeting he had had with Chávez last night. He had told the president that he thought the situation was very grave: "We think tomorrow's strike is going to be very strong, because today's was certainly a success." Usón knew because he had been keeping tabs on the strike, flying around the country with the minister of interior relations, the minister of the environment, and the minister of justice to see who was working and who wasn't. "Tomorrow we will be talking about a massive number of people in the metropolitan area," Usón said. "President, we have forty-eight difficult hours ahead, but if we can make it to Friday night without violence, we will make it through this because by Saturday and Sunday this strike will collapse in on itself, and on Monday we'll wake up with our country back."

Chávez had told his friend not to worry, that tomorrow, April 11, would be a day when he would exercise "maximum tolerance."

"President, because you say so, I will sleep peacefully tonight," and Usón had left the palace.

Now, looking out at the people amassing around Miraflores, Usón was beginning to lose the tranquil feeling he had the night before. He had felt a jolt of apprehension when he heard that the march was really coming, then relief when President Chávez had fired (or, technically, accepted the resignation of) the new board of directors of PDVSA that he had recently appointed. It was a move that they hoped would defuse the situation, but as Usón watched the approaching march on TV, he realized that it had had no impact. The problem, Usón realized, was no longer who controlled PDVSA. The problem had become Hugo Chávez.

Usón called the vice president, Diosdado Cabello, and the minister of information to tell them that they should send emissaries to the leaders of the march and be open to receiving their proposals. Maybe that would head off a confrontation. The vice president told him that this had already been taken care of.

Then Usón had to address more immediate concerns. His head of personnel was telling him that many of his employees were requesting permission to go home for the day. They knew that the march was coming and they wanted to be as far away from Miraflores as possible when it arrived.

To assuage people's fears, Usón began going from floor to floor asking people to remain calm and telling them they would be perfectly safe. He started on the eleventh floor and began working his way down. It seemed to be working. Usón had an unexpectedly gentle demeanor for someone who had spent his life in the military. He was a short, pudgy man with brown skin and a face that looked more round than it really was because of the big 1970s-style eyeglasses he wore—the kind with the little tint of amber in them. He spoke easily and with confidence. He was so gregarious you immediately sensed that he was trustworthy because it seemed that a man who talked so much and so openly couldn't possibly have anything to hide. The combination of his appearance and his character had a disarming effect on people.

When Usón reached the fourth floor, someone said to him, Minister, have you seen what the people down in the street have in their hands? Usón realized that from his office on the eleventh floor it was impossible to make out such detail. He went to the window and saw that the Chávez supporters were carrying rocks, sticks, chains, baseball bats, and metal pipes. Again, Usón's apprehension spiked.

He continued down to the ground floor and out into the street. On the opposite corner, in front of the Ministry of Exterior Relations, he saw a National Guardsman. Usón asked for his commanding officer. The soldier told him they had set up a command post in the Santa Capilla church. There Usón found the commanding officer, a colonel, who assured him that everything was under control. They planned to stop the marchers and keep everyone separated. "Don't worry, General," he said. And from what Usón could see, that's what the troops were doing, staying in front of the Chávez supporters.

Feeling a little better about things, Usón started to head back to the Central Bank. Then he noticed an MVR activist (a Chávez party member) with his red beret, carrying a soda bottle crate, but instead of empty bottles, it was filled with Molotov cocktails. Things are definitely not good, Usón said to himself, especially when the National Guard are twenty yards away and are doing nothing.

Once back inside the Central Bank, Usón gave the order to evacuate the building. He had security close the front doors and begin to send people out the basement exits. Usón told everyone to go straight home and not to hang around to see what would happen.

Although most people could see the growing possibility of bloodshed, Usón had more reason than most to worry. Two events in the past week had heightened his fear that the regime was willing to use violence as a political tool. The first was a high-level meeting held last Sunday, April 7—the same day that Chávez had publicly fired the PDVSA managers on his TV program. In attendance were Chávez, most of the cabinet, Attorney General Isaías Rodríguez, and the military high command—including Generals Vásquez Velasco, Commander of the Army, and Manuel Rosendo, the head of the Unified Command of the National Armed Forces (CUFAN).

The president began the meeting by saying that the strike the opposition planned was treasonous and he asked for opinions on how to counteract it and the marches. This began a discussion about how to best defend the palace, the process of declaring a state of emergency, cutting the signals of the anti-Chávez TV stations and, if necessary, to impose martial law.

The president asked General Rosendo to give a detailed outline of Plan Avila, a secret military operation for taking control of the streets. Using Plan Avila to quell civil unrest made the high command very uncomfortable because the last time it had been implemented was to stop large public protests during the Caracazo of 1989, when hundreds (and many believe thousands) of civilians had been massacred in the streets by the army.

While Rosendo was discussing Plan Avila, a group of Chávez's party officials entered the meeting. It was Deputy Cilia Flores (chair of the Political Command of the Bolivarian Revolution), Guillermo García Ponce (a veteran hard-liner who had worked with the communist guerrillas in the 1960s), and Freddy Bernal (one of the principal organizers of the Bolivarian Circles and a local mayor). This group was the Tactical Command for the Revolution (Commando Tactico de la Revolución), or CTR, and it controlled much of Chávez's political machine.

Uncomfortable glances were passed among the generals, and Rosendo abruptly changed the subject. Information about Plan Avila was secret and not to be discussed openly.

Usón noticed that with these new arrivals the tone of the meeting instantly changed, as did the attitude of the president. Before the appearance of the Tactical Command, Chávez had been behaving like the president of Venezuela and the commander in chief of the armed forces—his two primary roles. It had been a discussion of how the government would weather the storm. But now Chávez was transformed: He was now the leader of the Bolivarian Revolution, a very different role. The meeting, too, was no longer about what was best for the government of Venezuela; it was about what was best for the revolution. For Usón this meant that Chávez's options were greatly limited. He could not say things in front of these people that he could say among his generals, for, in a way, he was outnumbered and could easily lose face.

The Tactical Command steered the meeting toward their plans to employ the Bolivarian Circles as a paramilitary force to stop the marches and defend the president, specifically by organizing them into brigades. Then they discussed a plan to have the National Guard storm the central offices of PDVSA in Chuao to take control of the oil company by force. They also spoke of launching an aggressive information campaign on both the public and private TV stations, including having loyalists fill the highways with cars and then broadcasting the images on TV to make it look as if people were working.

In another plan to head off the strike, the president of PDVSA, Gastón Parra, suggested giving out a bonus to each PDVSA employee who did not join the strike. He said he could disburse 200 billion bolivares, or 1.5 million per employee (about $172,000 and $1,200 per employee, respectively).

This proposal irritated Usón for several reasons: First of all, in recent weeks Parra had not been sending PDVSA's promised contributions to the treasury (which constituted half of all government revenue), claiming that the oil company was experiencing "cash flow problems." The fact that Parra had enough money to pay a loyalty bonus meant that he had not been honest. Usón needed that money. He had already been forced to delay many payments, including government paychecks, which was causing labor tensions. It was also beginning to look as if they wouldn't meet their payments on the foreign debt. The internal debt, too, was being financed by the sale of bonds that no one was buying. Then there was Chávez's new minimum wage: That morning the president had announced a 20 percent increase in the minimum wage. Last night Chávez had called Usón and asked him if he could increase the minimum wage by 16 percent, which Usón had said was impossible; 12 percent was the maximum that could be funded, yet the president had gone ahead and made the announcement anyway. The increase would be effective May 1—twenty days from now! How were they going to pay for it?

Usón turned on Gastón Parra. "How is it that you can offer these people that kind of money, when we should be using it to pay teachers' salaries or medicines in the hospitals or food in the schools?"

But Chávez cut him off, telling Usón that this was a political meeting of ministers, not a discussion of administrative issues. In over twenty-five years of friendship, it was the first time that Usón could remember Chávez raising his voice in front of him.

As Usón sat quietly for the rest of the meeting, he reflected that the Tactical Command was considering everything imaginable to try to keep control of the situation, which signaled to Usón that the situation was the exact opposite—out of control. He also feared that Chávez was losing control over the more radical members of his party.

The other incident haunting Usón about the prospect of violence was a conversation he had just last night with a close adviser to Chávez, General Jacinto Pérez. Pérez had been one of Usón's and Chávez's professors at the Military Academy and now his office was located right next to the president's. The previous evening, when Usón had gone to give his report on the strike, he had to wait for a time outside Chávez's office. Pérez was there working, and he and Usón began to talk about the situation. Pérez, a military historian, confided that the revolution was in a crisis and that it needed to rejuvenate itself. Then he said something that shocked Usón. Pérez told him that the revolution needed to be cleaned, purified with blood. When he heard that, Usón, knowing how this man had the president's ear, wondered what he had been telling Chávez.

Now, as Usón watched the armed loyalists grouping around Miraflores, he began to wonder what the government had planned. What exactly were the orders the National Guard had been given? And what orders did the Bolivarian Circles have?

By 12:30 there were well over a thousand Chávez supporters around the palace and more were arriving every minute. They created a human barrier blocking every possible route the march might take. The National Guard was in position, too, having set up cordons blocking all the major avenues to the palace. All, that is, except for the narrow stairs under the Llaguno Overpass, where the bulk of the Circulos Bolivarianos had congregated. This, as it turns out, was where most of the killing would take place.

4 | The Perfect Opportunity for a Coup

12:00 NOON

Inside the palace, Hugo Chávez was informed that the march had left Chuao and was on its way to Miraflores. He was convinced that this was part of a plan by his opponents to stage a coup d'état. After all, Chávez knew how coups worked; the coup he had led against President Carlos Andrés Pérez in February 1992 had taught him that the chances of success were much higher if it coincided with some sort of popular uprising—if the conspirators could strike during a moment of popular discontent and take advantage of the chaos, it would be much easier to take and consolidate power. Just such an event had presented itself to Chávez in 1989 when riots broke out in response to the economic reforms of newly elected President Pérez. The result was the bloody Caracazo. Although the event had been the perfect opportunity for Chávez and his co-conspirators, it had caught them completely unprepared. Chávez himself was sick at the time with rubella. Ironically, Chávez's co-conspirators in the army had been obliged to help the same government they had been plotting to overthrow as they viciously oppressed the populace.

In the end, it was not until February 4, 1992, almost three years later, that they could stage their coup. And that coup, Chávez felt, had failed in part because the civilian component was lacking. He had had a truck filled with guns ready for all the civilians he had hoped would join his coup, but none of them showed up, not even the ones who had known their plans in advance.

Now, as the march made its way to Miraflores, Chávez was certain that his enemies would use this as the destabilizing event to try to oust him. Within the military, rumors of conspiracy were everywhere. Most were junior officers who posed no serious threat, but Chávez knew of one group led by Admiral Héctor Ramírez Pérez who did pose a legitimate threat. Luckily for Chávez one of the men attending their meetings was General Vásquez Velasco, the head of the army, who was telling Chávez everything. However Chávez had decided not to arrest them. Not yet. The right moment had not yet come, and perhaps, he thought, he could use their conspiracy to his advantage. More pressing than Admiral Ramírez Pérez was a report he had just received that General Medina—the staunchly anti-Chávez military attaché to Washington—was suddenly back in Caracas and might be part of an insurrection.

Indeed, it seemed as if everyone was against him. The church, the media, the labor unions, business leaders, and many in the military. For weeks they had been talking, openly, about his removal. The DISIP, his secret police, had been monitoring many of the meetings where leaders like Carmona and Ortega and rich businesspeople and religious leaders sat around and planned out how they would rule the country once he was gone. They seemed to treat the collapse of his presidency as a foregone conclusion. It was no longer a question of if he would lose power, just a matter of how. Could the opposition, invoking article 350 of the new constitution, force him from office because all sectors of the populace felt that his regime was "contrary to the values, principals and democratic ideals of the country"? Would the military take power in a coup? Or would Chávez himself bow to the incredible pressure and resign?

But Chávez was not going without a fight. Ever since he was twenty-three years old, when he had founded his revolutionary movement, the Liberation Army of the Venezuelan People (El Ejercito de Liberación del Pueblo de Venezuela), he had been fighting to remake Venezuela, to wrest power from the "oligarchy"—the corrupt political elite—and to set the nation on the course that he felt that the Great Liberator, Simón Bolívar, had always wanted. The revolution was his life.

He picked a walkie-talkie off his desk. He still had his trump card. Plan Avila. The nuclear option.

It was a dangerous move because the military was divided over Chávez's nepotism (his compatriots in the 1992 coup were promoted ahead of their non-*chavista* peers) and his soft stance on the Colombian guerrilla group, the FARC, which was operating within Venezuela. To order Plan Avila would be asking the high command to break the law for him because the army was expressly prohibited from controlling civilians—only the National Guard could do that. This was something that was added into the new constitution of 1999 specifically to prevent another Caracazo, to keep the military from massacring the population. What's more, the constitution clearly stated that if an order from a superior officer (the president included) violated the constitution, then that order should not be obeyed.

But more important in the minds of many generals was a famous Venezuelan mantra, a quote from Simón Bolívar, The Great Liberator of South America, a mantra that had been violated during the Caracazo: *Maldito el soldado que vuelva las armas contra el pueblo*. Damned is the soldier who turns his arms against his own people. No commander could put his troops into the streets without thinking of that passage. After all, the army had no crowd control equipment. Unlike the police and the National Guard, it had no gas masks, no riot shields, no batons, and no training in crowd control. Its only tools for controlling the march were assault rifles.

Chávez turned on the walkie-talkie. He had set up a special radio system known as the "Shark Network" to keep him in contact with his most trusted military leaders in the event of a crisis. Included in the network were the heads of the Army, the National Guard, the DISIP, Military Intelligence, and his Battalion Commanders.

Shark One [President Chávez]: Shark Eight, tell me if you copy. This is Shark One.

Shark Eight [Lieutenant Colonel Cepeda]: Yes, Mr. President, this is the commander speaking.

He ordered Plan Avila.

5 | Rumors and Paranoia

2:00 P.M.

By now rumors of the government's collapse were everywhere. The major networks were getting unconfirmed reports that Chávez had resigned, been arrested, was fleeing to Cuba, that the military had revolted, that the military high command had resigned, etcetera.

At just after two o'clock the military high command, led by Generals Lucas Rincón, Efraín Vásquez Velasco, and Manuel Rosendo, held a press conference to dispel the rumors: They assured the nation that Chávez was still the president, that he had not been arrested, and that he could continue to count on the support of the armed forces. "The president can be found in his office," Rincón said. "I categorically deny that the high command has resigned. We have here all of the members of the military high command and we are evaluating minute by minute the changing situation. Besides a few areas of disturbance, the situation in the country is normal."

6 | The Silence

"OK," Malvina said to Gorka, "if everyone is going to Miraflores and you want to go, no problem. But before we do I need something to drink because without water I'm not walking anywhere." It was a five-mile walk to the palace, so Malvina and Gorka headed over to the shade near the radio tower, got a drink, and rested awhile before joining the march.

Nestled tightly into a small valley about thirty miles from the Caribbean coast, Caracas had grown into one of the most densely populated areas in Latin America. The geographic limitations meant that the city had to be built upwards—a nine-mile-long corridor of high-rise office and apartment buildings. The metro area, which wasn't much more than the valley and an offshoot to the south, held over 3.1 million people. Yet, despite its towering skyscrapers and excellent subway, Caracas was a city that felt past its prime. Like the rest of Venezuela, its development had come to a standstill almost two decades ago when the oil boom ended. Now all of its buildings looked dated and unkempt, moss growing thick down their sides. In the rainy season it felt as if the greenery was gaining ground; finding footholds in the roads and balconies; eroding and cracking the concrete, metal, and asphalt, slowly undoing all that human labor.

However, the most striking thing about Caracas was not the skyscrapers, but the shantytowns. They climbed up almost every slope of the valley—great labyrinths of cheap brick homes that spread for miles. The little brown boxes, called *ranchos*, scaled the most precarious slopes of the valley, sometimes stacked up two and three stories high. Haphazard and ugly in the day, the shantytowns became beautiful at night. Connected to the grid by pirated electricity, the hills around Caracas came alive with little white lights. Looking up from the city below, this second constellation of light seemed to meld with the stars above. The city was a microcosm of Venezuela. It had thrived on oil money until that money ran out; since then the only thing that had grown were the shantytowns, which every day seemed to encroach closer and closer on the city.

A little after one o'clock Malvina and Gorka got off the highway at Bolívar Avenue. Here they suddenly felt the atmosphere change. They were entering pro-Chávez turf, or, as Gorka called it, "Apache territory." This was El Centro, the old business district of Caracas. But despite the change, Malvina still felt strong simply because of the crowd; after all, she thought, what could they do against so many of us?

Shortly, they came to an area where there was tear gas in the air, but whatever had happened here, it had ended awhile ago. "Let's go home because people are saying there is a lot more tear gas ahead," Malvina said.

But Gorka didn't feel the gas. "Naw, let's keep going," he said. "*Ni un paso atrás!*" he added. It was the opposition's rallying call: "Not one step back." "*Echarle pichón.* Let's go for it. No fear."

"No, with plenty of fear," she corrected him, "but let's keep going."

Just then, as if to answer their tear gas worries, an older woman appeared with an enormous jug of vinegar, which counteracts the effects of tear gas. She was handing it out to everyone. *Here you go, darling, take some.* People were soaking the front of their shirts with it. Malvina poured some of it on the red stripe of her flag so she could swab her eyes with it if she needed to. From then on, she kept that part of the flag wadded in her fist so it wouldn't dry out.

They were now entering El Silencio—The Silence—the old heart of Caracas. It was so-named because all the land around Miraflores had originally been parkland. Historical paintings of the area showed rolling meadows where people came to walk and have picnics. Today, however, El Silencio was a tightly packed urban jungle made up of high-rise business and apartment buildings. It was one of the noisiest and most congested areas of the city, and its name had taken on a certain irony.

Finally, they came to the intersection of Baralt Avenue. They were only about six blocks from the palace now, and the march was beginning to branch off and take one of three routes: The simplest was to continue straight for two more blocks until you reached El Calvario, then take a right up the New Republic Viaduct. The second way was to continue for one more block, then take a right up Eighth Street past Fermín Toro High School, but this street was much narrower than the viaduct. Lastly, you could turn right here at Baralt, which was a big six-lane road, but Malvina knew that to get up to Urdaneta Avenue (and to Miraflores) you had to take the very narrow stairs under the Llaguno Overpass and that bottleneck would make it slow going.

"Shouldn't we go up to the next block?" Malvina asked.

Gorka shrugged. "Nobody's going that way."

All right, she thought, if this was the way everyone was going, fine.

It was a seemingly insignificant decision that would change her life forever.

Malvina wasn't a leader, she didn't ever go first, but by now the yellow-shirted Primero Justicia crowd had spread out so much that there were only four or five of them carrying the big party banner, and suddenly there she was, in front of everyone.

They only made it a block up Baralt before they came under a barrage of rocks being thrown by angry Chávez supporters. Rocks didn't even describe these things, Malvina thought, they were more like boulders. Gigantic! It was too much for them, and Malvina, Gorka, and a small group from Primero Justicia turned off at the Pedrera corner to take refuge.

Out of the hail of stones, Malvina tried to take in the scene: On the other side of the street they could see a squad of Metropolitan Police officers taking cover around the corner of the National Building. They had two big police trucks they called *ballenas*, or whales—armored trucks with water cannons. Malvina wondered why the police weren't doing anything. Come on, she thought. All these *chavistas*, Chávez lovers, are throwing rocks at people, and all the police did was jump out, shoot some tear gas, and hide again.

"You guys stay here," Gorka said, "I'm going to check things out," and he went back out into the street. Now it was Malvina, two women, and a man named José María waiting for Gorka. Suddenly Malvina saw a man who looked like a photographer collapse right in front of her, right on the opposite curb. It looked like he had been hit with a rock. The man had on a black photographer's vest and a big camera. A crowd of people rushed up to help him. Oh, no, Malvina thought, this is too dangerous, and she came out from behind the newspaper stand to look for Gorka, to call him back. She stood there in the open on her tiptoes, her hand shading her eyes to look for him, then something smashed into her face and everything went dark.

7 | The Shooting Begins

Mike Merhi was walking west on Sixth Avenue in the opposition crowd with his eighteen-year-old son, Jesús, when they came to Baralt Avenue and the march began to fan out like a river reaching a delta. Up ahead, toward the New Republic Viaduct, Mike and Jesús could see that the march was beginning to back up and some people were even coming back. Word was going around that National Guard troops had stopped the march with tear gas on the viaduct and on Eighth Street.

In response, people started heading up Baralt Avenue, and Mike and Jesús went with them. They knew it was not the best way, but this was the way most people were going, and they weren't about to turn back now.

They had gotten up early this morning to get everything ready for the big march. They were men on a mission: They had their whistles, water bottles, and comfortable clothes for walking. Mike had on a shirt that had the colors of the national flag. It wasn't one of the popular flag shirts that many marchers wore, but it was the closest thing that Mike owned. Jesús had put on his favorite black Nike shirt. Then they had driven to Altamira, Jesús waving his Venezuelan flag out the window while Mike honked the horn. Marching to Chuao, they had met Mike's brother, Ali, and then the three of them had gone along shouting, singing, and talking.

When Jesús, Ali, and Mike had reached Chuao, it had been completely jam-packed with people. They never got close enough to even see the stage or hear anything that was said; there were just too many people. But many were chanting, "*Vamos a Miraflores, vamos a Miraflores!*" Many bodies, one mind.

Mike was not originally from Venezuela. In fact, his real name wasn't Mike, it was Mohamad. He had picked up the nickname when he emigrated from Lebanon in 1975 during Venezuela's big oil boom. He was immensely proud of Jesús Mohamad, the child of his first marriage, a handsome kid with a dark complexion. He was slight and lean like Mike, but strong and good-looking, with dark eyes and a head of thick black hair. Girls were always calling the house for him. He won medals in swimming and played drums in a band. He was in his last semester of high school and had made a little business of fixing computers and designing Web pages. Mike had named him Jesús Mohamad to symbolize the bridge between his Islamic roots and his new Christian home and to show that all human beings were brothers, regardless of religion. But Mike's ideas of brotherhood and patriotism seemed very much under attack by Hugo Chávez's revolution. *Revolution*, Mike mused, that was Chávez's word. Everything was for *la revolución*! But what did it mean? The truth was nobody knew. Chávez would never say. Was it socialist, communist? It certainly wasn't capitalist, Mike thought. Under Chávez, the economy had quickly taken a steep downturn, much of it due to the uncertainty created by his rhetoric.

When the march began to go to Miraflores, Mike and Jesus hadn't hesitated, but Ali had decided to go home. Now on Baralt Avenue, things started to happen quickly. Up ahead they could see a hail of rocks and people retreating with cuts and bruises.

They had to move slower now, more cautiously, but there were still so many of them that there seemed no way the *chavistas* could stop them. The noise, too, was much more intense. The sound of whistles and pots and pans had been replaced by shouting and screaming. There were so many rocks in the air that Mike and Jesús decided to take cover, Mike behind a light post and Jesús behind a skinny tree. They waited for a short time, and in an odd moment Mike recognized a friend in the crowd, Gustavo Tovar. They spoke for a few minutes, all the while looking about nervously. Then they all moved up the left side of the street together.

In front of them was an incredible scene: They were only a few blocks from Miraflores, but the way was completely barred by hundreds of the president's loyal supporters, hardcore *chavistas*, and they were throwing everything they could at Mike and his fellow marchers, an unremitting hail of rocks, bottles, and Molotov cocktails—which were landing and splashing into flames on the blacktop. Mike could see the *chavistas* waving sticks and makeshift shields above their heads. Mike knew that these must be the government's thugs, the Circulos Bolivarianos. Then he saw that they were throwing tear gas canisters, too. How did they get so much tear gas? he thought.

Between the opposing factions was an open space of about forty meters, a no-man's-land filled with garbage and spiraling plumes of tear gas. The two groups were surging against each other, one group would push forward and the other would fall back, then the other would push forward—but always leaving a space between them. The police were there, too. They had two armored trucks and were trying to keep the two groups apart with tear gas and water cannons, but with little success.

Just then Mike saw a photographer suddenly fall to the ground. He was on the far side of the street, only about twenty-five feet away. The man was dressed in an off-white Oxford with a black vest and a nice camera around his neck. He was trotting along when he fell forward almost as if he was doing a somersault. His head slammed into the pavement, and people rushed over to help him. Mike could see there was a bloody smudge on his forehead. "He must have been hit in the head with a rock," Mike thought.

There were more loud thumps in the air, rising above the din—a *doom, doom, doom* sound—and he thought it must be the police firing their *perdigones* (shotguns with plastic shot) at the *chavistas*. Then he saw a woman near the photographer, a very tall woman with short blond hair and a bright yellow T-shirt, suddenly collapse. It looked as if she had been hit with a rock, too. Up the street he saw another man stumble, and now, very loud, he heard the *doom, doom, doom*. Almost as one, he, Jesús, and his friend Gustavo realized what was happening. They ran for cover.

8 | Into the Fray

Gorka had left Malvina behind a newspaper stand to go and scout ahead. The crowd was chanting, "Not one step back, not one step back!" And Gorka was all for that. Yes, there were rocks and tear gas, he thought, but we haven't come this far to turn back now. This president has to go! He put his handheld flag in his back pocket so that his hands would be free (just in case), and he ran into the crowd shouting, "Get out, Chávez!" and "Not one step back!"

Looking up Baralt Avenue he could see a big pack of the *chavistas*. The street sloped upward so that the *chavistas* had the advantage of higher ground. Gorka had to shuffle and dodge rocks as he ran up the right side of the street past the armored trucks and the McDonald's. He was going to move further up the street, but the Metropolitan Police were shooting tear gas canisters over their heads, and the wind—the way it was channeled through the tall buildings—was bringing the gas right back down on them. Gorka had never felt tear gas before. He thought it would be like smoke and that he could tough it out. But it hit him hard. He immediately had trouble breathing and tears began streaming down his cheeks. He headed back to the corner where he had left Malvina and the others.

As he jogged back down the street he took out his flag so that people wouldn't mistake him for a *chavista*. As he came past the armored truck with the water cannon, he noticed a photographer laid out on the concrete, bleeding from the head. The size of his camera stuck in Gorka's mind, it was immense. Gorka went to see if he needed help. He was unconscious and Gorka checked for vital signs. Several other people came up and huddled around them. Just then, by some odd instinct, Gorka looked over to where he had left Malvina. He saw a huddle of Primero Justicia shirts; they were trying to pick someone up off the pavement. Gorka felt a horrible sinking in his stomach. The person on the ground had shoes and pants exactly like Malvina's. *Oh, no,* he thought.

He ran over and found Malvina bleeding from the face. They were still out in the open, so they picked her up and took her down a side street and propped her against the entrance to the Metro station—a modern redbrick building.

Everyone was shouting, and Gorka couldn't focus on anything. The noise from the street had changed. He could still hear the people chanting, *Ni un paso atrás,* but there was now screaming and cursing; a television crew was trying to film Malvina; the police were shooting up the street; and there was the bang of what sounded like fireworks. It was overwhelming.

He took out a handkerchief and put it on the wound for a moment, then took it off to see if the bleeding had stopped. It hadn't, so he did it again. *This didn't make sense,* he thought. There was so much blood, and the hole, it was very round, like a half-inch circle. He had never seen a cheek bleed like this. It was coming out in spurts like it was from an artery. Gorka turned to José María and the other Primero Justicia people "What happened? Was it an *alambre*, a rock, what?" An *alambre* (a wire) was a stick with a big nail in one end, which many of the *chavistas* were wielding like hatchets.

They said she had just fallen and that they thought she had been hit with a rock.

Gorka was confused, but he knew one thing: He had to get her out of here.

9 | Journalists in the Crossfire

Rafael Fuenmayor and his crew were filming the injured photographer when they saw Malvina collapse.

Rafael was a reporter for CMT, the smallest of the private TV stations in Caracas. He was a big guy, built like a linebacker, with short black hair that he kept slicked back. He wore wire-framed glasses and a suit when he worked, and these days, due to the increase in violence toward journalists, he had a Kevlar vest on under his jacket. He and his crew—a cameraman and one technician—had been working since five-thirty that morning covering the march, running all over the city trying to keep up with everything that was happening. They had beaten the march to The Silence, arriving around one o'clock. By then, there had already been a hundred or so presidential supporters around the Llaguno Overpass and another group of several hundred more up Eighth Street.

Then the marchers began to arrive, pouring out around the towers of The Silence. It seemed to Rafael that in the time it took to close his eyes and open them again, the place was full of people. At that moment he realized that when they had filmed the march that morning, he had only seen a small piece of it. He had never imagined that there would be so many people, and seeing them made his stomach tighten with anxiety. He sensed that something bad was going to happen—something ugly—because all these people had decided to go to Miraflores regardless of what might happen to them.

Unlike most people in the march, Rafael knew that shots had been fired. Not long before, he had filmed the very first gunshot victim on Baralt Avenue, an undercover detective for the DISIP who was shot in the head. The man's ID had said he was part of the president's escort, Tony Velasquez—*Caravana Presidencial*. Velasquez was dressed up like a journalist and had been shot farther up the street, closer to the Llaguno Overpass.

So when Rafael saw the photographer collapse, followed a moment later by the tall blond in the Primero Justicia shirt, he knew it was possible they had been shot, too. The wounded photographer particularly worried him because he was clearly a journalist: He had a camera with a telephoto lens and a vest, a *chaleco*—the kind with lots of pockets that is very popular with reporters. Rafael recalled that the undercover DISIP officer also had on a similar *chaleco,* and he had seen another photographer with a big camera injured earlier. It looked to him as if journalists were being singled out as targets.

A group of people had picked up the wounded man and were carrying him down University Avenue. In the confusion, Fuenmayor did not get close enough to see his face. It wasn't until much later that he learned that it was a friend of his, Jorge Tortoza, a forty-eight-year-old photographer for the newspaper *2001*.

Rafael turned back to Malvina. Her friends had propped her against the wall of the Metro station and a man was pressing a handkerchief against her face. Her eyes were closed and Rafael wondered if she were dead.

"This woman from Primero Justicia appears to have been injured in the face here at Pedrera corner on Baralt Avenue," he narrated. He glanced from the camera down at Malvina. Suddenly Malvina's eyes opened wide with fright. Rafael stopped midsentence, clearly startled. Malvina looked as if she had just woken up from a nightmare.

10 | Malvina's Motorcycle Ride

All things considered, Malvina Pesate felt pretty good. A bullet had struck her left cheek just to the side of her mouth and exited out the back of her neck—a little to the left of the spine. She had instantly fainted, but only for a few seconds. When she came to, she assumed she had been hit with a rock. For her, being shot wasn't really in the realm of possibility; of the dozens of marches that had taken place over the past year no one had ever been shot. The whole side of her face was numb, as if she had just been to the dentist and shot up with Novocain, but other than that, she really didn't feel all that bad. The way her body was reacting . . . it felt like she was in a sort of dreamland, sedated, as if she were outside her body watching herself. She felt someone pulling at her arm. "Come on," Gorka was saying, "we have to get you out of here." One thing was for sure: She didn't feel like going anywhere. "No, I'm cool here," she mumbled, sounding like her mouth was full of marbles. The pulling on her arm became more insistent. "Stop pulling me," she mumbled, "*Estoy bien*," I'm fine. "It doesn't hurt." Then she blacked out again.

Gorka and José María stood her up, and she came around again. Gorka didn't like the way her eyes were rolling around, it frightened him.

About twenty feet down the side street, a brigade of motorcycle cops had parked their bikes. Gorka ran down to them. "I need an ambulance," he told one of the officers.

The officer said the quickest way to get her to a hospital was on a motorcycle. Gorka agreed, anything.

By the time they got the bike ready, Malvina was conscious and walking with a little help from José María. That was good. She was trying to keep Gorka's handkerchief pressed to her face. No one had yet noticed the exit wound at the back of her neck.

"Get her on the bike," the policeman said.

"No," Malvina whined, "motorcycle, no."

"Come on," Gorka said.

Malvina shook her head, "*Moto*, no!" She didn't like motorcycles.

"Get on the bike *now!*" Gorka demanded.

Malvina relented. OK, fine, she thought, if that's what you want, sure. She let them put her on the bike and Gorka got behind her so she wouldn't fall—three on a bike—and off they sped.

She closed her eyes and tried not to look. She was afraid she might try to jump off out of pure fear. The bike was racing, roaring down the street, block after block. Then suddenly the policeman slammed on the brakes near the big tree by the National Library. There was a police truck there and they wanted to take Malvina to the hospital in it. She was still in a dreamy state, but functioning. With some effort, they got her into the high bed of the truck. Gorka told the truck driver that they had to get her to a hospital fast. "Don't stop, just go," Gorka said. "She's hurt bad and I think we're losing her. Go to Caracas Clinic; her brother is a doctor there. But please, hurry."

"OK, got it," the driver said, clearly excited, and without another word took off, leaving Gorka standing there in the street.

From the back of the truck Malvina watched as Gorka ran after them. She signaled and mumbled *ugh, ugh,* to the four police officers sitting in the truck with her. It reminded her of a scene from a cartoon. He was right there behind the truck running, but he couldn't reach it. Finally, one of the police officers shouted, "Stop!" The driver slammed on the brakes, and Gorka was sent flying into the back of the truck.

11 | The March Keeps Coming

After the gunfire started on Baralt Avenue Mike Merhi, Jesús, and Gustavo Tovar retreated about a quarter block and were taking cover behind a newspaper stand and a tree. After a few minutes, the gunfire died down and the *chavistas* fell back toward the Llaguno Overpass. Why did they fall back? Mike asked himself. And where were the gunmen? Were they in the street or on the rooftops?

Despite the gunfire, the march was still trying to push forward. A group of men nearby began calling for them to continue up the street. "Let's go! Let's go while we can!"

Mike hesitated. "But, Gustavo, they are shooting at us and we are unarmed."

Gustavo nodded in agreement, "Yes, but that is exactly why we have to keep going. If we stop now, then they will know they can use violence and win."

Jesús nodded in agreement. He repeated the opposition's mantra, "*Ni un paso atrás.*" Not one step backward. Mike agreed, he didn't want to turn back either, not now. They had come this far, and he did not want to retreat before the *chavistas*. How dare they shoot at them.

But he didn't want Jesús going. There was no need to put him in harm's way. "Stay here behind this tree and wait for us," Mike told him. Then

Mike and Gustavo moved up the left side of the street, along the curb by the National Building. They made it about halfway up to the Muñoz corner when they began to see bodies on the ground, some moving, some not. Although there were still many people and the noise was incredible, they had also entered a surreal, muted space in the center of the maelstrom, where the thick clouds of tear gas cut visibility. On the far curb he glimpsed a woman bleeding from the head and staggering around. Then the shooting reached a new intensity, and Mike and Gustavo took cover behind a tin blue kiosk. There were bullets flying everywhere and Mike could hear the supersonic hiss of them whizzing by. He dared not even stick his head out to look.

Mike wasn't sure how long they had been hiding there, maybe five minutes, but he was losing his perception of time. Suddenly he was consumed by smoke. A tear gas canister must have landed right next to him. He never even saw it because the gas instantly blinded him. As if being stuck in the middle of a firefight wasn't bad enough, now he was completely helpless, pinned down behind this cheap tin kiosk, without a weapon, deafened by the noise, and now unable to see or breathe, unable to do anything. He called out to Gustavo, but he got no reply. So he huddled there, terrified, unable to collect himself. Now and then he heard a sharp ping as a bullet smacked into the tin kiosk.

⸙

"Ahh, not so hard," Malvina mumbled. Gorka was sitting beside her in the police truck, pushing the handkerchief against her cheek.

"Here," he said as she fidgeted, "you do it." Malvina took the handkerchief. The whole left side of her face was asleep, but it still hurt when he pressed like that.

Again Gorka was struck by how much blood there was. He didn't understand. Blood was coming out in squirts, like in the movies. There was blood all over her chin and shirt, and all over his shirt, too, and the handkerchief was now thoroughly soaked. He knew she needed help fast, but the truck seemed to be going all over the city.

The police officers in the back of the truck asked what had happened. "It looks like a bullet wound," a policewoman said.

"No, it was a rock," Gorka said, but that was when he began to suspect the truth.

Finally they stopped. Gorka looked out. They were in front of the Red Cross center. The driver had taken them to the wrong place. Malvina began to protest. She would walk to the Caracas Clinic if she had to, but she was not going to the Red Cross. Gorka got out and explained to the driver that they had to go to the Caracas Clinic, that Malvina's brother was a doctor there. "OK, no problem," the driver said, still anxious to please. Luckily the clinic was only three blocks away.

12 | Andrés Trujillo

Andrés Trujillo had been standing in the middle of the intersection when Jorge Tortoza and Malvina were shot. He had lost the girl he had been marching with, Libia, when they had been tear-gassed by the police on Bolívar Avenue. Now he was alone, marching just behind some girls who were carrying a banner from the Primero Justicia party. He had just told them to be careful, because people with banners made juicy targets for the rock-throwing *chavistas*.

When the first shots rang out, people began shouting. *"Es plomo, es plomo!"* It's lead! It's lead! But even though they knew they were in danger, few people ran. A sort of collective euphoria came over them. The massive march, this immense collection of souls, had somehow intoxicated them and no matter what, they were going to get to the palace.

After the initial shooting subsided, the hail of rocks picked up again. Andrés found himself grabbing rocks and throwing them back. At first this reaction surprised him—the fury he felt. But he realized that this day could not be considered in a vacuum. His disappointment, frustration, and rage with the government had been building for a long time. The way Chávez was treating the people of PDVSA, his disregard for the law and the democratic process, his policies that were ruining the country, all filled

Andrés with indignation. And now this new affront: He wanted to get to the palace to protest, and the damn *chavistas* were trying to stop him.

Unlike many Venezuelans who had initially endorsed Chávez then later come to regret it, Andrés had never liked the man. He was one of the original *escuálidos* (anti-Chávez). For the twenty-eight-year-old graphic designer, Chávez had shown his true colors in 1992 when he had staged a coup against democratically elected President Carlos Andrés Pérez. He had broken the law, violated the constitution, and been responsible for many deaths. That had never sat well with Andrés. He felt that Chávez was a murderer. Yes, there was corruption in Venezuela, but you didn't fix it by breaking the law. Andrés knew that not everyone felt like he did. In his house, among his seven brothers and sisters, they often fought about Chávez, especially during the campaign. Andrés did everything he could to convince his family and friends that Chávez was not to be trusted. He couldn't believe that he had actually become president.

But many people loved Chávez and they had handed him a lot of power. Too much power. And they had let him bend a lot of laws in the name of the "national crisis."

But four months ago, in November 2001, when Chávez had exercised the Enabling Law and imposed forty-nine laws by decree, it had marked a turning point in public sentiment toward the president. It had shocked many people, *chavista* and anti-*chavista* alike. While it was true that the authority to pass these laws without legislative approval had been granted to Chávez one year earlier as part of certain "emergency powers" deemed necessary by the abysmal state of the economy, Andrés saw this as an outrageous abuse of power. Chávez waited until the last day he had the privilege, and then he didn't simply enact one or two laws, but forty-nine. The new laws included changes in the tax code, including a 0.5 percent tax on all bank withdrawals; a new hydrocarbon law; a fishing law; and a major restructuring of the government ministries and other public institutions. But perhaps the most controversial change was a land reform law that gave the government the right to expropriate private land that it deemed "idle." The wording of the law was so vague that the government could legally take any land it wanted—which it did. While some land was legitimately reclaimed and given to the poor, the government began to use the law as part of a patronage system, bestowing land titles on loyal party members even if the land was already owned by someone else. Critics were also quick to point out how, curiously, none of the nearly 50 percent of Venezuelan territory owned by the government was redistributed to the poor. The land reform law also caused bitter controversy (and several deaths) when thousands of squatters descended on land and demanded protection to live there under the new law. No one in Andrés's family owned land, but three of his brothers lost their jobs because the land they had been working was overrun by squatters.

The government's staunch refusal to reconsider any of these laws led to the first national strike on December 10, 2001. "All those who intend to strike, derail, or sabotage your Bolivarian Revolution are condemned to failure," Chávez had said before the strike. But people went on strike anyway, shutting down approximately 90 percent of the economy. It had been the biggest strike in the nation's history, larger than the one that helped topple the dictatorship of General Marco Pérez Jiménez in 1958.

Now Andrés and the other marchers moved up about half a block, taking up the slack left by the retreating *chavistas*. He could see a cordon of National Guard troops blocking the way east toward the palace. They weren't getting involved, just watching, as if, Andrés thought, they were waiting for orders. Andrés was struck by how many women were in the march. Many were just as enraged as any of the men. They were fierce: hurling rocks with all their might, and screaming obscenities through gritted teeth. *Malditos chavistas!* Just then a woman with a portable radio called out that Chávez had started a special broadcast, or *cadena*. A loud outcry went up from the marchers. By law, all the networks and radio stations had to broadcast the president's address, effectively blocking out all the coverage of what was happening.

It was only a few minutes after the special broadcast began that the gunfire picked up again. Andrés couldn't help thinking that it was on cue now that Chávez was on the air. He could hear the hiss of bullets flying by. He was amazed, yet, at the same time, detached. For some reason, for his adrenaline or his anger, it wasn't sinking in that these things flying around him were bullets.

But the marchers began to disperse under the gunfire. Andrés saw a boy standing on the corner get hit. The police, still in the middle of the two groups, yelled at them to go back down the street, but few people paid attention. Soon Andrés realized that he and a bunch of the other marchers had gone so far up the street that they were much closer to the *chavistas* than to the rest of the march. He could see them up there with chains, sticks, and pistols.

He recalled earlier that morning when they were marching along the highway. A group of *chavistas* in taxis and on motorcycles had gone by shouting, "We are waiting for you up there."

A woman next to Andrés had said, "They are going to do something to us."

"Señora," Andrés had said, "what can they do to us; to all these people? We're too many."

But now he was beginning to see what the *chavistas* meant. If we get close enough there is going to be a slaughter, he thought. He turned to the three girls with the Primero Justicia banner who were still next to him, "That banner is going to be more useful if you break it and we take out the poles," he said. The girls saw the wisdom of this and took out the poles, which were long, and broke them in two and passed them out, one for each of the three girls and one for Andrés.

Just then the police moved their armored trucks up the street. They were trying to put more space between the two opposing groups, and had also begun returning fire at some of the pro-Chávez gunmen. As the police pushed forward, a big mass of marchers, including Andrés, moved up behind them, shouting and throwing rocks. Now they were beyond the Muñoz corner—just a block and half from the Llaguno Overpass. The street was covered with detritus that the retreating *chavistas* had left behind: baseball bats, chains, broken wooden boxes, soft drink crates, and tons of orange and mandarin peels (rubbing the peels under the eyes lessens the effects of tear gas). He had lost track of the Primero Justicia girls and was staying behind one of the *ballenas*—the armored trucks— then stepping out to throw rocks. A teenage boy who was huddled next to him said, "I'll pass you the rocks and you throw them." The kid looked like he was in high school, maybe seventeen or eighteen years old, *un chamo*. He had on black jeans and a black Nike shirt with a pink whistle around his neck. Andrés agreed. The kid gathered up the rocks and passed them to Andrés, who threw them up at the *chavistas*.

Andrés heard an almost constant ping of bullets hitting the armor of the truck. There came a moment when he stepped out from behind the truck to throw another rock and when he came back for more rocks he found the kid sprawled out on the street with a thick pool of blood forming around his head. That was when Andrés broke out of his adrenalized rage. *That could be me. People are dying.* The kid's eyes were open but not focusing on anything and the blood, it was so thick it reminded him of spaghetti sauce. Just then a policeman came up. "Run!" he demanded. "Get back down the street." The policeman moved toward the boy.

Between going and staying, helping and fighting, Andrés found himself backpedaling down the street, trying to keep his eyes on the *chavista* crowd. He didn't see the boy again, but would later learn that it was Mike Merhi's son, Jesús, who had disobeyed his father's orders to stay behind.

Just as he was about to turn and break into a run, Andrés got hit on the upper thigh near his groin. At first he thought he had just been hit really hard with a rock because he didn't feel any pain. He tried to walk, but couldn't, so he hopped over to the curb by the McDonald's, but once there he collapsed and couldn't get up again. He looked himself over, then felt along his leg. Nothing. He didn't see any blood. Then a policeman came up. "What's wrong?" he asked.

"They got me with a rock and I can't get up." The policeman grabbed him under the arms; then another policeman came and grabbed his legs, and they carried him back down to the Pedrera corner and put him on the ground. Now, as he looked himself over again, he saw that his faded jeans were covered in blood all along the groin. Oh, shit, he thought, the rock crushed one of my balls. Then he noticed a hole in his jeans. He'd been shot.

He asked the police to put him in a nearby ambulance. It already had four wounded inside. The paramedic asked him where he was hurt. Andrés indicated the blood stains around his groin, and the paramedic quickly made room for him.

The paramedic took off his pants and his underwear. The good news was that it wasn't his testicle, but there was a hole in his leg. When the paramedic looked at the wound, he quickly grabbed his radio: "Possible femoral artery . . ." he said.

The paramedic kept talking, but Andrés didn't hear, he had gone deaf with fear. *Possible femoral artery.* I'm dead, he thought. He'd seen enough movies to know a rupture of that artery, the main branch of the iliac artery that provides blood to the leg, is often fatal. He tried not to believe it. He was bleeding, but not like he imagined that a femoral rupture would bleed. As a boy, he had fainted many times due to a glucose deficiency, so he knew what it felt like when you were going to pass out, and this didn't feel like that. No, he told himself again, it can't be that bad.

There was a kid next to him who was screaming in pain, and another man who was moaning and cursing. He told the paramedic to help the other people in the ambulance. "You are worse off than they are," the paramedic retorted. But by now Andrés had convinced himself that it was not fatal. "No, take care of them," he said. "I'm not going to die today."

Just then Andrés's cell phone began to ring. It was in his fanny pack which the paramedic had removed. It kept ringing. The paramedic, frantically moving from patient to patient, swore he was going to throw it out the window, but Andrés convinced him to pass it to him. It was his friend Claudio. "Claudio, they shot me. I'm in a white-and-red ambulance and they are taking me to Vargas Hospital."

"Andrés, *no me jodas*!" Don't fuck with me.

"It's true. They shot me. I can't talk. They are taking me to Vargas."

As soon as Andrés hung up, he began to worry about two things: First, Claudio might still think he was joking—they often played tricks on each other. Second, even if Claudio believed him, would he be able to find him? White-and-red ambulance? Duh.

13 | The Marathon Runner

About forty yards up the street from where Andrés Trujillo had been shot, Douglas Romero was doing everything in his power to keep the march from getting to the palace. Douglas was a diehard *chavista* and proud of it. Although the police were legitimately trying to separate the two groups to prevent bloodshed, that wasn't how Douglas and his fellow Chávez supporters saw it. They believed the police were trying to help the march by breaking through their lines so that the protesters could surround the palace. Douglas didn't trust the police because they were under the juris-diction of the mayor of Caracas, Alfredo Peña, a former Chávez ally who had defected to the opposition.

Douglas was from the Petare barrio—a sprawling shantytown in west-ern Caracas and one of the biggest slums in Latin America. One of seven brothers and sisters, the thirty-eight-year-old first-grade teacher was also a marathon runner. Douglas ran nearly every day. He ran in the botanical gardens, in Eastern Park, and even up the dauntingly steep Avila, the pic-turesque sierra that cuts between Caracas and the Caribbean. Douglas had won several marathons, seven of them in under three hours and one in just two hours and twenty-seven minutes. He hoped to one day run one of the great international marathons like New York or Boston, and dreamed of running up Fifth Avenue and through Central Park.

Douglas had always been a Marxist and a socialist. His father had been a communist and his uncle had died fighting with the National Liberation Armed Forces (FALN), a leftist guerrilla group that had been active in Venezuela in the 1960s and 1970s. Douglas felt that communism was the logical system for a country like Venezuela because it had so much oil wealth. He had studied the works of Simón Bolívar and had found they had much in common with Marx. The class struggle, the similarities be-tween the oligarchy that Bolívar spoke of and the bourgeoisie, resonated strongly with Douglas. When Chávez spoke of the Bolivarian Revolution, Douglas knew exactly where he was coming from.

But Douglas had been taken with Chávez even before he knew the man's politics. Chávez's famous "for now" speech after his 1992 coup attempt had amazed Douglas. Chávez had come on TV and, looking the nation straight in the eye, admitted to exactly what he had done. Here, for the first time that Douglas could remember, someone was taking responsibility for his actions. This was simply unheard of in Venezuela, where corrupt politicians and gen-erals were always lying and cheating to absolve themselves of the things they had done. And here was Chávez, a man of the people. He went into crowds, he hugged people, and he spoke to them like he was one of them.

The fact that Chávez had a military background was a plus in Douglas's eyes. Like many Venezuelans, Douglas perceived Chávez's red beret as an allusion to the days when General Marco Pérez Jiménez had ruled the country. Although Pérez Jiménez had been a right-wing dictator, his eleven-year rule, which ended in 1958, was remembered with great nostalgia in Venezuela as a sort of golden age. Many of Venezuela's greatest public works had been constructed (thanks in no small part to the president's willingness to use convict labor) and crime, which was now so rampant, had been virtually nonexistent. Chávez, Douglas felt, could do what Pérez Jiménez had done, but this time from the left.

Douglas had arrived in El Silencio to support Chávez in the early afternoon and had been walking up University Avenue when he found himself in the middle of the confrontation, but on the wrong side. He, too, had been on the Pedrera corner when Jorge Tortoza and Malvina had been hit. Just moments before, he had seen another man with a black "Quicksilver" head wrap get shot just a meter in front of him. The man immediately began to spit up blood, but Douglas didn't hesitate to help him. At that moment, his political affiliation was irrelevant; this was simply another human being. Soon, other men carried him away, but Douglas feared (correctly) that the man was already dead. The bullet had punctured his lungs and heart.

Eventually Douglas made his way up Baralt Avenue to the pro-Chávez crowd, and together they tried to repel the marchers and the police. Douglas wasn't in a Bolivarian Circle, but now he was fighting with them in what had become a free-for-all. He and his compatriots felt outnumbered by the police and the marchers. In Douglas's eyes they had to use every weapon at their disposal. If you had a stick in your hand, you used a stick, if you had a gun, you used a gun. It was *vale todo*, anything goes.

Suddenly the police surged forward and Douglas turned to run. As he was retreating, a bullet struck him in the back of the thigh just above the knee. He felt his leg lurch forward as if someone had kicked his heel, then the leg gave out from under him. People quickly picked him up and carried him down Urdaneta Avenue to the medical tents across from Miraflores. They put a tourniquet on his leg before loading him into an ambulance bound for Vargas Hospital.

At about this time freelance journalist Francisco Toro arrived on Baralt Avenue with his camerawoman, Megan Folsom, and Hamish, their oversized, redheaded Scottish translator. They were in Venezuela from the United States to do a project about land reform and even though the march had little to do with that—*nada que ver*—they still wanted to get some footage of what they suspected was history in the making.

But by the time they got to Baralt—amid loud explosions that sounded like gunfire—their enthusiasm for good footage was wearing thin. Francisco was jumpy as hell and wanted to get out of there as soon as possible. Megan, however, felt it was too important to miss. They were only there a few minutes when a man walked up to them and put his hand over Megan's camera. "No, you can't film me," he said. "I just came to tell you that you should get out of here. You'll be picked off in particular because of the camera. Get out, now."

That was all they needed to hear. Looking around, they had no doubt that this man was telling the truth. They turned around and went straight home.

It was only later that night that the full magnitude of it sunk in—Jorge Tortoza and six other journalists were shot that afternoon. But when Francisco tried to see if they had captured the mysterious man on film, they hadn't. Whoever he was, whether an undercover DISIP officer or a guardian angel, Francisco realized he had probably saved Megan's life and quite possibly his own.

14 | The Letters of General Rosendo

2:45 P.M.

Before he began his emergency broadcast, Hugo Chávez had been scrambling to implement Plan Avila, but he couldn't give the order to just any general; he could not circumvent the chain of command. Chávez had to

give the order to the head of the Unified Command of the National
Armed Forces (CUFAN), General Manuel Rosendo, the only man authorized to carry out the plan. And at the moment, the general was furious.

He had just found out about the Shark Radio Network—both that it
existed and, even worse, that he wasn't in it; he hadn't even been given a
radio. Completely inexplicable, he thought. *I am the commander of the
Unified Armed Forces, the supreme commander of Venezuela's military,
responsible for national security and I'm not included in the network?* It
was a blatant violation of military procedure, most importantly because
communications had to be secret. This was an open network. Anyone with
a radio scanner could listen in, and many people were.

General Rosendo was not the type of man that you wanted to upset.
The highest ranking officer in the Venezuelan military was a massive, barrel-
chested hulk of a man, with brown skin and a full round face. Rosendo
was built like a sumo wrestler, and the opposition, making fun of his girth,
often referred to him as *Rotundo*. In reality he was not that overweight, it
was more the way that his round head was cradled in his thick neck that
gave him the appearance of being fat, especially when he was on TV.

While he might not fit the physical profile of the commander of the
armed forces, intellectually Rosendo was exactly what you would expect. He
was confident, professional, and pointedly frank. He was endowed with a
sharp analytical mind and during his thirty years in the military was consis-
tently at the top of his class. He had been an instructor at the Military Academy, at the School of Infantry, at the School of Artillery, at the School of
Engineering, at the School of Electronics and Communication, and at the
School for the National Guard. He knew his military science and on his watch
things were done by the book. He had been invited to the Inter-American
School of Defense in Washington, D.C., where he had both taught and taken
classes. There he received highest merits and was named Teacher of the Year
in 1989—the best among eighteen participating countries.

But despite all his teaching and education, the opposition considered
him (like they considered most *chavistas*) an uncouth redneck—part of the
underclass, society's dregs, and, even worse, *communist* rednecks, who had,
by some twist of fate, managed to take control of the country.

Rosendo's reputation as a redneck was exacerbated by the fact that he
was a Zuliano, from the Venezuelan state of Zulia. Zulia was considered the

Hazzard County of Venezuela, hillbilly heaven. Isolated from the rest of the nation on the western frontier, Zulianos had their own diet, traditional music called *gaita*, and an amazing expletive-filled dialect: They all cussed like sailors. Over the course of history a very intense rivalry had developed between Zulianos and the rest of Venezuela for two important reasons. First, and much to the chagrin of the more aristocratic Caraqueños (Caracas residents), Zulia had become the breadbasket of Venezuela. Second, and much more importantly, it was the epicenter of the oil industry. It was here along the shores of Lake Maracaibo that the first big gushers were discovered in the early 1920s—forever changing Venezuela's relationship to the world. (Rosendo had, in fact, been born and raised in an oil camp.)

Rosendo's close friendship with Hugo Chávez began in 1971 at the Military Academy. Although Chávez was now technically Rosendo's superior, Chávez had only reached as far as lieutenant colonel in the army and so had a great respect for Rosendo's insights. In fact, Rosendo often played the part of mentor to Chávez. Rosendo felt that in many ways he was still trying to bring Chávez up right. The problem, Rosendo felt, was that the president had surrounded himself with people who didn't have the country's best interests in mind.

Rosendo's feelings about Chávez's advisers were more than the typical disdain that generals have for undisciplined and unorganized civilians. He felt that they were not only useless, they were the principal saboteurs of the regime—sycophants interested only in gaining political favors and getting rich. Rosendo kept pushing Chávez to get rid of them, but the president would never do it. They were loyal to him and Chávez put a very high premium on that. Instead, the president shuffled them from one ministry to another, even if they were completely inept at their jobs—a true *vergüenza*. It just infuriated Rosendo. Three years into the regime, some of these ministers had already held four or five different positions. People like Lucas Rincón and Diosdado Cabello. At the same time, good people quit or were pushed out, but Chávez didn't seem to care. He thought he could fix it all with money. If there was not enough agricultural production, for example, it didn't matter, Chávez would just import, regardless of the cost and the fact that it was destroying jobs. And he wanted to use the military for everything. Rosendo told him he couldn't keep doing things that way. In contrast to his politburo of advisers, Rosendo told Chávez what he felt—

exactly. That was just the way he was; if Rosendo thought Chávez had screwed up, he'd tell him, without sugar coating. Soldier to soldier. Unfortunately, the president increasingly did not like what his old friend had to say. A distance was growing between the two men. And what was dividing them was the meaning of the Bolivarian Revolution.

Like General Usón, Rosendo had been at the special cabinet meeting on Sunday, April 7, with the Tactical Command, and had been similarly disturbed by what he had seen and heard. But the part of the meeting that most infuriated Rosendo was the acquiescence of the attorney general, Isaías Rodríguez, particularly when the Tactical Command began talking about using the Bolivarian Circles as a paramilitary force to disrupt opposition marches. Unbelievable, Rosendo had thought. Here is a group of government officials—National Assembly deputies, mayors, and governors—proposing a violent action against the populace, and the attorney general, who is the head of the Department of Justice and not beholden to the executive, and whose very job it is to ensure that no one is above the law, is sitting there listening and makes absolutely no objection to the plan. When the outrageous proposition was first put forward, Rosendo had expected the attorney general to protest, but when he failed to do so it became clear that Rodríguez approved the idea, everything they had planned, with his silence.

Indeed, as the battle between Chávez and the opposition escalated, it began to seem to Rosendo that Chávez actually wanted a confrontation, that he had picked the fight with PDVSA in order to precipitate a crisis. He had certainly been aware of the mounting public resentment and the growing power of the opposition. He had dozens of opportunities to defuse the situation, yet had chosen a path that led to disaster.

Since November Rosendo had been sending the president personal letters that outlined what he felt was the best way to handle the country's problems. At the end of November, in an effort to defuse the first national strike planned for December 10—protesting the Enabling Law—Rosendo had written a long letter to Chávez: *Take advantage of the 6th of December, when you will celebrate three years since your popular election, to make a new call to bring all Venezuelans to you. Based on the national constitution, ask the National Assembly to study the forty-nine laws that were approved through the 'Enabling law,' and let them present the recommendations that they feel are convenient.* Chávez had not heeded his advice.

Just the previous night, Rosendo had met with Chávez. Rosendo had been very worried about the plan to have the National Guard take PDVSA by force. He told the president that the plan was dangerous, would have disastrous consequences if it did not go smoothly, and even if it did go smoothly, it would likely be a public relations nightmare. That afternoon Rosendo had met with General Francisco Belisario, the head of the National Guard, and General Rincón, the inspector general, and voiced his concerns. This was not what the armed forces were for, Rosendo had said, and he anticipated many wounded and God knew how many dead. But the two generals insisted that taking control of PDVSA was the only course of action.

Realizing that he was not going to persuade them, Rosendo decided to talk to Chávez personally. By now, it was only hours before the operation was scheduled to be launched. Finally the president conceded. He would make sure that Belisario aborted the assault. Rosendo was relieved. It was one of the rare moments in recent history when Chávez had listened to him.

It was then that Chávez said something that Rosendo would never forget.

"Rosendo, we are going to direct the operations from here [Miraflores]."

"What operations?" Rosendo asked.

"Plan Avila," Chávez said. "And I have my rifle ready to put lead in anyone who tries to stop this revolution that has cost me so much."

Rosendo had shaken his head in disbelief, then laughed. It was trademark Chávez. "The president is loco," he said, then headed for home.

Even though the plan to storm PDVSA had been aborted Rosendo remained worried and, once at home, called his family together. Being a part of the Chávez regime was not easy for his family. Because Chávez was so unpopular, Rosendo and his family had to be very careful in public. Something as trivial as going out to eat at a restaurant had become impossible because they were often heckled and harassed. When people in the opposition saw them, they almost always started a *cacerolazo*—banging their silverware against their dishes until he and his family left the restaurant. As a consequence, he kept his family on base most of the time.

Now Rosendo told his family that the next few days might be very difficult. Then he wrote another long letter to the president, wherein he weighed the probable outcomes in the days ahead: What might happen if the strike continued? What if they declared a state of emergency? What would happen if they used the armed forces for public order? And what would happen if they had to implement Plan Avila?

> Concerning the employment of the armed forces in Plan Sovereignty or Avila . . . this situation, if it presents itself, will leave us in very bad standing and also runs the risk that the officers will not heed its execution or it will induce an obligation to act with violence.
>
> Of particular interest is the fact that in accordance with article 329 of the Bolivarian Constitution of Venezuela, only the National Guard may participate in the conducting of operations which demand the maintenance of the public order.

Rosendo had sent the letter first thing this morning.

Rosendo was with a group of the military high command at the Fort Tiuna military base in eastern Caracas when he found out about the Shark Radio Network and that Chávez was trying to reach him. He called the president by phone. By now it was around 3 p.m. and Chávez was preparing for his national broadcast. The president immediately asked him to implement Plan Avila.

Rosendo reminded Chávez that the law prohibited the use of the military in this type of situation and that he could not follow the order. But there were other reasons why Rosendo didn't want Plan Avila to go into effect. First, who would the military control? In Rosendo's opinion, it was not the march that needed to be controlled, it was the armed Bolivarian Circles around the palace. They were the ones who were most likely to become violent. Earlier, he had received a call that confirmed his worst fears about them from his personal assistant, Captain Michael O'Bryan. He said that he had just overheard Defense Minister José Vicente Rangel giving Freddy Bernal orders that the Bolivarian Circles arm themselves and prepare to attack the opposition marchers: *Freddy, the march has already started for Miraflores. Our people need to be armed with rocks and sticks and knives. Announce on the state television station [Channel 8] that the shantytowns are armed, that will scare them.* The captain was shocked by the news. He had several family members in the opposition march and was panicked that they would be hurt.

Second, Rosendo was well aware that if he did call out the troops and there was a bloodbath, he would likely be blamed. He knew how the commanding officers had been persecuted after the Caracazo for following President Pérez's orders—the last time Plan Avila was executed. If he did this, his future was clear. He could stop the march, but people would die, and he knew that Chávez wouldn't hesitate to offer him up as a sacrificial lamb. He had a clear vision of his fate: standing in front of the International Court of Justice in the Hague, a killer, an assassin. No, Rosendo thought, *the president is mistaken if he thinks I am going to use the armed forces for this. This is not what they are for. This goes against everything I believe in.*

Damned is the soldier who turns his arms against his own people.

"Did you get my letter?" Rosendo asked Chávez.

"Yes, I have it," Chávez said. "I am getting ready for a special broadcast and I'm going to talk about some of it [on the air]."

Rosendo reminded Chávez that his troops were not equipped to deal with crowd control and many of them were very young and inexperienced. He recommended that Chávez call out more National Guard troops—which totaled four thousand soldiers in the CORE-5 division, including armor—as they were the appropriate body to handle the situation.

Displeased with Rosendo, Chávez hung up.

Rosendo and General Lucas Rincón turned their attention to the opposition leadership. If they could talk to the leaders of the march—Dr. Pedro Carmona and Carlos Ortega—they might be able to get the march to turn back before things got worse.

In fact, General Rincón (who had also refused to implement Plan Avila) had been trying to reach the opposition leaders since the march left Chuao and had already spoken to Ortega. Ortega seemed open to dialogue and was willing to meet with Rincón and the other military leaders. But Ortega didn't like it when Rincón pressed to know exactly where he was. Ortega grew suspicious and hung up on him. "Do you think I'm going to tell him where I am?" Ortega said to his aide. "Fuck that. They'll arrest us all."

A few phone calls later and Rosendo's aide had Ortega on the phone again. The labor leader said he was waiting for Rosendo, Rincón, and Vásquez Velasco at the nearby Coliseo Hotel. Rosendo called Ortega directly to say that Rincón couldn't come (he was still upset by their earlier argument and refused to talk) but that he and Vásquez Velasco would come right away.

Now Ortega addressed him caustically. Unlike Rosendo, Ortega knew that there were dead on Baralt Avenue and he blamed Chávez and the military. "I want to know how the armed forces are going to pay me back for the seven dead we have?"

This was the first that Rosendo had heard of any dead. "If that's true, I'm sorry, but I don't have an answer for you, since I'm not capable of bringing them back. What I want is to talk so that we can avoid any more damage. Anyway, if it is true, I'm sorry if it prevents us from talking." Ortega hung up on him.

Rosendo sat back for a moment, thinking. The fact that people were dying sank in, as did the fact that Ortega was putting the blame on him and the military. And while Rosendo did feel responsible, he knew that the burden lay heaviest on Chávez's shoulders. Again, it struck Rosendo that Chávez must have wanted this. Knowing all that he knew, Chávez had wanted the crisis to reach this point because he had certainly done nothing to stop it.

When Rosendo told the high command about the conversation with Ortega and that there were seven dead, Defense Minister Rangel replied, "It isn't seven dead, it's only one, and it's one of ours."

Rosendo had had enough. "Minister, for me it is a Venezuelan, regardless of what side they are on. And I'm ashamed of the negligence of this high command."

Rincón tried to calm Rosendo down. "Now is not the time to pick fights," he told him. The generals turned on the TV and saw several wounded, including the replay of photographer Jorge Tortoza being fatally shot.

Soon Ortega and Rincón were talking on the phone again, but now Ortega didn't want to negotiate, he wanted the military to stop what was happening. "You have the historic opportunity of being a hero for the nation," Ortega told Rincón. "I haven't got guns or a uniform to stop this bloody barbarity. You're the general. It's up to you."

Ortega closed his cell phone and took a drag from his cigarette. "I was pretty tough on him, eh?" he said to his aides. "Shit, I'm giving the orders." The people in the room laughed.

A while later Rosendo's assistant informed him that President Chávez was on the phone and wanted to speak with him. Rosendo waved him off. He wasn't going to answer it. By now Chávez's national broadcast had started; Rosendo was watching him live on TV, so whoever was on the phone was not Chávez.

15 | The Mild-Mannered Lawyer

On South Eighth Street, a block west of the fighting on Baralt Avenue, a friend of Andrés Trujillo's, Carlos Ciordia, was trying desperately to get to the palace. The march had split into three prongs and he was in the middle one. But here, instead of facing *chavistas,* it was the National Guard who were blocking the way. They had set up a cordon at the bottom of the hill that sloped up to the palace and were holding the marchers back with tear gas. The marchers responded by throwing rocks at the soldiers, and soon the soldiers responded in kind. Behind the troops, leading up to Miraflores, was a large mass of Chávez loyalists who were cheering the soldiers on as if they were their hometown baseball team.

Truth be told, Carlos had never thought of himself as a violent person and definitely not someone who would throw rocks at a demonstration. The slight thirty-seven-year-old lawyer preferred to talk and debate. Yet he suddenly found himself with his shirt wrapped over his muzzle like a bandit, shouting and throwing rocks as hard as he could.

In the middle of the melee, Carlos saw a group of his friends, some he had known since grade school. One of them was Andrés León, who was a councilman for Bandera Roja, or Red Flag, one of the communist parties that had once been part of Chávez's coalition. Since they were kids León had been a troublemaker, the most radical of the group, always spurring the rest of them to mischief. "Carlos? Carlos, is that you?" Andrés León asked with mock incredulity, obviously pleasantly surprised by Carlos's transformation. "I didn't recognize you."

"I don't recognize myself," Carlos replied. "This is no time for games. Get some rocks or they're going to fuck us."

Carlos's younger sister, Patricia, had also undergone the metamorphosis. She simply amazed Carlos: a tiny woman, *superchiquita*, he had never seen her behave violently (he didn't even think she cared much about politics). But when the National Guard had started shooting tear gas canisters at the crowd, she had become enraged. She was screaming, *Ni un paso atrás!* and hurling rocks. All the women Carlos saw were like that, in a complete fury at anyone or anything that blocked their path to the palace.

Incredibly, Carlos had initially thought the march would make a good family outing, a good way for them to do some bonding. That morning his parents had told him they wanted to go, and he knew that his sister was already planning on marching, so he thought they should all go together. He left his wife at home with his three girls and went with his parents, his sister, and her friend Aris.

In Altamira they had met Andrés Trujillo and his friend Libia. Already, people were talking about going to Miraflores. Andrés was particularly vocal about this, noting that walking from one predominantly anti-Chávez neighborhood to another was not going to accomplish anything.

Yet Carlos noticed that while everyone was saying, "Let's go to Miraflores," no one was actually doing it. They seemed to be all talk and no action, and pretty soon they began to make fun of themselves. "Come on," Carlos would say and start walking in the direction of the palace. "Are you coming?"

"Oh, yeah, sure. I'm with you, man," they would say, but no one would really follow him so he would stop and come back. They laughed at themselves. All bark and no bite.

Like Mike Merhi and Jesús, Carlos and his family never got close enough to the stage to see or hear anything that was going on, so they milled around chanting and banging their pots and pans. Finally, Andrés gave up. "We're not going to accomplish anything unless we go to Miraflores," he said, "*nada.*" He was hungry and wanted to eat. "If you really end up going to Miraflores, call me," he said. "Besides, if we have to overthrow Chávez, we will need our stomachs full," and he and Libia went to get some food.

When the march had started for Miraflores, Carlos was pleasantly surprised. He thought, the *sifrinos* (the snooty, rich people) have finally decided to protest at the president's door.

As they headed to Miraflores, Carlos had no illusions about what going to the palace meant. Everyone knew that when they got to Miraflores there would be people with sticks and rocks and bottles. But when he talked to other people about this—when he considered the potential disaster—Carlos thought, how many people can they have up there? A thousand? Five thousand? OK, they kill the first ten thousand of us, but the other 990,000 behind them are going to make it. And with this thinking they all walked, chanted, waved their flags, and blew their whistles. Between people with portable radios and people talking on cell phones with friends at home watching TV, they were constantly getting news of what was going on and what was waiting for them.

When they got to El Silencio, Carlos's mother wanted to go up Baralt Avenue, but Carlos refused. He was thinking of the stairs going up to Urdaneta Avenue. He thought, those stairs are only three feet wide and there is no way all these people are going to fit. They are going to kill us on those stairs. "Let's go over one more block and go up," Carlos said, "it'll be safer."

When they got to South Eighth Street by the Fermín Toro High School, they found the way blocked by a cordon of Metropolitan Police. About half a block behind them were soldiers from the National Guard, and about fifty yards behind *them* were the *chavistas*—all blocking the way to Miraflores. The police were keeping the marchers not only from going up to the palace, but also from turning down the side streets, so very quickly the street got backed up with marchers. Then the National Guard began shooting tear gas canisters into the crowd, arcing them over the police. Three tear gas canisters landed at Carlos's mother's feet—somehow among the thousands of protestors, it seemed that the National Guard had singled her out. She was overwhelmed and couldn't breathe. Luckily, the people living in the apartments along the street began to throw down pieces of cloth doused in vinegar to the marchers. Carlos helped his mother inhale through the cloth. When she could finally breathe easier, she said, "Damn, it's a good thing we came the safe way."

The tear gas had pushed them and the rest of the crowd back about half a block, but now they tried to move forward again. When they were near the Marcos Parra corner, they began to hear shots. But Carlos noticed how people didn't run. With so many people around and no one sure where the shots were coming from, people just froze for a few seconds and looked around. "There are snipers!" someone shouted. Everyone was looking for them. On top of the National Building, down toward Baralt Avenue, Carlos saw several men with guns—two with rifles and one with a handgun. People in the crowd started calling to the police that there were armed men on the roof. The police moved down toward Baralt, where it appeared most of the shots were coming from. Now that the wall of police that had been separating the marchers from the National Guard was gone, the marchers moved up and the melee began. At first, the protestors pushed the soldiers back up the hill toward the *chavistas*, but the soldiers retaliated by launching canister after canister of tear gas, which left long jet streams of white smoke hanging in the air.

In this section of Caracas, the manhole covers for the phone company are made of cement. Carlos saw a group of people prying one up and trying to smash it to make rocks. Carlos, ever the lawyer, chastised them: "Hey, that's public property! You shouldn't do that."

Seeing how intense things were getting, Carlos, Patricia, and Aris took their parents down University Avenue toward El Calvario to look for cover. Halfway down the block, they tucked their parents into the doorway of a building with a long awning so that snipers wouldn't be able to see them. Luckily the wind was blowing from the west that day, so the tear gas wouldn't come their way. Then Carlos and Patricia and Aris went back out into the street.

The exchange of tear gas and rocks between the marchers and the National Guard was becoming increasingly vicious. People in the apartments were still throwing down rags soaked in vinegar and even plastic bottles full of it. This surprised Carlos because he had thought that this part of Caracas was 100 percent *chavista*. He soaked his own shirt in vinegar and wrapped it over his nose. Pretty soon he, Patricia, and Aris had lost themselves in the passion of the fight. And this was a rock fight. Thousands of people were throwing rocks simultaneously—creating crisscrossing swarms in the air. Not twenty minutes after Carlos had so diligently defended public property and scolded people for destroying manhole covers, he himself was taking apart the walls of the Fermín Toro High School. He was picking up big chunks of the wall and throwing them as hard as he could.

The Chávez supporters were also throwing rocks and bottles at the marchers over the heads of the troops. Carlos wondered why the National Guard weren't shooting tear gas at them? It also infuriated him that the National Guard didn't seem to care about the snipers. It was the police who had gone down to the National Building, but the soldiers had done nothing.

There was so much noise, so much confusion, and Carlos noticed how different people were reacting to the situation. Some turned aggressive, others became hysterical, and others became paralyzed with fear and walked around weeping. There were people trying to organize others in their attacks, just as there were people trying to convince others to go home. In general, when people weren't running from the tear gas, they tended to congregate near those who had portable radios to hear what was going on.

Before long, the marchers made a rough barricade to keep the National Guard from advancing: big rocks, garbage, and—oddly—an old desk that they set on fire. Carlos and the girls were still on University Avenue— on the left flank of the battle—while most of the march was still on Eighth Street.

Carlos put his back to (what was left of) the wall of the high school. They could tell that the soldiers were just around the corner so they began lobbing rocks over the wall onto them.

In response, a group of soldiers took cover behind the entrance to the Silencio Metro station on the far side of the street. Carlos could see the soldiers through an art deco fence made up of small metal triangles. That's when he saw one soldier pull out his pistol and shoot three quick rounds into the crowd that was coming up Eighth Street. Carlos was perpendicular to him and realized that if the soldier turned, he would have a clean shot at him, too. *This thing is serious*, Carlos thought. It also made him angry. The National Guard were famous for being abusive and he suspected that the soldier had put himself behind the entrance to the Metro tunnel so that no one would see him fire.

He, Patricia, and Aris regrouped with his parents under the awning. "That fucker just started an emergency broadcast," Carlos's father said.

"What time is it?" Carlos asked.

"Three forty-five," his father replied.

"No wonder I'm so hungry," Carlos's mom said. "If you guys want we can go down to the Candelaria and get something to eat."

Carlos was incredulous. *How can she be thinking about eating?* he thought. "Oh, sure, Mom, let's just go for a little walk and get something to eat." His mother shrugged off his sarcasm.

After the emergency broadcast started, Carlos could hear the gunfire pick up; not where they were but one block over, on Baralt Avenue. Then a cheer went through the crowd when they heard that the TV stations had split the screen, letting the rest of Venezuela know what was really going on.

Soon Carlos was back in the fray, lobbing rocks over the wall of the high school at the National Guard. He was in a rhythm now; he would grab some rocks (careful to watch for incoming), take aim, throw, then return to scavenge for more. Suddenly his phone started ringing. "A miracle call." To receive any phone call during a march was considered a phenomenon because so many people in close proximity messed up the signal. It was the first call he had gotten all day. It was Claudio, a mutual friend of his and Andrés Trujillo. He said that Andrés had been shot.

Carlos didn't believe him. "Who told you he was shot?" he asked.

"I called him," Claudio said. "He was in an ambulance."

Jesus Christ, Carlos thought, Andrés has been shot. He suddenly felt very vulnerable.

Claudio asked him how to get to Vargas Hospital. Carlos considered for a moment explaining this just as you would explain directions to anyone—"go up two blocks then take a right before the Cota Mil"—but in this dizzy maelstrom of rocks and tear gas he quickly abandoned the idea. "Take a taxi and get him out of there as fast as you can. Take him to Caracas Clinic or Centro Médico."

Carlos hung up, still processing the information.

He ran back to his parents and quickly told them the news, but then he was right back in the fight, throwing Hail Marys over the wall at the National Guard. After a rock whizzed close to his head, Carlos returned fire with another rock. As he watched his "rock" go flying he recognized its shape. Oh, no, he thought. Did I just do what I think I did? He quickly patted himself down. Fuck! He had just chucked his cell phone over the wall.

16 | Juan Querales

A block west of Carlos Ciordia, Nade Makagonov, a local college student, was sitting on the steps of El Calvario when a fat man sitting just behind her was shot through the stomach. Nade thought she saw the shooter: a man dressed in black on a nearby rooftop with a FAL (the standard issue assault rifle for the Venezuelan military).

Until now the wide, tall steps of El Calvario had functioned like the grandstand for people—mostly opposition marchers—watching the confrontation. They cheered and booed and hollered advice as if they were at a baseball game.

After the man was shot, Nade, like many of the spectators, ran, but some stayed to help the wounded man. Among those who ran was Juan Querales, a twenty-five-year-old telephone operator for CANTV, the national phone company. Juan was a very handsome man with a square jaw accentuated by a black goatee. He wasn't really a part of the opposition and hadn't picked sides. He and his sister, Yamileth, had come down to El Silencio around 2:30 p.m. just to see what was going on. Watching it on TV, Juan had been swept up by the magnitude of it. This was worth getting involved in.

As they were running from El Calvario toward Eighth Street, Yamileth stumbled and fell. As Juan was helping her to her feet, they saw a girl get shot in the face. She was right next to them. Juan picked her up. Her face was covered in blood. "Meet me down at O'Leary Plaza, by the second palm tree," Juan told his sister, then they split up. Juan took the girl toward a group of police officers, and Yamileth turned and ran for O'Leary Plaza.

As Juan was carrying the girl he was shot. The 9-mm round entered his leg and "tumbled," or changed direction on impact, cutting his femoral artery, then twisting up into his abdomen and doing extensive damage.

He later died at Vargas Hospital. He survived the surgery but he had lost too much blood.

17 | Hugo Chávez and the Special Broadcast

At 3:45 p.m. Chávez began his special broadcast. The broadcast had two purposes. Ostensibly it was to reassure the nation and maintain the calm. But by going on the air, Chávez could also block out the news coverage of what was happening in the streets. That would give the National Guard and his secret police time to get to the different broadcasting towers around the city and cut their signals.

He would weather this thing. He would find a way out. After all, politics ran thick in his blood. His great-great-grandfather had been a leader in the civil wars that had ravaged Venezuela during the nineteenth century, and in 1914 his great-grandfather, Colonel Pedro Pérez, had led an uprising against Venezuela's most infamous dictator, Juan Vicente Gómez. When the rebellion failed, Pérez was arrested and later died in prison. As a boy, Hugo Chávez was regaled with stories about his rebellious antecedents and quickly developed a keen sense of history and, perhaps more importantly, of his own place in it. He had a passion for learning about the past, a passion that was fostered not only by his parents, who were both schoolteachers, but by his grandmother who lived with them. It was she who told him the exciting stories of the wars between the rival caudillos that had raged through Venezuela in the nineteenth century, stories that left young Hugo mesmerized.

The man who would one day be president was born Hugo Rafael Chávez Frías on July 28, 1954, in the small town of Sabaneta and was one of six boys. In 1971, at the age of seventeen, Chávez entered the Military Academy, but not for the reasons you might expect. "I dreamed of being a professional baseball player. I didn't enter the military academy because I wanted to be a soldier, but because that was the only way to get to Caracas," he later said. As a lieutenant, his first assignments were in counterinsurgency: It was his job to hunt down and eradicate the various guerrilla groups operating in Venezuela at the time. But Chávez quickly found that he empathized with the guerrillas. He was about to leave the army in disgust when he discovered that his brother, Adán, was secretly working with the communist guerrillas. Adán introduced him to their leader, Douglas Bravo. Chávez later said, "He inspired me and I realized I wouldn't be leaving the army. I discovered ideological meaning in civic-military work and the possibilities for underground work, a phase that lasted several years." Chávez became part of a program started by the communists in the 1960s to spread their ideology within the military. He ultimately spent most of his military career conspiring with and learning from the same guerrilla leaders he was purportedly wiping out. When he became a statesman, his policies would closely adhere to the leftist doctrine of the guerrilla, who had borrowed heavily from the Cuban Revolution since they had been inspired, and often funded, by Havana.

By 1977, the twenty-three-year-old lieutenant had formed his own insurgency group—the Liberation Army of the Venezuelan People (El Ejercito de Liberación del Pueblo de Venezuela). It began as just Chávez and some of his close friends, but before long Chávez, drawing on his love of history, was building and refining his ideas about the movement. What arose was the concept of a leftist revolutionary movement that had the military as its centerpiece, a movement where the military would establish a government that was a mix of civilian and military leaders. And why was the military to be the crux of this movement? In Venezuela (as in many countries in Latin America) the military was deemed one of the few, if not the only, institution that really worked, and a more egalitarian institution at last. The military elite was limited in Venezuela, so the armed forces were viewed as more representative of the population than the political class. Consequently the military, especially the army, was seen as a sort of bodyguard for democracy. When the country's rulers veered too far from the wishes of the populace, there was an expectation that the military—whether by threatening or actually staging a coup—would and should step in to correct the course of the ship of state. It was with this thinking that Chávez saw his mandate: to lead just such a movement.

Over the next fifteen years Chávez would study, come into contact with, and sometimes form and break alliances with many leftist insurgency groups in Venezuela and throughout Latin America. He ended up building a long alliance with Douglas Bravo, and the two worked closely together for

nearly a decade, Chávez learning much from the charismatic and venerable Bravo. But shortly before Chávez's coup attempt in 1992 they parted
ways, ostensibly over the role of civilians in a possible uprising.

Another important influence on Chávez was General Omar Torríjos of
Panama, also a left-wing military leader. Of particular interest to Chávez
was how Torríjos (and later Manuel Noriega) had formed civilian paramilitary groups called Dignity Battalions. While in Panama, Chávez had seen
these civilian groups being trained in insurgency tactics. Chávez thought
this would be ideal for his movement and proposed it to one of the political parties he was allied with, the Radical Cause.

"We made suggestions over the years to [the Radical Cause] that they
should form 'dignity battalions,' made up of civilians from the shanty
towns, and led by genuine community leaders," Chávez said. "We provided materials about different weapons, and we gave classes in the use of
arms, though we couldn't provide them with arms for obvious reasons. We
were under constant surveillance."

These were the forerunners of the militant Bolivarian Circles that
would play such an important role in the violence of April 11. In addition
to these Bolivarian Circles, Chávez embraced other leftist guerrilla groups
that were already in existence (like the Tupamaro in Caracas) and appointed advisers to work with them. Often these advisers were the same
Bolivarian Circle leaders who had received military training in Cuba.

By 1980 Hugo Chávez was back at the Military Academy, but now as
an instructor, the perfect position for him to recruit cadets to his movement. In the end, many of them joined his 1992 attempt to overthrow the
government. They formed an important core of support for Chávez, not
only during the coup, but during his political campaign as well. Because
he had been their instructor, he was both a leader and a father to them.
They had known and respected him from the beginning, during their military formation, and hence their loyalty to Chávez was very strong.

Then came the coup of 1992 and Chávez's imprisonment. When
Chávez was pardoned and released in 1994, still not much more than a
cult figure, unemployed and penniless, he was taken in by Luis Miquilena,
an old communist fox who had been active in Venezuelan politics since the
1930s. Trained as a lawyer, Miquilena had been a student leader, a union
leader, and had helped found the very influential anti-Stalinist communist

party in Venezuela in 1946. A tireless reformer, he had been imprisoned for a total of eleven years at various times throughout his life.

Miquilena became Chávez's political mentor. Indeed, Miquilena's advice and experience were critical in launching Chávez as a political candidate. Once Chávez was in office, Miquilena became the most important civilian in the regime, serving as president of the Constitutional Assembly and then helping Chávez restructure the judicial system.

Following the advice of public relations advisers, Chávez intentionally spoke as little as possible about the details of his revolution during the presidential campaign, saying that these important political details would be clarified by the Constitutional Assembly, which would, of course, be representative of the population. In this, and in many other regards, Chávez was very astute. By keeping the specifics of the revolution as general as possible he simply let the wave of popular discontent against the two traditional parties carry him into office. Clearly, Chávez was a skilled populist and his platform—which blasted Venezuela's rich oligarchy and denounced neoliberal economics and its Washington advocates—expertly capitalized on the poor's widespread feelings of neglect. Yet, even though Chávez presented himself as the champion of the poor, he was also able to carry (at least at first) many of the middle and upper class who also felt that the political elites had squandered their chances at effective rule. Many of Chávez's initial programs to help the poor were very progressive. He funded school lunch and breakfast programs at impoverished schools and began an initiative called Plan Bolívar 2000 that built and renovated schools, nurseries, housing blocks, and roads (often with the help of the military).

Even in physical appearance Chávez seemed more in line with the populace. He had full lips, curly hair, and brown skin—a mix of the white, black, and Indian that is characteristic among Venezuelans. The fact that he had tried to overthrow the government also bolstered Chávez's status as a reformer and added a romanticism to his rise to power: He had stood up to a corrupt system, had gone to jail for his beliefs, but now had a chance at the presidency through the ballot box.

So many of Hugo Chávez's political icons—from his most influential high school teacher, to Douglas Bravo, to Luis Miquilena, to Fidel Castro—were communists that allegations that he, too, was a communist were not long in surfacing. Though Chávez denied this upon taking office in 1999, most of his political appointments were either former leftist guerrillas and communists or comrades from the military. The initial government confrontations with the private sector—attacks on the press, clashes with the church, and attempts to control the economy (i.e., the means of production, by trying to control first the labor unions and then important businesses like PDVSA)—were viewed as standard operating procedure for an authoritarian communist regime. Additionally, it did not go unnoticed that Fidel Castro had also declared that he was not a communist while he was busy consolidating power.

The president's greatest political attribute was his skill as a speaker. Hugo Chávez was an excellent orator. He was relaxed, confident, and inspiring. His speeches, Wagnerian in length, would run for hours. His weekly talk show, "*Hello, President*" (*Aló Presidente*) often lasted six hours. Chávez himself liked to make jokes about his verbosity. "It's now 10:40 and we are going to be here until tomorrow, that is, until early in the morning. Go get yourself some coffee . . . or green tea, which is also good." When Hugo Chávez smiled at you, it was hard not to smile back. He was often self-deprecating, calling himself "ugly" and "a little uncouth." But again, his man-on-the-street style appealed to many and was, in a word, charming.

The most common topics in Chávez's speeches were always the same: Simón Bolívar and Jesus. They were the chorus and leitmotif of every presentation. A devout Catholic, Chávez wore a hundred-year-old scapular (two small pieces of cloth tied by string and worn on the back and chest under the clothes by some Catholics), that he inherited from his great-grandfather, Colonel Pedro Pérez—the one who had tried to overthrow Gómez—and it seemed no coincidence that his weekly TV program was held on Sunday. With Chávez's preacher-like style, the event was very much like a religious service. "Beautiful Jesus," he began one program holding a painting of the crucifixion. "Jesus, my commander. This Jesus with his luminous gaze, with his courage as he faces his tragedy like a man, but with godly grandeur. We ask God and we ask this Jesus who was crucified, this Jesus who was resurrected, this Jesus who was redeemed, that he gives us all that we need."

Then there was Simón Bolívar, whom Chávez simply referred to as "the father." Chávez felt a spiritual connection to the Great Liberator. He believed that history was repeating itself and that he was the Bolívar of the twenty-first century. So profoundly did Chávez feel this that he often set a place at the table for Bolívar and it was not uncommon for him, often while entertaining diplomats, to produce Simón Bolívar's sword and ask his company if they could feel Bolívar's presence in the room.

Although separated by almost two hundred years, Chávez's political platform followed Bolívar's quite closely. Chávez's fervent nationalism, his distrust of the United States, and his desire to create a pan-American alliance all stemmed from the beliefs of Simón Bolívar. The renaming of Venezuela to the "Bolivarian Republic of Venezuela" stipulated in the 1999 constitution was suggestive of Chávez's desire to re-create Gran Colómbia—the short-lived union of Colombia, Panama, Ecuador, and Venezuela established after Bolívar's war of independence from Spain.

Not surprisingly, Chávez's revolutionary movement was originally called the Bolivarian Revolutionary Movement-200 (Movimiento Bolivariano Revolucionario-200 or MBR-200). The "200" being a nod to Chávez's belief in the cyclical nature of history and the two-hundred-year anniversary of Bolívar's birth in 1783. Indeed, when he and his fellow conspirators made their secret oath, it was on Aventino Hill in Maracay where Simón Bolívar had made his vow to overthrow Spanish power.

Chávez's references to Bolívar and Jesus were so common that the two seemed to blur into one another; each was both a political and spiritual leader. By coopting Bolívar, the father of Venezuela, and Jesus, the son of God, Chávez appealed both to strong nationalists and the devout Roman Catholic population in Venezuela.

This was Chávez's forte: his ability to tap into people's emotions and belief systems. He made you feel like you were a part of something bigger; that you were playing a role in history by joining the cause.

While the presidents before Chávez cast themselves as magicians—men who promised to transform Venezuela with the magic of petrodollars—Chávez cast himself as the mystical reincarnation of Simón Bolívar; a savior who had come to rescue Venezuela from its spiraling socioeconomic decline. The result was that many of Chávez's supporters behaved more like religious fanatics than members of a political party.

Now, as the violence began to escalate outside the palace, Chávez knew he was facing the greatest battle of his administration. In that battle, the media would play a crucial role. Simón Bolívar, even in his day, had seen the importance of the media. "The press is the artillery of ideas," he had said. It was a lesson that Chávez had taken to heart and the reason why, on coming into office, he had transformed the state-owned TV station, VTV, into a twenty-four-hour infomercial for the revolution and also why he had coopted the private channels with his *cadenas*. By law, all TV and radio stations had to broadcast these official announcements.

He started the special broadcast. All across the country, people who had been sitting glued to their televisions watching the escalating violence suddenly saw a government logo come on the screen accompanied by the sound of trumpets. "This is a special announcement from the Ministry of Information and Communication." A moment later President Chávez appeared in his office in Miraflores. He was dressed in a suit and sat at a huge desk decorated with gold emblems on its seams and corners. Behind him was a large portrait of Simón Bolívar and the Venezuelan flag.

Very good afternoon, my dear fellow countrymen and -women of Venezuela. Here we are in the government palace of Miraflores. Here we are, as always, facing our responsibilities. I have taken the decision when—according to my watch—it is fifteen minutes to four in the afternoon, to call this special radio and television broadcast in order to send a message to all Venezuelans. And here I want to begin. This message is directed at all Venezuelans, and especially I ask God that those Venezuelans—a minority, of course, in how many they number, not that we are slighting them in any way, for they are Venezuelans, too—a minority of Venezuelans who appear to not want to hear, who appear to not want to see, who appear to not want to accept a reality. As the Bible says, I invoke the name of God to begin this message with His help, with His guidance, and His illumination. The word of God says—the Bible—that the voice of the people is the word of God. With this invocation, with this spiritual elevation, I want to begin this message, I repeat, to all Venezuelans, to all Venezuelans in all of the national territory.

The whole country is witness since three years ago now, not since yesterday, since three years ago, of the huge endeavor that the government is managing with dignity, that it is pursuing in every way, in the political [arena]. We passed the difficult year of 1999 in a political debate that was fiery and, as I always say, unlimited. But it was a debate that now you can see was constructive. The Constitutional Assembly was elected, the people came out, [and] every sector of the country participated in the national debate, there we did not disrespect anyone, no one was pushed aside, everyone made use of their rights to express themselves: individuals, political groups, economic groups, social groups, the whole country, religious groups, nongovernmental organizations gave their opinions and by decision of the majority, as we are all witness to, on the 15th of December of 1999, this national project, this Magna Carta that governs Venezuelan life by the will of the great majority of us, was born.

Chavez paused.

'99 was the year of the Constitutional Assembly and the beginning of this peaceful, democratic, tolerant, open, reflexive, constructive revolution, not in any way destructive, if not a revolution that we have said one thousand and one times, of love, of dreams for the future generations of Venezuelans so that we rise out of the tragedy that we had fallen into, all Venezuelans but especially the weakest, especially the poorest. But this is an endeavor of all of the classes including the highest. I have said it many times, the middle classes, the lower classes, the marginal sectors, the dream that we have and I have personally is that Venezuela, in the middle-term—I have said it an infinite number of times—will be a great country of a great middle class.

18 | The Conference Call

After Finance Minister General Usón ordered the evacuation of the Central Bank (shortly after one o'clock), it was only about twenty minutes before he began to feel tear gas in the air. He had ordered the employees to leave in groups of thirty, but by two o'clock it had become too dangerous to go into the street. Usón ordered the building sealed—no one got in or out—which left a little over thirty people inside—a skeleton crew. Presently, they began to hear loud detonations. Usón told his people to stay away from the windows.

The Central Bank was a huge high-rise in the heart of El Silencio. The bank had a main building and a large annex with a garage for all the ministry vehicles. The annex extended right up to the Llaguno Overpass and Baralt Avenue on the north side, where some of the fiercest fighting was taking place.

The ministry also had its own health clinic, an ambulance, and a paramedic on duty (and the man on duty today luckily happened to be a registered nurse and a firefighter, too). About forty-five minutes after the first detonations, the paramedic called Usón to say that the clinic was receiving wounded from the street violence outside and asked him to come down. Usón checked his watch, he had an important conference call with a group of seventy private investors in New York City at 3:30. The political crisis had made the investors very worried about Venezuela's financial stability, and they wanted Usón's reassurance that the country was still a sound investment. If he missed the call, the government could lose a lot of money.

Calculating that he would have time to check on the wounded, he went down to the ground floor and out to the annex where the paramedic had set up an improvised area for emergency care. Four doctors were helping the paramedic tend to the wounded in the carport beside the ambulance—which they were raiding for supplies. Bags of plasma were hanging from the roof of the carport on coat hangers, their tubes running down into the bodies of the wounded.

There were about twenty people wounded by blunt instruments and about seven gunshot victims. A few of the victims had red streaks on their cheeks—war paint—which meant they were the more militant Chávez supporters, but it appeared to Usón that the majority of the victims were normal people who had come to see what was going on, people who had left work because of all the commotion. He saw one man who had been shot in the back with a shotgun at point-blank range. The shot had perforated the man's lungs—Usón could hear it in the way the man rasped for air. He also had another bullet wound, and the people who had brought him in claimed that he had been shot a second time while he was lying on the ground. Usón suspected that this shot, the coup de grâce, was intended to put the man out of his misery. He wasn't dead yet, but it seemed impossible that he could survive. He was bleeding from the mouth, and the shotgun had left him like a sieve.

Usón couldn't help thinking that it was the National Guard who carried shotguns and sidearms.

The doctors and paramedics tried to evacuate the injured to nearby hospitals, but as soon as they had cleared them out, more wounded replaced them—they were the closest first aid to the Llaguno Overpass.

As he was inspecting the wounded, the doctors and the paramedic cautioned Usón not to go out from under the awning because they were being shot at from the rooftops. As Usón looked closer he could see that the thin fiberglass awning had bullet holes in it. Snipers on nearby rooftops were taking shots at the carport, likely knowing full well that there were wounded people there. Usón thought of all the leg wounds he had seen and the downward trajectory of the shots and realized their wounds had likely been inflicted by snipers.

Usón checked his watch again. He had to get back for the conference call. By the time he reached his office, Chávez had started his emergency broadcast. As Usón and his staff got ready for the call, he feared they would never be able to pull it off. Even though they were on the eleventh floor, the noise from the street was unmistakable—sirens, gunfire, fireworks, and people shouting, cursing, and screaming. He was sure the investors would be able to hear it as clear as day. They started the call. A representative from one investment bank said he had heard a rumor that Chávez had fled the country. "No," Usón replied, "he's addressing the nation right now from the palace." The investors remained skeptical; they were worried about the possibility that oil production might be interrupted. Usón did his best to calm them down. Finally the call ended. Had they heard all the noise in the street? Did they believe him? It looked like they bought it.

Now Usón turned his attention to the *cadena*. He quickly realized that Chávez would say one thing when what was really happening was exactly the opposite. Hugo, what are you doing? Usón thought. What are you thinking? You have a slaughter in the streets that I am witnessing firsthand, and you aren't saying anything. In fact, you're saying that the country is fine.

At that moment, the TV screen split—showing the image of the president on the left side and the live reporting of the violence on the right. The sound remained the oration of the president. When he saw that, and saw the disparity between what Chávez was saying and what has really happening, Usón began to speculate that perhaps the emergency broadcast had been previously recorded.

Pass me that walkie-talkie, it's that I have a walkie-talkie here. We have a network and I am checking the situation, worried, of course. Who wouldn't be worried, of course? Worried, checking with the officials and the troops that are taking care of the palace because, of course, I have ordered a cordon, to make a big buffer of protection, not just for the palace, and this is not for me, not me. The last thing I think about is myself. I am thinking about all these people that are here, [and] more than anything about the mass that is there outside. Because it is the same attitude as the instigators in Maracay that Didalco Bolívar told me about last night how we did not go over there. They were saying that we were, that Chávez, ordered the [National] Guard, that [we] were going to order a march of Bolivarian Circles, etc. Now [the opposition] has grasped on [to the idea] that the Bolivarian Circles are circles of violence. We condemn violence. I condemn violence and have given precise instructions that the people that follow me do not use violence; that they do not fall into provocations.

19 | The Media War

Within fifteen minutes of the beginning of Chávez's broadcast, the private TV stations decided to split the screen in two, showing Chávez on the left side of the screen (as well his audio), and the continuing violence in El Silencio on the right side.

In Venezuela there are four major private broadcasters (Venevisión, Radio Caracas, Televen, and Globovisión), which Chávez referred to collectively as "the four horsemen of the apocalypse." One smaller broadcaster, CMT, also covered the news. The option to split the screen had been under discussion for a while as a strategy to combat what these five broadcasters felt was Chávez's abuse of the *cadenas*. Since taking office in 1999 Chávez had held 437 special broadcasts. Incredibly, in just the last two days, between Sunday and Monday, the government had held 35 special broadcasts which had taken up fifteen hours of broadcasting time on more than three hundred radio and TV stations. Not only had it cut into the broadcasters' ability to do business, they saw it as an overt attempt to block the independent news coverage of the strike. By Tuesday the broadcasters felt that something had to be done so they agreed to begin splitting the screen; however, they would not split the screen during a presidential address. They would maintain that courtesy to the president, at least. All other government broadcasts by ministers and other spokespersons would, however, be split.

It was only a few hours after their meeting that they implemented the first split, during a broadcast by the labor minister, María Cristina Iglesias. It got an immediate response from Miraflores. The government was livid, and the next day (yesterday, April 10), the minister of defense, José Vicente Rangel, invited the five media heads to Miraflores. Abdel Güerere, the director of CMT, remembers Rangel telling them that splitting the screen was a violation of the law and that he would not permit it. But Güerere and the other station heads were unyielding—the split would stay. Rangel had not been pleased.

Later that day, the owner of Venevisión, Gustavo Cisneros, and the president of Radio Caracas (RCTV), Marcel Granier, had been invited to lunch with the president today, the 11th, but the two men had refused the invitation on the grounds that any agreement had to be between all of the station heads and not just two. The situation was growing increasingly tense. On Monday, a group of DISIP officers had been seen casing the Volcano—one of the four broadcasting towers in Caracas located high in the hills. National Guard troops had also beefed up their presence in the Avila, where the other transmission towers were located. The broadcasters knew that the government was planning to cut their signals.

Now, with the beginning of the president's broadcast and just as the march was reaching Miraflores and the violence was escalating (they had already seen Jorge Tortoza and Malvina Pesate hit) the major networks quickly contacted each other. Concerned that Chávez was trying to block out the most important political event in years as well as a potential government massacre, they decided to split the screen . . . yes, even though it was the president.

The acrimonious battle between the media and the president was about to reach its apex. It was a fight that had been steadily escalating since Chávez had taken office. The president had started out by calling the opposition press "distorted" and "unfair" and its journalists "unpatriotic" and "counter-revolutionary." Shortly, he became more vocal. Perhaps due to his military training, the president seemed to take every criticism as an attack that had to be countered. "If they attack me, let them watch out, they'll get as good as they give," he said. Soon the president was attacking specific journalists: When an unfavorable editorial appeared in the *Washington Post,* Chávez claimed that the editor of the daily *El Universal* was responsible. "I know where you move, I know who you meet with, I know you are behind this editorial," the president said on TV. "They are waging a media war against us," he later said. "The aim is to try to halt the Bolivarian Revolution."

The conflict grew increasingly bitter. When the president held a press conference in Maracay, the journalists in attendance refused to ask questions as a form of protest.

In June 2001, the Chávez-appointed Supreme Court moved to legally control the media with a ruling that called for "timely, truthful and impartial information" on the part of the media. It also stipulated that the press could be held accountable for "false news or news that is manipulated by the use of half truths." Watchdog groups criticized the ruling, noting that it violated the American Convention on Human Rights, which stipulates a right to information of all kinds. But with the ruling, Chávez was better positioned to rein in the media and he swore to revoke the broadcasting licenses of those stations that did not behave. That same month he made some of his most direct threats to date. Concerning the foreign press, Chávez said, "Any foreigner who comes here and says anything offensive against the nation or the government or the president or the people will be expelled from Venezuela."

During 2001 there was a steady deterioration of relations between the two camps. The more the president criticized the media, the more they published material about the president trying to limit their freedom of speech and the more anti-Chávez they became. In response, Chávez began to exercise his right to the special broadcasts more and more. The fact that the economy was continuing to deteriorate and people were becoming disenchanted with Chávez's reforms only gave the opposition press more ammunition.

Both sides were becoming more extreme, more biased. The conflict was becoming very personal, too. From the media owners on down to the reporters in the streets, they all felt besieged by Chávez and had become emotionally involved. As a result, by April 11 many media outlets had not only lost their perspective but were actively participating in political events. Many ran opposition ads gratis, had encouraged participation in the strike and march, and had stopped their regular programming to cover the crisis. They emphasized all things bad about Chávez and omitted the good. Their coverage gave the opposition an invaluable push in swaying public opinion against the president.

It is important to note that the media were also playing another critical role. With all the separate powers of the government beholden to Chávez—especially the Justice Department, the Supreme Court, and the Defender of the People—the media had become the only check on the Chávez regime. No case could be won against the government because all the prosecutors and all the judges had been appointed by the president. In effect, the investigative reporting that the media were doing became the only policing (as toothless as it was) of the Chávez government.

January 2002 saw the first concerted attacks against the media. The first was on January 7, when a group of over one hundred Chávez supporters held a rally, then assaulted the office of *El Universal* newspaper. On January 20, a news crew from Globovisión was attacked while recording *Aló Presidente,* and on January 31, a bomb was thrown at the offices of the paper *Así Es la Noticia.*

Being a journalist in Venezuela had become a dangerous job. And those covering the march on April 11 were in no way rested and fresh. All the political upheaval of the past months, and especially the last week, had worn them out. Abdel Güerere saw the telltale signs of chronic fatigue in his employees: They were running on very little sleep and were emotionally stressed. Whenever they went into pro-Chávez areas they were insulted and threatened, which added to their paranoia and fatigue. His news crews had become afraid for their lives.

Now, by splitting the screen during Chávez's *cadena,* the media had launched their latest volley. The decision had a huge impact: It made Chavez appear completely disconnected from the reality on the ground, where people were running, screaming, and pleading for help in front of the cameras.

But Chávez's counterstrike against the private media was only minutes away.

In Miraflores, Chávez upped the ante:

Well, I am going to make an aside in order to explain to the country a particular situation that has to do with this presidential message.

To the owners of the private channels, the situation is this: At this moment the national stations, Channels 2, 4, and 10, are off the air. For what reason are they off the air? There are other channels that we are considering and we will be taking measures appropriate for them. [The other two channels, Globovisión and CMT were also off by this time.] This is an aside that I feel obliged to make during this message to the nation. The result is, well, the country knows very well what a few don't know. The radio electric signal as they call it; the signal by which my voice goes out so that you can hear it; the signal by which this image goes out so you can see this [picture of] Bolívar that is here, this flag that is here, this is the signal, it is a signal that belongs to the state. . . . Those three channels are, at this moment, off the air. Until when? I don't know. This is a procedure that the minister of infrastructure, Eliécer Hurtado Soucre, initiated the day before yesterday, since these stations began; and you saw how we have put up with it. You are witnesses of how much we have put up with. Yesterday we received I don't know how many calls to the palace. Last night I stayed to review them. I don't know how many: five hundred, six hundred. I don't know. And do you know what the majority of people say? The people have asked this: "Close them down, Chávez. Do it, Chávez." One woman told me, "Chávez, I am eighty years old, my love. May God bless you. Do it, Papá." And I have put up with them so much. I have put up with them until the very limit. But one can't tolerate the folly, the insensitivity of these men that are the media owners, to know that the signal is not theirs. And knowing that they have an obligation to the constitution and the law.

—◦∞◦—

In order to shut down the four major broadcasters and CMT, the government had to cut the signals from four separate transmission points around Caracas: Mecedores, the Cuño, Avila 5, and, the farthest of the four, the Volcano. The National Guard took care of the first three and the DISIP took care of the Volcano. All over Venezuela millions of people watching the march and the president's speech on TV suddenly saw nothing but a blue screen with a scrolling marquee that said the station was off the air.

But what the government did not take into account was that these were only the UHF and VHF broadcasts. The secret police had been fooled by a lone TV technician who manned the transmission station high on the Volcano. Even though Abdel Güerere had specifically told the man that if anyone showed up with a gun, to do exactly what they wanted, the man— a true engineer—did not want to risk damaging the transmitter. If you just shut down a transmitter like that, there is a good chance you will damage it when you turn it on again—something that can take months and hundreds of thousands of dollars to fix. Instead, the engineer only cut the UHF and VHF signals to the antenna, pointed to a nearby TV screen filled with snow, and declared the stations off the air. The secret police believed him. However, anyone with cable, a big satellite dish, or DirecTV could still watch the news, which represented millions and millions of viewers—including people living in the shantytowns where DirecTV dishes dotted the hillsides.

Additionally, two of the major networks, RCTV and Venevisión, had set up hidden UHF transmission centers for just such an emergency. Within a half hour of going down, they had these clandestine transmitters up and running—the signal was weak, but many people could still get reception.

Meanwhile at the government station, VTV, in the Los Ruices district of eastern Caracas, the workers were beginning to flee for their lives. During the second coup attempt in 1992, led by Admiral Hernán Gruber (and supported by Chávez from jail), VTV had been stormed by the insurgents. Jesse Chacón, one of Chávez's men, had led the assault, which had been one of the bloodiest phases of the coup. Many station employees had been wounded and two killed when the National Guard tried to take the building back from the conspirators. Memories of the conflict were vivid in the minds of the station employees and they did not want to hang around to see if history was going to repeat itself. They left in shifts according to the importance of their work. Administrative people went first. Last were the engineers and the master operators. By the end of the afternoon the station was completely abandoned, its doors left open.

People who tuned in to VTV that afternoon saw a thirty-year-old nature documentary on ducks.

20 | The Tape

~ 4:00 P.M.

Meanwhile, Luis Fernández was about to become one of the most famous TV reporters in Venezuelan history. Luis was a young man of twenty-eight with light skin and a gentle face under a broad forehead.

He was standing on the roof of the seven-story apartment building that sat kitty-corner to Miraflores. It was an excellent spot from which to film what was going on, and in fact, his was the only camera crew to get this close to the palace. The rest of the reporters had arrived too late to get past the cordons of police and National Guard troops. Fortunately for Luis and his crew, they had already been working in El Silencio when they got the call that the march was coming their way.

From the rooftop he could see almost everything. He was on the northeast corner of the Urdaneta Avenue and Eighth Street intersection. On his right was the White Palace, which was headquarters of the Casa Militar, or Military House—the security detail for the president and his honor guard. Miraflores was across the street on his right. A stage had been set up in front of the main entrance and government spokespeople were taking turns rallying the crowd. A huge yellow banner above the stage read, "A VENEZUELA NO LA PARA NADIE" (NO ONE STOPS VENEZUELA). Directly across the street from him was the Ministry of the Environment. Between the ministry and Miraflores he could see straight down Eighth Street, where the march was in its heated skirmish with the National Guard (Carlos Ciordia somewhere among them). One block down Urdaneta Avenue, on his left, was the Llaguno Overpass. The block and a half from the overpass to the stage was filled with Chávez's supporters. They were thickest in front of the stage and on the overpass; they had also filled the half block leading down Eighth Street behind the National Guard and were taunting the marchers.

On top of the Ministry of the Environment were two men with rifles and one with a pistol. On the roof of the White Palace there was an officer in beige fatigues looking down Eighth Street with binoculars. Also in the parking area in front of the White Palace there were several hospital tents set up—big igloos with paramedics and an ambulance nearby. It struck Luis as strange that they would have all these paramedics there, as if they were expecting trouble. He also didn't like the fact that one of the government spokespersons on the stage was telling people they should be ready to defend the revolution with their blood.

There were eight people in his film crew: His cameraman, Julio Rodríguez; two technicians for transmissions; two technicians for the microwave antennae; Luis's assistant; a producer; and a security guard. They had arrived together around noon. Down on the street they had been insulted and heckled by the Chávez supporters. Luis considered these the normal insults that came whenever he covered government functions. He worked for Venevisión, the private channel owned by billionaire magnate Gustavo Cisneros—one of the richest men in South America and owner of many TV stations, including Univision in the United States and DirecTV Latina; the Caracas baseball team, Los Leones; and the second largest brewery in Venezuela, Regional. Cisneros had also been a friend of President Chávez and had contributed to his campaign, but like many others, their relationship had turned sour as the media war escalated and they were now bitter enemies (although their wives were not). Chávez often blamed the ills of the country on people like Cisneros, often referring to him by name. He also blamed Venevisión for treasonously inciting civil unrest. As a result, those loyal to Chávez had little love for Venevisión.

Once on the roof, Luis's team set up their microwave antennae and began broadcasting live. Soon a soldier from the Casa Militar came and told them they couldn't film there. He threatened to arrest them. Luis knew the man had no right to stop them from filming and became angry. "No, you can't kick me out," he said. "I am doing my job." His film crew backed him up. Then he told his cameraman to turn the camera on the soldier. When he did, and Luis began to narrate that this man was trying to arrest them, the man became frightened and began to retreat toward the stairs. Luis pushed his advantage and pursued the man, pretending to interview him. They reached the staircase but the cables from the camera wouldn't reach that far. Now out of sight of the camera, the man turned on Luis and slammed him against the wall. Then, with a laugh, he left.

By now the march had divided into its three prongs: one up New Republic Viaduct, the other up Eighth Street, and the third up Baralt Avenue. Luis could see the conflicts on New Republic and Eighth Street, but his view of Baralt was blocked by the tall buildings.

When the government cut the signals for the TV stations, Luis could no longer transmit his footage to Venevisión. The crew had to switch to tape, and anything they recorded would have to be hand-delivered to the station before it could be broadcast. That morning they had packed three tapes, but they had already filled two and sent them back to the station. Luis took out their only remaining tape and told his cameraman to take only the shots he deemed indispensable.

For a while they stayed on the northwest corner of the roof, closest to the intersection, because most of the action was down on Eighth Street between the marchers and the National Guard. Then Luis saw a group of men carrying a wounded man up from the skirmish to the hospital tent. Luis suspected he was from the opposition because he saw them carry him through the National Guard troops. He looked like he had been injured in the leg.

While all this was going on, Chávez's special broadcast was still being piped through the sound system on the stage:

So they think they can come here? For what? I am making a call to them and I ask God to send a thunderbolt of reflection to them, to those that have become like mad blind people because of their beliefs, of what sort I don't know, and so they try to come here like this. I say, what could happen when it is 4:30 in the afternoon, twenty-three minutes before five in the afternoon? This is not going to happen. Of course, it isn't going to happen. But what could occur if we permit this march with all of the anxiety that it brings and the injected [tension] that they have put into it in these last few days—whether live or through the media—to come here to the palace? What for? What are they coming here for? Without a doubt it is with a provocative attitude that is very irresponsible, and those that are responsible for this are the spokespersons and those that came out this morning to say that the march was to go to Miraflores.

It was then that Luis heard a series of shots coming from the direction of Baralt Avenue. He realized he had been focusing all his attention on Eighth Street and had forgotten about the Llaguno Overpass. He glanced down that way and saw a group of gunmen on the overpass shooting onto Baralt Avenue. He quickly grabbed his cameraman.

Luis could clearly see three sets of gunmen: one group on each end of the overpass, and a third group of three or four men on their stomachs or kneeling in the center of the bridge. At the back of the overpass was a group of boys and men setting off fireworks and breaking bottles, seemingly to simulate (or mask) the sound of gunfire.

His cameraman focused on the cluster of gunmen on the far side of the overpass. In the midst of the gunfire most of the other pedestrians had either run away or got down on the pavement. This gave Luis's cameraman an unobstructed view of the far group of shooters. The men were huddled behind a redbrick building at the end of the bridge.

Luis watched as a tall man in black pants and a white shirt stepped out from behind the building and began firing down into the street. His name was Richard Peñalver—a city councilman for Freddy Bernal and part of Chávez's Tactical Command for the Revolution.

A man on the near side of the bridge, who had been lying down for cover, stood and waved his hands at the gunmen, apparently trying to get them to stop. One of the gunmen shouted and gesticulated back at the man, as if to say this was something that had to be done and that he should get down.

There was a metal hand railing along the overpass: two thick cylinders with thin perpendicular rods connecting them. Luis watched as a man with a gun jogged up to the railing. He wore blue jeans, a white shirt, and a black vest. He leaned over the railing and fired six or seven quick shots down Baralt Avenue. He then stepped back for a moment and peered down the street looking for a target, then stepped up to the railing again and fired two more shots. His gun jammed, and he pulled back the slide to clear the chamber and then fired until the gun was empty. He stepped back to reload. His name was Rafael Cabrices and he worked for the Ministry of the Environment.

Lying on their stomachs on the overpass were several more gunmen shooting into the street. One of these—a man in a brown jacket—was about three feet from the railing and was holding up his pistol with one hand and shooting blindly. With the gun raised above his head like that, it seemed impossible that all the shots could make it through the railing without ricocheting.

The gunmen on their feet were taking turns stepping up to the railing and shooting. Most of them appeared disorganized and unsure of themselves, and only a few like Peñalver and Cabrices were confident with a gun. They were ducking and diving, apparently watching out for return fire. But in the middle of it all there was a thick man with dark features, curly black-red hair, and a green leather jacket who was telling the gunmen what to do. He would point out targets, motion for them to get closer to the railing, and twice he was seen talking in Peñalver's ear as the man prepared to shoot. Luis also saw him handing out ammunition.

Luis could not see into Baralt Avenue where all the bullets were going because of the angle, but he knew that there were people there. Not ten minutes ago he had spoken with his colleague Elianta Quintero, who was down on Baralt. He was suddenly afraid of what might be happening down there, and he was especially afraid for the reporters because many of them were his friends. Whether you worked for a pro- or anti-Chávez station or newspaper, reporters tended to know each other because they were often reporting the same stories at the same places and, more often than not, they were bored out of their minds while they waited for something to happen. To stave off the boredom, they talked and became friends.

The gunmen continued firing. Most would jump out and shoot, then get back behind cover. But some of them were bold and stayed out on the overpass shooting, not bothering to take cover. They would empty their pistols, reload, and resume shooting. Another cluster of gunmen on the near side of the bridge were also firing into the street, although they would not be captured on Luis's video.

The whole scene amazed Luis. He told his cameraman to be careful, but to tape all he could. Luis suspected that time was getting short. He had a feeling that there were many people who did not want him to see what he was seeing and, to be honest, he was amazed that the Casa Militar had let them stay up here this long. What's more, there were about fifteen people on the roof with them—Chávez supporters who appeared to live in the building—who began pressuring Luis and his team to get out. They began insulting the journalists and saying they were *desgraciados*, unwanted, bastards.

He tried to calm them down, but at the same time, his film crew was getting very nervous. They knew all the stories of journalists being attacked by Chávez supporters and could feel the tension growing. Ironically, their security guard seemed the most frightened of them all. Luis's crew told him he was crazy for wanting to stay there any longer, but he did his best to keep them calm. He realized the importance of the footage they had just taken. Civilians shooting guns like that? He had never recorded anything like it in his life.

Suddenly someone was wounded down on the street and there was a big commotion. Coming from the direction of the Llaguno Overpass was a group of men carrying a wounded man. He was wearing beige pants with a black belt and had on a beige shirt that had been pulled up to his shoulders. He was limp and his face was covered in blood. His name was Erasmo Sánchez. He was a fifty-eight-year-old nurse and a Chávez supporter who—just before being shot—had been lying on the near side of the Llaguno Overpass aiming his pistol at the Metropolitan Police. Among the men who were carrying Sánchez was again the man with the black-red hair and the green leather jacket. He abruptly stopped, and they put Sánchez down. The crowd got thick around them as people rushed to get a look, and it was impossible for Luis to see or film exactly what they were doing. Then the man in the green leather jacket pushed his way out of the crowd and, looking up at a nearby building, motioned to someone there. It was difficult to see if he was making a thumbs up or thumbs down motion, but he was definitely signaling someone. Then he ran back toward the overpass.

The wounded Sánchez was still lying in the street when one of the government supporters picked him up and began running with him. Another man kept his legs from bouncing. They rushed him to the medical tents that were just across the street from where Luis was filming them. They quickly stripped off the man's pants and shirt and a group of paramedics and firefighters began administering first aid. They tried to wipe the blood off his face. The bullet had struck him near the left eye and appeared to have come out the right side of his neck. The paramedics were putting pressure on the neck. A big firefighter with a black vest straddled Sánchez and stuck his finger into the man's cheek up to the knuckle. Another paramedic was trying to put an IV in his arm while another brought oxygen, but the big firefighter was already shaking his head. Sánchez was already dead.

It took several minutes for Luis to realize that this was real. For some reason he didn't accept that there were really people wounded. He wanted to believe that it was fake, like some sort of paramedic training exercise.

Someone on the stage was speaking now, cutting off Chávez's broadcast. The man, out of breath and almost hysterical, was addressing the crowd: "We are not going to fall into provocations! Comrades! Comrades! We are publicly denouncing [the fact] that some of Peña's police from Chacao and Baruta are shooting at our people there on the Llaguno Overpass. Please, comrades, don't panic! We are going to continue here."

"Peña" was Caracas Mayor Alfredo Peña, a man who had initially been a close ally of Chávez and whom the president helped get into office. A short, balding, middle-aged man with a high voice, Peña had been one of the framers of the new constitution. Before entering politics he had worked for over thirty years as a journalist—he had a daily radio show, then a TV program, on Venevisión. Unfortunately, Peña's relationship with Chávez had turned sour when they began to fight over the technicalities of the revolution, particularly the role of the Metropolitan Police. Chávez was worried that they could be a threat to him because the police were a large armed force, so he insisted that Peña appoint a military officer to lead them. Peña refused on the grounds that such an appointment would violate the law. Thereafter, relations between Chávez and Peña quickly deteriorated. As was typical of Chávez's reaction to defectors, he labeled Peña a traitor and took every opportunity to blame all of Caracas's problems on him. In the current ultrapoliticized climate, everything associated with Caracas's municipal government—the schools, the hospitals, and the police—was branded an enemy of the revolution. The police, in particular, were now viewed by Chávez loyalists as henchmen of the opposition.

Luis started to give a commentary on what was happening but it did not tape well. There was too much going on, too much noise from the street, and his voice could barely be heard.

They gave up and again focused the camera on the Llaguno Overpass. There were still men with guns there but they were no longer shooting into the street. On the side of the brick building where the gunmen had taken cover, someone had written some graffiti: "Peña is with the CIA." Then Luis and his cameraman jogged back to the corner of the roof closest to Miraflores. Again, Luis noticed the officers on the roof of the White Palace across the street looking at him, and he wondered how long he had.

Now there were more wounded *chavistas* arriving at the medical tents. The small igloo tent just below them was full, so the paramedics were treating people on the pavement outside. Luis could see a group of paramedics frantically trying to resuscitate a young man with black hair. His eyes were wide open and unblinking. It appeared that he had been shot in the head and a thick pool of blood was expanding out from his right ear. It suddenly struck Luis as more than a coincidence that as soon as these gunmen had started shooting, all of these progovernment victims had begun to appear.

Other paramedics brought in another young man with a chest wound. By now the first victim they had seen carried to the tents, Sánchez, had been pushed to one side, while the paramedics scrambled to keep up with the wounded. Another young man in a red sweater with a bandage on his forehead lay on another stretcher. He seemed surprisingly calm, propped up on one elbow and checking his cell phone while these gruesome images surrounded him.

"Everyone remain calm!" someone was shouting from the stage, although the inflection in the man's voice was anything but. There were many people grabbing for the microphone. One man snatched it and began screaming and cursing the *escuálidos*. Then another man took the mike and tried to get the crowd chanting: *No pasarán! No pasarán!* (They won't get through!). Slowly the crowd took up the cheer.

Suddenly, another soldier appeared on the rooftop and told Luis and the other civilians they had to leave immediately. The soldier was a very young man and was wearing green fatigues and had a white earpiece. Luis began to argue with him. The soldier put his finger to his earpiece and looked over to the roof of the White Palace where his commanding officer was apparently speaking to him, then he began to wag his finger at Luis as if to say, *no way*. He reached out and put his hand over the camera lens. The cameraman stepped back. Luis began to talk into his cell phone, telling people at the station that a soldier from the Casa Militar was violating their rights to free speech. At the same time, his cameraman was trying to film it all, pretending they were transmitting live instead of taping. Luis, of course, wasn't really talking to anyone. His cell phone didn't even have a signal, but he was hoping he could scare the officer away. He thought for a moment it might work, but now the government supporters who were on the roof stepped up their harassment.

"We are here, as you can see, in front of the Miraflores Palace," Luis said, trying to resume his commentary, but his voice was tremulous and he was visibly frightened and distracted. It seemed that at any moment things might get violent.

Then a man in a yellow shirt tried to snatch the microphone from him.

"You can't! You can't!" Luis said, trying to slip away.

"Yes, I can. Yes, I can," the man said, and began pushing him toward the staircase. Just then someone began pulling at the cables of their equipment. The battery for the camera got disconnected and they lost power. Luis gave up. There was nothing else they could do now. He told his crew it was time to go.

But that was easier said than done. Many people down on the street knew they had been filming on the roof. Now with the violence, they would be even more aggressive. There was no way they could just walk out of here. Luis was sure they would be lynched.

And the tape. Everything was on that tape. They had to make sure it made it back to the station.

They got off the roof and into the stairwell. The soldier wanted to escort them out of the building but Luis knew that he couldn't protect them. Finally he convinced the soldier that they would not try to film anymore, but that they needed to stay in the building. Then, very slowly, he and his crew began descending the stairs.

They couldn't figure out what to do. He asked his cameraman for the tape, hid it in his clothes, then realized that if someone grabbed them, he would be the first person they searched. He gave it back to the cameraman, who gave it to someone else in the crew.

They found an apartment with an open door and ducked inside, only to come rushing out a few seconds later as the residents shouted and cursed at them. "*Fuera!*" they shouted. When they got to the second floor a woman came out of her apartment. "Pssst. . . . They are going to kill you down there," she said. "Come on."

Luis realized they had been saved.

21 | Fighting for the Revolution

Dr. Alberto Espidel was standing just a few feet from the Llaguno Overpass when the gunmen started shooting. Much later he would remember April 11 as a series of shocks—stunning events that filled him with fear. This was the first shock: Venezuelans were shooting at other Venezuelans. It had come to this.

Espidel was the head of the intensive care unit at Vargas Hospital—one of the oldest public hospitals in the country. At forty-six, Espidel was a healthy-looking man with short salt-and-pepper hair and a thick mustache. He had the thickness of body and arms typical of Venezuelan men but had avoided the extra weight that comes from the carb-heavy diet of rice, yucca, and fried plantain. He had a quick smile and was known around the hospital for his good bedside manner: He was friendly and energetic and took the extra time to both listen and explain things thoroughly. He was married with two sons, Joan and César, aged twenty and twelve. The eldest, Joan, who was studying law, was standing next to him.

That morning around nine o'clock, Espidel got a call from an MVR party representative asking him to join the vigil around Miraflores. Espidel knew it was possible that the march might come—the TV and radio stations had been saying so for days—and Espidel felt that it was important to help Chávez if it did, although he had to admit he wasn't exactly sure *how* he would help if the march did come. Regardless, at ten o'clock, he had left the hospital to meet his family at the Llaguno Overpass. To show their solidarity, both Espidel and Joan wore their red Chávez paratrooper berets.

Espidel's conviction that Venezuela needed a major cultural restructuring had come long before Hugo Chávez arrived on the scene. In fact, it had started in the 1970s while he was a medical student at Venezuelan Central University in Caracas. Back then the university was home to an important counterculture, much like the 1960s peace movement in the United States. The students were committed to social equality, the alleviation of poverty, socialized medicine, land reform, and the removal of the U.S. military presence in the region. Espidel joined them in protesting against U.S. involvement in Latin America and especially the war in Vietnam. He could still recall going to rallies and shouting, "Yankee go home!"

But by the end of the 1970s Espidel saw that the counterculture was dying. He looked around at many of his colleagues and it seemed as if they had given up. They said, "Hey, I'm a doctor now. I'm a professional." And all the talk about the poor and social justice wasn't important anymore. In fact, many of the people who had been revolutionary in the 1960s and 1970s were now working for the same corrupt two-party system of Acción Democrática and Copei that they had previously spoken out against. They had big houses and liked to travel to Miami. They didn't worry about the poor anymore.

But Espidel was different. He hadn't given up on those ideas. In fact, his conviction grew when, after med school, he went to work in the Amazon basin with Pacentia Rural—a program that sent young doctors into the interior to provide health care for indigenous groups. For Espidel it was the culminating experience of his life. For the first time he saw how differently people could live. Primitive, yes, but Espidel quickly saw that in many ways it was better than the way people lived in the cities. It was a new way to look at being human. Soon Espidel learned to live like them, simply. He got up in the morning and helped people. He found it ironic: The indigenous people were the ones that most others considered poor, yet he began to see that theirs, in many ways, was a much healthier way to live. Here he didn't see hypertension, cardiovascular disease, or many of the other disorders that were so common in Caracas.

The experience changed him. He found the beauty of the place, the simplicity, and the natural rhythm of life very inspiring. It affected his soul and changed the way he treated people. He no longer rushed through life. In the jungle it seemed as if time didn't exist, so he made himself get into the habit of taking his time with people. And he no longer worried about money. He liked money, sure, and needed it for his house and his family, but it wasn't as important as it had been before.

When he returned to Caracas, he was again startled by the contrast. He saw a country that was very poor in culture, a place where people weren't interested in reading, in art; a place obscenely materialistic; that sold its oil to buy unnecessary marks of opulence.

He also noticed the lack of community spirit that he had felt among the Indians. This was 1975 and Venezuela was at the apex of the biggest oil boom in history, yet there was no sense of social responsibility. Everyone was out for themselves.

As for many Venezuelans, the Caracazo of 1989 had been a critical juncture in Espidel's life. But for him, the details of the crisis showed how blatant the elite's disregard for the poor had become. The violence had started when newly elected President Carlos Andrés Pérez, bowing to the pressure of international lenders, began implementing austerity measures that caused a sharp rise in the cost of many goods and services—most importantly gasoline. Bus drivers, anticipating the increase, quadrupled their fares. The result was that many working people suddenly had to spend half their day's wage simply to pay the bus fare to get to work. Spontaneous riots broke out. First, people burned buses; then they began looting stores. Within hours, the unrest had snowballed into a massive wave of looting and arson. With a very heavy hand, the military put down the uprising. Although the government says that only eight hundred people were killed, most people believe the true number was many times that. For Espidel the significance was clear: If the poor misbehaved, the oligarchy would put them in their place.

Espidel felt that Chávez was the first president in forty years who represented real change. He was working hard to wrest power from the elite, but he was finding it very difficult. Espidel felt that Chávez needed more time. You can't just undo forty years of corruption and injustice in a few years. Espidel believed in Chávez's project, his revolution. Yes, he realized that there were contradictions and that it had done some bad things, but, in the end, he supported it anyway because he felt there was a greater good to be achieved. It was more important to revolutionize Venezuelan culture than to worry about every deed and method that Chávez performed.

All that morning the tension in the crowd around the palace had been growing. The media coverage was nonstop—TV, radio, newspapers. All morning people had been talking about the possibility of a confrontation. Espidel was standing on Llaguno Overpass when the news began to pass through the crowd that Carlos Ortega had told the people to go to Miraflores. It hit Espidel like a pulse of electricity. Everyone was talking about it. How can this be? Espidel thought. It was crazy. Didn't they know we were here? Didn't they know that the [National Guard] were here, too?

There were many barrios, or shantytowns, nearby. The supporters around the palace began calling other people by cell phone. Things were generally unorganized, but they knew they would need more help. He saw Freddy Bernal, a member of Chávez's inner circle and the principal organizer of the Circulos Bolivarianos. Espidel expected him to be giving orders, talking to the people, but he wasn't.

Now there was gunfire. Quickly, much of the crowd bolted, looking for cover, but two dozen or so people (mostly men) remained, laid out on the overpass on their stomachs or squatting down. He saw men with pistols taking cover behind a building then taking turns stepping up to the overpass railing and shooting into the street below. There were also a few gunmen in the middle of the overpass, sprawled out on their stomachs trying to aim between the bars of the railing. All the men had pistols, and he could tell by the way they were taking cover that they were being shot at, too.

It was a critical moment. His wife, her sister, and her mother were safely down the street at the Carmelitas corner. Only he and Joan were in danger. They could run or they could stay. Espidel quickly made up his mind. No, he thought, grabbing Joan's wrist, we are going to fight. "Come on," he said to Joan, "you and I are going to save this revolution," and he led him down the narrow steps toward Baralt Avenue. He figured that the more people they had on the street below the overpass, the harder it would be for the police to push through.

"Be alert and always stay behind me," he said to Joan. "If you see people aiming downward, watch out for ricochets."

In a very short time he saw about twenty-four wounded, and he and Joan helped carry three gunshot victims up the narrow stairs to the medical tents in front of Miraflores. Up and down the steps they went. Rushing from victim to victim.

Espidel was frustrated because he had no equipment. He had blood on his hands and splattered across his clothes, but the blood didn't bother him because Caracas is a very violent city and he had seen plenty of gunshot wounds. As a doctor, he knew what he should be doing (putting an IV in them and trying to stabilize them), but he had no equipment, and there was no way and no time. So he just did a quick check of their pulse and breathing, and tried to make sure that they were carried right. "Don't bend the neck," he told people. "Press on the wound, support the spine."

The firefight seemed to him to be between the police, shooting from doorways and from behind their armored trucks, and the pro-Chávez gunmen—who were interspersed with many unarmed Chávez supporters.

The pro-Chávez fighters were operating in packs. There was a Bolivarian Circle from Libertador and the Simón Bolívar Coordinating Group. There was also a group of the Tupamaro, a leftist guerrilla group that had its home in the barrio called 23 de Enero, near Miraflores.

Sometime before five o'clock Espidel and Joan were back near Miraflores when someone cut into the president's broadcast playing over the loudspeakers. "Some of Peña's police from Chacao and Baruta are shooting at our people there on the Llaguno Overpass. Please, comrades, don't panic!" Espidel remembered that two of the victims he'd seen had head wounds where the entrance wound looked as if it had come from above, making him suspect snipers.

This was Espidel's second shock that day: that his wife, Sabrina, could be injured or killed in the melee. So he and Joan headed east down Urdaneta Avenue to find her, her sister, and her mother.

They found them on the Carmelitas corner—the same corner where
the Central Bank was located and where General Usón had recently finished his conference call with New York investors. They took refuge in a
nearby church and waited until the shooting died down.

22 | Taking It All In

Rafael Fuenmayor, the husky reporter from CMT who had seen Malvina
collapse, was exhausted. The confrontation had been going on for close to
two hours now, and he and his crew were still running around. And they
were literally *running*, because to stay still for too long would not be
healthy. They kept doing a circuit from Baralt Avenue to the National Assembly, to Eighth Street, then back to Baralt. They must have done it
twenty times. The shooting would get heavy then die down, get heavy,
then die down, but he could always hear shots from somewhere. The worst
had been behind one of the *ballenas*, the armored police trucks on Baralt,
a constant *ding-ding-ding-ding-ding-ding-ding* as lead peppered the armored plating. The sound was almost benevolent and reminded Rafael of
being under a tin roof in a hard rain.

It seemed to him that the gunfire was coming either down Baralt Avenue or from snipers up in the buildings. Now and then he saw muzzle
flashes from the Llaguno Overpass. At one point his cameraman swore he
had been hit. Rafael looked him over carefully and found nothing wrong
with him. Perhaps he had just been nicked by a rock, Rafael thought. It
would not be until many hours later, when they were back at the station,
that his cameraman would find a bullet embedded in his camera. He had
been holding the camera on his shoulder when he felt the impact and now
he could see that if the bullet had made it a centimeter farther, it would
have come out the other side of the camera and into his head. The camera,
amazingly, had never stopped working.

For close to an hour after the shooting started, Rafael saw new marchers arriving, unaware of what was going on. They would come up the street to a little past Pedrera corner and realize they were walking into a firefight, then disperse into the side streets. But as soon as they ran, they were replaced by the marchers behind them. People just kept coming and coming—perhaps aware that *something* was going on up ahead, yet still determined to get to Miraflores. It was like meat being pushed into a grinder. People were marching forward, not realizing that just twenty yards ahead of them others were being shot.

Rafael and his crew had filmed all sorts of things: people vomiting from the effects of tear gas; men on top of the National building; a girl with a tattoo on her left arm with a head wound walking with a blood-soaked T-shirt pressed to her forehead as a policeman with a shotgun tried to get her to an ambulance. Rafael himself had inhaled his share of tear gas and had to cut his commentary short more than once because it overwhelmed him. Like all the other film crews, they could no longer send their footage directly to the station. They were taping. His commentary was jumbled and the sound was bad, half the time he was out of breath from running.

As the afternoon wore on, the reality of the gunfire sank in, and the two groups moved farther and farther apart. At one point, earlier in the afternoon, the opposition marchers had almost reached Piñango corner, just a block from the Llaguno Overpass. By late afternoon they were being kept well below Pedrera corner, the same place where Malvina Pesate and Jorge Tortoza had been shot, while the *chavistas* were now staying on and below the Llaguno Overpass. Three blocks of wreckage separated the groups. By now, everyone knew that people were being killed. The only life in this no-man's-land was the Metropolitan Police. Four armored trucks were halfway between the two groups and the police—now crouched down around the trucks or in doorways—were still exchanging fire with the gunmen on and below the overpass.

⁂

All told, the gun battle on Baralt Avenue would last from 2 p.m. until about 5:30 p.m.—over three hours—but gunshots would be heard until well after 8. The first person injured by gunfire was the undercover DISIP (secret police) officer, Tony Velásquez, and the first fatality was thirty-four-year-old Jesús Orlando Arellano, who was shot through the heart and lung on the Pedrera corner in front of Douglas Romero just before Jorge Tortoza and Malvina Pesate were hit. (Photos of the dying Arellano were the last pictures on Tortoza's camera.) An amateur video captured Arellano's killer: a man with a red bandana over his nose kneeling and shooting a revolver from behind a kiosk on the opposite side of the street.

When Officer Carlos Rodríguez, who was in charge of Metropolitan Police operations in El Silencio, was informed of the gunmen on Baralt just before three o'clock, he ordered that the armored trucks be moved up the street between the marchers and the *chavistas* in order to keep them separated. Once this was done, the number of opposition casualties dropped off rapidly.

The pro-Chávez gunmen (close to sixty of them) were still interspersed within the pro-Chávez crowd as they threw rocks, Molotov cocktails, and tear gas. While most of the marchers stayed back, hundreds (like Andrés Trujillo) were still determined to get to the palace and surged up around the police. At this point, around 3 p.m., the police were still using mostly tear gas to keep the two groups apart, but were also using rubber bullets and polyurethane buckshot against the pro-Chávez crowd. Still other officers were beginning to return fire against the pro-Chávez gunmen. (In Venezuela, when an officer is fired upon he has the right to respond with deadly force; there is no need to request permission from a superior.)

When the police did move up to create the buffer between the two groups, many in the pro-Chávez camp (including Douglas Romero) perceived this as an assault—that the police were trying to help the marchers—and responded with more force. Hence, as the afternoon wore on and as the distance between the two groups of civilians grew, the battle increasingly became a firefight between the pro-Chávez gunmen and the Metropolitan Police. By late afternoon the police had been reinforced by SWAT-type units better trained to handle the gunmen, including police snipers, two of which could be seen prone on the roof of the armored trucks selecting targets, one with an AR-15 rifle.

It is important to note that the police did not try to take the Llaguno Overpass or completely drive back the armed Chávez supporters. Instead, they stayed between the two groups, acting as a buffer, returning selective fire at the armed *chavistas*. This is significant because the police were by far the largest armed force on the scene, with over one thousand officers (compared to fewer than two hundred National Guardsmen). If the police had really resolved to push back the Chávez supporters so that the march could reach Miraflores—as the Chávez regime would later claim—they could have easily done so. More, if the police had been involved in such a conspiracy, they would not have blocked and tear gassed the march on Bolívar Avenue before it reached El Silencio. They also would not have picked Baralt Avenue to launch such an assault because Urdaneta Avenue—and hence Miraflores—is accessible only on foot from Baralt Avenue and their most important asset, the armored police trucks, couldn't pass that way.

During this last phase of the conflict—the last hour of fighting—the pro-Chávez side sustained many wounded. In fact, in the last forty-five minutes, when the march had been effectively turned away, the pro-Chávez side suffered all of their fatalities. It is clear that the Metropolitan Police shot many of them, like Erasmo Sánchez, who had been firing at the police. Others were possibly hit by friendly fire from the Chávez supporters' haphazard shooting. This explains most of the pro-Chávez fatalities on Baralt Avenue, but there were others who were allegedly shot just in front of Miraflores, in the very heart of the pro-Chávez zone where it was impossible for them to have been shot by the Metropolitan Police and where there was no opposition presence. The question of who was responsible for these shootings would become the great unsolved mystery of April 11. The government would claim that the victims were hit by opposition snipers trying to spark mayhem and clear the way for the march. But how would anti-Chávez snipers get in the windows and rooftops of buildings already controlled by Chávez's security forces, the Casa Militar? In contrast, the opposition would claim that the government intentionally waited until late in the afternoon, then shot its own people so that the events of the day would appear to the world as a clash between equally violent forces. But would the Chávez regime go to such extreme lengths to garner political sympathy? The answer would never become clear.

23 | Mystery Gunman

It was just about five o'clock when Antonio Návas was hit. He was standing near the Bolero corner next to Miraflores when it happened.

He had come down to the palace that afternoon to support Chávez. Antonio was a former DISIP officer who worked as a bodyguard for the Cisneros people, the owners of Venevisión. Even though he worked for people in the opposition, he was still a *chavista*, and it wasn't simply because his brother worked security at Miraflores. Antonio felt that Chávez wasn't like the other Venezuelan presidents. This president helped people; he was one of them. He had programs for students and gave financial credits to the poor.

As the march got closer, different government leaders got up on stage to rally the crowd: MVR Deputy Cilia Flores and the minister of defense, José Vicente Rangel. But Antonio could see that people were worried. And there was a lot of dialogue that Antonio didn't agree with. People talking about violence. There were women and children there, after all. Many people had taken red lipstick and marked their faces—one stripe on each cheek—as if they were Indians getting ready for battle. Antonio was also worried about what the opposition might do. You didn't know if they might start shooting or maybe one of them would put on a shirt like a Bolivarian Circle member and start killing their own people to blame it on us.

He decided to go down to the Llaguno Overpass. He took the steps down to Baralt and saw about 150 people in a melee with the police. He saw wounded—one man bleeding from his leg, another with a wound in the shoulder—and he saw people who looked like they were dead. He also saw the Chávez supporters throwing rocks and firing guns. Frightened, he ran back to the palace. From then on he stayed near the stage where there were more National Guardsmen to protect the crowd. How did I end up here? he thought. How did Venezuela end up here?

Things were turning *feo*, ugly, and he saw more wounded being carried to the hospital tents. (On the rooftop above him, Luis Fernández was busy filming.) Antonio's cell phone began ringing. It was his stepfather,

Antonio Álvarez. He answered the phone and was in the process of turning around when the bullet slammed into the back of his head below his right ear. It struck him at an odd angle. The bullet perforated his skull, wisped past his lower brain, broke his jaw, blew out his teeth, then came out his right cheek.

At first he thought the shot had come from the front, from down Eighth Street where the National Guard were fighting it out with the marchers, but later the government's ballistics experts would tell him the shot probably came from Hotel Ausonia, which he didn't think was right either. In the end, because he was turning at the moment he was hit, he was never really sure.

But he knew immediately that he had been shot. People rushed up to help, shouting that he had been shot in the head and was dying. The pain was excruciating and he was very frightened. He felt dizzy and had an incredible headache. He could see people standing over him, but he couldn't talk. They carried him to the hospital tents. In and around the tents he could see six or seven wounded. He watched as the paramedics tried to save one man with a head wound. Antonio tried to turn his head away from all this. Up on the lawn toward the White Palace he saw a young man standing with his arms crossed on the inside of the black ornate fence. His name was Nelson Zambrano. He was twenty-three years old and had begun working in the palace archives just two weeks before. He was looking down at Antonio, and for a moment their eyes met. Suddenly, Zambrano collapsed and Antonio watched as his body rolled down the grassy embankment toward him. Other witnesses would say that Zambrano had simply fainted, but he had been shot in the neck, the bullet entering the tenth vertebra and killing him.

A soldier from the Casa Militar, thinking the shot had come from the Hotel Ausonia, began shooting in that direction.

Soon Antonio was evacuated in an ambulance.

Crelia de Caro and her husband, Luis Alberto Caro, had been part of the vigil around Miraflores on April 9 and 10, but they had both agreed not to go to Miraflores today, on April 11. Crelia had a feeling that something bad was going to happen and as a good Catholic she was keeping a candle lit by the small altar to Jesus she kept in her house. Crelia hoped that God and the Virgin Mary would look after the president and that the Holy Spirit would give him the wisdom to move forward with his revolutionary project. Her husband had teased Crelia about her bad portent at the breakfast table that morning: When she pulled a long hair out of his eyebrow, he acted as if he had been mortally wounded. "It hurts," he cried. "Can't you see how the blood is coming out of me?"

There was no blood, she knew, just a bit of water that had been left on her hands from preparing *arepas*.

Instead of going to Miraflores, Crelia and Luis Alberto planned to spend a quiet day in their home in Catia la Mar, a town on the Caribbean coast about forty-five minutes from Caracas. Crelia was forty-seven and a housewife, while Luis Alberto was ten years older. He supported the family working as a refrigerator technician for the Madosa Company, a job he had held for fifteen years. They had three children and two grandchildren.

To Luis Alberto's consternation, Madosa had joined the strike, so there was no work, and he soon became restless sitting in the house.

Both Crelia and Luis Alberto were very devoted to Chávez, and Luis Alberto had even joined the Tactical Command for the MVR near their home. They both believed in Chávez. Luis Alberto saw the revolution as something vital for the future of the country. What Chávez was doing was for his children and for their children.

As the day wore on, Luis Alberto became increasingly impatient. After lunch—having watched all the happenings around Miraflores on the news—he announced that he was going to take a little drive, which Crelia interpreted to mean around the neighborhood.

It wasn't until a little after three o'clock that she got a call from her niece, who had learned that Luis Alberto and their son, Luber, had gone to Caracas and were in front of Miraflores. By now the TV stations were talking about dead and wounded and gunmen and snipers. Crelia felt a jolt of fear. She watched the violence on TV with mounting apprehension.

Late in the afternoon Crelia got a call that confirmed her worst fears. It was a friend of Luis Alberto's: "Señora, your husband has fallen near Miraflores." Crelia began to weep. She was very startled, but part of her didn't really believe what she had heard. It couldn't really be true.

With more frantic phone calls the details began to become clear. Luis Alberto and their son had separated once at Miraflores. When the wounded began arriving, Luber had actually seen his father being hurried to the hospital tents by a group of men, but he hadn't recognized him. It wasn't until well after five o'clock that a stranger had come questioning Luber about his father. He took Luber to the tents and asked him to identify one of the bodies. No, Luber told him, this bloody dead person who had been shot through the nose was not his father. Luber had turned and walked away. But then he came back. He had to be sure. After cleaning off the blood with his hand, he resigned himself to the truth. It was his father.

Back in Vargas, Crelia was in a state of shock. Her daughter, Laydi, and her granddaughter soon arrived at her house. On hearing the news, the little girl went to the window and began crying, "Papi, Papi," calling for her grandfather.

24 | At the Caracas Clinic

Meanwhile, Gorka Lacasa was anxiously waiting in radiography at the Caracas Clinic. Malvina's brother, Israel, had arrived from the march to take care of her. That had made Gorka feel better for a while. He knew she was getting excellent attention now, but he didn't understand what was taking so long. They kept taking her in and out of radiography. They would get the results, then send her right back in for more tests and scans.

At last, Malvina's brother took him aside and explained what had happened. When Malvina had arrived, the ER staff had quickly noticed that there was much too much blood for a blow from a rock. Malvina had also complained that the nape of her neck hurt. That was when they found the exit wound and took her for X-rays and an MRI. They realized it was a gunshot wound but had to do another MRI to make sure there were no remaining bullet fragments; luckily, there weren't. The bullet had broken Malvina's upper jaw (the inferior maxillary)—shattering it like a car windshield—then changed trajectory slightly and exited out the top of her neck on the left side. The bullet, her brother said, had missed both her carotid artery and her jugular vein by a quarter of a millimeter. He assured Gorka that she was going to be OK. It was a miracle that she was alive, he said; then he left to check on her again.

There was a TV on in the hallway, and Gorka could see Chávez, still doing his special broadcast, saying that everything was fine and not to be alarmed. With all that has happened, he thought, almost getting killed, Malvina almost dying, and this freak is still going on and on. That was when it all caught up with Gorka. Suddenly everything that had happened overcame him. He began to cry.

He went in to see Malvina. When she saw the tears on Gorka's cheeks, she said, "Don't cry. I'm fine." Then, impressed by his display of emotion, she teased him, "Now I'm sure you love me."

Most of the time it didn't bother Gorka that he and Malvina had never gotten married. They were together and loyal to each other; that was what was important. But Gorka thought about it now, that he should have married her a long time ago. Malvina had one condition for Gorka: It was a running joke that he had to propose to her on top of a *tepui*, one of the massive plateaus that rise out of the jungle deep in Venezuela's interior. This was quite a tall order because getting to the top of one of the *tepui* meant either hiking for five days or taking a helicopter. Gorka had always promised her that one day he would. Now he planned not to wait so long.

—◦◦◦◦—

With a little help from nepotism, Malvina received exceptional care at the Caracas Clinic. She would remember being almost overwhelmed by attention. Friends of her brothers from every specialty coming to see her, checking her over, giving their opinion. She would find out later that even in the operating room there had been neurologists and other specialists coming in and observing, giving advice, and trying to help.

Malvina's jaw was wired shut for six weeks, and she had to learn to eat through a straw. She began physical therapy immediately. Without it, there was a risk that the swelling would constrict her windpipe. In order not to alarm her, it was agreed that no one would tell her she had been shot, and she continued believing she'd been hit with a rock.

25 | Inside Vargas Hospital

Vargas Hospital was scarcely seven blocks from the fighting and would bear the brunt of the casualties. Over one hundred years old, the hospital had been added onto dozens of times, eventually becoming a massive labyrinth of twisting corridors and disjointed buildings that consumed three city blocks. Walking through the hospital you could be surrounded in the chaotic world of a bustling inner-city hospital one moment and the next moment find yourself in an abandoned, water-filled basement. In its heyday, it had been the best hospital in Venezuela and here and there you could see the remnants of this proud past—beautiful Doric columns, trellised archways, ornate fish-head rainspouts. But the years had not been good to Vargas, and it was now literally crumbling, buckling under the burden of Venezuela's appalling poverty, skyrocketing violence, and chronic government underfunding. The paint was peeling from the walls in long strips, there was thick mold on the ceiling tiles, and black smudges disfigured the walls.

This dilapidated state was typical of Venezuela's public hospitals, long neglected by the traditional ruling parties that came before Chávez. But in addition to suffering from this systemic disregard, Vargas Hospital was also a victim of the political battle between Chávez and Mayor Peña.

Due to Venezuela's overly centralized government, public hospitals like Vargas were heavily dependent on the federal government for funding, even though they were technically under the jurisdiction of the local municipality. This was because virtually all government revenue—taxes and oil income—went straight to the federal government before being redistributed back to the states and municipalities. As in most countries, the legislature was supposed to control government monies, but in Venezuela the reality was that this power was held by the Ministry of Finance (headed by General Usón), which was controlled by the president. If the president did not approve of the leader of a specific state or municipality, the funds were stalled or blocked altogether. This abuse of power was not new to the Chávez administration, but Chávez—in part due to the rancor he felt against those who opposed him—made the tactic into an art form.

For the hospital, the quarrel was a disaster. As Chávez put the squeeze on Peña, the flow of funds to the hospital had been reduced to a trickle. The result was that each day the hospital had less and less to work with. Most months the federal portion of employee paychecks went unpaid.

The ER whiteboard read:

> There is no: PL equipment
> electrodes for external pacemakers,
> fuses for ventilators and BiPAP,
> EKG paper
> Bilumen and Trilumen Catheters

Taped to an old HP inkjet printer was a note that read: "There is no toner! Not here or anywhere else in the hospital and I am not going to buy any more." Although incredibly low on equipment and supplies, Vargas Hospital did several things very well and one of these was treat gunshot wounds. Due to its location in the inner city, it received between 95 and 110 gunshot patients in any given week; 75 percent of the broken bones that the hospital treated were caused by bullets. Venezuela's two-decade-long economic crisis had led to a staggering surge in violent crime, which had transformed Vargas into more of a war hospital than anything else. By necessity, the staff, and particularly the surgeons, had become experts in treating gunshot wounds.

Dr. Pablo Rausseo was in charge of emergency medicine at Vargas Hospital on the afternoon of April 11. He himself had gone to the march that morning and walked the scheduled route from Altamira to Chuao, but since he was due at the hospital at one o'clock, he and his wife had gone home to have lunch before he headed to work.

While they were eating, they watched the news coverage switch back and forth between the march moving closer and closer to the palace and the government supporters and National Guard waiting for them. Rausseo could see that many of the president's supporters had sticks and rocks, so he knew they could expect people with beating injuries—cuts and concussions and a few broken limbs—plus those suffering from tear gas inhalation.

Earlier that morning, at around eight o'clock, Rausseo and his boss, Dr. Ricardo Serbenescu, had set up a contingency plan in case there was a confrontation. They added staff and set up a triage system:

Green—Injuries can wait
Yellow—Noncritical injuries but can become critical
Red—Critical
Black—Nonrecoverable injury

When Rausseo got to the hospital, he made additional preparations. Extra stretchers, beds, blood. He even had a couple of stretchers put in a small room as an interim morgue. He knew it was probably unnecessary. There had been a lot of big marches in the past year and there hadn't been any fatalities.

Rausseo was surprised when the first patient was a gunshot victim, a young man with a single shot to the head. He looked very young and had thick black hair. Rausseo guessed he was seventeen or eighteen. He was coded black—a nonrecoverable injury. The bullet had passed through his head, entering the forehead, exposing the brain, and making a large exit wound at the back of the head. He lived about fifteen minutes, his breathing erratic, then died. The young man was later identified as Mike Merhi's son, Jesús.

More wounded began to arrive. He could tell by their dress—their T-shirts, their flags and whistles—that they were marchers for the opposition. Rausseo realized that the additional staff he had requested was not going to be enough and began making calls for more help.

Dr. Ricardo Serbenescu was working in his private office when he got the call from Vargas. He switched on the TV and saw the footage of the photographer Jorge Tortoza being shot in the head. He immediately headed for the hospital.

Dr. Serbenescu was a tall man with a light mustache, small chin, and a receding hairline. As the Chief of Emergency Care at the hospital he was soft-spoken, gentle, and professional—very even keel—which, in his line of work, was necessary. Many doctors couldn't handle emergency medicine. He, however, had learned how to deal with it and he didn't let it get to him . . . most of the time. He hadn't planned on going into emergency care—he had wanted to be an internist—but there had been a need for people to specialize in emergency care; public violence was on the rise. In the end, he had come to like it, in part because issues can be resolved quickly. You weren't spending months and months working with patients.

When Serbenescu arrived at the hospital, he found it surrounded by a massive crowd shouting and yelling. At first he figured they were either from the opposition or the government engaged in some sort of protest. But when he got closer he realized they had congregated there to see what was going on and to help in any way they could. He could hear them shouting, "Here's another wounded!" "Watch out!" "Coming through!"

Inside was total chaos. He had never seen so many wounded before. There was no place to put them, and many were just lying on the floor in the hallways. The staff couldn't keep up with the stream of casualties brought in by pickup trucks—three or four wounded in each truck bed. There was blood everywhere. Not only were there the shouts and cries of the patients, but Serbenescu could tell that his staff was also very frightened; they didn't know what was happening and their emotions were taking over. Serbenescu felt it too. He was too young to have worked during the Caracazo, so this was new to him, but he knew that when circumstances become too distressing, it generated uncertainty about what to do next. Inaction. He had to make sure his people stayed focused on their work.

Even though his colleague, Dr. Rausseo, had done all he could to get ready, this was much more than they could have ever prepared for. They were going to need a lot more supplies: more blood, more plasma, more gloves, just about everything he could think of. Serbenescu had been quietly hoarding supplies here and there over the last several months—supplies that he knew they might need in the case of a "real" emergency. He had put them in boxes and locked them in a special room. He was the only one with the key. This, he realized, was a real emergency.

After he retrieved the extra supplies, he divided his staff into teams: each with a surgeon, nurses, residents, and different specialists. He assigned the upstairs operating room for all the broken bones. But even with his hoarded supplies, he knew that they were going to run out of blood. He made calls to the mayor's office, the blood bank, and the Red Cross asking for help. When they ran out, they started taking blood from the nurses and residents.

The surgeons were pulling a lot of handgun bullets from the victims, mostly 9-mm rounds, but they were also removing a lot of .308-caliber (762 NATO) rounds that could only have been fired from a Belgian FAL, the assault rifle used exclusively by the Venezuelan military, most likely by the National Guard troops loyal to Chávez.

Dr. Rausseo was struck by the damage these rounds were doing. It was not uncommon for a patient with four or even five wounds from a .38 to recover as long as the bullets didn't hit anything vital. But the military rounds were tearing these people up. They thought they could save a pregnant woman who was shot in the shoulder at a downward angle. It didn't look that serious at first, but when they got inside they found the bullet had traveled down into her abdomen and done too much damage to her organs. They couldn't save her. Her name was Josefina Rengifo and she was nineteen years old.

Rausseo also noticed a disproportional number of leg wounds, mostly the 9-mm rounds, usually entering from the back of the leg. Rausseo guessed that this was from the bullet's falling trajectory as people ran from the gunmen.

There was a reporter who came in saying that he had been shot in the chest. His name was Jonathan Pérez and he worked for the daily *Tal Cual*. The bullet had pierced his wrist and struck his chest near the heart. He had blood all over his shirt, and Rausseo could tell he was very frightened. But when they took off his shirt and examined the wound, it was only a fraction of an inch deep. They checked the vest the reporter had been wearing and found the bullet embedded in his cell phone, which he had— contrary to custom—placed in his chest pocket.

As the afternoon wore on, they began to get more wounded from the progovernment side. People with red berets, red T-shirts, Long Live Chávez headbands.

More and more staff arrived, including many residents. This was graduation weekend for the medical students and dozens of them came in to help in any way they could.

All the bullets that the surgeons removed were taken by the attorney general's office as evidence. They were never seen again.

26 | Andrés Trujillo in Vargas

Andrés Trujillo, who had been shot through the leg near Mike Merhi's son, Jesús, was crammed next to another wounded man when the ambulance doors opened onto what looked like the loading dock of a rundown restaurant. This was the emergency entrance to Vargas. There were many people around: a newspaper photographer snapping pictures, a radio journalist, doctors, nurses, and many, many gawkers.

Once inside, Andrés was stripped and examined. A doctor started giving the nurse instructions. Andrés heard him ask for something.

"We're out of that," the nurse replied.

"OK, then give him *toxoide*," said the doctor.

"There is no *toxoide*," she said.

"OK, take an X-ray," he said.

"Hold on, Doctor, 'cause I think we are out of X-ray plates," and she went to check.

The doctor turned to Andrés, "Wherever you end up, tell them to inject you with *toxoide*."

"I feel like I'm going to pass out," Andrés said. "How am I gonna tell anyone anything?" The doctor took a roll of medical tape, tore off a piece, wrote something on it, then stuck it to Andrés's chest and left. "Inject with *toxoide*," it said.

A nurse put an IV in his arm, and soon another wounded young man arrived. He had a head wound, yet was still conscious and cursing. "Why the hell did they do this to us? Goddamned *desgracia'os*!" Andrés tried to talk to him. He looked pretty young, probably about twenty, but was not the same boy Andrés had seen on Baralt Avenue. He had a shocked and distant look in his eyes. "They really let us have it!" the boy said. *"Que bolas!"* A doctor and two young residents—a man and a woman—triaged the boy. "Leave him," the doctor said, "he isn't a priority." But Andrés noticed that the residents both had tears in their eyes, and the woman resident told the doctor they had to give him such-and-such medicine. "No," the doctor said. "We have to optimize our resources. He isn't a priority." The boy kept cursing, "Motherfucking Chávez! Why did you do this to us?"

A nurse was nervously running to and fro, and she accidentally knocked out Andrés's IV. By the time she had set up the IV again and Andrés had turned to the wounded boy, he was dead. The woman resident began crying over the body. "We should have done something to save him," she said, and began to run through all the possible procedures one is supposed to follow, other things they might have done. That was it for Andrés. The confidence that he had in the ambulance—that this was not his day to die—was gone. He dug out his cell phone and called his friend Claudio. It was hard to get a signal, but he finally got through. "Please, do whatever you have to, but you have to get me the hell out of here." No one had put anything on the wound to slow the bleeding and he could hear his blood dripping to the floor. He was starting to shiver from the cold and he had become very weak and scared. He knew that at any moment he might pass out. *I can't pass out here*, he said to himself, *if I do, I'll die. No, I can't pass out here.*

Andrés noticed that there were many young residents. Many of them were walking around with tears in their eyes. Some, at least, were keeping busy, but others were pacing around in a state of shock. The older doctors had hard looks on their faces and knew how to handle the situation, but most of the residents were completely beside themselves. One of these residents stayed with Andrés. A big man, he was built like a weight lifter and had black hair and a goatee. He was apparently too inexperienced to know what to do, so he just kept watch over Andrés. "Damn, it's really messed up, dude," he said, putting his hand on Andrés's shoulder and touching his hair. When Andrés said he was cold, the resident went and found a thin hospital gown and draped it over him.

Every now and then a nurse would come in with a little folder and take down his name, ID number, and other personal information. Then a little while later another nurse would come around with a different notebook and ask for the same information. This happened five times.

A nurse returned to announce that they had some X-ray plates, and Andrés was soon wheeled into the X-ray room. The results were a relief. "He's all right," the doctor told the residents. The bone had not been broken, and the bullet had missed his femoral artery. "He isn't a priority." Somehow this phrase was less than reassuring. It echoed what the doctor had said about his young neighbor only minutes before he stopped breathing.

Andrés was left in the main corridor outside one of the operating rooms. Seven or eight other wounded surrounded him. Some were on stretchers like Andrés, others were sitting in bloodied plastic chairs, still others were lying on the floor. On his left, through two swinging stainless steel doors, was an operating room. The screams coming from inside that room were incredible. Terrible, terrible sounds. Andrés had never heard screams like that. And the doctors, too, were shouting and screaming and arguing with each other about what to do. Twice he heard a doctor say, "He's dead. Bring in the next one." And they would wheel the body out covered in a sheet.

Andrés was starting to lose it. He felt light-headed and his vision was getting blurry. He had to get out of here before he fainted. He tried to call Claudio again—to call anyone—but his cell phone was dead. The minutes dragged on and on and on.

How had things got so fucked up? he thought. He remembered back to this morning, when he and Libia had joined the march on its way to Miraflores. It had been so amazing; such an incredible feeling to be a part of this thing. The energy. He thought about all the people, so many people: women and children and old ladies; fat people, thin people, rich people, and poor people who smelled bad. Every type of person you could imagine, but they had all been happy. People were dancing and chanting and waving flags and banging pots and pans. They really felt like they were going to accomplish something; they were going to get Chávez out. It reminded Andrés of an epic Hollywood movie, the ones with thousands of extras, when the tide of events caused a great movement of people. And when they had begun singing the national anthem, Andrés found he had tears running down his cheeks.

Andrés turned and noticed a man in a suit and tie looking for someone among the wounded. Andrés recognized him: He was a *chavista* and a councillor for the Baruta municipality. The person he was looking for turned out to be the boy on the stretcher next to him. "Could you ask your dad if he could lend me his phone?" Andrés asked the boy. He was worried that the man might say no, somehow knowing that Andrés was an *escuálido*. But the man didn't hesitate and immediately handed over his cell phone.

He called Claudio again and told him what was going on. Claudio was outside the hospital but they wouldn't let him in. "Do what you have to, but get me out of here!" Andrés said. He knew he sounded hysterical which, in fact, he was. If freaking out was what it took, so be it.

⚬⚬⚬

Lying on a cot on the floor beside Andrés was Douglas Romero, the marathon runner who had been shot in the leg fighting against Andrés and the police on Baralt Avenue. The medics outside Miraflores had put a tourniquet on his leg and the bleeding was under control, but he, too, was waiting to go into the emergency operating room. As he lay there among the other wounded, listening to Andrés call for help, he was disgusted. Yes, it was a horrible scene—Douglas had never seen death like this before— but still, the doctors were doing everything they could. In fact, Douglas was impressed by how well they were handling the crisis. And here was this *escuálido,* this petit bourgeois, crying for help like a baby.

⚬⚬⚬

Just when Andrés didn't think he could stay awake a second longer, Claudio appeared. "Your family is waiting outside. Can you walk?" Andrés said he didn't know. Claudio went to find the director of the hospital, who told him that he could not release Andrés. But Claudio knew one of the doctors who worked there and with his help they negotiated Andrés's release.

Claudio and Andrés's brother, Pepe, got him up and loaded him into the back of Pepe's Cherokee and they rushed him to the Caracas Medical Center, a private hospital. Just as at Vargas, there was a crowd and news crews there, and Andrés's arrival was broadcast on RCTV. On his chest you could see the white strip of medical tape on which the Vargas doctor had written his instructions.

As they were pushing him down the hall toward the ER, Andrés said to himself, "Here I can pass out," and he did. He closed his eyes and was immediately unconscious. When he came around, he could hear people arguing about his insurance. There was some problem because his insurance didn't cover "civil unrest." Andrés remembered an older doctor saying, "We are going to attend to these people without conditions and the hospital will cover their costs because these people were defending democracy, defending us. They are heroes." Then Andrés lost consciousness again.

He woke up a short time later feeling a little stronger. Soon a doctor came in. "Your leg isn't responding," he said to Andrés. It was true, his leg wasn't as numb as before, but he couldn't move it. "The bullet probably nicked your sciatic nerve. We are going to have to operate if, in an hour and a half, it hasn't begun to respond." He explained the procedure and told Andrés that if they had to operate, there was a very high probability that he would lose the leg.

Andrés thought perhaps the doctor told him this to scare him, to somehow shock him and his leg into working. He became very frightened. Another doctor came in and began a long set of nerve tests. She would prick his foot with a needle, and he was supposed to tell her when he felt it. He couldn't feel anything. He thought he would just lie to her, but she set up a little apron across his chest so he couldn't see what she was doing. Finally, after forty-five minutes, he began to feel the prick of the needle. "He can feel it," she told the other doctor, "and I can tell he isn't faking it."

Andrés would keep his leg.

⚬⚬⚬

Douglas Romero, who stayed in Vargas Hospital, would not be so lucky. He, too, would keep his leg, but he suffered permanent nerve damage below the knee. His days as a competitive marathoner were over.

27 | The March Turns Back

The next time Carlos Ciordia returned to check on his parents, he saw that several tear gas canisters had landed right where they had been. They were gone. *Shit, I lost them,* he thought. He, too, had been hit with a big dose of tear gas and had to wait until his head cleared, then he went looking for them.

That's when he ran into Elías Santana, one of the opposition leaders.

"What should we do?" Carlos asked him.

"We have to leave," he remembered Santana saying. "They are killing people and it is irresponsible for us to stay. We have to go."

"But people don't want to leave," Carlos said.

Soon after that, he began to hear opposition leaders speaking from the back of a pickup truck loaded with sound equipment asking everyone to fall back to the O'Leary Plaza.

Finally, Carlos found his sister and parents in the entrance to the Metro. By now his mother had had enough. "*Vamos, vamos, vamos,*" she said.

But Carlos said he wanted to stay.

His mother objected. "You have three daughters," she said.

But Carlos wasn't going to fall for that. "And when you get home, tell them I love them," he said. He knew, somehow, that this was a pivotal moment for the country and if they really wanted Chávez out, if the opposition really wanted to take back their country, they had to have the gumption to keep fighting. His family descended the steps into the Metro station, and Carlos went back to the fight.

By now it was after five o'clock and the National Guard was pushing the marchers west down Fourth Street toward El Calvario. After protesting all morning and fighting for close to four hours, the opposition was running out of steam. People were still chanting, *ni un paso atrás,* but now they were undoubtedly moving backward. Then the National Guard made a huge lunge forward, shooting an enormous quantity of tear gas. Earlier Carlos had told people not to run from the tear gas, but he himself was running now. It seemed that he covered the three hundred meters from El Calvario to San Martin Avenue in about ten seconds. He felt as if he was being asphyxiated. After that, everyone started heading for home. The fight had gone out of the opposition.

But Carlos didn't want to believe that it was all going to end this way, so he made his way back toward El Calvario, stopping at O'Leary Plaza. There were maybe fifteen hundred marchers still milling around, but they were the last. There was still tear gas there, and Carlos picked up the canisters and threw them into the fountain. He could hear rapid gunfire nearby. There were rumors going around that a column of tanks had been sent to protect the marchers and that they should wait, but few people were. By the failing light, Carlos guessed it was close to six o'clock.

He sat there by the fountain for a time, crying, and thinking, *what a tragedy, what an obscene injustice that they were living through this.*

———

On Bolívar Avenue, Mike Merhi was trudging eastward with the rest of the defeated marchers. He had fallen in with them as they retraced the route they had taken a few hours ago, but it was a very different scene now. Where before he felt strength in the crowd, now he felt despair. Everyone seemed depressed, defeated. He passed by a woman crying to her friends, "Where is the army? They are killing us, shooting at us, and the army didn't do a thing."

Mike honestly didn't know how long he had been trapped on Baralt Avenue behind the tin blue kiosk after he got teargassed. He had been completely blinded, helpless, and had to wait a long time before he could make it back down the street. As he had stumbled along, a police officer had screamed at him to run or he would be killed, but he was so disoriented that he only managed a pathetic jog. That was when he saw a man next to him get shot in the back.

He finally made it a safe distance down Baralt Avenue and his vision began to clear. It was in front of the Korda Modas store that he began calling Jesús. He could tell by how quickly the voice mail came on that Jesús's phone must be turned off. He must have lost it, Mike thought. It must have fallen off his belt when he ran off. As he walked, Mike kept turning around, scanning the crowd in the hope that he might see Jesús. He'd walk a bit, try to call, then walk a bit farther and try again—four, five, six times—each time leaving a message. "I am heading back toward the Metro station. Try to meet me there." Mike would leave seventeen messages for Jesús that afternoon.

It was well after five o'clock by the time he reached the Capitolio Metro station. Entering the coolness of the subway tunnel Mike suddenly felt very alone. On the train back to Altamira he overheard some people talking about a young man they had seen shot. Mike felt a fresh rush of adrenaline. His heart beating fast, he quickly took a photo of Jesús out of his wallet to show them. "No," they said, looking at the picture, "that isn't him."

He got back to his car, hoping that Jesús would be there waiting for him. He wasn't. Mike drove around Altamira for a while looking for him—driving in circles—once, twice, thinking that Jesús would arrive any minute. Finally, he headed for home. At this point, Mike wasn't too worried. He kept telling himself that Jesús was probably already back at the house.

28 | The Book Man

Back on Eighth Street there was still a small group of marchers fighting it out with the National Guard. By now there was garbage and debris and smoking tires strewn over the street. Tear gas canisters, some of them still emitting weak plumes of smoke, littered the pavement. The sun was fading over Caracas, and the shadows had grown long.

One of the marchers who refused to give up the fight was Jhonnie Palencia. Palencia was a twenty-nine-year-old mattress-factory worker from a small mountain town about three hours east of Caracas called Ocumare del Tuy. He had grown up poor, in a *rancho*, a small brick house with no running water. The house actually had a toilet, but to flush it you had to

dump a bucket of water into it that sent the waste out into the ravine behind the house.

Despite being poor, Palencia was making something of himself: He was
becoming an important leader in his community. He had served his
mandatory two years in the army, which had given him discipline and a
strong desire for self-improvement. In the mattress factory Palencia was
known as the Book Man—*el hombre de los libros*—because he was always
studying some book. Sometimes he studied the Bible, but mostly he just
read whatever he could get his hands on. He was taking classes in industrial engineering and was very active in the local chapter of Bandera Roja
(Red Flag), one of the communist parties, and had run as their candidate
for the local council.

But Palencia didn't go around preaching his beliefs. He was naturally
very taciturn. Somewhat paradoxically, his quietness had a charming effect
on people, and he made friends not because he was outgoing, but because
he was a good listener. He worked hard and did his schoolwork; then,
when he had time, he would sit under the lime tree in front of his house
and read. People knew they could find him there and often came to talk to
him and ask for advice. He was their lanky small-town Buddha.

Palencia was adamantly anti-Chávez. He had attended all the marches
and had even convinced the owners of the mattress factory to join in the
first strike in December.

For this march, he had made a giant banner that said, *Fuera Chávez!*
(Get out, Chávez!). Yesterday afternoon he had taken the three-hour bus
ride from Ocumare del Tuy to Caracas so that he and his cousin, Wilmer
Bastidos, could attend the Red Flag meeting at the headquarters of CTV,
the national labor union. (The party was so confident of Chávez's inevitable fall that they were already making plans for how to work with the
transitional government.) At sunset last night Palencia and Bastidos were
in Chuao at the PDVSA rally. Then they spent the night on cots in CTV
headquarters. In the morning they joined the march.

When the National Guard had made its big advance, Wilmer and
many of the others had run. "They are killing people," Wilmer had said,
because he had seen one person shot. But Jhonnie stayed and was now one
of the last people still fighting. He was near the Metro stop, throwing

rocks at the National Guard. Just as he was about to throw one—at the moment that his head and arm were arched back—a bullet caught him under the chin and passed out the top of his head. He was dead instantly. The bullet that killed him was from the military's standard-issue FAL, which meant that he had almost certainly been killed by the National Guard or one of the honor guards in Miraflores.

When Gabriel Osorio, a photographer for *Primicia Magazine*, saw Palencia lying in the plaza he thought it might be his colleague from Reuters, Emilio Guzman. "They have killed Emilio!" he shouted. After moving cautiously most of the way toward the body, he made a final scramble over to Palencia and lay flat on the sidewalk. He was doing everything he could to make himself as small as possible. He had seen the barrel of a FAL sticking through the wall of the Miraflores parking garage and knew there were snipers around. He had already heard that one photographer had been killed and another wounded. He did not want to be next.

Now he could see that this was not Emilio. He watched the man closely to see if his rib cage was rising and falling, but he was so nervous and his own heart was beating so fast that he couldn't tell. Then he noticed the blood—it was pouring out of the body, filling the cracks in the brick sidewalk and getting closer and closer to Gabriel. Many years later he would still remember the blood with the little yellow flowers from a nearby tree floating in it; it was burned into his memory. He wanted to run, but he hesitated, remembering a quote from the famous World War II photographer Robert Capa: "If your photos aren't good enough, you're not close enough." He checked his fear a moment longer, leaned in for a picture, and then ran.

The National Guard soon pushed forward, putting Palencia in their territory and out of reach of any marchers who could have retrieved the body. All night he lay there on his side in his blue jeans, black T-shirt, and running shoes. On his back was his lime green backpack with his toothbrush, two batteries for his cell phone, and the paperback book he had been reading.

29 | How They Got the Tape Out

A block away from the body of Jhonnie Palencia, Luis Fernández and his film crew were still holed up in the apartment building across from Miraflores. After the woman had opened up her apartment to them, they crowded in. Unfortunately, most of the people in the apartment were *chavistas,* but two—the woman and her niece—were not.

Quickly, Luis and his crew decided that the best way to get out of the building was to dress everyone except Luis and their personal security guard like *chavistas* (Luis was too recognizable) and have them sneak out with the tape. Luis and the security guard would stay until things settled down. If necessary, Venevisión would send some security personnel to escort them out later.

The woman who had saved them helped paint the crew's faces with red lipstick. Then they hid all of their equipment in the apartment and left the building.

Luis waited, feeling like a war correspondent trapped behind enemy lines. Outside he could hear gunshots and people shouting and screaming. Chávez's voice could still be heard over the loudspeakers. At first the people in the apartment were very civil and even offered him coffee. But the situation became increasingly tense. The woman's neighbors began telling her that she had to get Luis out of there. Soon the other people in the apartment began to argue about him. One man, the same man in the yellow shirt who had tried to get him off the roof, was getting more and more worked up. He was drinking and soon began cussing at Luis.

A while later, word went around that the DISIP were searching for snipers in the Hotel Ausonia, the building directly behind them. This surprised Luis because he hadn't seen anyone shooting from the hotel.

It wasn't long before Luis saw his footage on TV. It showed the gunmen on the overpass shooting, and the station had added little arrows pointing to all the guns in the men's hands, then they cut to the footage that Luis's colleague Elianta Quintero had taken down on Baralt Avenue at about the same time. Next they showed the footage of the wounded government supporters around the medical tent.

Now the *chavistas* in the apartment began threatening Luis. The man in the yellow shirt spat on the TV and cursed the anchorman. "*Maldito!*" he said, then turned to Luis. "This is all your fault!" Luis became very nervous. These people are going to kill me, he thought. And he wasn't worried just about the people in the apartment with him. He knew there were people outside who had noticed that he hadn't left and might come in looking for him. His security guard was very nervous, too, and didn't know how to handle the situation.

Luis went to the bathroom and locked himself inside. He began to worry about his family and about never seeing them again. Shortly, the woman's niece, who had been sticking up for him, asked to come into the bathroom and began talking to him. Slowly, she was able to calm him down. She told him to try to relax, that she would talk to the men in the apartment. She left and Luis could hear her talking to the others. He began to breathe easier.

Finally, around nine o'clock, some people from Venevisión security came and got him out. They had a car waiting for him, but even in the car, as they drove through abandoned streets strewn with the wreckage from the fight, he did not feel safe. It wasn't until they got to Venevisión that he began to feel a sense of relief.

While he knew that the footage they had taken was extraordinary, he suspected that other film crews had taken similar footage or even the same footage from a different angle. The gunmen were right there on the overpass; surely someone else had seen them. He was wrong. Except for one amateur video, the only footage that captured the Llaguno Overpass shooters had been taken by his crew. His footage caused a wave of resentment and indignation against President Chávez, and many Venezuelans who had been sitting on the fence turned their backs on him. When combined with the other footage of wounded falling and dying, and the masses of panicked people running, it made for a damning indictment. For the first time in their lives, Venezuelans were watching the oppression and killing of other Venezuelans for political reasons.

PART TWO
COLLAPSE

1 | The Reluctant Gorilla

At 5:25 p.m. Hugo Chávez finished his emergency broadcast with one last plea for calm and then headed for his office. His advisers told him that gunfire could still be heard around the palace, and the president, suspecting that he might come under attack by rebelling military units, changed out of his suit and into his green camouflaged fatigues. Then he got his rifle and sidearm and called Brazilian president Henrique Cardoso in Brasília to inform him of the situation.

Where did he go from here? His fear was that the *golpistas*—or "coupsters"—would storm the palace at any time. Thinking back to 1992 and his own coup attempt against President Pérez, he knew that he would attack now. But who was conspiring with whom? Who were the officers he could count on? Had he underestimated the conspiracy of Admiral Héctor Ramírez Pérez? Should he have arrested them sooner? Would other officers rally behind them because of what had happened today?

His attempt at a media blackout had failed, and that was critical. With the private TV stations still broadcasting, his support was disintegrating by the minute.

His best hope for survival still lay in implementing Plan Avila—in getting whatever military support he could around himself and the palace. He had to get Rosendo to execute Plan Avila.

Chávez got back on the radio.

Shark One [President Chávez]: OK. Look, I'm trying to reach Rosendo by various avenues—right now by phone—but I haven't been able to talk to him. I've been here for half an hour. Have you had contact with him? Over.

Shark Six [General Jorge García Carneiro]: No, negative. I'm here and I haven't had contact with him for about forty minutes.

Shark One: OK, then, look . . . [Chávez hesitated, obviously unsure of himself] activate Plan Avila. Tell me if you copy, over.

Shark Six: Copy. Put in effect Plan Avila, uh, I'm proceeding now.

Shark One: Hold for me, hold for me. Tell me if you copy, over.

Shark Six: Yes, yes, I am waiting for your instructions. Don't worry. I am waiting for your instructions.

Shark One: Hold for me; it looks like they have Rosendo here on the phone. He doesn't have a radio. I'm calling here, by phone . . . [In the background the president could be heard giving commands to his advisers, but Rosendo was not on the line. Then Chávez addressed Carneiro again.] OK, look, I am ordering you to put Plan Avila into effect, and the first movement that we are going to do is bring the Ayala Battalion to take positions.

Shark Six: Those are reserves and can be placed wherever you order them.

Shark One: Then send them here to the palace, to the surroundings, to take positions and tell the commander that he will be under my orders here. Over.

Shark Six: Very good. Understood. At this moment then the Ayala Battalion will go out. We'll use . . . up until now the most convenient way would be to use the tunnels to come down on Sucre Avenue and then come down there, do you hear?

Shark One: Right, I copy. OK, coordinate with [the commander of the Military Police, General José] Vietri who is here so that you can coordinate positions. One group for dissuasion, another group can be in reserve on the patio, etc. Tell me if you copy. Over.

Shark Six: Affirmative . . .

General Jorge García Carneiro was the commander of the Army's Third Division, but more important, he was eternally loyal to Chávez. The two men had graduated from the Military Academy together in 1975. Chávez knew that even if his highest generals would not follow his orders, Carneiro would.

At the Fort Tiuna military base, Carneiro put on his bulletproof vest and began organizing the tanks of the Ayala Battalion for deployment around Miraflores. Then he called General Rosendo. "*Mi General,* the president ordered me to activate Plan Avila. I am taking out the tanks."

"Then all the dead from here on out are your responsibility," Rosendo told him, "because no one ordered you to do it." He reminded Carneiro that while Chávez had rights and privileges as president, he wasn't omnipotent and couldn't simply do whatever he wanted. Even if the order didn't violate the constitution it still had to come from Rosendo and he had decided he was not going to give it.

General Andrés Cárdenas was sitting in his office when he noticed tanks going by his window; he came out to investigate. Carneiro told Cárdenas he was implementing Plan Avila. "Do you think I am going to let the *adecos* return to power?" Carneiro asked, referring to Acción Democrática, one of the two parties that had controlled Venezuela before Chávez. "Are you with the Bolivarian Revolution or not?"

Trying to conceal his alarm from Carneiro, General Cárdenas headed straight for the army's central command. To him it seemed that the tanks were being called out to stop a peaceful march. *Damned is the soldier who turns his arms against his own people.* He knew that the public would not forgive them for another *Caracazo.* Once in central command, Cárdenas and the second commander of the army, General José Ruíz, tried to verify the order with his superiors—Inspector General Rincón, and General Vásquez Velasco, the head of the army. Vásquez Velasco was not there, but Cárdenas felt better after he had spoken with General Rincón, who assured him that the tanks should not go out. (Chávez had also ordered Rincón—who was technically Rosendo's superior—to implement Plan Avila earlier, but the inspector general had stalled, saying he had to get back to Fort Tiuna. When Chávez called him again, Rincón had said he couldn't implement Plan Avila because "it wasn't convenient.")

It was now after six o'clock and word that Carneiro was implementing Plan Avila was spreading across the base. Generals began calling and meeting with each other trying to figure out what they should do; like Cárdenas, they needed direction, clarification; they needed to know what role the military should or should not be playing in the escalating violence they were watching on TV. (There was, it must be remembered, a time delay. Even though most of the violence was now over, few people realized it, as much of the footage was just arriving—on tape—to the TV stations.) The generals were asking themselves: Is Carneiro acting only on Chávez's orders? How many troops were being called out? How would they manage the march once deployed? And, of course, many wondered about their friends and families who were in the march. The officers needed to hear from the head of the army, General Vásquez Velasco.

But General Efraín Vásquez Velasco was not to be found. Earlier in the afternoon he had decided to resign. It was a decision he had been agonizing over for the past four months, ever since Chávez had appointed him to the army's highest office in December. The way Chávez was handling the crisis proved to him that he could not, in good conscience, continue to support him. He called his wife, Gladys, and told her he was on his way to Miraflores to tell the president in person.

While people like General Rosendo could not understand why Chávez kept doing things that incited discontent, Vásquez Velasco had learned that it was all part of a very logical strategy on Chávez's part. It was divide and conquer. His divisive policies forced the discontents into the open, so that Chávez knew who was loyal and who was not; who was trustworthy enough to command troops, and who would be sent to the exterior for "training."

Chávez was politicizing the army, in much the same way he was politicizing PDVSA—he wanted to be sure that everyone in a position of power was loyal to him. It was a process that began as soon as Chávez entered office, and military promotions were at the heart of the strategy. Under Venezuela's old constitution, promotions had effectively been usurped by the Venezuelan Senate—then controlled by the two main political parties, Copei and Acción Democrática. Under the pretext of ending corruption, Chávez's new constitution gave control of promotions directly to the president. But like many of Chávez's reforms, the new system only increased graft. Now he simply promoted those he knew were loyal to him—like General Carneiro—sometimes promoting them two and three times in a year. He tended to ignore the rest. In this way Chávez hoped to lessen the chance of a coup, as it was only these ardent *chavistas* who were given control of troops. But other officers, who were often more talented and qualified, were being passed over for promotion and becoming resentful.

However, the issue of promotions was small compared to what was really ripping the armed forces apart—the role of the military in the revolution. The president had always dreamed of a socialist Venezuela with a strong military at its core. But Chávez's radical changes quickly alienated much of the armed forces. Here again, it was Chávez's enthusiastic embracing of Fidel Castro and the Cuban model that was the root of the problem.

To understand this rift, it is important to remember that the primary purpose of the Venezuelan military has always been counterinsurgency, to stop guerrilla groups from forming in Venezuela, and to keep foreign guerrillas—like Colombia's FARC and the ELN (National Liberation Army)—out of the national territory. A country like Venezuela does not have to worry about a full-scale invasion from a foreign power. Conversely, like all of its neighbors, it does not have the resources to launch a war of aggression, either. In this part of the world, power and influence are won through low-intensity conflicts, asymmetrical warfare, radio propaganda, and guerrilla warfare. And Cuban influence has long played a role in these guerrilla movements. In an effort to export his own revolution, Castro had been funding most of the insurgency movements in the region for decades. In fact, Fidel Castro had closely watched Venezuela since coming to power in 1959. Throughout the 1960s the young dictator led a crusade to export his revolution to Venezuela, a country he saw as an inexhaustible breadbasket of natural resources and a beachhead into the rest of South America. At that time representative democracy was just taking root in Venezuela after the fall of the Pérez Jiménez dictatorship in 1958, and the old divisions among the radically diverse political parties meant the infant democracy was on shaky footing, something that Castro hoped to exploit. In 1962, Cuban-sponsored FALN guerrillas tried to overthrow the government of President Rómulo Betancourt at Carúpano. Then, in 1966, the FALN struck again (along with sympathetic army officers) against President Raúl Leoni. Both attempts were put down by the Venezuelan armed forces.

The ties between the Venezuelan FALN and Castro were hardly subtle. Large caches of weapons were delivered to the guerrillas from Cuba (and sometimes intercepted by Venezuelan authorities). In 1966 a group of Cuban militiamen entered Venezuela through Falcon State along the coast, and in May 1967 a small invasion force led by Cuban officers was captured on the Venezuelan beach of Machurucuto in a sort of PG-13 version of the Bay of Pigs. It was a mostly bloodless affair with the exception of Briones Montoto, Castro's personal chief of security, who was captured, attempted to escape, and was shot to death. Castro's overt meddling in Venezuelan affairs caused President Betancourt to break all political ties with Castro in December 1961 and to recommend Cuba's expulsion from the Organization of American States.

As a result of this history, Venezuelan officers had been taught from day one of their military training that leftist guerrillas (i.e., pro-Castro guerrillas) were the greatest threat to their country and that their single most important goal was to hunt them down and kill them. But under Chávez, the paradigm had shifted; former guerrillas and guerrilla sympathizers were now in power, and the military was being asked to turn a blind eye to—and in some cases assist—their biggest adversaries.

Worse for them was that shortly after Chávez took office FARC training camps began to appear along the border in Venezuelan territory. A camp of one hundred huts known as Resumidero was built and another, called Asamblea, with twenty-five houses and Internet access, went up near the border town of Machíques. And it was not simply that Chávez looked away while the guerrillas did as they willed: He was directing the military to help the guerrillas—supplying ammunition for their raids into Colombia as well as issuing them Venezuelan identity cards to allow them free rein within Venezuela. Bolivarian Circle members were even sent to the camps to receive training from the guerrillas.

More infuriating to much of the Venezuelan military was that under Chávez they were expected to work with the Cuban military. As part of an initiative called Plan Bolívar 2000, Cuban military units were brought into the bases and barracks to work alongside their Venezuelan counterparts. At the same time, Venezuelan intelligence services were expected to open their file cabinets and hard drives to Cuban military advisers.

For many officers it was hard to imagine a more profound betrayal. Their Caesar was Brutus. Fidel Castro, after forty years of covert activity, armed insurgency, influence peddling, gunrunning, and propagandizing, had won. Castro was getting all the Venezuelan oil he could use (was even exporting it himself to get hard currency), and with the massive influx of Cuban advisers into Venezuela and with the cooperation of the FARC, Castro was setting up a huge South American base camp to export the Cuban Revolution throughout the hemisphere. The inroads that Castro had tried for decades to accomplish through armed revolt had finally come to him through the Venezuelan ballot box.

Not surprisingly, many Venezuelan officers were furious about the situation and were desperate to get Chávez out. Vásquez Velasco had been feeding the president information about several budding conspiracies. But when, month after month, Chávez failed to act on the information, Vásquez Velasco came to believe it was because Chávez intended to use an uprising as an excuse to gain more power—to consolidate control of the military and to keep soldiers permanently in the streets. That past December, Chávez had told the general that he anticipated a coup in the coming year, but that he wasn't worried; he would control it, and then he would rule Venezuela the way it should be ruled. The general had soon come to learn that it was true: A group of officers in the navy and the air force led by Admiral Ramírez Pérez were planning something and they had let Vásquez Velasco in on their meetings. But neither he nor Chávez considered them a serious threat.

Unlike Rosendo, Vásquez Velasco was not an imposing figure. He had a disappointing chin between heavy, swollen cheeks. He was a bureaucrat general, a man who had graduated with a computer engineering degree from American University in Washington, D.C.—Phi Beta Kappa. He had a distinguished career, but he had always played by the book, obeyed orders, was reliable. Chávez had appointed him for this very reason. He would do as Chávez commanded.

But in February, during a meeting of the high command, Vásquez Velasco had told Chavez that the army was demoralized because of his political meddling. Chávez had given Vásquez Velasco a hard look and dismissed the other generals in the room. The two had argued: Chávez reminded Vásquez Velasco that he was the *jefe*; as the president of the country, he had control of the army, it was in the palm of his hand, and he would do with it what he willed. Vásquez Velasco told him, no. "I am the *jefe* of the army, you put me here to do a job, and I appreciate that . . . you,

you are a politician, you are the president, the leader of Venezuela, not the chief of the army; leave that to the generals so that the army can stay apolitical, so that it can continue to represent the people."

Vásquez Velasco remembered the president's reply: *I'm not going to fight with you. Just remember that when I need to put the troops in the street that we are going to take them out,* patria o muerte. Fatherland or death.

That was when General Vásquez Velasco began to feel manipulated and used. He sensed he was becoming a pawn for a *caudillo,* a military strongman. He was becoming the strongman's surly gorilla. Under the trappings of honor and country, he had come to the army's highest post, but it was a charade, a shiny veneer to cover what was really underneath—the dirt of oppression. Might makes right. The prospect of violence was particularly unsettling for Vásquez Velasco because he was an advocate of human rights and had even founded the Office of Human Rights in the army.

Never had this sense of manipulation been stronger than during the previous Sunday's special meeting in Miraflores with the military high command and the Tactical Command for the Revolution. Like Generals Rosendo and Usón, Vásquez Velasco had sat and listened as the others planned to cut the TV station's signals, to call out the troops, and to use the Bolivarian Circles to attack opposition marches. As he listened to them he realized that he was expendable, and that when the moment came to call out the troops, he would be blamed for everything that went wrong.

Now, April 11, everything they had discussed was actually happening. When the march had headed toward Miraflores, Vásquez Velasco had called Inspector General Rincón and told him that Chávez needed to address the nation immediately and tell them he was firing the new board of directors of PDVSA; they had to defuse this thing. But Rincón hadn't even bothered to pass the message on to the president, knowing that Chávez wouldn't like it. Chávez kept the announcement about PDVSA to himself. He didn't announce it publicly and he let the march come. That was when Vásquez Velasco suspected that Chávez wanted the march to reach Miraflores; that he wanted to teach the opposition a lesson.

Then, at two o'clock, Rincón had ordered Vásquez Velasco and the other officers of the high command into that ridiculous press conference where they had assured the public that everything was under control and that nothing unusual was happening. *¡Mentiras!* Lies. They already knew there was a confrontation with lots of tear gas. By three o'clock it was clear that the National Guard was holding back the march. Vásquez Velasco had been working with Rosendo and Rincón as they tried to negotiate with the leaders of the opposition—Ortega and Carmona. The plan was that Vásquez Velasco would get his car and then he and Rosendo would go and meet Ortega, but when he returned with the car, Vásquez Velasco found Rosendo's personal assistant, Captain O'Bryan, sitting on the floor weeping. The captain said his family was in the march and that he had heard Defense Minister Rangel order the Bolivarian Circles to attack. (Even though he was the minister of defense, Rangel had more faith in the loyal Bolivarian Circles than the military.) Vásquez Velasco couldn't believe it, but then again, he supposed that with all that he knew, it shouldn't have surprised him. He asked where Rosendo was, and O'Bryan explained that the meeting with Ortega was off; Ortega had hung up on Rosendo. That was when Vásquez Velasco decided he had to go to Miraflores himself to talk to Chávez. Face to face. *Esto no puede ser.* This just can't be.

By now Chávez was in the middle of his national broadcast. As Vásquez Velasco's driver was trying to make his way through traffic to get off the enormous base—which was the size of a small city—he realized that the main gate had been closed, even though he had given no such order. Something was wrong. Then he saw two infantry groups from the Bolívar Battalion in formation on an open field. They were armed and looked as if they were getting ready to deploy. He flushed with rage, and suddenly felt like a man returning to his house to find that vandals had rearranged his furniture. His troops, *his men* were being given orders without his knowledge.

"What is this battalion doing out?" he demanded of General Carneiro.

"I have them out to control them," Carneiro explained.

"What do you mean to control them? To control them, you keep them inside their barracks." Vásquez Velasco's eyes narrowed on the man; he knew Carneiro and Chávez were very close.

Carneiro countered that these troops could still rebel. The truth was that Carneiro had gotten wind of Rosendo's refusal to implement Plan Avila and was waiting for Chávez to give him the green light.

"Look, there is no military coup here," Vásquez Velasco said.

"No, General, it's just that the situation is very, very complicated."

"OK, I want you to go down to the main gate, get control there, and then contact me." Just then Vásquez Velasco received a call from General Néstor González González, an intense soldier's soldier with a bald head and piercing eyes. It was González González who had held a damning press conference last night denouncing Chávez for letting the FARC operate in Venezuelan territory. González González said he was with a group of other generals in the command post of the Army School and they needed to speak with him immediately. Vásquez Velasco could tell by González González's tone that it was urgent.

Once at the Army School, González González and the other generals updated Vásquez Velasco on the situation around Miraflores. *Mi general*, they are attacking the march. We have reports of shots being fired and several gunshot victims, but we don't know if they're dead or just wounded, and we believe the president is going to call out the army to put down the march.

I'm not going to permit that, Vásquez Velasco thought, knowing that the order was illegal and violated the constitution.

"I will go to Miraflores and tell Chávez that I won't allow it," Vásquez Velasco told them.

"And what if he doesn't listen to you?" one of the generals asked.

"Then I'll resign."

That answer aroused a chorus of protest. No, general, you cannot desert us now, they said. They pointed out that if he resigned, the president would call out the troops anyway. But if you stay, they said, if you stand up to Chávez, you may be able to stop it. Now is not the right time to resign.

It was at this moment that Vice Admiral Bernabé Carrero's walkie-talkie crackled to life. It was six o'clock.

Shark Six: Copy. Put in effect Plan Avila, uh, I'm proceeding now.

Shark One: Hold for me, hold for me. Tell me if you copy, over.

Shark Six: Yes, yes, I am waiting for your instructions. Don't worry. I am waiting for your instructions.

Vásquez Velasco's equivocation about resigning quickly evaporated. The president cannot call my subordinates and give orders, he thought, I am the commander of the army. I am responsible for whatever happens out there. *When the moment comes and the troops are called out, I am going to be blamed for everything that goes wrong.*

"Get me Carneiro!" he ordered.

Word came back that Carneiro, rather than securing the main gate as ordered, had opened the gates and sent out a company of tanks (about twenty), which were now en route to Miraflores.

"Get me the commander of those tanks," Vásquez Velasco barked.

Commander Ismar Cepeda was leading the tanks. General Ruíz, the second commander of the army, got through to him and ordered him to return to the fort. Cepeda complied immediately and soon the tanks were on their way back. The generals breathed a sigh of relief.

Next Vásquez Velasco ordered a nationwide military lockdown. He first ordered General Ruíz to reinforce all of the gates on base to make sure that no one else could leave. All troops were confined to their barracks. Then he had General Cárdenas send a message to every army base in the country, reiterating an order that Vásquez Velasco had given about a month ago—that any order to mobilize troops had to be in writing. In the general's eyes, the lockdown would do two things: It would keep loyalist troops from repressing the march, and it would keep any potentially rebellious troops from attacking Chávez in Miraflores.

It was at about this time that Luis Fernández's footage of the Llaguno Overpass gunmen began to hit the airwaves, confirming to Vásquez Velasco and the other generals that Chávez had ordered the Bolivarian Circles to attack the march. The generals were all in agreement that the army needed to pull its support of the president in order to avert a possible massacre. (What they didn't realize was that by then the conflict was all but over in El Silencio.) As General Cárdenas contacted each of the country's commanders he would remember that each one voiced his support for Vásquez Velasco, including General Raúl Baduel, one of the four founding members of Chávez's original revolutionary program, MBR-200, and a close friend of the president. Baduel asked how the president fared, but ultimately—for now—he went along with Vásquez Velasco and the rest of the army commanders.

Although he had only been commander of the army for four months, the military leaders were lining up behind Vásquez Velasco.

He and the other generals assessed the situation. It was clear that the rogue commander was Carneiro—he had ordered the tanks out—and that they had to control him. Vice Admiral Carrero was assigned the task of taking him into custody. He, Cárdenas, and an armed escort went to find him. By now, Chávez had learned that Vásquez Velasco and the other generals were holed up in the command center for the Army School, and he ordered Carneiro to have them all arrested. Each camp was trying to arrest the other at the same time.

In the end, it was the generals who prevailed and there was no confrontation. Carneiro agreed to go with Carrero and Cárdenas to General Rincón's office, where many members of the high command were beginning to converge.

Vásquez Velasco did not go to Rincón's office, but did try to call him to tell him that he had stopped Carneiro and refused to use the army to suppress the march. But by now it was after 7:00 p.m. and Rincón, Carneiro, Rosendo, and a group of other military leaders had already taken a helicopter to Miraflores under Chávez's instructions. Whether intentional or not, it was convenient for Vásquez Velasco not to talk to Rincón. As his superior, Rincón was certainly not happy with Vásquez Velasco. As a loyal *chavista* who had been with Chávez from the beginning, Rincón knew that if the president went down, he would likely go down with him. While it was true that Rincón had also refused to implement Plan Avila, he was not going to completely turn his back on Chávez. In fact, it wasn't long before Rincón was ordering General Ruíz, the man just below Vásquez Velasco, to take command of the army because it was clear that Vásquez Velasco would not follow Chávez's orders. But General Ruíz had already sided with Vásquez Velasco. He informed Rincón that army commanders across the nation had also sided with Vásquez Velasco and were keeping their men in the barracks.

Suddenly, Vásquez Velasco was the most powerful man in Venezuela.

⁂

By early evening, people watching TV began to see the country's military, political, business, and labor leaders announcing their condemnation of the violence and Hugo Chávez. At 6:30 p.m. it was the business and labor leaders. At 6:45 it was Vice Admiral Ramírez Pérez and about ten other high-ranking officers saying they refused to recognize Chávez as the legitimate ruler. They also demanded that the high command resign immediately. Then the head of the National Guard made a similar announcement. Chávez was on the ropes and was getting hammered hard.

At 8:00 p.m. Vásquez Velasco weighed in. It would be the most crushing blow yet.

It was a short announcement of thirteen points which began by stating that the rights of the people as outlined in the constitution had been grossly violated.

> The military high command had the time to avert disaster but did not take the necessary steps. Further, the government has fostered and armed the Bolivarian Circles and manipulated them into committing crimes. They have also manipulated officers of the Armed Forces for political ends. . . . Further, the authority of the General Commander of the Army has been desecrated by the President of the Republic who gave direct orders to the Commander of the Infantry's Third Division and other military authorities without taking into account Army Command. Today we ask for forgiveness from the Venezuelan people for the events that have occurred and that your Armed Forces were unable to perform their duties. The function of the National Armed Forces is not to assault the people or to take to the streets to fight against Venezuelans. As the General Commander of the Army, I am the legitimate leader of all of the troops of this branch and as such I have ordered all of my commanders from my fort and [the forts] throughout the country to stay in their barracks. This is not a coup d'état. This is not an insubordination. It is a position of solidarity with all the people of Venezuela.
>
> Mister President, I was loyal until the end, but the violation of human rights and the killing that took place today cannot be tolerated.
>
> I evoke articles, 25, 328 and 350 of the Constitution of the Bolivarian Republic of Venezuela which oblige me to make this decision.

Vásquez Velasco's announcement was followed shortly by a similar announcement from the head of the air force, and a short while later by statements from leaders of the navy. As with Vásquez Velasco, these leaders appeared before the cameras with a contingent of other officers standing behind them. It made for a powerful scene; Chávez had lost control of the military. Perhaps only one defection could possibly be more damaging . . . a personal betrayal . . . one from someone much closer to the president.

That defection was just minutes away.

2 | Dr. Frankenstein

At about 8:30 p.m. Chávez's political mentor, Luis Miquilena, went to the headquarters of Venevisión to make a public announcement. Miquilena had served as the president of the Constitutional Assembly, as the minister of justice and the interior, and was currently the national coordinator for Chávez's party, the MVR. He was unquestionably the most important civilian who supported the Chávez government. What he was about to do was not an easy thing. Not simply because he was about to turn his back on Hugo Chávez—a man who had become like a son to him—but because doing so would mean that much of his life's work had been wasted. It meant that most of the things he had been fighting for—for nearly seventy years—would not come to pass in his lifetime. He would never see Venezuela become the country he knew it could be; never see his socialist vision become a reality.

It was a hard lesson for Miquilena, a bitter apostasy. Long ago he had come to understand that at the heart of Venezuela's problems was its class disparity, the plight of the poor was a ticking time bomb. Over the past four decades Miquilena had watched that bomb grow larger and larger as the neglect and abandonment of the underprivileged steadily increased at the hands of the ruling elite. The best way to defuse the bomb, he felt, was a whole new constitution—to wipe the slate clean and start anew—and in 1989 he had begun a mass movement along with Douglas Bravo and many other former guerrilla fighters to push for a constitutional assembly. But the movement lacked political will. It needed a leader. Miquilena knew that Hugo Chávez could be that leader. With the right guidance Chávez could be an icon for the changing times. What's more, Miquilena saw that many of his own aspirations could finally be fulfilled through Hugo Chávez. That was why he invited the young man to live in his house after he was released from prison. That was why he had used all of his connections to build the political alliances that got Chávez into office.

In 1999, with Chávez in power, Miquilena finally realized his dream of creating a new constitution—overseeing the process personally as the Constitutional Assembly's president. But just a year into Chávez's term, Miquilena began to worry. Chávez was changing.

At first he had been open to criticism; a man of understanding, of dialogue, who talked to the people, and it was this conduct that made it possible for him to unite many different sectors during the campaign. He had united MAS (Movement to Socialism), PCV (the official communist party), PPT (Fatherland for All), Red Flag (also communist), independent sectors, and industrial and business leaders. They had all been excited about change, they didn't want to repeat the past, and they wanted a decent government that was free of corruption.

But when Chávez got to power, Miquilena saw him go through a radical transformation. It began when Chávez began attacking the media. Miquilena knew that no government got along with the press, but to handle the press you had to explain yourself as much as possible and accept the criticism when it was fitting. But Chávez felt like he was being attacked, so he counterattacked. Many felt that it was just a difference of style, but Miquilena believed it was more than that. When a president mistreats a newspaper or a journalist it is very dangerous because he is limiting the right of citizens to criticize and be heard, and that can have far-reaching consequences.

When Miquilena saw how the president wanted to undermine and control the other powers within the government, the rift between them widened. Miquilena told Chávez that he had fought his whole life for a real democracy. I haven't fought to be a minister, he said, I have fought so you could be president. I have fought to change Venezuelan society, so that there could be a democratic regime, where you, as president, would respect the citizens, the power of the law, and so that you would act within the autonomy of the executive while respecting the other powers. Because that has never truly existed in Venezuela.

Chávez's response to the first national strike in December 2001 had further pushed the two men apart. The opposition's reason for holding the strike had been to send a clear message that the majority of the population wanted Chávez to renegotiate the forty-nine laws created under the Enabling Law. However, instead of heeding the message, Chávez had moved in the opposite direction, refusing to negotiate and refusing to resubmit the laws to the National Assembly for review. He attacked the opposition leadership and prepared for a long, drawn-out battle. This reaction alienated many moderates in the party, including Miquilena, who shortly thereafter announced his retirement.

And today? What Miquilena had seen today filled him with both anger and regret. It had been a peaceful march, and the government could have managed the situation with civility. But Miquilena knew that Chávez had greatly resented the idea of a march ever arriving at Miraflores, which was all that the opposition wanted—to demonstrate in front of the palace. There was no reason to repress it with violence, which, in turn, had caused the army to defy Chávez's orders, which they had every responsibility to do because Miquilena's constitution established in article 45 that if an order of a superior officer violates the constitution—which this order certainly did—then they did not have to follow that order. Miquilena knew this was no coup. It was an act of disobedience.

As for the violence by government supporters, Miquilena honestly didn't know of the Bolivarian Circles as armed groups, but he *did* know that the Chávez government had contracted armed mercenaries, which they kept as a sort of "shock brigade" to be deployed at opportune moments. Over time the regime had been building and enhancing them. They, Miquilena felt, helped intensify the growing hatred in the country.

The opposition sometimes referred to Miquilena as "Dr. Frankenstein" because he had created a monster that he could not control. Now Miquilena himself had to admit that it was true. Chávez, he was realizing, had become his great sin, a sin that he now had to confess to.

In the headquarters of Venevisión, Miquilena prepared to give his press conference. With little preamble, he announced that he no longer supported the Chávez regime. "I solemnly declare that it is very difficult that a government of this nature could ever count on the possibility of help on my part," Miquilena said. He added that the regime "had ended up stained in blood," and that to sit by and not take action against what Chávez was doing would be both cowardly and criminal. Lastly, he pressed for an institutional solution to the crisis and open dialogue between the opposition, the military, and the government.

With those words, Chávez lost control of both the legislative and judicial branches of the government as large chunks of Chávez's political coalition sided with Miquilena over Chávez. In the Supreme Court, the defection of Miquilena meant that justices were now split between *chavistas* and *miquilenistas,* with one justice on the fence.

3 | General Usón's Big Decision

While these events were unfolding, Finance Minister General Usón and his remaining staff were still waiting in the Central Bank for the violence to die down. They stayed there until well after sunset. Then General Usón took steps to get everyone still in the building home safely. He took people down to the northern exit and saw them off. When he returned to his office, he began watching the steady stream of pronouncements against Chávez on TV—Vásquez Velasco, then the leaders of the National Guard, and finally, Luis Miquilena. With those defections it was clear to Usón that Chávez's political and military base had crumbled. He had lost control of Venezuela.

General Usón had had a long relationship with Hugo Chávez but the events of the day and the past few weeks were making him reconsider whether he, too, could still be a part of his movement.

Usón had first met Chávez at the Military Academy in 1973. Chávez was two years ahead of him, which meant that Chávez's graduation class (the outgoing class) spent much of their time training Usón's class.

After graduation the two men had gone their separate ways, but three years later, in 1980, they were both back at the Military Academy as instructors. Usón and Chávez were part of a three-man team that oversaw the final year of training for the cadets. The third man on that team was Captain Lucas Rincón, who would later become General Rincón, Inspector General of the Armed Forces.

In this trio, Usón took care of the administrative functions: He organized the promotions, ordered uniforms, and balanced the books. It was Hugo Chávez who was in charge of cadet orientation. He was an excellent instructor—dedicated and very concerned with the success of his students. But the thing that most impressed Usón was how brilliant Chávez was at using symbols to persuade people. When he would sit and talk to the cadets he would do it below an acacia tree on the academy grounds because the hymn of the military academy had a verse about acacia and oak trees. And he would talk about the Great Liberator, Simón Bolívar, and how it was believed he had bivouacked his entire army under the great acacia Samán de Güere near Maracay. The cadets would be transfixed. And during their tenure at the academy, Usón noticed how much Chávez's speaking skills improved, so much so that Usón would take the time to go and listen to him lecture.

While the two men remained friends, Usón never took a part in (nor was he ever invited to join) the group of officers who masterminded the 1992 coup. While Chávez was in jail for his coup attempt, Usón had approached his boss for permission to see him, but he was flatly denied. His boss cited two reasons: First, anyone who visited Chávez in jail was marked as a potential conspirator and, second, Usón's friendship with the lieutenant colonel had already raised suspicions in Military Intelligence and the visit would likely be the death knell of his career.

But once Chávez was elected, they didn't have to worry anymore. In October 2000, President Chávez had named Usón the head of the Central Budget Office, where he worked to keep government spending at a minimum. He soon found that it was not an easy job. Usón discovered that the new administration was overspending because much of the president's staff was new to government. While the president had great charisma and a tremendous capacity to communicate, he had no ability to organize. This, coupled with a very short attention span, made him difficult to work with. In meetings, Chávez didn't like to focus on the details. He knew they were important, but he was not comfortable talking about them. Instead, he would go on for hours about transcendental things—the ideas of the revolution and history. And the meetings would run late into the night but not resolve anything.

Chávez was also very spontaneous and often announced new government programs that had just occurred to him during speeches or during his weekly TV program, *Aló Presidente*. He was a man who was truly worried about society, especially about the poor, and he launched some very interesting programs, but they were rarely transformed into real projects because new ideas would overtake them. The result was that few decisions were ever made and even when they were, they were usually done too hastily and ended up wasting money.

Corruption was a problem, too, because with so many new projects and missions being created and so much money moving around, it was easy for people to steal public funds. The worst example of this was the Unique Social Fund (El Fondo Único Social), that became a model for corruption and waste that Chávez let quietly slip under the radar of auditory control.

Usón had been in the Budget Office for a little over a year and a half before he was made minister of finance—in fact, he had been in his new post for only thirty-eight days on April 11. During his time in the Budget Office the most significant event had been the terrorist attacks of 9/11. They had presented a critical opportunity for Chávez to define his ambivalent stance toward the United States, Venezuela's biggest trading partner. But Usón felt that Chávez made a crucial error in criticizing the United States and saying that the attacks were a consequence of America's imperialist past finally catching up with it. Usón had immediately felt a change in the attitude of the banks and international lending agencies he worked with. Although world sentiment toward the United States would shift as it waged its war on terror, in the aftermath of the attacks the globe was unified behind the United States. Chávez's comments ignited protests and the very first *cacerolazos* (casserole strikes). For the first time, people were coming out into the streets to protest against the president.

Now, as the events of the day replayed through his mind, Usón thought back to when Chávez had offered him the post of finance minister. He had been blunt with Chávez. "Look, *Presidente,* if a time comes when I am no longer in agreement with you, then I will resign, and when I do it, I'll do it personally and I'll tell you why." Now Usón realized that that moment had come. All that had happened today and in the past few weeks only reinforced his own personal doubts. It had been a slow disenchantment. A slow erosion. A slow realization that even though Chávez might truly believe the things that he said, the reality would never match the rhetoric.

He would go to Miraflores and resign.

4 | Finding Jesús Mohamad

It wasn't until Mike Merhi got home and found that his son, Jesús, wasn't there that he really began to worry. Up until then, he had been telling himself that they had just gotten separated. Jesús wasn't answering his cell phone because he must have lost it in the confusion. But upon arriving at the house, Mike realized that something had to be very wrong. He called his brother, Ali, who told him that most of the wounded had been taken to Vargas, but when Mike tried to call the hospital, he had trouble getting through and when he finally did get through the line would suddenly get cut off. He called Gustavo Tovar and Ali, and they all went to Vargas together.

The hospital was in a state of chaos. Hundreds of people had gathered outside but the guards were not letting anyone in. The three men slowly pushed their way to the front of the crowd. Mike explained to the guard that they were looking for his son, that he might be one of the wounded, and the guard let them in. The wounded were everywhere—on gurneys, on the floor, in chairs, crouched in the hallways. Mike spoke to some of them, asking if they had seen Jesús. Some of them asked him for money because they said they had no way to pay the doctors. He gave them all the small bills he had.

Mike felt like he was going crazy. He was so tired and afraid. Every young man he looked at he thought might be Jesús. They searched through the hospital but couldn't find him. Finally, Gustavo said that he was going to check in the basement. A fresh feeling of terror ran through

Mike. In the basement was the morgue. He knew he couldn't go himself, so he just nodded. Go ahead.

After a while Mike began to talk to a nurse. She told him that she had a notebook that listed all the people who had been checked into the hospital. By now Gustavo had returned from the basement, having found nothing, and began to help Mike review the list of names. Then Mike saw his son's name with the word *deceased* beside it.

Gustavo, looking over his shoulder, saw it, too. Mike would remember how cold he suddenly felt, as if everything inside his body was frozen. Ali began to weep. Mike just stood there. He didn't know how to react to such a blow.

5 | Stuck in the Middle

By nine o'clock things were beginning to settle down at Vargas Hospital and by ten o'clock many of the doctors, exhausted but still running on adrenaline, sat down to talk. Most were outraged at the government, but more than anything, they were very angry about the senseless loss of life. There seemed to be no good reason for it. Sixteen dead. Seventy-five wounded. Most of the victims had been very young, and many of the survivors were going to be permanently disabled. Dr. Serbenescu was saddened by it all, especially the death of Mike Merhi's son, Jesús. Yes, Serbenescu had tough skin, but sometimes, often at unexpected moments, he had a sudden emotional response to what he saw in the ER. That's how it had been with Jesús. A young man like that, so healthy. The boy had been in a state of agony, but there was nothing they could do for him.

Serbenescu felt that what he had seen today had changed him. Today, the political polarization that was rupturing Venezuelan society had reached out and touched him. He understood now what a political conflict like this could mean for Venezuela; what human beings were willing to do to each other in the name of ideology. In this job, where he dealt with violence every day, Serbenescu always had his finger on the pulse of public discontent. Now he knew that the violence was not going to subside. No, he thought, from here it is only going to get worse. It would come out in different ways—marches, crime, assassinations—but more was coming. The political situation would drive it, exacerbated by the media on one side and the government on the other. People would get more and more and more worked up.

At that moment—thinking about the carnage he had seen today—one thing was very clear to Serbenescu: His emergency room was going to stay very busy.

⋙

At 9:50 p.m., in an effort to deflect criticism, government spokespersons announced that the day's violence had been perpetrated by snipers from Bandera Roja, Red Flag, one of the communist parties that was now opposed to Chávez.

No evidence would ever surface to support this claim.

6 | Weighing Exile

Dr. Espidel—who, with his son, had given first aid to the wounded under the Llaguno Overpass—had found sanctuary with his family in a little chapel across the street from General Usón's office. When the gunfire died down, they headed back to the stage in front of Miraflores.

By now everything was very quiet. A feeling of depression had entered the crowd. It was now well after sunset. Espidel felt out of touch with what was happening; he still didn't understand what it all meant. Some party officials were speaking on the platform—Freddy Bernal, the leader of the Bolivarian Circles; the ministers of health and environment; and a few deputies from the National Assembly. Espidel remembered them saying things like, "Everybody be calm, don't worry. Everything is fine." But Espidel didn't believe them. He was afraid that President Chávez had been overthrown. Many people had left, and the president's honor guard had retreated to the palace and the barracks across the street. Even worse, they weren't getting any more information from the pro-Chávez radio stations.

Espidel called his mother on his cell phone. She confirmed that all the pro-Chávez news services were down and she said that the military was no longer recognizing Chávez as the legitimate leader of Venezuela.

Around eight o'clock the speakers on the platform began telling the crowd to go home. Feeling confused and depressed, Espidel and his family walked down Baralt Avenue until they found a taxi.

"What's the matter with you?" the taxi driver asked. "Chávez is gone!" he said enthusiastically.

"How do you know?" Espidel asked.

"It's all over the TV," he said, meaning the private stations. Espidel refused to believe it. How could it be?

When he and his family finally got home, he switched on the government TV channel. Nothing. He couldn't believe it. The state TV station was off the air. The first shock of the day had been the gun battle from the Llaguno Overpass. The second had been the fear that his wife Sabrina was in danger. This was the third shock—the government channel was down. It was over for Chávez. He remembered back to the overthrow of right-wing dictator Pérez Jiménez in 1958. Espidel's grandfather told him that losing control of the TV stations was what had sealed Pérez Jiménez's fate. If Chávez had lost control of the media, he had lost control of the country.

At around midnight, Dr. Espidel began to see postings for people on TV, suspects from the Llaguno Overpass as well as members of Chávez's inner circle—ministers and National Assembly deputies. They were asking for any information about the whereabouts of these people. Espidel knew that the witch hunt had begun. That was the fourth shock. *Are people going to come to my house and take us away?* In his neighborhood, people knew that he was a *chavista*. When people had their *cacerolazos* and were out banging their pots and pans, they had surely noticed that he and his family never participated. What's more, Espidel had relatives who were in important positions in the Chávez regime. If they went after them, they would likely come after Espidel as well.

Maybe someone was going to come and get us, someone who was angry and felt cheated by Chávez. The TV was depicting everything that had happened as Chávez's fault, saying that the Llaguno Overpass gunmen had been firing into the crowd. The opposition was out for blood.

Espidel gathered his family together. He didn't know what to do, but he was beginning to wonder if they should flee the country.

7 | The Pistol

When General Francisco Usón walked into the president's office around 10:30 to resign as finance minister, he found Chávez sitting between two ministers: Ramón Rodríguez Chacín, the interior and justice minister, and José Vicente Rangel, the defense minister. The president was wearing his camouflage fatigues and was sitting with his forearms on the desk. Usón noticed that he was very nervous. He looked defeated and melancholy and seemed almost oblivious to the urgings of his advisers: Rangel was pushing for resistance, while Chacín was urging moderation and negotiation.

Usón was struck by how few people were in Miraflores. These were the only two men with Chávez at such a critical time? Where were all the government leaders? Where were Chávez's political allies? Yes, there were a few roaming around the halls, and he had seen several members of the military high command, but the palace was much too quiet.

As Usón took in the scene, he saw something that made him pause. On the president's desk he noticed a pack of cigarettes, a lighter, an ashtray, a cup of coffee, and a pistol. *That pistol isn't there for self-defense*, Usón thought. *A gun on the table like that is a choice.* The president had Rangel

on one side, wanting a fight, and Chacín on the other, recommending sur-
render. The pistol was in the middle. It was another way out.

The president shook Usón's hand in greeting then they began to talk
about the situation.

"You acted badly, *Presidente,*" Usón said.

"The fault belongs to the *golpistas,*" replied Chávez, referring to the
coup plotters.

"That's possible, but you didn't know how to handle the situation."

"I disagree," Chávez said.

Although Usón didn't blame Chávez directly for the deaths (he didn't
think that Chávez had ordered anyone to pull the trigger), he had still
turned a blind eye to a violence that he knew would occur. Usón felt that the
Bolivarian Circles, with their radical and irrational leaders like Lina Ron,
had gotten out of control and were eating the regime alive from the inside.

"I have decided to resign my post," Usón said.

"*Entiendo,*" Chávez said, I understand. "It is your decision."

"I think it would be well if you resigned, too."

"I am thinking about it," Chávez said.

Rangel interrupted, "*Presidente,* we must resist to the last bullet." Usón
was stunned that Rangel was considering a fight and told him so. When
Usón first arrived he had seen the honor guard preparing for a siege. They
were mounting machine guns and preparing antitank weapons and rocket
launchers in the guard posts around the palace. Usón had also noticed that
the mass of Bolivarian Circles and other loyalists that had been surrounding the palace was gone. "There is no one outside capable of defending
you," Usón told the president, "and if someone told you they were, then
they were lying." Usón warned Chávez and Rangel that they had to be sure
there wasn't a confrontation between opposing military units, but it was
also important to avoid a confrontation between the military and the people, whether it be people coming to support Chávez or people coming to
force him out.

The president appeared to be listening to him, but he also seemed too
overwhelmed to make a decision.

Then Usón explained that as a brigadier general on active duty and
given the circumstances, he had to present himself to central command.

"Go and report in, then," Chávez said.

Usón glanced again at the pistol on the desk.

"Don't lose hope," he said. "Your project has failed, but you could amend your errors and get another chance."

As Usón left the office he picked up his own pistol, which he had left with the president's personal assistant. The pistol on Chávez's desk still weighed on his mind. Chávez *was* the Bolivarian Revolution. If he died, he would become a martyr like Ché Guevara, and the revolution would live on. Usón didn't want that, but perhaps Chávez, now feeling defeated and betrayed, did.

"Look," Usón told the assistant, "as soon as you get the chance, get that gun away from the president."

At 11:50 p.m. another domino fell. The leaders of the secret police (the DISIP) announced that they no longer recognized Hugo Chávez as the president of Venezuela; their duty was to the people of Venezuela, not the government.

8 | Guillermo García Ponce

In the corridors of Miraflores the remaining staffers waited; there was nothing else they could do. Yes, many of them had fled, fearing a military attack, but others had stayed. Some, like Guillermo García Ponce, had decided to stay with Chávez until the very end, no matter how bitter that end might be. That would be García Ponce's way: forever loyal to *the cause*.

He was an old man, seventy-nine years old, his back was bent, his pale skin splotched, and his head almost bald. But while he outwardly showed his age, his mind was as piercing and perspicacious as ever. García Ponce had, as they say in Venezuela, *cuatro dedos de frente,* four fingers of forehead—literally and figuratively. He was a smart man. His was a mind formed by a life of constant struggle, of persistent persecution, of being labeled "other"—the radical, the communist. He had spent his life on the outside, always fighting to wake the masses, to stir them to revolution. Along the way he had fought dictators, military juntas, right-wing governments, and, when necessary, left-wing governments that weren't left enough.

He shared a great deal with his contemporary Luis Miquilena, a man who had been, until just a few hours ago, a loyal friend and ally. Like Miquilena, García Ponce was one of Venezuela's most prominent communists, and over the course of half a century the two men had often worked, rallied, protested, plotted, and even served jail time together. When Chávez came to power both Miquilena and García Ponce had assumed pivotal roles in the regime: Miquilena took the more prominent position as the godfather, the venerable political adviser, and García Ponce worked within the MVR as part of the Tactical Command for the Revolution.

García Ponce had risen to prominence in Venezuela's Communist Party (PCV) in the late 1950s and the 1960s. Inspired by the Cuban Revolution in 1959, the PCV, with García Ponce as one of its leaders, began working with Castro to overthrow the young Venezuelan democracy and set up a socialist state. But when the Carúpano coup attempt failed in 1962 and the links between the coup, Castro, and the PCV came to light, President Betancourt outlawed the party, forcing it underground. In response, García Ponce, along with other PCV leaders like Pompeyo Márquez and Teodoro Petkoff, quickly formed the FALN (National Liberation Armed Forces) and began a guerrilla war against the government that would continue for most of the decade. They sabotaged oil pipelines, assassinated police officers, robbed banks, bombed a Sears Roebuck warehouse, burned the U.S. military mission in Caracas, and hijacked a government-owned 3,127-ton freighter and sailed it to Brazil.

But García Ponce was leading a double life: In addition to being the deputy general of the FALN, he was also a member of congress. However, in October 1963, the Betancourt government initiated a massive crackdown on the FALN. García Ponce was arrested along with many other guerrilla leaders (including Pompeyo Márquez and Teodoro Petkoff) and thrown into the military prison of San Carlos in Caracas.

As García Ponce and the other FALN leadership waited in their prison cells, hundreds of their comrades were arrested and tortured. At the same time other friends and comrades were being killed in skirmishes with security forces or in training accidents. With their networks collapsing and popular support toward the guerrillas waning, the FALN leaders realized their rebellion was in a crisis. If they were to save it, they had to get out of jail.

So they planned a prison break, a stunning escape that would be remembered as one of the most famous in Venezuelan history.

A young Syrian Marxist named Nehemet Simón spearheaded the effort: He bought an *abasto* (a convenient store and coffee shop) near the prison, and while he served coffee and *pastelitos* to the off-duty prison guards, his comrades dug a sixty-meter tunnel toward the prison.

But the work was slow going. The air in the tunnel was pestilent and made the workers sick. Twice they discovered they had lost their bearings underground. In the end, a tunnel they hoped would take a few months to complete ended up taking three and a half years. As García Ponce, Márquez, and Petkoff waited impatiently in their cells, every week brought more despairing news: more comrades killed in combat, more arrests, more tortures. The men heard fantastic stories of the ruthlessness of Venezuela's counterterrorist forces—the army, Digipol, Sifa. Stories of friends found hung in their cells . . . "suicides," or comrades who were arrested, tortured, and executed. To cover up the murders, the officers would often take the body to a local motel, fire a few shots into the air, and then say that the suspect had been killed while resisting arrest.

By the time the tunnel was ready in February 1967, three of García Ponce's four brothers were in jail for rebellion (his mother went to visit a different one every day of the week except Tuesday), and Simón had become such good friends with the prison officials that he hosted a party in the shop for them and put the captain of the guard in the seat of honor—directly on top of the hole to the tunnel. By now Luis Miquilena was also in jail at San Carlos, but in a different section of the prison, so he could not be included in the breakout.

On February 5, the three men made their escape, and Simón drove them out of the *abasto* garage in the back of his station wagon. The newspapers declared it the most amazing prison break in history and the tunnel became a tourist attraction. Simón immediately fled the country, but the other men stayed, living in safe houses and working clandestinely for the resistance.

Yet, even though García Ponce, Petkoff, and Márquez had escaped, the resistance was still collapsing, principally because the FALN never gained broad popular support among those they had hoped would be their political base—the poor. Ironically, the armed insurgency had the opposite effect it intended. As the radical offshoot of Acción Democrática, the FALN made AD appear much more moderate, the lesser of two evils in the eyes of the right. The guerrillas also unified the armed forces by giving them a common enemy, thereby diminishing internal squabbling and keeping the military from meddling in politics.

Another blow to the FALN was the loss of its financial support from Cuba. By the late 1960s Castro's patriot games throughout the developing world were causing the Kremlin considerable embarrassment as it tried to negotiate détente with the United States; finally First Secretary Leonid Brezhnev decided he had had enough and reined in Castro by threatening to pull Soviet subsidies to Cuba if he didn't behave. Castro reluctantly complied, and the flow of money and arms to the FALN came to an abrupt halt.

At the end of the 1960s the FALN was a weak and emaciated organization. In fact, García Ponce and his comrades were exonerated in 1969 because the movement no longer posed a threat to the powers that were. The communist party had even been legalized the previous year by the more moderate President Rafael Caldera.

But the woes of the Venezuelan communists were not quite over. In 1971 the PCV split into pro- and anti-Soviet camps, largely in response to the Soviet invasion of Czechoslovakia. Petkoff and Márquez went with the anti-Soviet group, which was christened the Movement toward Socialism (El Movimiento al Socialismo, or MAS). MAS became the larger of the two groups and much more mainstream. García Ponce remained with the PCV. He was, and would remain, the hard-liner. The fundamentalist. The most extreme, the most devout, and often the most radical of the communists.

The cost of this infighting was apparent in the 1973 presidential elections when each of the three socialist parties—Popular Unity (which included PCV), MAS, and URD (Democratic Republican Union)—ran a separate candidate, none of which gained more than 5.1 percent of the vote.

———

Given the communists' long history of struggle, for Miquilena to go to Venevisión—what García Ponce considered the den of the fascists—and say those things, that their government was "stained in blood," was an incredible shock. He considered it an unprecedented act of treachery and a complete betrayal of all that they had fought for their whole lives.

Miquilena had certainly tricked them, García Ponce thought, even veterans like himself, people who had known him for more than half a century. He had duped them all. How altruistic it had seemed when Miquilena had "helped" Chávez after his release from prison. But now García Ponce saw that it had been a false generosity, a generosity to advance Miquilena's selfish goals. García Ponce kept asking himself, why? Why had Miquilena done this? For García Ponce it was clear that Miquilena must still be part of the old system, full of the vices and corruption of the old guard. He had just been slow to see it. Miquilena was not truly part of the "the project." How could he be? How could he really be for the revolution? No, he was just a mixture of businessman and social climber, out to enrich himself through his political contacts.

⣿

As the Miraflores staffers waited anxiously in the palace, they split into two groups: one staying in the secretary's office watching the news, and another out in the garden congregated around the fountain. García Ponce stayed mostly with the former. It was around nine o'clock when José Vicente Rangel came into the corridor and told them, "It's an uprising of the generals."

That had got them working the phones to get the word out, but no one's cell phone could get a signal. Why? To García Ponce it all seemed part of the plan, part of the operation to silence them. They kept trying. Eventually, some of the journalists from Channel 8 contacted CNN, and others were able to reach Telemundo, Channel 1 in Colombia, and a station in Mexico.

Every few minutes more generals and politicians were coming on TV to denounce Chávez. As García Ponce watched, his suspicion solidified that it was all part of a plot by the coupsters. Everything pointed to it.

Earlier that day, at 3:15 p.m., when García Ponce had heard the first gunshots, he had gone outside to investigate and found that the medical tents were already full of wounded. García Ponce saw people motioning toward the rooftops; some of them grabbed him and tried to protect him, saying that there were snipers.

He was sure that the snipers were no accident. They were another part of this premeditated plan, a plan that needed some pretext—dead bodies, blood, violence—to justify a coup d'état. The peaceful and democratic road taken by Chávez meant that the "coupsters" had no other options. García Ponce was adamant: Under Chávez there was not one political prisoner, not one person persecuted, not a single outlawed party, not one censured newspaper. There was wide liberty of expression and political organization. Chávez was the legitimate and democratic president, chosen by the people by an overwhelming majority.

So there was no valid reason for such an uprising. And because there was no legitimate reason to overthrow him, García Ponce believed a reason had to be created. The conflict with PDVSA had been intentionally prolonged in order to rally the marchers and get them to come to Miraflores; along the way they had been protected by the Metropolitan Police, who, when necessary, helped clear the way; and finally, the snipers had been brought in to create blood and bodies. Meanwhile, the seditious generals had waited in ambush in their garrisons, ready to pounce.

García Ponce knew that the opposition had been preparing this for months. He was sure that they had laboratories for creating rumors, for psychological warfare, laboratories run by experts trained by the international intelligence services. These labs had been one of the most effective weapons for the conspirators. They planted the most absurd, yet at the same time most credible, rumors in the minds of high-level military and civilian leaders. Over time, as more and more and more people believed these lies, it created a kind of alternate, or "virtual," reality. Fueled by newspapers like *El Nacional* and *El Universal* and TV channels like Globovisión and Venevisión, the generals had become confident that Chávez was about to fall and were ready to advance their fascist plot.

Now, in the palace, García Ponce and the other staffers kept talking about what they should do. Some wanted to spirit Chávez to the nearby city of Maracay, but the idea was soon dismissed. They had thought they could use the tanks sent out by General Carneiro as escorts, but when they were recalled by Vásquez Velasco it made the move too dangerous. He knew that José Vicente Rangel was pushing for a fight, but García Ponce saw this as senseless self-destruction. What would they gain by the death of President Chávez and his comrades at the hands of these generals? No, in his opinion, the priority must be to safeguard Chávez's life. The president should not give in, but he shouldn't put his life in danger, either.

"The CIA is behind all this," a woman said. "Everybody knows it; we have been saying this, we have documents." By chance, there was a film crew inside the palace, a group of Irish filmmakers working on a documentary about Chávez. Even though they had only planned to do a biography, they were now getting some amazing footage of the regime in crisis. At that moment, they came up to García Ponce and started asking questions, but he was exhausted and didn't have a clear answer for them. "Our adversaries were too powerful," he said, then trailed off, "and we did not have enough time."

Still they waited. Generals Usón and Rosendo came and then left the palace. Then Chávez asked to be left alone. The staff reluctantly complied. At that moment García Ponce couldn't help but think how Chávez, seeing himself betrayed and abandoned, might come to the same conclusion that Chilean president Salvador Allende had come to in 1973 when he was besieged by Augusto Pinochet. One staffer, Jorge Giordani, stayed rigid the whole time Chávez was by himself, anticipating the gunshot that would crack the silence.

9 | Negotiating for the Nation

Earlier, just before eight o'clock, General Manuel Rosendo, the man who had refused to implement Plan Avila, had flown to Miraflores in an army helicopter to turn in his resignation. Rosendo met with Chávez, several members of the military high command, and General Hurtado. When Rosendo saw that the president was in his camouflage fatigues and was armed, he remembered Chávez's comment from the night before. *And I have my rifle ready to give lead to anyone that tries to stop this revolution that has cost me so much.*

While some of the generals were talking of this as a coup d'état, Rosendo disagreed, this was not a coup, it was a *desconocimiento*, a disowning, a spontaneous refusal by the military and civilian leaders to recognize Chávez as the legitimate president.

Vice Admiral Carrero also offered up his resignation to Chávez. Earlier that day he, too, had overheard Defense Minister José Rangel giving orders to Chávez supporters around the palace, telling them to come with sticks and clubs. The vice admiral said he no longer wanted to be part of a government that advocated violence like that.

Chávez, for his part, said he had no knowledge of any such order and would not condone it if there had been one. For Rosendo, Carrero's claim confirmed what his assistant, Captain O'Bryan, had told him earlier that morning when he had overheard Rangel giving similar instructions to Freddy Bernal. The more Rosendo considered what had happened, the more he blamed Chávez. Today Venezuela had experienced its worst violation of human rights since the Caracazo of 1989. But it was more than negligence on Chávez's part, more than the fact that he had not heeded Rosendo's advice. *He, Hugo Chávez,* was responsible for these human rights offenses.

Rosendo turned to President Chávez. "I have also come to turn in my resignation," he said. He told the president that he had made a great effort to avoid this crisis and yet it had occurred anyway. Therefore, he didn't feel that he could remain the head of the supreme command (CUFAN). Then he said, with trademark candor, that he could no longer work with a military high command that was so inept and so incompetent that it couldn't find solutions to the simplest problems.

At first, Chávez did not want Rosendo to resign and told him so. But Rosendo said he would stay only if Chávez was willing to do four things, one of which was disarm the Bolivarian Circles. "You know, I had been collecting information on the Bolivarian Circles," Rosendo said. "Before today, all I had was a lot information that suggested they were armed, but today I had a demonstration, and now my suspicion has become hard intelligence."

Chávez shook his head. I cannot guarantee that they won't defend me, Chávez said. He preferred to accept Rosendo's resignation to making sure the Bolivarian Circles were disarmed. But I will accept it only on one condition, the president said. Chávez wanted Rosendo to help him negotiate with the military—the brass on both sides respected and feared Rosendo. Rosendo agreed. He and General Hurtado would go to Fort Tiuna. At the same time, Vice Admiral Carrero—who also said he would not resign until the situation was under control—would go the Vargas coast to talk with the naval commanders.

Once at Fort Tiuna, Rosendo was relieved to find that the troops were all in their barracks and there was no confrontation between pro- and anti-Chávez units as they had feared. They met with the army generals in the command center, and Rosendo delivered his message from Chávez: The president is willing to wipe the slate clean and start over. He is ready to act as if nothing has happened today, that you have not showed disloyalty. He will forgive you. What's more, he is willing to take the necessary steps to make things right. He is willing to dismiss his ministers and the vice president and hold roundtable discussions to work with the opposition. He's ready to change.

But the generals flatly refused.

Forgive me?! Vásquez Velasco thought when he heard Rosendo's offer, forgive me for what? I haven't done anything wrong. The president is responsible for the dead, so why is he blaming me?

The generals responded with a counteroffer: Tell the president that he can leave the country and we will guarantee his safety and the safety of his family.

Next Rosendo and Hurtado went to the Ministry of Defense. Here a large group of officers of various ranks had gathered. General Hurtado told them of Chávez's offer as well as the response of the army generals. Here again, the officers told Rosendo and Hurtado that there would be no negotiations, but they were undecided on what to do with Chávez. At first they insisted that the deaths of the afternoon were the president's responsibility and said he would have to stand trial for human rights abuses. But some of the generals, including General Carlos Alfonso, said they were willing to let Chávez go just as the army had proposed.

Rosendo told Vice Admiral Héctor Ramírez Pérez, the ranking officer, that he should bring everyone to a consensus, then he and Hurtado headed back to Miraflores.

When they returned from negotiating with the other generals, Rosendo told Chávez, "One response is that if you leave the country, they will guarantee your security and that of your family." Rosendo didn't tell Chávez about the dissension between the generals nor that some of them were insisting that he stand trial.

Chávez said he would agree only if Rosendo personally guaranteed his life and his safe passage out of Venezuela. Rosendo agreed.

"Where do you want to go?" he asked.

"Cuba," the president said.

Rosendo assured the president, "I will make the arrangements to get you to Cuba."

Rosendo then called General Vásquez Velasco. "Vásquez, the president has accepted the offer to leave the country. Send a plane to Maiquetía [airport]."

"OK," General Vásquez Velasco said, "I will make the arrangements," and he told Rosendo he would contact him when everything was ready.

Rosendo put down the phone. Chávez was going to resign. Rosendo pondered the implications of it. He felt that Chávez was acting to prevent more bloodshed; he didn't want the military to tear itself (and the country) apart. That was good.

10 | Chávez Falls

While these events were unfolding, the entire nation was waiting in a state of extreme agitation, trying to anticipate what was going to happen next. The TV networks could barely keep up with the news. It seemed that every thirty minutes another important figure, including many military leaders, was holding a press conference to denounce Chávez, many calling for his immediate resignation. The networks played the footage from the violence, especially from the Llaguno Overpass, over and over, as well as other high-impact bits of news—the cutting of the TV signals, Chávez's out-of-touch emergency broadcast, Chávez ordering Plan Avila over Shark Radio, Miquilena's press conference. It was all ratcheting up the pressure. Where was the cabinet? Why didn't Chávez address the nation again? One thing was becoming increasingly clear: Whoever was in control, it was not Hugo Chávez.

The possibility of regime change meant that people everywhere began jockeying for positions. Venezuela, like many developing countries, is a place where the wealth of the nation flows from the coffers of the state. Even if you exclude PDVSA and all its subcontractors, the Venezuelan government is by far the country's largest employer. What's more, most private companies survive only by remaining in good standing with the government. In short, the state is the teat from which most Venezuelans, directly or indirectly, suckle. Accordingly, regime change means that everyone who doesn't want to lose her or his livelihood has to cater to the politics of the new rulers.

For the *escuálidos,* the approaching fall of Chávez was welcomed with glee. They had endured over three years of *chavismo* and had been excluded from the power and access they felt entitled to. Now their time had come. Those who were quick and clever stood to reap tremendous spoils from Chávez's fall.

For the *chavistas* the regime change could mean many things. For those closest to Chávez the immediate priority was survival. Many of them, like Vice President Diosdado Cabello and other cabinet members, went into hiding. Others sought asylum at foreign embassies. Those who were further from Chávez did everything they could to distance themselves from him and his party. And they began rehearsing their stories—how they had never really liked Chávez. They had just needed the money.

Sometime after midnight, a prominent newspaper journalist decided to see if MVR deputy Juan Barreto, one of Chávez's highest lieutenants and the man who had rallied the Bolivarian Circles around the palace that afternoon, happened to have his cell phone on.

"Juan, is that you?"

"Who is this?"

The two men were speaking in whispers although neither one knew why.

"What are you doing?" the journalist asked him.

"Ah, we are in hiding."

"What are you going to do?"

The journalist remembered Barreto replying, "I don't know, but at least it looks like we got rid of *el loco*."

The people of Venezuela stayed glued to their TV sets late into the night. At 1:00 a.m. the news media began reporting that President Chávez would turn himself over to the military. Soon thereafter General Vásquez Velasco confirmed that they were negotiating for the removal of the president.

By 2:30 a.m. thousands upon thousands of people had come out into the streets to celebrate the fall of Chávez. "Se fue! Se fue!" they shouted (He's gone!). They made long caravans of cars and drove around blasting their horns.

But at the same hour there were reports that vehicles owned by the private TV stations were being attacked by loyal Chávez supporters.

At 3:20 a.m. came the news that everyone was expecting. Inspector General of the Armed Forces Lucas Rincón, the military's highest official and a man whom everyone considered Chávez's closest adviser, announced that the president had resigned:

People of Venezuela, good morning. The members of the military high command of the National Armed Forces of the Bolivarian Republic of Venezuela deplore the regrettable events that occurred yesterday. Before these facts they have asked the president of the republic to resign his post, which he has accepted.

The members of the military high command are, as of this moment, tendering our resignations, which we will turn in to whatever officials are named by the new authorities. Finally, I want to call on the glorious people of Venezuela to stay calm and to exercise an exemplary civility and reject all provocations to violence and disorder. Have faith in your armed forces.

The announcement was soon verified by the rest of the military high command. A short time later, around 4:00 a.m., President Chávez was taken from Miraflores to Fort Tiuna, escorted by General Rosendo. It was broadcast live to the nation. That made it plain to everyone: Hugo Chávez had lost power. According to the constitution, the vice president would become president for thirty days until new elections were held. But the vice president was in hiding, and it was rumored that he, too, had resigned, further exacerbating the power vacuum.

At 4:51 a.m., Dr. Pedro Carmona appeared on television and announced that he would assume the presidency of Venezuela as part of a civilian-military transitional government.

As the sun rose over Caracas that morning, Venezuela and the world awoke to the news that South America's oldest democracy had a new president.

11 | Reactions

That night Andrés Trujillo's mother stayed with him in the hospital. Despite all that had happened—being shot on Baralt Avenue, the chaos at Vargas Hospital, almost losing his leg—Andrés couldn't sleep. He was not very religious, but for some reason he wanted to pray. So he and his mother prayed together. Late in the night they watched Lucas Rincón announce that Chávez had resigned. Andrés felt an incredible joy. He turned to his mother and said, "There were many killed, many wounded, and a lot of blood, but it was worth it." Soon he fell off to sleep.

—✽—

Antonio Návas, the Chávez supporter who had been shot through the jaw in front of Miraflores, was also in the hospital. The news that Chávez had resigned scared him because he was afraid that someone might come and finish him off. There were rumors going around that security forces from the new government were going to the hospitals claiming they needed to take the wounded to private clinics but were really "disappearing" them.

Then the Tupamaro, the urban guerrilla group that controlled the neighborhood called 23 de Enero, came to the hospital to act as security for the government victims. That made Antonio feel better.

In the morning the director of the hospital came to him. The director was also a *chavista* and was taking special care of the people who had been wounded. He told Antonio that many people like him had risked their lives and been wounded or killed, simply because they wanted a president that would really help them and listen to them.

The director, too, was worried about Antonio's safety, so around ten that morning, a doctor and a nurse snuck him out the back entrance to the hospital. At this point, because of the number of wounded, he had only been given basic first aid along with some X-rays. They had not had time to operate on his fractured jaw, so Antonio went home as he was, feeling it was better to wait until things cooled down than to risk being in a hospital.

12 | Venevisión

While it seemed to the world that Hugo Chávez had resigned in disgrace and handed control over to the military, this was not exactly . . . not quite the case.

Rewind now to the previous night; it is nine o'clock in the headquarters of Venevisión, where Luis Miquilena has just made his announcement that he no longer supports Hugo Chávez.

The top floor of the TV station had been converted into a cross between a penthouse and a bunker: a luxurious conference room with a huge TV and a terrace that led to a helipad so that, if necessary, people could be evacuated. In this room a critical meeting was taking place. In attendance were over twenty opposition leaders, including Gustavo Cisneros, the billionaire owner of Venevisión, Dr. Pedro Carmona, and Carlos Ortega.

Carmona and Ortega were the yin and yang of the opposition. Each, in his own way, personified the organization that they represented. As the head of the business guild Fedecámaras, Carmona, was an elderly gentleman who represented the more aristocratic business and political elite. He was a short man with light skin and an almost bald crown (except for a band of gray hair that ran from ear to ear at the back). Trained as an economist, he had been a career diplomat, living throughout Europe and Latin America, and eventually becoming Venezuela's ambassador to Peru. In 1985 he had retired from the foreign service and gone into the private sector. Since then he had served on the boards of several large companies and trade associations. He was well spoken and respected among the elite and had the air that he would be quite at home in the rich Caracas suburbs of Altamira and Country Club. He spoke French and had over twenty-five hundred flight hours as an amateur pilot.

In contrast, Ortega, the head of Venezuela's enormous labor union, the CTV, was a burly former oil worker with a pocked complexion. He spoke like the workmen he represented and was not at all shy about using expletives. He was the type of guy you'd expect to find in a bar with a string of empty cerveza bottles in front of him talking politics in his raspy smoker's voice.

When they held press conferences together—sometimes twice a day in recent months—Carmona wore a suit and tie. Ortega wore jeans and a short-sleeved shirt. They were opposites, but together they represented a large spectrum of Venezuela's population and their camaraderie was essential in giving the opposition its united front against Chávez.

Earlier that afternoon—after Ortega had blasted Generals Rosendo and Rincón for not doing more to stop the bloodshed—Carmona and Ortega had met at a house in the Floresta neighborhood. The two men talked privately about how an interim government should be formed. It was a reiteration of what they had been talking about for many months—a nine-person group, or junta, made up of four military men, one from each branch of the armed forces, and five civilians. In their initial planning Carmona and Ortega had decided not to participate in the junta; they both felt more efficacious in their current roles as the business and labor leaders of the country.

Now at the meeting in Venevisión, the opposition leaders spoke about the makeup of the interim government and, more importantly, they agreed that whatever happened they needed to follow the letter of the constitution. But despite this talk of the constitution and legality, some in the room were planning how they would abuse the power they would soon be given and how they would cut out their colleagues when they divided up the spoils.

After a while Carmona said that he was very fatigued and asked if he could be allowed to sleep a few hours before continuing the discussion in the morning. As Carmona was getting on the elevator, journalist Rafael Poleo spoke to him.

"Are you going to sleep at your house?"

"No," Carmona replied, "I'm going to the Four Seasons to shower and change."

After Carmona had gone, the meeting resumed. It wasn't long before Poleo received a call. It was from a contact at Fort Tiuna. Poleo informed the group that he had just been told that Carmona was out at the base—along with a young millionaire named Isaac Pérez Recao—meeting with the military leaders. They were setting up a new government.

The group was shocked. "He's fucked us!" someone said. Ortega began punching numbers into his cell phone. He got through to Carmona. "Look here," Ortega said, "I thought you were a trustworthy man!" Ortega made it clear he felt he was being betrayed and that whatever Carmona did, it would not be supported by the Confederation of Venezuelan Workers (CTV). When Ortega hung up, he called another number and demanded to speak with General Vásquez Velasco. According to witnesses in the room, it appeared that the general was trying to sooth Ortega and invited him to come down to the base to participate in what they were doing.

"I'm not going anywhere!" Ortega said. "I'm not getting into this and you can't count on me!" Ortega got up and made a few more calls. After a while he said that he was tired and needed to rest. "Why don't you go?" someone in the room asked. "They are making the new government."

"I'm not going to whitewash what they are doing," Ortega said. "Besides, this thing won't last." The leader of the opposition's most powerful body, the CTV, had just withdrawn his support for the interim government.

To understand why the opposition was disintegrating so quickly, it is necessary to understand the business and political elite who made up its leadership.

At the time of the coup, Hugo Chávez was using two terms to refer to the opposition: *la oligarquía* and *los escuálidos*. "The oligarchy" referred to those who had traditionally held power: the business and political elite. It was these people who Chávez claimed had grown outrageously rich off Venezuela's oil wealth but turned their backs on the needs of the masses. According to Chávez, the oligarchs fought his reforms tooth and nail because he put their cozy way of life at risk.

The other term, *escuálido*, literally means "weak," "pale," or "thin." The word was meant to imply that the opposition was a small minority out of touch with the needs of the country. It also had the connotation of a rich, lazy brat.

Both terms effectively played off the common perception that in Venezuela (as in much of Latin America) a small elite controlled all the wealth. Further, the terms helped Chávez compress Venezuela's complex social problems into a simple conflict between rich and poor. This dichotomy, with Chávez as the champion of the poor, allowed him to place the blame for many of the country's ills on the oligarchy (a charge that was not always unjustified). Any problems with his social programs, any allegation of corruption, anything at all that made him look bad was usually blamed on the oligarchs. According to Chávez, the oligarchs were on a devious mission to stop the revolution, most notably by infiltrating his government or by subverting it through the businesses they owned (e.g., the newspapers and TV stations).

Granted, the oligarchs certainly existed—they were a class of citizens that fit the most extreme stereotypes of materialism and shallowness. They loved to flaunt their wealth—luxury SUVs, ostentatious jewelry, thousand-dollar handbags—and seemed completely oblivious to the sprawling poverty that was all around them. Looking on them from below they were easy to hate.

However, the situation was not nearly as simple as Chávez contended: Many of these "oligarchs" were very active in social programs and profoundly patriotic. They were businesspeople who funded schools in poor neighborhoods; doctors who went into the shantytowns and gave free care; and attorneys who dedicated themselves to public service.

What's more, one could not simply say that the rich hated Chávez and the poor loved him. Many oligarchs—including the heads of the private media—had helped Chávez into office and many remained loyal through the April 11 crisis. As for the poor, statistics showed that in 2002, over 60 percent of Venezuelans lived in poverty. Yet, on April 11, Chávez's approval rating was estimated at below 30 percent; therefore, many of the poor were actually against him at the time. While Chávez's popularity would rebound after the coup, his reputation as the defender of the poor was still largely a campaign promise.

Further complicating the issue was race. In Venezuela 68 percent of the population is mestizo (of mixed blood), 21 percent is Caucasian, and a very small percentage is African-Venezuelan. As in many places in Latin America, skin color is lighter in the higher social classes. The darker you are, the more you are perceived as poor. Although Venezuelans don't like to admit it, there is a great deal of racism superimposed on the class disparity—racism becomes elitism and vice versa. The darker-skinned Hugo Chávez physically represented his targeted constituency, the poor. His declaration of war against the oligarchy had strong racial overtones—it was a backlash against the historic racism/elitism that had prevailed in Venezuela. Just as the old regimes had discriminated against people with darker skin, so the Chávez regime discriminated against the lighter-skinned Venezuelans. Some viewed this as affirmative action, while others saw it as reverse discrimination and racism.

Mixed into this complex situation was the interesting fact that a significant chunk of Venezuela's upper and middle class are immigrants or children of immigrants, many of whom come from humble origins—like Mike Merhi, Malvina Pesate, and Gorka Lacasa. Many newcomers feel a certain condescension toward "native" Venezuelans, whom they view as less industrious. After all, these newcomers were able to make it in Venezuela, so they ask themselves what is wrong with the other Venezuelans? In return, many "native" Venezuelans consider the new arrivals sly, greedy foreigners out to get rich off their country's natural resources.

All these factors—political rhetoric, racism, immigration—contribute to Venezuela's class tensions.

But perhaps the greatest irony, however, is that much of the animosity toward the "oligarchs" comes not from poorer people wanting to get rid of them, but from poorer people wanting to *be* them. The oligarchs are, after all, the Venezuelan dream. This is, we must remember, a petrostate, a country that is not only sustained by oil but where everyone feels they have a right to oil wealth, a place where politicians have—for close to a century now—fed into the fantasy of quick wealth by promising voters that, if elected, they will make them rich. This promise has led to a great self-deception in the Venezuelan psyche—the belief that the state, as supreme owner of the oil, has an obligation to make all its citizens as rich as the oligarchs; instilling in them the delusion that Venezuela is only a few steps away from being an oil emirate, a Qatar-like state where instead of paying taxes, citizens are given a handsome check by the government each year.

So pervasive is the oil/oligarch dream that not even Chávez and his most devout socialist comrades are immune. It wasn't long after Chávez was elected that the president's mother, Elena, who raised her six boys in a shack with a dirt floor, began appearing in the newspapers with Coqui, her poodle, wearing designer clothes and a cumbersome amount of gold jewelry. Ironically, it is the former guerrilla fighters who now drive SUVs, get breast implants, and wrinkle their noses at the proletariat. Now they are the *nouveaux riches.*

—◆◆◆—

Enter Isaac Pérez Recao, a thirty-two-year-old businessman, heir to one of the largest fortunes in Venezuela and an important player in the interim government that was about to take power. His family dynasty had major interests in construction and had built many shopping malls around Venezuela, as well as two in North Carolina. They owned big bingo clubs and they had large stakes in many of Venezuela's oil subcontractors, including Venoco—of which Pedro Carmona had long served as a member of the board before becoming president of Fedecámaras. The family owned luxury cars, planes, sailboats, and helicopters.

Isaac was a young man fascinated by the military: guns, martial arts, the whole bit. He trained with his squad of bodyguards as if they were a real military unit—from target shooting to skydiving. In the words of one Venezuelan journalist, Isaac was a Rambo wannabe; another described him as "a yuppie with guns." There was, however, a personal reason for his obsession with security. The family's immense wealth made them ideal targets for criminals and several family members had been kidnapped and ransomed. Isaac took it upon himself to be the head of family security.

Isaac's family business and his hobbies had given him extensive contacts in the government, private industry, and the military—and not just with the influential Carmona. It was rumored that he was financing a group of dissident military officers who wanted to overthrow Chávez. What was certain was that he was bankrolling many opposition activities and had been meeting with the opposition leaders for months. He often hosted the meetings and would give members whatever they needed to do their work—he would loan them his bodyguards, let them use cars from his personal fleet, and even transport them around on his private jet. On April 11, for example, he flew General Enrique Medina—Venezuela's devoutly anti-Chávez military attaché in Washington and a man that Chávez suspected of conspiracy—from Miami to Venezuela on the family plane.

Ironically, the same favors Isaac now lavished on the opposition he had once lavished on the *chavistas*. He had financed Chávez's party during the presidential campaign, let bigwig *chavistas* use his helicopter, and even let Chávez himself use his armored cars. During the Vargas floods, he had also used his helicopter to help the government rescue people from flooded areas.

But by April 11, Isaac had developed a deep personal wrath against Chávez and all those who represented *chavismo*. He felt that these three years of Chávez had cost him and his family (and the family business) dearly. And like many of the opposition leadership, he felt that all Venezuelans *must* feel the same way—that virtually everyone wanted Chávez destroyed. This would be his error. His ethnocentrism and sense of privilege would blind him to the greater significance of *chavismo*.

Still, Isaac Pérez Recao, a man few Venezuelans had ever heard of, was about to have his day in the sun.

13 | A Strange Sort of Coup

Just as the opposition leaders were beginning to feud over how the transitional government should be led, things in Miraflores were not going as smoothly as most of the world perceived either. After Rosendo hung up the phone with Vásquez Velasco with the understanding that the army would get a plane ready for Chávez's trip to Cuba, the agreement between Chávez and the military ran into problems.

On the mind of the Miraflores staffers was how to ensure the president's safety. García Ponce suspected a trap—that the generals really wanted to take Chávez out of the country and turn him over to the Americans. Then, using whatever pretext they wanted, they could keep him in jail (as George Bush Senior had done with Manuel Noriega of Panama). Sitting in a prison in the United States, Chávez would no longer be a problem for the mighty economic powers; with him gone they could once again "sink their fangs into Venezuela's petroleum."

To ensure that the generals played fair, Defense Minister José Vicente Rangel proposed that the resignation take place at one of the TV stations in the presence of representatives from the church who could guarantee Chávez's safety. Rangel called Omar Camero, the owner of the TV station Televen, while Ramón Chacín, the minister of justice and the interior, called Archbishop Baltasar Porras, president of the Venezuelan Episcopal Conference, and Bishop José Luis Azuaje.

Archbishop Porras would remember that it was half past midnight when he got the call from Chacín. After a few minutes, Chávez came on the line. The president greeted him formally and said that in light of everything that had happened, he was ready to leave the country. *Some are in agreement and some aren't, Chávez said, but it is my decision. I don't want any more blood spilled, although here in the palace we are sufficiently armed to defend ourselves against any attack, but I don't want it to come to that.*

The archbishop was very surprised that the president had called him, but agreed to help Chávez in any way he could.

What I am asking of you, Chávez said, *is that you escort me to the steps of the plane or even accompany me* [to Cuba] *if necessary.*

The archbishop said he would do whatever was necessary. The plan was to meet at Televen, formalize the resignation, and then go to the airport.

To fulfill his part of the bargain Vásquez Velasco sent Generals Enrique Medina, Rommel Fuenmayor, and Nestor González González to the station to oversee the resignation. Before long Rosendo received a call from Fuenmayor, who said they were at Televen with Archbishop Porras and the other generals waiting for Chávez. Rosendo told Fuenmayor that this wasn't the plan the president had agreed to—these weren't the generals he wanted to turn himself in to—but Fuenmayor insisted that this was the decision and that he was sending the resignation letter by fax.

Rosendo told Fuenmayor that he would tell the president, but when he did, Chávez, predictably, said he didn't trust *these* generals and that, even though they had the archbishop with them, they had not guaranteed him anything. Chávez was particularly suspicious of Medina, whom he suspected of plotting against him and who, in Chávez's mind, might possibly have orchestrated this whole thing. It is also quite possible that Chávez didn't know whether these three generals were acting on Vásquez Velasco's orders, or that he suspected they might deviate from the army commander's instructions. That was the problem: So many generals were pressuring Chávez that it was unclear who was with whom and who really had control.

It was about this time that Hugo Chávez finally got through to the man whose advice he most valued. It was 1:38 a.m. in Caracas.

"What forces do you have there with you?" Fidel Castro asked.

Referring to the honor guard, Chávez said, "Between two hundred and three hundred exhausted men."

"Any tanks?"

"No, there were some, but they withdrew them back to their base." Chávez went on to give Castro more details of the situation and the state of the negotiations with the generals.

"Can I give you my honest opinion?"

Chávez said yes.

Echoing the advice of Chacín and General Usón, Castro recommended against a fight. "Lay down conditions for an honorable agreement and save the life of the men you have, which are the men that are most loyal to you. Don't sacrifice them, or sacrifice yourself."

The two men talked for a while and agreed that it would be best if Chávez left the country, at least temporarily. Castro even offered to send some planes to get him. Once in Cuba they would figure out a way to fight this. Castro then told Chávez not to resign if he could; that it was better if he simply left the country.

Soon thereafter, Colonel Silvino Bustillos and Generals Luis Camacho Kairuz and Juvenal Barráez arrived at the palace from Televen with the original resignation letter for Chávez to sign. Chávez was in his office with the president of the National Assembly Willian Lara, José Vicente Rangel, Aristóbulo Istúriz, and Chacín.

"*Como está, paisano?*" Chávez said to Kairuz.

"Trying to get through this difficult time," Kairuz replied.

Chávez went to a sofa and Bustillos gave him the resignation letter. He was smoking one cigarette after another. Finally, he said he would only sign when his exit from the country had been guaranteed. "In cases like this, tradition dictates that the deposed leader leaves the country. I think it is best that I am gone before dawn."

The generals pressed him to sign now.

"Don't sign, Hugo," Jóse Vicente Rangel said, "that way it will be a coup d'état."

Chávez nodded. He was exhausted and a part of him wanted to sign, to get it over with, but he was still not ready. He would not sign. First, he had to make sure there wasn't a double cross—that he and his family made it out of the country safely. Second, there was Castro—*try not to resign*. But there was a third reason: Chávez was starting to develop a deeper under-standing of what was really going on here; he was beginning to see that perhaps this "coup" was not as well orchestrated as he had initially be-lieved. This realization was coming slowly, in bits and pieces, and it was, ironically, coming to him from the den of the coupsters themselves, from Fort Tiuna, from a man who was there with the rebelling generals, a man who was trusted by both sides: General Usón.

One of the first things that struck General Francisco Usón when he reported to the military command at Fort Tiuna was that Pedro Carmona was sitting in the chair of the commander of the army. For Usón this was completely inappropriate; an insult. What's more, Isaac Pérez Recao and Daniel Romero were sitting at a table naming their friends as new government ministers. "For [minister of] defense put down Héctor Ramírez Pérez, the vice admiral," Isaac said.

The scene was a mess, complete disorder. And there was a strange disconnect between what the civilians were doing and what the officers were doing. They were each in their own separate worlds, each at opposite ends of the building, and neither was working with the other.

"You intend to run the country with those people out there?" Usón asked Vásquez Velasco. "That out there smells like Carlos Andrés Pérez and people aren't going to accept it," he said, referring to the Venezuelan president who was impeached in 1994. He was in an office with Vásquez Velasco and a big crowd of generals. Usón urged them to include *chavistas* in the transitional government and he named a few moderates in the party who he thought would be acceptable to both sides. But Usón was told that this would not be possible, because those decisions had already been made.

Usón then went back to see the civilian group and spoke to Carmona. "I don't know who is going to be president of this country in the next few hours," Usón said, "but let me tell you something. Even though I have resigned as Finance Minister, I'm still the only one authorized to sign [government transactions] who is still in the country. Tomorrow, the twelfth, we have to make payment on the debt. We also have to put the system in motion for paying the public employees because Monday is the fifteenth, and I think this government will start very badly if it begins with a labor dispute."

Carmona, seeing the wisdom of Usón's words, told him to go to the Ministry of Finance and take care of it.

It had been about 11:30 p.m. when Chávez had started calling Usón to find out what was going on. Usón still had the ministry cell phone, which was part of a private government network. The president called him five or six times over the next four hours. He kept asking about what was happening, saying he needed to talk to Vásquez Velasco. Usón was trying to act as messenger between Chávez and the military high command, but the generals and admirals were shut away in an office deliberating among themselves.

"I need them to put me on a plane so I can get out of the country," Chávez said. He seemed very distressed, in a state of shock. He wanted a guarantee that he and his family would be allowed to leave Venezuela. Usón noticed that this was all he was focused on. He wasn't talking about anybody else and he wasn't concerned about designating a successor or what would happen to the revolution. He had realized that his government had collapsed. In addition, Usón suspected that no one around Chávez had the wherewithal to help him control the situation. Adding to the confusion was the fact that the vice president and the majority of Chávez's cabinet and advisers had gone into hiding.

"Look, president," Usón said to Chávez, "the situation is this: Things are very disorganized here. They can't come to an agreement." Finally, Usón forced his way into the generals' meeting and handed Vásquez Velasco his cell phone, explaining that the president had been waiting for half an hour to talk to him. Vásquez Velasco took the call. But Usón could tell by listening that Vásquez Velasco was still unsure of things, too. (Emblematic of the government's complete disarray, this was the first time that Chávez had actually spoken with Vásquez Velasco since the crisis began.)

Usón, knowing Chávez as he did, suspected that the president was drawing important conclusions from all this. Chávez was beginning to realize that the military hadn't planned this. The president had assumed that this was a coup d'état in the classic sense, like those that had occurred in Guatemala and Chile, well planned and likely backed by the United States. He had assumed that the military had been working together for months, were united, and had each step planned out. But now Chávez was beginning to realize that it was something that the military was not controlling and if the military couldn't control it, then perhaps there was an opportunity for him. He could smell it.

14 | Leaving Miraflores

Having failed to get Chávez's signature on the resignation letter, General Kairuz, General Barráez, and Colonel Bustillos left Miraflores and headed back to Fort Tiuna. It was now after 3:20 a.m., and General Lucas Rincón had already announced that Chávez had resigned on national TV.

Chávez had told Rincón not to make the announcement until all his conditions were met, but Rincón, terrified that a bloody confrontation between pro- and anti-Chávez military units was imminent, had jumped the gun. He hoped that saying that Chávez had agreed to the military's demands would defuse the situation. Yet to the rest of Venezuela such an announcement by Chávez's most trusted aide was gospel—Chávez was out!

Almost immediately, some of the generals began calling Miraflores to pressure Chávez; they had had enough and wanted this thing wrapped up. What's more, they said, the deal had changed. Bolstered by Rincón's announcement, they saw little need to cater any further to Chávez's whims. He would be placed under arrest and there was no guarantee of his safe passage out of the country. It wasn't long before General Fuenmayor himself called, having received word that Chávez had refused to sign the resignation letter. The air force general was enraged and made it clear that if Chávez wasn't out of Miraflores in a hurry, he would demolish the palace with his squadron of F-16s. He gave the president fifteen minutes.

When Rosendo told Chávez of the change, the president reiterated that Rosendo had to guarantee his life. Rosendo once again assured Chávez that he would. Then Chávez reluctantly agreed to be taken into custody.

Rosendo could see the incredible stress that Chávez was under. It was obvious that he was very concerned about being killed. He kept asking Rosendo for advice and solace. But Rosendo's sympathy only went so far. "President, you have made the best decision because this crisis can't take any more of you. The best thing for you to do is to get out of the country and let the Venezuelan people set the nation's course as they will, because the people, *el pueblo*, have had enough of you."

It was the kind of unsolicited commentary that Rosendo was famous for—as blunt as a drill sergeant—and Chávez would remember it.

It was then that Chávez called for his parents, who were in the palace, and told them of his decision to turn himself over to the dissident generals. "It looks like we're leaving, Mamá."

"All right," his mother said, "we're leaving [too], my darling. But don't worry because your house is waiting for you. The little house in Barinas, we'll live there. . . . We will always be the same family." The two tried to console their son, reminding him that he still had the opportunity to be an important international leader.

⌘

Word of Fuenmayor's air-strike ultimatum ran through the corridors of Miraflores like wildfire. Upon hearing the news many people fled the palace, but not García Ponce. While frightened, he didn't flee. He would continue to take his chances with Chávez.

Ana Elisa Osorio, the minister of the environment, came out of Chávez's office and spoke to the crowd of about twenty remaining staffers. The minister was a slim, blond middle-aged woman with white skin and a small chin that now quivered with emotion. She spoke softly, directly to one of the men in front, but the crowd hung on her every word. "Politically, for the record this was a coup d'état. It isn't that he resigned because the president did not resign. He didn't resign and so he is under arrest." Then she spoke louder, addressing them all. "It's that it's a coup; let the world know!"

The group applauded. The Irish film crew—still working inside the palace—recorded it all.

A few minutes later General Hurtado opened the door to the president's office. "The president will say goodbye now," he announced. "Line up double file. We are going to do it quickly. We don't have much time."

They began to sing the national anthem. *"Gloria al bravo Pueblo que el yugo lanzó, la ley respetando la virtud y honor."*

When Chávez appeared, they started chanting, "Chávez! Chávez!" It was a difficult moment for everyone—tired and exhausted they surged around him, their leader, their hope. They shouted words of faith and encouragement. Men hugged him, women kissed his cheek, they didn't want to let him go. He made his way slowly through them; in one hand he carried a small crucifix. "I'll only be gone for a little while," he said. "We'll return!"

Out in the courtyard more people crowded up to say good-bye, then he got into a limousine with Generals Hurtado and Rosendo and headed for Fort Tiuna.

After he had gone soldiers wept.

15 | The Empty, Empty Hole

Many miles away in the mountain village of Ocumare del Tuy, in a small four-room shack, Catalina Palencia sat in the darkness. Gray moonlight streaked in from her open front door. Still no Jhonnie.

Once more, she went to the door and looked out at the dirt road that ran by the house. She knew if she stood there long enough, she would start to imagine a figure there, her Jhonnie, walking up the lane. Three or four times she was sure she saw him, but it was only the darkness playing tricks on her.

She told herself she should go to bed, but she knew she would just lie there, so she stayed where she was, watching as the night wind stirred the trees and shadows.

Where was he? The boy he had gone to Caracas with had returned to the village around 7:00 p.m. He'd come by the house looking for Jhonnie and seemed surprised that he wasn't already home. He told Catalina how they had marched with the opposition, but near the palace, on Eighth Street, they had seen a man get shot and gotten separated.

Now, looking out at the road, Catalina put her hand to her brow and stared into the darkness. She was a small woman with brown skin and short, curly brown hair. She had a face that told you, without regrets or pity, that she had a hard life. A face that was rugged and worn, with deep rings under her eyes that gave her a perpetual weary look. Her house was a *rancho*, a brick shack with a tin roof. There was no plumbing or telephone.

Sheets hung in the doorways to give a little privacy to the bedrooms. On the bare-brick wall in the living room was a plaque that Jhonnie had earned in the air force, a Hello Kitty sticker, and a few framed pictures of Catalina's other six children. Her only furniture consisted of a small homemade table with three mismatched chairs, a wooden sofa, and a broken refrigerator. Still, Catalina thought, she did all right, the best she could do working sporadically as a maid and selling keno tickets. Luckily all her kids were grown and could take care of themselves.

As she stood there in her doorway Catalina didn't know—couldn't have imagined—just how much harder her life was about to become. That her quiet son, "the Book Man," lay dead beside the El Silencio Metro stop, shot by the National Guard. How tomorrow she would see his body on TV, still lying there. How she would be lied to by the police and told that he was not dead. Then, when it was undeniable, she would be told that he had not been killed on April 11. And then, when that had been proven they would claim that he had not been fighting against Chávez, rather defending him—how the government would claim him as their martyr, a loyal patriot killed by the "murderous" opposition. How his picture would appear in all the newspapers, and how Catalina would collect all the clippings—even the pictures that showed his corpse in full color. And how Chávez would say on national TV that anyone who went to the police or newspapers saying the government had used violence, anyone who said they lost a family member on April 11 at the hands of the National Guard or the Bolivarian Circles was a traitor to his or her country. And how Catalina would fight anyway, how she would get a lawyer to work for free, but how, in the end, no judge would hear her case, and no one would ever be held accountable for her son's death.

But all of that was to come. In a few hours it would begin. Now she waited under the equatorial stars, looking into the darkness for her son. Waiting to see him emerge from the shadows, tired and weary, as he made his way up the lane.

Catalina lay down on the concrete floor just inside the doorway. He would have to step over her when he came in, and that would surely wake her. Then she would know he was home. Then she could really sleep.

16 | Coup or Resignation?

Hugo Chávez, General Rosendo, and General Hurtado rode in silence to the military base. It was only after they were inside the main gate that Chávez finally spoke. "Once again under arrest," he said, "just like ten years ago. And to think that I am going to turn over power to this pack of *escuálidos*."

It was 4:00 a.m.

Three things struck Rosendo when they arrived at headquarters. First, people were very sober as if collectively mourning the loss of life, but at the same time they seemed tranquil. The military had not massacred the people and there was relief at that. Last, Rosendo noticed a certain relief that Chávez had resigned.

Archbishop Baltasar Porras, the man whom Chávez had called to guarantee his safety while he negotiated with the generals, was waiting for them. The president greeted the archbishop, asked for his blessing, and said he was sorry for all the negative things he had said about him (Chávez had once accused the archbishop of keeping the devil under his frock). Without hesitating the archbishop blessed Chávez and embraced him. The archbishop saw before him a beaten man. Yet, at the same time, Chávez had a serenity about him; he seemed resigned to his fate.

Chávez then greeted Bishop José Luis Azuaje, who also blessed and embraced him. Then General Rosendo took his leave: "OK, Mr. President, I am going to retire," he said. "You asked me to bring you here and I have done it." It was now up to the archbishop and the bishop to guarantee Chávez's life. Rosendo headed back to his house on the base.

With one cleric on each side and surrounded by armed soldiers, Chávez was taken to the top floor of the army command. He greeted everyone and if he recognized a soldier, he called him by name and asked after his family.

General Vásquez Velasco was surprised to hear that Chávez was on the base. He thought the resignation had already taken place. On seeing the president, Vásquez Velasco felt oddly sorry for him. He looked over-whelmed, defeated, and Vásquez Velasco suspected that Chávez had put on his military uniform for that very reason: to invoke sympathy. Pathetic, Vásquez Velasco thought to himself. How can this be? How is it that a president abandons his people? He should have stayed in Miraflores and negotiated from there, fought, struggled for his ideas, for what he wanted. But instead he took the easy road. *Me voy de Venezuela.* I am going; I am running . . . abandoning my people. And on top of all that I am going out dressed like a soldier, as a snub to the other officers.

Vásquez Velasco shook his head.

"I understand that you have just resigned," he said.

Chávez denied this. "*Bueno,* General, you know my terms."

"Yes, you want a plane to go to Cuba . . . then Lucas [Rincón] will have your signed resignation?"

"Everything that I need to turn in to you I will give you on the plane."

Vásquez Velasco exhaled loudly. He could see that Chávez was trying to manipulate him. The general pressed him, but Chávez cut him off.

"I repeat. I'll give it to you on the plane."

The military leaders (about twenty-five of them), including Usón, Vásquez Velasco, and the archbishop and the bishop gathered around Chávez in the conference room at the Headquarters of the Army. Also there were Generals Ovidio Poggioli, Carlos Martínez, and Medina. By now it was well after four in the morning and Chávez again made his plea. "I am ready to resign, *if* you guarantee me what I am asking which is passage out of the country and the safety of my family. If you can guar-antee me that, I am willing to resign."

The room was quiet for a moment. Finally, one of the officers said, "President, you cannot leave because you are going to be put on trial for the human rights offenses that occurred with the slaughter of Venezuelans."

"You have changed the rules of the game on me," Chávez said. "What Rosendo and Hurtado talked about with Efraín [Vásquez Velasco] was that I would sign the resignation, if you let me leave the country. That was the understanding. But now you say that I am in your custody, which is to say that I will be under arrest. You will have arrested a popularly elected president. Well, I'm not going to argue about that. Now that I am here I am in your hands, you will have to do what you think is convenient. . . . I am not in a position to argue, nevertheless I think I am less of a problem for you if you let me leave the country, and I will be a bigger problem for you if I stay in the country, but *you* have control."

General Usón agreed with Chávez on this, but for a different reason. He had been sitting quietly in the corner, but now he pressed the generals to let the president go in exchange for the signed resignation because to do otherwise was to really have a coup. There was no historic precedent for arresting a sitting head of state, and the people would certainly see it as a breach of the military's role in upholding democracy, which, Usón had to admit, it would be.

Again the generals pushed Chávez to sign. A palpable tension filled the air. Usón felt that this was the critical moment and he could tell that Chávez saw his opportunity. What Chávez had suspected in Miraflores while talking on the phone with Usón was now obvious—this was no well-planned coup. The generals were divided and without a clear leader. Yes, Vásquez Velasco might have rank and respect, but he was not controlling all of them, and they clearly had not planned any of this and certainly hadn't planned to attack Miraflores.

What's more, Chávez knew what it was like to be jailed and, to put it mildly, he didn't like it. If he was going to be put on trial, it would be better if he was the president, with all its influence and legal privileges, than to be a normal citizen, which was exactly what he would be if he resigned. He wasn't going to make it easy on them.

"I am not going to resign," Chávez said, and he said it so emphatically that it was clear to Usón that the negotiations were over. Then Chávez turned to Admiral Ramírez Pérez. "You, Admiral, are making a coup d'état against a president."

Acting on the counsel of Alan Brewer Cariás—one of Carmona's legal advisers—some of the generals said that the signed resignation wasn't even necessary. General Rincón's announcement had been enough to legally prove that Chávez was out. Thinking of the need to quickly fill the power vacuum, General González González said, "We have to move forward. We can't continue arguing."

Feeling that there were too many people in the room, the top officers of each of the branches of the armed forces decided to meet privately to discuss Chávez's fate. But in the meantime, General González González ordered Chávez to take off his uniform. To many of these men Chávez was a disgrace to the uniform. He had once led a coup, betrayed his country, been thrown in a military prison for two years, and discharged in 1994. The fact that he still paraded around the country in his uniform was seen as an affront to many of these career officers . . . an affront they didn't have to put up with it anymore.

Chávez had brought a small suitcase with him and, after it was searched by the soldiers, he put on sweatpants and a T-shirt. He had also packed a brand new pair of gym shoes and after he emerged from the changing room he lifted himself onto his toes and said to the clerics, "They fit nice."

While Chávez and the clerics waited for the generals to make their decision, Chávez asked for coffee and some cigarettes. He tried the coffee but didn't like it and pushed it aside. Chávez still had his cell phone and while they were waiting, he got a call from his wife, Marisabel. Chávez urged her to stay calm and said that he was fine, that he had the two archbishops looking after him. After he had hung up, he set the phone on the table. A few minutes later Bishop Azuaje's phone rang. It was Marisabel calling back. She was sobbing. "Take care of Hugo," she said.

Then Chávez confided to Archbishop Porras: "*Bueno,* I am here in their hands. . . . I have provided them with everything they need. What's more, I told them that I would dismiss [Vice President] Diosdado [Cabello] because I know he wouldn't be able to lead because he wouldn't be accepted by everyone, and to make it easy for them, I proposed putting it there [in the document], the dismissal of Diosdado and the whole cabinet and my resignation."

"What a shame that things are ending this way," Archbishop Porras said, "with all these deaths."

Chávez responded that the deaths were caused by the opposition, by people who wanted to destabilize his government. "It wasn't us," he said, but rather Bandera Roja, Acción Democrática, and the police that had masterminded it all.

True to their word, the archbishop and the bishop stayed by Chávez's side. They talked of many things—Chávez's childhood, the military academy, and his time in the army. The clerics did their best just to listen, to let Chávez talk. Yet both noticed how—as more time passed—Chávez seemed to be losing heart. Every now and then he looked to be on the verge of tears, but then would pinch his nose between his eyes and hold them back.

But Chávez's fortitude had its limits. He was losing hope and was increasingly confident that his captors might do much worse than put him in jail. Yes, he had stood up to them and refused to sign, but in so doing had he merely pushed them into a corner where their best option was to kill him?

The heads of the separate branches of the military—Carlos Martínez (army), Héctor Ramírez Pérez (navy), Pedro Pereira Olivares (air force)—met with Vásquez Velasco in his office to decide what to do with Chávez. But they could not reach an agreement. For them, there was no question that Chávez was out; what concerned them was how the armed forces would be perceived if they let him leave the country. There had been many human rights violations and many deaths (no one knew the exact number yet, and few really understood what had happened); letting Chávez go without finding out seemed irresponsible. Would people view them as being complicit with the killings if they let Chávez leave without a trial? Would they be labeled as "the generals who let Chávez get away"? Yet getting Chávez out of the country quickly had its advantages.

Personally, Vásquez Velasco wanted Chávez out of the country. Echoing General Rosendo, he felt that Chávez had to go so that Venezuela could pick up the pieces and get on with its future.

But at the same time, Vásquez Velasco knew that it was not his right or privilege to tell the president he had to go or he had to stay. He was just a soldier after all, as were the rest of the men in the room. With that thinking he suggested that they wait. "There is no consensus and it will soon be dawn," he said. "I propose that we keep him under custody in order to ensure his safety. We can leave it to the transitional government to decide Chávez's fate. Tomorrow will be another day." The other generals agreed, principally because it would protect them. It would take the onus of the decision off the military.

They returned to the conference room and took their seats. Vásquez Velasco took the folder with the letter of resignation and once again insisted that Chávez sign.

"I'm not signing anything," Chávez said, then repeated: "I am in your hands and you can do with me whatever you think is convenient."

"Then I am informing you that from this moment you are in the custody of the national armed forces," replied Vásquez Velasco. The negotiations were over.

Before being led away, Chávez said good-bye to the archbishop and the bishop. By now he was quite certain that he didn't have long to live; his emotions finally took over and he broke down a little, a tear forming on his cheek. He asked them to forgive him, to forgive him for not having built a better relationship with the church. He asked them to have all the other clergy pray for him, too. "*Dénme su bendición*," he said. Give me your blessing.

Then he was taken away.

Hugo Chávez, president of Venezuela, passes soldiers outside of the Museum of Military History in Caracas in early 2002. *AFP/ Getty Images.*

No single photograph was able to capture the opposition march in its entirety. This photo shows a little over half of what was the largest civic protest in the history of Venezuela. *Courtesy of El Universal.*

The march was full of banners playing off Chávez's recent firing (*despedidos*) of employees of the national oil company, PDVSA. *Photo by Daniel Hernandez, courtesy of Cadena Capriles.*

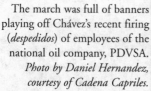

Malvina Pesáte, Joyce Ruth, and Gorka Lacasa on the morning of April 11. This photo was taken just a few hours before Malvina was shot in the face. *Courtesy of Sammy Eppel and Malvina Pesáte.*

The march arrives at the headquarters of the national oil company, PDVSA. This was where the march was officially scheduled to end. *Photo by Jose Diaz, courtesy of Cadena Capriles.*

As the march approached Miraflores, Chávez supporters gathered around the palace to defend their president. In this photo National Assembly Deputy Juan Barreto (right), a close ally of Chávez, speaks to supporters. *Photo by Gabriel Osorio, courtesy of Orinoquiafoto.*

President Chávez sips coffee buttressed by his two highest military officers—General Rosendo on his right and General Rincon on his left. On April 11, both men would refuse the president's orders to use the military against the march. *Photo by Douglas Blanco. Courtesy of Cadena Capriles.*

The first gunshot victim on Baralt Avenue was undercover Secret Police (DISIP) officer Tony Velasquez, who may have been shot because he was dressed like a journalist. *Courtesy of El Universal.*

Point of view: opposition. On Baralt Avenue the march found the way blocked by Chávez loyalists. The Metropolitan Police tried to keep the two groups apart. *Courtesy of Cadena Capriles.*

Point of view: *chavista*. On Baralt Avenue Chávez supporters try to keep the marchers from reaching the Presidential Palace. *Courtesy of Cadena Capriles.*

Vale Todo. On Baralt Avenue the outnumbered Chávez supporters used every means available to stop the huge march from surrounding the palace. *Courtesy of El Universal.*

On Baralt Avenue Chávez supporters light a Molotov cocktail. *Courtesy of Cadena Capriles.*

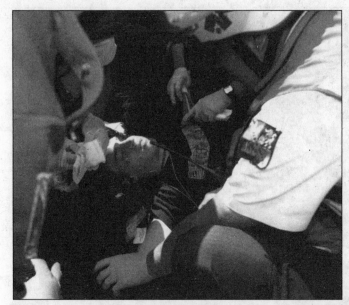

Mike Merhi's 18-year-old son, Jesús Mohamad, lies mortally wounded on Baralt Avenue. *Courtesy of El Universal.*

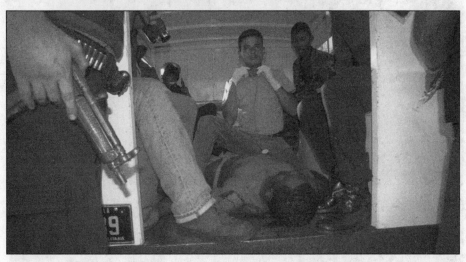

The fatally wounded photographer Jorge Tortoza arrives at Vargas Hospital in a police truck. *Courtesy of Cadena Capriles.*

Dr. Alberto Espidel was on the Llaguno overpass supporting President Chávez when the shooting started. *Photo by author.*

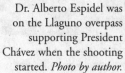

A block away from Baralt Avenue, on Eighth Street, National Guard troops loyal to Chávez shoot shotguns with plastic shot and teargas into the opposition crowd. These troops were also videotaped shooting their 9mm pistols into the crowd. *Courtesy of Cadena Capriles.*

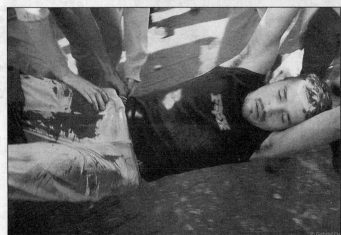

Juan Querales, who wasn't aligned with either the opposition of the government, was shot near El Calvario. He later bled to death in Vargas Hospital. *Ramón Lepage/ Orinoquiaphoto.*

Photographer Gabriel Osorio's picture of Jhonnie Palencia. Osorio ran into the line of fire thinking Palencia was a fellow photographer. Photo by Gabriel Osorio, courtesy of Orinoquiafoto.

Wounded begin
to arrive at
Vargas Hospital.
*Courtesy of
Cadena Capriles.*

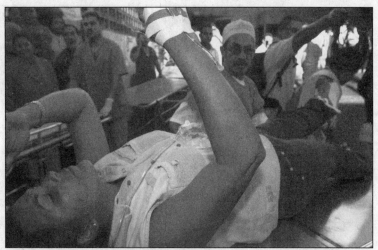

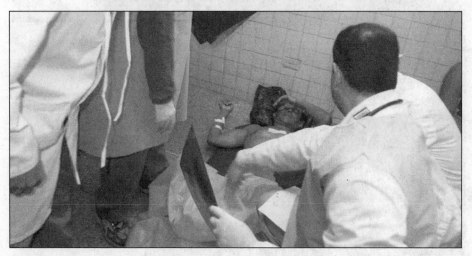

Dr. Serbenescu (with his back to the camera) attends to a wounded man in Vargas Hospital.
Courtesy of Cadena Capriles.

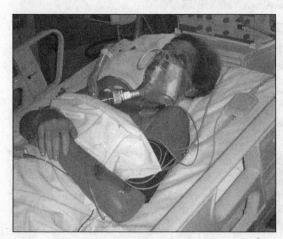

Malvina Pesáte in intensive
care at the Caracas Clinic
after reconstructive surgery
on her face. *Courtesy of
Malvina Pesáte.*

A frame from Luis Fernández's video showing pro-Chávez gunmen shooting onto Baralt Avenue. The footage would tip popular support against Chávez. *Enhancement made by Angel Echeverria, courtesy of Cadena Capriles.*

Venevisión reporter Luis Fernández (left) struggles with Chávez supporters as they try to kick him and his crew off a rooftop near Miraflores. *Luis Fernández.*

Dr. Pedro Carmona swears himself in as the interim president of Venezuela. Daniel Romero, who would read the declarations dissolving Venezuela's democratic institutions, stands on the far left. *Photo by Jorge Aguire, courtesy of Cadena Capriles.*

The Sleeper: General Raúl Baduel, a devout Taoist and founding member of Chávez's revolutionary movement, would lead the operation to rescue the president. *Photo by Hector Castillo, courtesy of Cadena Capriles.*

Army commander General Vásquez Velasco (with microphones) holds a press conference on April 13 pulling his support for Interim-President Carmona. To his left are Generals Rosendo and Carneiro. *Photo by Angel Echeverria, courtesy of Cadena Capriles.*

Chávez's Honor Guards—who were not replaced by the interim government—wave to supporters after retaking the palace on April 13. *AFP/Getty Images.*

After two days of imprisonment a victorious Hugo Chávez returns to the palace of Miraflores in the early morning hours of April 14. *Photo by Gabriel Osorio, courtesy of Orinoquiafoto.*

Catalina Palencia sits with her collection of newspaper articles about her son Jhonnie's death. *Photo by author.*

Carolina Campos and her Aunt Mílvida were both struck by the same bullet on Baralt Avenue. Like many of the government victims, they now work in the palace of Miraflores. *Photo by author.*

PART THREE

THE REGIME OF PEDRO CARMONA

April 12, 2002

1 | Backlash Part I

Throughout the night and early morning of April 12, thousands of people from all corners of Venezuela were on the move—packing up their things, gathering their children, and fleeing their homes. They knew Venezuelan history and they knew the backlash was coming. They left quickly, fearful that at any moment the police or army (under orders from the new government) might come and drive them away. These were the squatters, people who had invaded private lands at the encouragement of Chávez after the Enabling Law was passed. The president had wanted to redistribute some wealth from the rich to the poor; give them a fresh start. Now, without Chávez in power, there was no one to protect them. They knew they didn't have much time.

What they couldn't carry or load into cars was left behind.

⸺∞⸺

At dawn, the backlash against *chavismo* began. For three years the opposition had put up with the "cubanization" of their schools, Chávez's attacks on the media, and his economic policies, which had created a million new unemployed. Now all that frustration could be unleashed. In many places it was completely spontaneous, in other places it was not.

This had become the way of things in Venezuela. Whenever an unpopular regime was toppled there was always a backlash. Vengeance. "Justice." Similar backlashes had occurred after the fall of Marco Pérez Jiménez in 1958 and, most notably, after the death of Venezuela's most famous dictator, Juan Vicente Gómez. When Gómez died in 1935 it provoked a seven-day rampage that unleashed twenty-seven years of frustration: Mobs burned

whole neighborhoods, looted stores, massacred Gómez's friends and supporters, and destroyed statues and public works associated with his reign.
Backlashes had become a Venezuelan tradition.

No one knew exactly what the day might hold. Only one thing was certain: Today would be open season on all things Chávez.

———&———

The morning papers set the tone with a mixture of joyous exultation, sor-
row over the killings, and rage at Chávez. *El Universal*'s headline simply
read, "IT'S OVER!" in huge print.

El Nacional ran a front-page editorial blasting Chávez: "We already knew
about your mental problems and that you were not exactly courageous. . . .
But what we truly ignored was your lack of scruples in ordering your fol-
lowers to fire on defenseless people. . . . With that miserable and cruel act,
you committed your worst political error and your greatest betrayal of your
fatherland. . . . They say history elevates or buries men; for you it has re-
served a pit beside the Venezuelan leaders infamous for their atrocities."

———&———

By midmorning a massive manhunt for the Llaguno Overpass gunmen
and high-level *chavistas* believed to be complicit with yesterday's violence
was under way. It wasn't long before the police, the CICPC (the Venezuelan FBI), and the DISIP had arrested several men from Luis Fernández's
film. One was Henry Atencio. He worked as the chauffeur for Ana Elisa
Osorio, the minister of the environment.

Another suspect was Rafael Cabrices, also an employee of the Ministry
of the Environment. He was the man in the black vest seen stepping up to
the railing and emptying his pistol. When arrested, he broke down in front
of the police and news cameras. He pleaded for God's forgiveness for what
he had done and said that he was sure that the Lord had guided the bullets to prevent them from hitting anyone.

In the process of finding Cabrices and Atencio, the police also captured
Cabrices's cousin, Rafael Guédez, trying to get rid of a 9-mm pistol and
other evidence that implicated the two men.

The connection to the Ministry of the Environment led the CIPCP to search that ministry's office in Venezuela Plaza where they discovered a large cache of arms as well as munitions and bulletproof vests. The rumor that the Chávez regime had been training and arming its most loyal supporters—until now only speculation—was confirmed.

Another gunman in the video, Richard Peñalver, an adviser to Freddy Bernal (head of the Bolivarian Circles), had not yet been detained, but details from his past—namely, that he had served time for murder and robbery—had been discovered.

Acting on reports of high-caliber weapons being stockpiled at a government office near Miraflores in recent weeks, General Luis Camacho Kairuz and members of the CICPC also searched that office and found so many guns that they had to get a truck to transport them all. The office (part of the interior ministry) was located directly across the street from Miraflores; it was assumed by many that the weapons handed out to the Bolivarian Circles yesterday had come from here.

The discovery of the arms cache instantly made Ramón Chacín, the minister of justice and the interior, public enemy number one. Wisely, the minister had gone into hiding, but it wasn't long before a woman noticed him in her apartment building and called the police. (Chacín was the adviser who had been with Chávez in Miraflores urging negotiation while Defense Minister Rangel urged battle.) By the time the police arrived, word had spread through the neighborhood, and an angry mob had encircled the building. The police were able to enter the building and find Chacín, but now the problem was how to get him out without injury. As Chacín was rushed out of the building encircled by officers in black flak jackets, the crowd surged up. With painful slowness, the officers snaked their way through the sea of bodies. All the while the crowd clambered at Chacín, punching and scratching him. Finally, they loaded him into a police truck and took him away.

Young Isaac Pérez Recao was getting involved in the manhunt for *chavistas,* too.

Although it had not yet been announced to the public, Pérez Recao had named his friend, retired General Ovidio Poggioli, to head the secret police (DISIP). Poggioli had immediately returned the favor by giving Isaac the rank of DISIP superintendent. With his new badge in hand, Isaac and his band of deputized bodyguards began searching the city for wanted *chavistas.*

Outside the Cuban embassy an angry crowd of some 250 people gathered. Not only was Cuba blamed for usurping Venezuela's government and taking its oil, but a rumor had spread that many important *chavistas* were seeking asylum inside, including Vice President Diosdado Cabello.

That changed things. This wasn't just a protest against Cuban meddling in Venezuela's affairs. No, this was a siege. They weren't about to let Cabello and his cronies get away. As the crowd chanted, *"Ni un paso atrás,"* one protestor, interviewed by a news crew from RCTV, made the mob's intentions plain: "Look here, señores, you there inside—Diosdado Cabello and your 'combo.' You are going to have to eat the carpets! You are going to have to eat the chairs and tables that are there inside because they aren't going to let any food in; they aren't going to let any water in," he paused to take a breath. "We are going to cut the lights right after you see this transmission."

And they did. The crowd opened a manhole and cut the power. Then they cut off the water. They pelted the building with rocks and set an embassy car on fire. The only problem was that Diosdado Cabello was not inside—he was hiding on a farm in the state of Vargas. Fearful of imminent violence, Cuban ambassador Germán Sánchez called on municipal mayor Henrique Capriles to intervene, which he did. Archbishop Porras—the man who had safeguarded Chávez's life last night in Fort Tiuna—also came to help the Cubans and appease the crowd. Eventually, they dispersed.

At the headquarters of PDVSA, a new board of directors was named and its first action was to cancel all of the country's oil contracts with Cuba. It was a major blow to Cuba as it was Venezuelan oil that was keeping the economy afloat, just as Soviet subsidies had kept it afloat during the cold war.

Shortly after 10 a.m. Chávez's high lieutenant Juan Barreto began calling his contacts at the U.S. embassy. He was scared for his life and wanted to come in; he wanted political asylum. One embassy staffer remembered how frightened he sounded, almost on the verge of tears. Barreto said he was in hiding, but was sure that they were going to find him and torture him. His pleading surprised the staffer. This was one of the most militant and radical leaders of Chávez's political machine—someone who was always full of fire and brimstone about the revolution and often lashed out at the United States. Still, the staffer worked with him and spoke to him several more times that day, but in the end the embassy's consul general said that no one could be granted asylum because Venezuela was not on the current list of countries that the United States recognized with political persecution. The staffer was very sorry, but the embassy could not help Barreto.

Near Machiques—a little town on Venezuela's border with Colombia—Dr. Rafael Bohórquez took a drive through his dairy farm and found that all the squatters had gone. There had been about two hundred of them and they had made a little village on his land . . . were even in the midst of building a school. Now every house was deserted. He felt a tremendous sense of relief. He had been powerless to stop them because Chávez had kept the police from intervening. All he could do was sit and watch as they had slowly destroyed the farm his family had owned for over ninety years—cutting down his trees, damming his streams, and killing his cows.

Thank God it was over, he thought.

Oddly absent from the backlash that morning were the *saqueos*—the looting and pillaging of shops. In Venezuela, whenever there is a lapse in the state's ability to police the population, there is looting. Always. Oftentimes the looting is a form of political protest (such as the Caracazo in 1989, and the fall of dictators like Gómez and Pérez Jiménez), but other times it doesn't have a political impetus (as was the case following the Vargas floods in 1999). If people are confident no one can stop them, they loot. Given the historical precedents, one would have expected angry members of the opposition to be out looting on the morning of April 12, but they weren't.

The *afternoon* of April 12, however, would be a different story, and the looting would be sparked by the *chavistas*.

2 | Washington, D.C.

"Good morning. I want to give you a report on the president's day, and then I have a statement from the president about the recent events in the Middle East."

Over two thousand miles away in Washington, D.C., White House Press Secretary Ari Fleischer was beginning a forty-minute press briefing. It was exactly 12:30 p.m. in Washington. First he reported on the president's day so far: George W. Bush had already put in a call to Russian president Vladimir Putin and Italian prime minister Silvio Berlusconi about a NATO-Russian summit. He had also had a meeting with trade representative Bob Zoellick and the Olympic women's figure-skating gold medalist Sarah Hughes. Fleischer then explained that, during his morning meetings, the president had got word that there had been a suicide attack in Jerusalem; Fleischer expressed the president's condemnation of the violence.

When Fleischer opened the floor to questions, they focused mostly on the bombing. Secretary of State Colin Powell was in the Middle East working on a peace plan and was even scheduled to meet with Yasir Arafat.

The fact that the PLO, which Arafat ostensibly controlled, had taken responsibility for the attack now put the meeting in jeopardy.

"I would like to just call a pause to the Middle East for a second," one reporter said about halfway through the Q and A. "A very important event has happened in Venezuela. We have had the renunciation or forced [unintelligible] of President Chávez. Now, a new government has taken place. Venezuela is a very important country to the stability of the hemisphere; a democracy, and also the third-largest oil supplier to the United States. What does the White House think of the change of government in Venezuela?"

Fleischer was obviously ready for the question:

Let me share with you the administration's thoughts about what's taking place in Venezuela. It remains a somewhat fluid situation. But yesterday's events in Venezuela resulted in a change in the government and the assumption of a transitional authority until new elections can be held.

The details are still unclear. We know that the actions encouraged by the Chávez government provoked this crisis. According to the best information available, the Chávez government suppressed peaceful demonstrations. Government supporters, on orders from the Chávez government, fired on unarmed, peaceful protestors, resulting in 10 killed and 100 wounded [*sic*]. The Venezuelan military and the police refused to fire on the peaceful demonstrators and refused to support the government's role in such human rights violations. The government also tried to prevent independent news media from reporting on these events.

The results of these events are now that President Chávez has resigned the presidency. Before resigning, he dismissed the vice president and the cabinet, and a transitional civilian government has been installed. This government has promised early elections.

The United States will continue to monitor events. That is what took place, and the Venezuelan people expressed their right to peaceful protest. It was a very large protest that turned out. And the protest was met with violence.

"Will the United States government back a civilian government," the reporter asked, "although it's an interim one, to help Venezuela get back on its feet?"

"As I indicated, the events remain fluid. Events are underway still, as we speak. We are consulting with our OAS [Organization of American States] allies and reviewing the events on the ground. I think you'll have more developments and we'll share [them] with you as they warrant. So it's an ongoing story."

The questions returned to the Middle East for the next few minutes until another reporter came back to Venezuela.

"Ari, I understand there was a concern of the U.S. in regards to the policy of Mr. Hugo Chávez towards Iraq and Cuba. Is there any relief maybe because finally he's out of power and the Venezuelan people is electing a new democratic president?"

Fleischer answered:

At all times, these are issues that are the rights of the people of Venezuela to decide who will represent them. As I mentioned, this was a peaceful protest and the peaceful protestors were attacked and many of them were killed or injured as a result of the actions of the Chávez government, which also sought to repress coverage of the issue. The United States is, at all times, committed to democracy around the world and particularly, of course, in our hemisphere. That's why the president traveled to El Salvador and Peru just last month to highlight the importance of democracy.

It's, at all times, the position of the government to promote democracy and tranquility, and as I indicated, events are fluid in the region and this is an issue for the Venezuelan people to determine. . . . I think events took place on the ground there as they did . . . [Fleischer paused.] I think that played out for all to see, and it happened in a very quick fashion as a result of the message of the Venezuelan people.

The next questions steered the conversation back to the Middle East. Would the United Nations send an international force into the Palestinian territories? Was Saudi money being used to fund Palestinian attacks? What was Bush's initial reaction to today's bombing? Fleischer fielded the questions.

"I want to get back to Mr. Chávez one last time," a reporter said during a pause. "You said today from the podium that basically the actions that occurred yesterday were provoked by the Chávez people or people working for Chávez. Do you believe that the armed forces of Venezuela played a constructive role at the end? Because during the whole crisis, they were pretty much aloof and did not get involved. There was some criticism of certain members. But the armed forces seemed to have acted only at the last moment, after the bloodshed. Do you believe that they played a constructive role?"

"Here are the facts that we do know from yesterday's events," Fleischer said. "And that is that the Venezuelan military and police refused to fire on peaceful demonstrators and they refused to support the government's role in such human rights violations. That's the role that the military played. They refused to fire."

There were a few more questions about the Middle East, then the press briefing ended. It was 1:10 p.m. in Washington.

⸺∞⸺

At 3:00 p.m. in Caracas, Attorney General Isaías Rodríguez held his own press conference.

"This is a coup d'état," he said. "There is no doubt about it. There has been a violation of the Inter-American Democratic Charter and the Washington Protocol."

It was the first public statement that suggested that Chávez had not resigned; many people were shocked. Word was beginning to spread.

3 | Carmona's Decrees

Twenty-two-year-old college intern Isabel Muñoz was doing her daily chores at Televen TV when she got tapped to go to Miraflores: a lucky break for an intern. The crisis had taken its toll on the camera crews, who had been working nonstop since the strike began four days ago. They needed fresh legs. After sitting in the station for most of the past twenty-four hours, Isabel was glad to get out. And she had a personal interest in going to Miraflores. Her cousin was part of Chávez's honor guard, and they had lost contact with him. Her family was desperate for news. Once in Miraflores, Isabel hoped to find out what had happened to him.

Isabel was a very petite and pretty young woman with a round face, short black hair, and braces. She was so petite, in fact, that it was impossible for her to wear the bulletproof vests that the station insisted they put on when they were out in the streets—the thing made her knees buckle.

As she and the news crew headed to Miraflores, Isabel noticed how quiet and lonely the streets of Caracas were for a Friday morning. But being out in the sunshine was wonderful. She felt like someone who has just come out of her house after a hurricane has raged through—that feeling that, despite the destruction and debris that is all around, you are happy just to be alive and once again standing in the sun. A few of the cars they passed were honking their horns to the rhythm of "*Ni un paso atrás*," adding a festive feeling to the air. She saw no Chávez supporters. She figured they must be demoralized after yesterday's events; they had finally realized they were not a majority and felt (appropriately) vulnerable.

Yesterday, when the shooting had started in El Silencio, the station had gone crazy. *Completamente loco*. Suddenly it was not so much about covering the news, but about trying to account for all of their people that were down there. They were cut off. Cell phones and radios stopped working. From the station, El Silencio looked like a war zone. They knew their reporters were down there somewhere, but where?

With painful slowness the crews began to make their way back to the station. One by one. All of them were shaken and many of them were in shock. As they tried to tell their stories, some of them couldn't stop crying. The stories they told were amazing. All afternoon and late into the evening they waited nervously for the last stragglers to come in. Eventually they all made it back safe and sound.

Early this morning Isabel finally made it home for a few hours of rest, but she found she couldn't sleep. The station was where the action was and before long she was back at her desk working on *tortas* ("cakes")—collages of images that would be shown throughout the day. Then she got the call that a crew was being sent to Miraflores to cover the swearing in of Carmona. Isabel would be the microwave technician.

Getting through Miraflores security was easier than she had expected. The honor guard were known to be aggressive and manipulative with journalists—inspecting everything they had and delaying them, anything to make them uncomfortable. As it turned out, the first person in Miraflores she recognized was not a politician or a general, but a close friend of her cousin's, Lieutenant Andrés Torres from Chávez's presidential escort. Isabel had seen him a few times at barbecues. The lieutenant greeted her with a kiss on the cheek.

"Have you seen Eduardo?" she asked. The lieutenant said that he had been in the palace since yesterday and didn't know where her cousin was. When Isabel asked him what it had been like, he didn't want to talk about it, saying only that he was thankful that no one inside the palace had been wounded.

Then it struck her how strange it was that the lieutenant—this lieutenant—was in Miraflores in the first place. As part of Chávez's escort, he had been selected for his job because of his unwavering loyalty to the president, it didn't make sense that the new government would let him stay. "What are *you* doing here?" she asked. Andrés explained that, yes, they had been told to collect their things and leave, but that no one was really enforcing the order. "How bizarre," she thought. The new government, led by the opposition, was giving the security forces of the ousted president free rein of the palace?

When all of the equipment had been set up, Isabel took a better look around. She had never been in Miraflores before and it was exciting to see in person all the things that she had only caught glimpses of on TV. It was a beautiful place. The warm colonial Spanish palace was built around a magnificent central courtyard. There were elaborate patios and gardens, high archways and verandas, and statues and fountains by famous artists. It all came together to create a sublime little world in the middle of Caracas. Indeed, as she sat in the courtyard, Isabel felt as if she was in a movie about the nineteenth century.

As she looked around, she noticed that almost everyone was part of the opposition. OK, Isabel thought, that's to be expected, but still, she'd expected to see some "repentant *chavistas*"—Chávez supporters who had jumped ship to get good jobs in the new regime—but there were very few.

Things were very disorganized and everyone was free to go anywhere they wanted to. Isabel noticed a lot of foreigners there because, for once, the international press was paying attention to Venezuela. Isabel couldn't help but notice the differences between the international journalists and the Venezuelan ones. The Venezuelan news crews were very excited, ecstatic even. Being in Miraflores was very symbolic for them because of their struggle with Chávez; for them it had truly been a war. During the last three years Chávez had threatened them over and over again; he had used his Bolivarian thugs to attack them and bomb their offices; he had used his *cadenas* to block their news; and he had, in the final battle, tried to cut their signals to censor them. It had been an ugly war, but they had fought him; stood up to him. In the end it had been the media, they felt, that had helped tip the scales against the president. Now that it was all over, they could exhale, they had won. And now, right now, they were actually in Miraflores. They had taken it. Isabel saw that many reporters were clearly reveling in the victory; going around to rooms that had been off limits before and looking at the international journalists with chests inflated by pride. *We did this, ya know. Sabes?*

But for the international journalists, this was just another story. It was business. They kept insisting, over and over again, on seeing Chávez's letter of resignation. "That is the indispensable proof that he really resigned." "We have to see it." But the letter didn't appear and Isabel began to wonder if they had put too much faith in General Rincón's announcement. He may have been one of Chávez's closest advisers, but his statement was the only proof of Chávez's resignation.

Another thing that struck Isabel as strange—another difference between the international reporters and the Venezuelans—was that the Venezuelan reporters were both covering and participating in events. Some were going into closed meetings with the politicians, and that suggested that they were providing support to the new government. Not a good thing, Isabel thought.

Then she saw Carlos Ortega come into the courtyard. The reporters scrambled to interview him. They had no idea (no way of knowing) that he and the huge labor union he represented had pulled their support for Carmona. They still saw him as the Ortega of yesterday—the yin to Carmona's yang.

The labor leader made a few bland "business-as-usual" statements, all smiles, embracing and congratulating some of the opposition leaders, then he headed into one of the salons where cameras were not allowed.

In reality, Ortega was furious. He had come to the palace on his own accord to tell Carmona that he couldn't take over the presidency in this way. But Ortega got nowhere with the officials he met, including Carmona, and soon left even angrier than when he had arrived. In the end, the visit had only confirmed his worst fears. Now he was certain that the "fat cats" had hijacked the thing he had worked so hard to make. He had wanted a constitutional transition away from *chavismo* so that Venezuela could move into new territory—a better future. Now it was clear that he had merely liberated the country from Chávez so that the worst of the old guard could replace him.

Out in the courtyard Isabel saw Ortega go. He was visibly upset and refused to make a statement.

Ortega was from Coro, a small city just south of the Paraguaná peninsula in western Venezuela. And now he headed there—looking for peace and solitude. Excluded from the decision making, his anger soon melted into depression and a feeling of profound defeat. Once at home he locked himself away for many hours, refusing to talk to even family members, feeling that something that had been growing in Venezuela, something important, had died.

—∞—

Back at the palace Isabel and the other reporters waited. One hour . . . two hours . . . three hours. Still no official announcement from the transitional government. It was obvious to Isabel that things were very disorganized. They were told an announcement would be made at four, then at six. The new government was "finalizing some details of the document." Outside the high iron gates that surrounded Miraflores a small crowd had gathered and were singing the national anthem. They did not seem to be predominantly either *chavista* or *escuálido*—they were just curious about the new government.

Throughout the afternoon Isabel kept asking the other members of the honor guard if they had seen Eduardo, her cousin. They told her that he had been assigned to guard the armory, but they didn't know if he was still on duty or not. As she spoke to the soldiers, she confirmed that they were the same soldiers who had been here yesterday—the new government was being protected by loyal *chavistas*.

Finally, they were allowed to enter the Salón Ayacucho, the large hall where the transitional government would make its first announcements and Carmona would be sworn in. This was the moment when people all over Venezuela would see exactly how Carmona—an untested politician— was going to run things. How would Carmona follow the constitution, given that there had already been so many irregularities? There were about 120 people seated in front of a low stage. To the right were two long rows of military men—General Vásquez Velasco, General González González, and Vice Admiral Carlos Molina among them. Catholic Cardinal Ignacio Velasco sat grinning between two generals.

But more important than who was in the room was who was not. General Usón was absent. In fact, no representatives of the Left—not even the most moderate *chavistas*—were in attendance. Also absent was the multi- racial, multiclass component that had been so pronounced in yesterday's march. No one here looked like they lived in a shantytown, no one here looked like they did hard labor, no one to represent Jhonnie Palencia or Carlos Ortega's union workers.

The mood in the hall was very upbeat and, Isabel thought, almost eu- phoric. As the ceremony began, Isabel wondered who would swear Carmona in as president as she had heard that the head of the National Assembly, Willian Lara, was in hiding and refused to appear in public because he feared for his safety. She was surprised when Carmona swore himself in. Then Daniel Romero—Carmona's incoming attorney general dressed in an Ar- mani suit—began to list all the legal changes that would take effect immedi- ately. He announced that the name of the country would be reverted back to "The Republic of Venezuela" from "The *Bolivarian* Republic of Venezuela." Isabel had to admit that she was fine with that. She had always thought the name change was ridiculous. But as the proceedings continued, and as each new decree was made, she began to feel more and more uneasy.

Next to go were the forty-nine laws passed as part of the Enabling Law. For Isabel, it was not only what Romero was decreeing, but how the crowd was reacting that made her uncomfortable. They were cheering each announcement and pumping their fists as if it were a sporting event—each decree was like a home run. When it was announced that the National Assembly would be dissolved, Isabel turned to her colleague Ángela Mastrogiacomo and whispered, "Can they do that?" Looking at the thunderstruck faces of the other journalists, she got her answer. But the audience was ecstatic.

When it was announced that all of the state governors would be replaced, Isabel again turned to Ángela, "Can they do *that*?" A shrug. Regardless of legality, the crowd loved it and was now cheering itself into a frenzy. These, after all, were positions filled with *chavistas,* sometimes by questionable means.

But Romero was just getting warmed up. He had a long list of government offices that were to be liquidated. "The attorney general's office!" he called. The journalists couldn't contain themselves; this was too much. Cell phones and walkie-talkies were coming out as they frantically called their respective stations. Things were getting out of control. By now the applause was incessant—Romero had to shout to be heard. "The Supreme Court!" More cheers. People were on their feet. "The Office of the Defender of the People!" Isabel noticed a pair of older men embracing, tears of joy streaming down their cheeks. "The National Assembly and the National Election Council!" Now came the coup de grâce: The Venezuelan Constitution of 1999 would be revoked, and the country would revert back to the Constitution of 1958.

The crowd roared.

Sitting on the stage, President Carmona himself shook his fist, basking in the victory. He couldn't help but show a very inappropriate smirk. Elections for a new congress (with two houses as opposed to the single house under the 1999 constitution) would occur within ninety days, and it was Carmona's plan to have that body reestablish the separate powers—the Supreme Court, the attorney general's office, and so on. Presidential elections were promised within a year, and Carmona would not run, but in the meantime the interim government and a "consultative board" would run the country with complete impunity.

"Democracia! Democracia!" the crowd chanted.

Not content with the fall of Chávez, Carmona and his crew were going
to sweep away three years of *chavismo* in a single stroke.

—◦◦◦—

Someone in the audience who was not cheering was General Efraín
Vásquez Velasco, the head of the army. He turned to his assistant, "*Nos uti-
lizó!*" he said—He's used us!

Just that morning he had met with Carmona and told him that *this* was
exactly what he didn't want—*chavista* versus anti-*chavista*. He wanted the
military and the country to go back to the way it was before, as one country. "There's not going to be any persecution of the *chavistas* here," he'd
said. Carmona had assured him it would be a peaceful transition, but now
he was pouring salt in the wound—and trampling the constitution while
he did it. The interim president was only supposed to guide the country to
elections. Vásquez Velasco had picked Carmona so that they could keep a
civilian face on the transition; he had been quite sure that the people
would have protested a purely military government—seen it as a military
junta—so he had let Carmona (a man whom Vásquez Velasco had never
even met before last night) assume the face of that transition. Now
Vásquez Velasco knew he had made a serious mistake.

The general felt misled . . . misled and betrayed. It was he, Vásquez Velasco, who had put his neck on the line yesterday and kept the military
from massacring the marchers. It was he who had risked taking Carneiro
into custody and recalled the tanks. And what had they given him in return? Nothing. He was the obvious choice for the new minister of defense.
But they had just passed him over and named Vice Admiral Hectór
Ramírez Pérez instead, a navy man, and an officer with significantly less
experience than Vásquez Velasco.

He had been duped and he suddenly felt ridiculous sitting in this deliri-
ous throng of *escuálidos*. He could not permit the army to be a part of this;
he could not let the people think the army had condoned it. He had to get
back to his command and call the officers he needed to call. Then the military had to pull their support for Carmona; they had to refuse to recognize his decrees. Then they had to pick up the pieces, try to follow the
constitution as best they could.

As the meeting ended, mayhem ensued. Carmona left quickly and no one could interview him so the reporters surged forward to interview anyone they could. Within seconds the stage was packed with reporters sticking their microphones in people's faces and cameramen jockeying for the best angles.

Isabel found herself in the middle of it, getting pushed and shoved around. She was trying to get patched through to the station with her radio when an odd thing happened. Without realizing, she sat back in a chair to get out of the way of a cameraman. A microwave technician from one of the other stations gave her a funny look and said, "Did you notice where you're sitting?" She looked down, then stood bolt upright. She had been sitting in the *Silla Presidencial*—the president's chair. She turned bright red. "I didn't realize!" she said.

The man laughed. "The funny thing is that it demonstrates exactly what's happening in this country."

She gave him a quizzical look.

He helped her along: "That anybody can put their *culo* in the president's chair."

Upon leaving the conference room, Isabel found her cousin, Eduardo. She hugged him and wanted to know where he had been and why he hadn't called home, but Eduardo was too focused on what was happening. "*Que payasada es esta!*" he said. What a circus this is! "Everyone has gone crazy around here."

When he calmed down, he told her that yesterday had not been easy, especially because they had explicit orders to shoot *anyone* who tried to enter their "ring of security." He was fatigued to the point of exhaustion and said that his cell phone battery had died so he couldn't contact the family.

When it was time to leave the palace and head back to Televen, Isabel felt a new tension in the air. Carmona's decrees had changed things, and no one knew what would happen next. They could actually hear gunshots close by, but no one knew if they were in celebration or in anger. The other TV personnel were diligently donning their bulletproof vests. By now the crowd of people outside the palace had all but gone. Isabel guessed that they had gone home to watch the news. When they got to their car, the driver ordered them to lie flat and keep their heads down, then they flew back to Televen.

4 | Exile or Resistance?

Dr. Alberto Espidel—the *chavista* doctor who had given first aid to the wounded under the Llaguno Overpass with his son—had gotten up early that morning and gone to Vargas Hospital. He knew many wounded had been taken there, but he hadn't had his car yesterday so he hadn't gone. He had also been worried that he might be treated harshly at the hospital. His colleagues knew that he supported Chávez and with the way the news was being covered he feared some of them might react violently. Fortunately, when he arrived none of his colleagues bothered him. In fact, they were so happy that Chávez was gone that they weren't interested in arguing about politics anymore.

Espidel returned home at about two o'clock and called the family together—his wife and the boys, his sister, and his parents. He had decided it was best to leave the country, at least until things settled down. He suggested Curaçao or Aruba, but his family protested. They said that the people would probably not do anything to them and they didn't believe they would be attacked. Besides, to travel required American dollars, and they didn't have any.

As a family they decided not to go, but Espidel remained uneasy. They had heard about the persecution of ministers like Chacín, the rounding up of the Llaguno Overpass gunmen, as well as the protest outside the Cuban embassy. Espidel's nervousness turned to horror when he saw Carmona liquidate Venezuela's democratic institutions on national television. The most disturbing thing for him was the enthusiastic cheers from the audience. He again told his family that they should flee, but they insisted on staying.

The country was now literally without a constitution. The "government" could do anything it wanted without fear of recourse. Espidel began thinking about how he would defend himself and his family, if necessary. He didn't have a gun, but he knew where he might be able to find help— the place where any fight against the new government would surely begin: Catia, the neighborhood northeast of Miraflores. It was one of the most loyal (and militant) *chavista* neighborhoods. So Espidel told his son Joan to stay and take care of the family; then he headed to Catia.

There, on Andrés Bello Avenue, he found well over a hundred people protesting against the new government. They were shouting, "We will bring Chávez back!" Even more interesting, more intense, was that they were ready to fight. They were talking openly about forming a resistance movement. This was something new for Espidel: the thought of joining a resistance, a guerrilla group, to fight the new government.

Espidel went home feeling much better. The solidarity of his fellow *chavistas* had invigorated him. For the first time he felt a little more hopeful about the future.

<hr/>

When it came to the idea of forming a resistance, one man was way ahead of Espidel—Guillermo García Ponce. Ever since he had left Miraflores the night before, the veteran *chavista* had been thinking of little else.

Despite the urgings of many of his colleagues, he had decided not to go into hiding. The old socialist hard-liner preferred to stay at home where he could be easily contacted and, more importantly, work the phone. (Still, as a precaution he made up a small suitcase should he need to escape quickly.)

First he contacted Emma Ortega, a member of the Political Command for the Revolution. She said she was planning a rally in Plaza Bolívar to demand the safety of President Chávez. García Ponce said he would activate the Bolivarian Circles to help her. Then he called Hugo Chávez's brother, Adán, and the two of them set up an improvised headquarters where they could receive calls and coordinate the activities of the resistance.

He put in calls to the loyal governors of the states of Portuguesa and Lara. Then he received a call from José Albornoz, a leader of the PPT (Patria para Todos, the political party that had formed an alliance with Chávez's MVR party). Albornoz wanted to hold a big rally on Sunday to denounce the coup, but García Ponce told him that Sunday would be too late, the rally had to be tomorrow.

In the early afternoon, he and his family realized that someone had plastered posters all around the outside of their apartment. They said things like "Get out!" and "García Ponce is a murderer!" He knew exactly who had done it—a neighbor who was a devout member of Acción Democrática. A friend told him that this neighbor had been calling the Metropolitan Police all day trying to get them to come and arrest him. The police never came. García Ponce told his family to leave the posters there. Taking them down, he felt, would only show that they were afraid.

García Ponce's spirits lifted when he saw the announcement by Attorney General Isaías Rodríguez declaring that Chávez had not resigned. They quickly made copies of the speech and started distributing it.

Then came Carmona's decrees. For García Ponce it only confirmed what he had suspected all along—Venezuela's extreme right was taking over. Half of them were fascists, the other half irrational. This was the old guard rising up again; the old gang from Caracas's rich suburbs, the same people who had overseen Venezuela's political apartheid in the era before Chávez. In the audience he saw the executives of the banks and foreign companies. Behind them were those under the influence of the "rumor laboratories," and the anti-Chávez media: officials from PDVSA, primly dressed journalists, bureaucrats from the Mayor Peña's office, the good sons of Caracas's petite bourgeoisie, and a few renegades known for their opportunism.

As the day wore on, the plan for the resistance became more concrete: Mobilize the Bolivarian Circles and Chávez loyalists, get them into the streets to protest, and also get them in front of the military bases to show their opposition to a military regime. Buses were also organized to take protestors from the barrios to Miraflores and Fort Tiuna. The quasi-guerrilla groups Tupamaro and Simón Bolívar Coordinating Group joined in the operation.

Late in the afternoon, García Ponce sent an e-mail to a long list of international contacts:

The constitutional president of the Bolivarian Republic of Venezuela, Hugo Rafael Chávez Frías, has been imprisoned by a group of fascist high officials. The National Assembly, the Supreme Court, the attorney general's office, and the Office of the Defender of the People have been dissolved by force. The National Constitution has been abolished, and they have formed a junta without legitimacy, outside of the law and established democratic institutions. The police have launched a wave of persecution, seizures, and detentions. President Chávez has not resigned, as has been falsely reported. We request an international response to stop the silencing of President Chávez and that his family be allowed to visit him. We request respect for human rights and an end to the persecution of President Chávez's government ministers. We ask [the international community] to refute and deny that President Chávez and his government were responsible for the bloody incidents that occurred on April 11. On the contrary, the aggressors were snipers from the extreme right and the victims were supporters of President Chávez.

Sincerely, Guillermo García Ponce.

5 | Closing Down the National Assembly

At seven o'clock, National Guard troops arrived at the National Assembly to shut it down.

In a rare act of solidarity, assembly members from virtually all the political parties protested the closure.

"We reject this plutocratic government that makes its laws by decree," said Ernesto Alvarenga, a member of Chávez's MVR party. Pedro Pablo Alcántara, of Acción Democrática, also spoke out against the dissolution of the legislature. "We have to rebuild this country with everyone's help, not by snubbing the organizations that make a democracy." The head of the National Assembly, Willian Lara (MVR), said that Carmona's actions were proof that this was a coup d'état. "How can a regime call itself democratic if the first thing it does is dissolve the parliament?"

Despite the protests, the National Guard closed and locked the building. As they were forced out, a large group of pro-Chávez legislators gathered outside the tall black gates. They embraced before departing . . . and many wept.

6 | Backlash Part II

In the shantytowns of Caracas—in Catia and Petare—rioting and looting started to break out. *Saqueos.* Sporadically at first, but as night fell things began to escalate. Windows were shattered. Blowtorches were used to get through the steel-gated storefronts or—when that was too time-consuming—they were simply torn off with pickup trucks.

The looters were mostly *chavistas*. Their reasons were many: They were infuriated by Carmona's decrees, by the ousting of Chávez, because they had lost a leader they felt really cared about them. They also felt their momentum building as more people began to say that Chávez had not really resigned. Lastly, in the case of the Bolivarian Circles, they had been ordered to do so. Circle members marked businesses and storefronts with party symbols to guide the looting—if your door was marked, then you were a friend of the party and it was not sacked. If it was not marked, it was stripped to the last lightbulb.

While breaking into stores, some looters were shot by business owners or by their armed guards. Store owners also died trying to defend their businesses, and others—just employees or bystanders—got caught in the crossfire.

Nineteen-year-old Giovanni Rodríguez was working at the Full Carne butcher shop when the looters arrived. Not wanting to risk that the teen might identify them, the looters executed him.

Sixteen-year-old Ión Guerra was coming home from a party with his family sometime after midnight when he was struck in the head by a stray bullet. A group of armed men were taking advantage of the fact that the police were otherwise occupied and shooting at things for fun when they accidentally killed young Ión.

Just as looters were taking advantage of the chaos, so were some police officers. "Social cleansing" had been a growing phenomenon in Venezuela; a practice that had grown in step with the country's jagged increase in violent crime. Frustrated by an inept and largely corrupt judicial system (only three of every one hundred accused murderers were convicted), extralegal killings had become commonplace throughout the country. In fact, every major city in Venezuela had its own Vengador Anonimo, or "Anonymous Avenger"—a person, or group of people, who exterminated suspected criminals who had gone free. (*Anonymous Avenger* is the Spanish title of the *Death Wish* movies starring Charles Bronson, which are very popular in Venezuela.)

Particularly frustrating to police was a new law passed just as Chávez took office that stated that there had to be a preponderance of evidence simply to charge a suspect of a crime. And if they could not be charged immediately, they could not be held. While the law was intended to protect suspects from unlawful arrests, it meant that criminals had to be caught "red-handed," or *en flagrancia*, in order to be arrested. The new law worked particularly well for kidnappers and left the police with hundreds of cases in which witnesses could positively identify the kidnappers, yet the suspects went free. The rumor was that Chávez had supported the law to protect the Colombian FARC, which was operating in Venezuela, as kidnapping was its primary source of income. Regardless, Venezuela's kidnapping rate was now its highest in history.

For Venezuela's Anonymous Avengers—who most people agreed were off-duty police officers—the fall of Chávez and the disorder of the Carmona regime meant that the risk of reprisal for a "social-cleansing" killing was essentially zero.

In Caracas, two brothers, Rommy and Yurmi Nieto Laya, were left by a group of friends near the Las Adjuntas Metro stop just after one in the morning on April 13. A witness said that the boys were picked up by a patrol of Metropolitan Police. Early the next morning, the boys' father received a call saying that the boys had been killed in "a confrontation with police."

PART FOUR
CHÁVEZ RETURNS
April 13, 2002

1 | Sleeper

When Chávez first began his revolutionary movement—the Bolivarian Revolutionary Movement-200—it had been only four officers, all close friends.

It had started on December 17, 1982, the anniversary of Simón Bolívar's death. In the city of Maracay, one hundred kilometers west of Caracas, then-Captain Chávez had given a stirring speech to over a thousand soldiers commemorating the Great Liberator. But while he spoke, the higher-ranking officers had shifted uncomfortably in their seats, quite sure that Chávez's big mouth was getting him (and perhaps them) in trouble again—his speech called for radical changes in both the military and the government. However, the troops loved it, and when Colonel Manrique took the podium he said, "I want you to know that what Captain Chávez said was authorized by me." A lie. "I gave the order for him to give that speech, and everything he said, although he did not put it in writing, he told me yesterday." The colonel looked out at the crowd a moment, then decided it was best to add, "None of this is to leave the base!" Then he gave them the rest of the day off.

Chávez and his three friends decided to go for a long run in the foothills of the *cordillera de la costa*. As they jogged, they talked about the country's problems: They had a democracy but not one where everyone participated equally, where a better life was not really possible for the majority despite all the country's natural resources. Further, they felt that not to take action would make them accomplices of the current political system, accomplices by omission.

It was a long jog—six miles out and six miles back—and by the time the four men once again reached the outskirts of Maracay they were exhausted.

It was then that Chávez convinced the others to make a stop at Aventino Hill where a gigantic acacia tree known as the Samán de Güere stood. It was a historic spot because this was where Simón Bolívar had made his vow to overthrow Spanish power. The tree was still there and even had a few branches that still bore leaves. Exhausted but contented, each man took a leaf, and Chávez led them in a formal oath that paraphrased Bolívar's own oath. They decided that they would not be "accomplices by omission"; they would fight against the oppression they saw in Venezuela.

Thus was born the MBR-200.

During the Caracazo in 1989 one of the four men, Felipe Acosta, was killed. In 1992, ten years after taking their oath, two of the remaining men—Jesús Urdaneta and Hugo Chávez—participated in the coup attempt against President Carlos Andrés Pérez, and were subsequently arrested and thrown in jail for two years. But the fourth man managed to maintain his anonymity and continued his career in the army. In fact, the others insisted that there had only been three conspirators all along.

That fourth man was General Raúl Baduel and on April 13, 2002, he was the commander of Venezuela's elite 42nd Paratrooper Brigade—the best fighting force in Venezuela. Chávez's decision to promote Baduel to general and give him control of the paratroopers had puzzled many who did not know their connection, but it was a decision that was about to pay big dividends.

Baduel was a fascinating character; a devout Taoist, he believed in reincarnation, studied the martial art of aikido, and burned incense in his office while listening to Gregorian chants. Many people didn't know what to make of him: a career military officer who didn't believe in violence. Indeed, the reason Baduel had refused to join Chávez and the others in the 1992 coup was because he did not believe in using violence to overthrow a democratically elected government.

His military thinking was heavily influenced by Eastern classics like Sun Tzu's *The Art of War,* Lao Tse's *Tao Te Ching,* and Miyamoto Musashi's *Book of Five Rings,* which Baduel was often quoting at length. "The best soldier is not militant; the best fighter is not aggressive," or "The greatest skill consists in victory without a single drop of blood."

On the morning of April 13, General Baduel was in his office at the Maracay base with several battalion commanders. "If any of you are not ready to follow through with my decision to not recognize this de facto government, you can speak up now. I will not try to pressure you or judge you and you have my guarantee that I will not do anything against you."

Baduel had decided to go after Carmona. But unlike many people who also wanted to depose him, Baduel had the soldiers and the hardware to succeed.

In Venezuela, the city of Maracay represented the backbone of the country's military might, and Baduel had the support of virtually all the military leaders in town. At the moment they were all packed into his office. With the help of Generals Nelson Verde Graterol, Julio García Montoya, Pedro Torres Finol, and Luis Acevedo Quintero, and Admiral Orlando Maniglia, Baduel now controlled the Fourth Armored Division, which included four brigades, six battalions, four artillery groups, five tank battalions, and, perhaps most important, control of the Libertador Air Base, which safeguarded the nation's small fleet of F-16 fighter jets.

After getting the overwhelming support of these commanders, Baduel walked around the base visiting the men. He had to be sure he wasn't asking too much of them; that they wouldn't disobey his orders when the moment came. But on the contrary, they were excited, ready, and willing, anxious to be involved in what was happening. When he returned to his office, he found that someone had removed General Vásquez Velasco's portrait from the wall. That said it all. Vásquez Velasco's apparent complicity with the new regime—especially seeing him in Miraflores when Carmona read his decrees—had personally disgusted Baduel and many of the men. It was no way for a general to behave—disgracefully rubbing shoulders with Carmona and his cronies. The coincidence was too much for Baduel. This was a coup and Vásquez Velasco was certainly involved. On April 5 Baduel had written in his planner, "The coup is imminent."

Then there was Carmona. While Baduel was exceptionally tolerant of others, he—like Chávez—had a lifelong dislike for the oligarchs. The cause of the coup, in Baduel's eyes, was economic: The oligarchs were resisting the loss of their privileges, they didn't want to give up what they felt was their rightful allotment from the public coffers. It hadn't taken Baduel long to size up Carmona—a man who posed as a diplomat while he fomented exclusion and intolerance. He and his oligarch friends were dividing up the country as if it were the prize bull after a bullfight.

Baduel was also skeptical about Chávez's "resignation." He had talked to Chávez around midnight on April 11, and while his old friend had said he was considering going to Fort Tiuna to negotiate with the generals, he had never indicated that he planned to resign. Baduel remembered that Chávez was very worried that the military would start fighting itself. "My brother," Chávez had said to him, "I beseech you—it is more than an order—I beseech you *not* to turn yourself or your troops into a factor that will spill blood unnecessarily."

Respecting Chávez's wishes, Baduel had done just that, kept quiet . . . until now. But Carmona had gone too far. Resignation or no, Baduel had to act.

Back in his office, the group analyzed the situation and how best to proceed. They jotted down a manifesto in which they demanded the resignation of the "dictator Carmona," a return to constitutional order, reinstatement of the governmental powers, and that Chávez be allowed to return to Miraflores. They also requested access to the private media stations so that they could address the nation.

That last point would be particularly important. Drawing on his Taoist beliefs, Baduel wanted this operation to go off without bloodshed. Instead of sending the troops out, they intended to stay put and refuse any order from the new government—to deploy was the last thing they wanted. In such a battle, the media would be crucial. But as Baduel and his team tried to get access to the media, they found every door closed; every excuse was given to them—bad microwave antennas, not enough reporters, any pretext—not to broadcast their side.

Another top priority for Baduel and the officers was Chávez himself. Most of them assumed he was dead. *If* he wasn't, they needed to know where he was and who was holding him. All throughout the morning, the men made hundreds of phone calls—to subordinates, aides, civilians, journalists—trying to collect information and gain support. In the process, news of their insurrection was growing (at least within the military), and as it did, more and more officers were calling Baduel to voice their support of his mission.

By midafternoon Baduel had so much power at his command that he could have likely overcome Vásquez Velasco if it came to that. Fortunately, that was a contest that would not be necessary.

Back in Caracas in Fort Tiuna, Finance Minister General Usón was in General Vásquez Velasco's office.

"My General," Usón told Vásquez Velasco, "if you want to arrest me, go ahead, but I am not going to adhere to the orders of this government."

While it was true that Usón had decided on April 11 that he was not in agreement with Chávez, he had also decided after the liquidation of the democratic institutions that he was not in agreement with Carmona, either. Yes, he was continuing in his duties at the Ministry of Finance, but that was just to keep the country solvent. For Usón, Carmona's actions were inexcusable—who was Carmona to dissolve the Election Council or the Supreme Court? That was the moment he realized that there really was a coup d'état. In the confusion of April 11, Carmona and his allies had been quickest to fill the power vacuum and had stolen power from the rest of the opposition. This, Usón felt, was Vásquez Velasco's big mistake. He should have kept control of the situation. He should not have ceded so quickly to the civil-military group that Carmona represented. Once he did, he lost his ability to have a transitional government that followed a legal precedent.

"We are reevaluating the situation," Vásquez Velasco replied, "because we are not in agreement with this, either."

Since the moment Carmona had made his decrees, Vásquez Velasco had been working to get rid of him, too. He was still furious about the whole thing and the more he thought about it, the more it disgusted him. The decrees were one thing—Carmona had gone outside the law and hadn't consulted him, *him*, the one who had trusted him to set up a proper transitional government. Worse, Carmona had already selected his entire cabinet, proving to Vásquez Velasco that Carmona wanted much more than to be a transitional leader. He was planning on staying in power indefinitely.

Then Vásquez Velasco had received another blow—General Poggioli had come by his residence that morning and told him that Carmona wanted to send him to Madrid to be a military attaché. Once gone, they would appoint a new head of the army. "The name of the [new] commanding general of the army will be General Henry Lugo Peña," Poggioli said. Poggioli himself thought it was a terrible decision—given the precarious position of the Carmona government, it would likely cause a violent backlash within the military, further weakening Carmona.

In order to get the transitional government back on track, Vásquez Velasco had called Dr. Hermann Escarrá, a lawyer and one of the framers of the 1999 constitution, who agreed to advise him. Given that the vice president and the president of the National Assembly were both in hiding, Escarrá said, the chief justice of the Supreme Court, Iván Rincón, was next in the line of succession. The lawyer tried to convey that Vásquez Velasco's actions were critical. "The reestablishment of the constitution is in your hands, General," Escarrá said.

Shortly after ten, Vásquez Velasco called a meeting with his battalion commanders, plus General José Ruíz Guzmán and General Rosendo (Rosendo was the only person who had not officially resigned who was above Vásquez Velasco). But when Vásquez Velasco arrived at the conference room there were many generals there; the word had spread that they were going to speak out against Carmona. Everyone agreed that the army could not support Carmona, but the question became how to proceed. Some of the generals suggested that the army should just take control, but Vásquez Velasco said no. If he couldn't send out the troops on April 11, he couldn't do it now. Besides, the officers had to trust in their leaders, and he couldn't betray them now by illegally using the army to oust Carmona.

But even though they decided not to deploy the army, they still had many options. So, just like General Baduel and his group of officers in Maracay, Vásquez Velasco and the other generals sat down to make their plans.

2 | Escalating Violence

On April 12 and 13 there were fifty-six deaths in Venezuela from gunshot wounds, mostly in Caracas—a disproportionate number even for a country as violent as Venezuela. Authorities would later conclude that twenty-six of these were directly related to the political situation, yet this number is little more than a guess because a thorough investigation of the deaths was never made.

The looting that had started last night after Carmona's decrees was escalating and in some areas had snowballed out of control—in Petare, in Catia, in Antímano, in Montalban, and in La Florida shopping center. Hundreds of stores were sacked and burned, and by midafternoon tall spirals of black smoke could be seen all over Caracas. Although the looting was sparked by politics, motivations quickly became blurred as people joined the mobs to take advantage of the chaos, to enrich themselves. Even SUVs from rich neighborhoods were seen driving into the mobbed areas to fill up on free stuff.

The level of violence was also escalating. Many of the looters and Bolivarian Circles were armed, and when the Metropolitan Police arrived, gunfights often broke out. The *chavistas* still saw the Metropolitan Police as complicit with the new regime—they were convinced that the police had helped the march on April 11 and had killed many brave *chavistas*.

Metropolitan Police officer Mauricio Marín was on patrol when he got a request for backup from a group of officers that had gotten into a gunfight with a band of armed Chávez supporters in Catia. Marín arrived on the scene to help the officers when the twenty-two-year-old was shot in the head. Witnesses say that one of the Chávez loyalists had somehow gotten a FAL—the high-caliber assault rifle used exclusively by the Venezuelan military—and it was he who shot Marín. The young officer was still alive when they got him to the Caracas Clinic, but soon died.

The National Guard was in such a state of disarray at this point that it had no clear leader to give directives. Many police chiefs, feeling overwhelmed and that the National Guard were not doing their share to curb the violence, began recalling their officers from the more dangerous areas. For them, it was just not worth the risk, even though their withdrawal meant that complete anarchy ensued.

Confident of their impunity, some criminals used audacious levels of violence: In the Caracas suburb of Propatria, a group of armed men dressed up as soldiers and set up a bogus military checkpoint. In this way, they could search all the people who passed by—who were, by and large, looters burdened with their finds. When the "soldiers" fancied a particular piece of contraband, they took it. If the "owners" resisted, they were murdered, and all because the "soldiers" were too lazy to steal from the stores themselves. At a pet store in the Florida shopping center looters massacred all the animals. Two thirty-five-year-old turtles were dismembered, bags of food were dropped into fish tanks, and puppies were ripped to pieces and their blood smeared on the walls.

3 | The Blackout

When freelance reporter Francisco Toro's clock radio went off on the morning of April 13, it was to a pleasant documentary on the history of the *arepa*—the thick cornmeal pancake that is the staple of the Venezuelan diet. Hungry for some real news, Francisco changed the station. He found *This Week in Baseball* dubbed in Spanish and a Catholic mass, but no news.

Disappointed, he got up and turned on the TV. One station had *Animaniacs* and another was showing a Major League baseball game. The government station, VTV, was still down. Rolling his eyes, he turned to Globovisión—Venezuela's twenty-four-hour news station—but even here the news was old; nothing about Carmona, Chávez, the looting, *nada*.

That's it then, Francisco thought. Just forty-eight hours old and the coup's already stopped making headlines. With some relief he realized that politics under Carmona would be commendably boring. Just like it had been before Chávez.

But just then he got a call. "*Chamo,* I don't like the way this is going down. The witch hunt is still going on, and suddenly there is no news; who knows what could be happening?"

Francisco went back to the radio and started flipping the dial more aggressively. Nothing. But then he thought about it: If the anti-Chávez news media were not reporting, it must mean that the new anti-Chávez government was in trouble. By not covering the news they were, in effect, trying to prop up Carmona—trying to give the impression that everything was normal. Luckily for Francisco, he was a freelancer. He had come from the United States to work on a documentary film about land reform, which meant no boss, no one to tell him he couldn't go out into the streets, no one to tell him that it was "too dangerous." Admittedly, it was more risky than usual. He had heard about the looting and rioting in Petare and Chapellin, and he would later learn how some of the stations had told their news crews it was too dangerous go out. But this was still Caracas, not Beirut. So at about 11:30, he and Megan, his camerawoman, decided to go out and see what was happening.

It took them a while to find a taxi driver who was crazy enough to drive them around. They asked her to take them to Catia, but she refused. "Too much shooting." She would, however, take them to the entrance to Fort Tiuna.

Downtown Caracas was mostly deserted: very few cars and almost no pedestrians, except here and there on the street corners they saw little bands of *chavistas*—maybe five to fifteen in each group—holding pro-Chávez signs. Coming out of the tunnels near the military base, they got their first good look at the shantytowns on the west side. Small pockets of people had come together to wave flags and homemade signs demanding Chávez's return. Some cars tooted at them in support. Obviously something very important was happening, but the fact that the private stations refused to acknowledge it made it all particularly bizarre, unreal.

They arrived at the front gate of Fort Tiuna. Three heavy personnel carriers blocked the entrance with a line of MPs in front of them. Francisco guessed about a thousand *chavistas* had gathered in front of gate. They were about as angry as Francisco had ever seen anyone be angry. They were enraged by the blackout and grateful for the opportunity to explain what was happening to a camera.

For the protestors—many of who were Bolivarian Circle members assigned the goal of getting media attention (preferably international media attention)—Francisco and Megan were exactly what they had been waiting for. They surged up around them and hustled in front of each other to express their grievances.

A fat woman with a baseball cap started shouting into the camera, and when another man tried to speak over her shoulder, she rounded on him fiercely, "Shut up!" then turned back to the camera. "I LOVE VENEZUELA!" she shouted at the top of her voice. "And because I love Venezuela, I . . ." she gasped for breath she was so excited, "I need help from the international news media—ALL OF THEM—so that we can have JUSTICE!" Another man—equally impassioned—cried that those who had died on April 11 were *chavistas*; they had been killed by Mayor Alfredo Peña's police. He shook his fist violently as he spoke.

Francisco and Megan spent about an hour interviewing people. The atmosphere was tense and emotional. The soldiers didn't seem to have a clue as to what they were doing. Yet everyone was very friendly to them. At about 1:30, they took a taxi home. On the way, Francisco scanned the radio for news.

Nothing.

∞

Meanwhile, Dr. Alberto Espidel and his son Joan were driving around Catia trying to pick up one of the few pro-Chávez radio stations. They knew something was up and wanted some news, but all the TV stations were showing was cartoons. With the government TV station still down, radio was the only way for them to hear their side.

Espidel and his son had dressed to join the resistance: blue jeans, khaki military shirts, and black berets with silver stars on the front—in the style of the Argentine revolutionary Ché Guevara. They were ready to fight and were becoming more and more optimistic about the situation: A colleague of Espidel's had called saying that there were rumors that Baduel was going to rebel. Finally, they got within range of a pro-Chávez station and they heard that Chavez had not resigned and was being held prisoner.

Espidel and Joan decided to go back to the Llaguno Overpass near Miraflores. This was where he and the other party members had always met before. When they got to the overpass, they were surprised that there were no military or police anywhere around, and no National Guard, either. But people were starting to come. From all over the city people were starting to come to Miraflores to demand Chávez's return.

4 | Pressure

While the separate forces within the military were plotting against Carmona, international pressure was also mounting. Nineteen Latin American presidents had condemned the undemocratic actions of the regime and demanded speedy elections. Mexican president Vicente Fox said flatly that his government would not recognize Carmona. Argentine president Eduardo Duhalde gave his succinct assessment: "No one can consider [the Carmona government] legitimate."

The leaders were gathered together in San Jose, Costa Rica, for the Rio Group conference and had pushed aside their planned agenda to focus on events in Caracas. They called on the Organization of American States to open a full investigation into the events—a move that was also supported by the United States.

Only El Salvador voiced support for Venezuela's interim government.

In Caracas, there was—somewhat incredibly—still an atmosphere of jubilation and excitement inside Miraflores, albeit somewhat more subdued than the day before. When Carmona arrived at the palace that morning—just after first light—he was greeted with military honors. The head of the honor guard, Colonel Jesús Morao, announced, "Eyes to the president of the republic!" as the band played the national anthem.

At 9:00 a.m., Carmona had his first official visits from the Spanish ambassador Manuel Viturro de la Torre and U.S. ambassador Charles Shapiro.

At first glance, Charles Shapiro looked too young to be an ambassador. Even though he was fifty-one, he looked as if he were still in his thirties. Adding to his youthful aura was the fact that he liked to joke and play around. However, his humor sometimes rubbed people the wrong way, particularly among the Chávez crowd, who were always looking to discredit him. When a pro-Chávez journalist railed at him about the problems of "Yankee imperialism," Shapiro—playing off Venezuela's love of baseball—

said coolly that he, too, was adamantly against Yankee imperialism because the Yankees weren't his team. He was a Braves fan.

Shapiro had only been ambassador for six weeks before April 11 and had felt that things were going well between himself and Chávez. Although Chávez's relationship with his predecessor, Donna Hrinak, had soured, it was clear to Shapiro that Chávez had wanted a fresh start. Chávez had invited Shapiro to the palace and then to his residence. They had lunched together, and in Chávez's words, he had "put his cards on the table" for the new ambassador. Shapiro told him he also wanted a fresh start and lamented that the embassy staff was having a lot of trouble arranging meetings with government officials and asked the president to encourage more dialogue between his people and the embassy.

Then came April 11.

Like just about everyone else, Shapiro and Viturro de la Torre were operating under the assumption that Chávez had willingly resigned. Viturro de la Torre, who was the senior diplomat, led the meeting by handing Carmona a joint statement from the United States and Spain outlining both countries' concerns about the new government. Then they proceeded to review the statement's major points. First and foremost for Viturro de la Torre was Chávez's personal safety.

Shapiro then addressed the issue of yesterday's decrees. He told Carmona that dissolving the National Assembly had been a grave mistake, as it clearly violated the constitution. (It had also enraged many of the country's elected officials, not least of which those who had been summarily dismissed. Shapiro had actually got wind of Carmona's plan to dissolve the assembly before it was announced. One of the opposition assembly deputies had seen the draft of the decrees in Miraflores that morning and had called the embassy, furious about Carmona's plan. In response, Shapiro had called Carmona to urge him against it. But while Carmona had politely thanked Shapiro for sharing his views, he had done it anyway.) Now Shapiro told Carmona he needed to find a way to "undissolve" the Assembly as quickly as possible. Both the ambassadors reminded Carmona that the international community was watching closely and that Carmona should welcome a delegation from the Organization of American States. Shapiro also told Carmona that he had to stop any mob violence against the Cuban embassy and that Venezuela had diplomats posted in Cuba and that it was every government's responsibility to ensure the safety of all foreign diplomats.

Carmona did his best to reassure the ambassadors that he would proceed in a democratic and transparent way and that the de facto situation would end as soon as possible, as soon as they could hold a popular referendum—ninety days. Carmona said he would welcome a mission from the Organization of American States, and that he would make a request that very morning—which he later did.

The meeting lasted about a half hour. Carmona felt that the two men seemed relieved by his assurances, but he also noticed that neither Shapiro nor Viturro de la Torre said anything that would indicate if they truly supported or condemned his government.

Yet having Carmona in power would certainly make life easier for the United States. In contrast to the intractable Chávez, Carmona would be much easier to work with. Upon Shapiro's return to the embassy, staffers remembered how he had seemed pleased with the meeting. One of the major bones of contention between the United States and Chávez before the coup had been the issue of overflights—the right of U.S. military aircraft (AWACs) to fly in Venezuelan airspace, mostly for the purposes of drug interdiction, but also for intelligence gathering for operations in Colombia. Many countries in the region gave the U.S. overflight privileges because they welcomed the help in controlling drug trafficking, but Chavez had refused—most likely because of his alliance with the Colombian FARC. Under Carmona, it was plain that the privileges would be granted.

Around noon, Carmona met with the heads of all the private TV stations. The media heads agreed, in general, to help the interim president "move the country forward" (a euphemism for only showing pro-Carmona news), but with two important conditions: First, Carmona had to retract his unconstitutional announcements of yesterday; and second, he had to bring labor leader Carlos Ortega back into the fold so that the country could see that the workers were being properly represented. Carmona thought it would suffice if he gave the Venezuelan vice presidency to Manuel Cova, the secretary general of Ortega's labor union, but the media heads insisted that Ortega had to return. Once again, the media heads were trying to influence politics instead of covering it.

During the meeting, the new minister of defense, Admiral Héctor Ramírez Pérez, told the media heads that General Baduel was planning to hold an important press conference and suggested that the networks not televise it. When someone commented that the *international* networks would surely transmit it, one of the owners said, "It doesn't matter. Only a tiny number of people watch CNN."

In the end, none of the Venezuelan networks would show Baduel's announcement.

⎯⎯∞⎯⎯

At the same time that Carmona was meeting the media owners, the commander of his honor guard, Colonel Morao, was in a nearby room putting in a call to General Baduel. Morao had gotten wind of Baduel's plans and was calling to offer his help. (Just like the rest of the honor guards who were loyal to Chávez, Morao had not been replaced.) Once on the line, Baduel asked him for an update on the situation, then he asked if Morao would need reinforcements to retake the palace.

No, Morao said, he was confident that he could take the palace easily, without reinforcements.

In fact, Morao had been itching to do just that since yesterday. As tempting as it had been to seize Carmona and thereby cut off the head of the interim government, Morao didn't want bloodshed or a reprisal from forces loyal to Carmona. So he and his men had waited, playing it cool, acting as if everything were normal—even (although it was painful) presenting Carmona with military honors each morning when he arrived—all the while patiently planning how they would take over.

Now, with the tide shifting against Carmona, it would be easier to act.

Baduel told Morao that as soon as he was ready, he should proceed.

⎯⎯∞⎯⎯

By the time the meeting between Carmona and the media heads came to a close, they could feel that things were not quite right. The crowd of protestors outside was growing, and the rumors about Baduel and Vásquez Velasco seemed very real. The media heads left the palace quickly, making vague references to pressing business elsewhere, and hastily agreed that if all went well, they would return later, when Carlos Ortega had arrived.

But Carlos Ortega would never arrive. Ortega was still in his hometown of Coro, where he had fled the day before. The billionaire owner of Venevisión, Gustavo Cisneros, was assigned the task of bringing the labor leader back to Caracas and sent his private plane to get him. But Ortega never got on board. He remained firm in his refusal to work with Carmona.

By now Guillermo García Ponce had also got wind of Baduel's plans and he began pulling out all the stops—if they were going to topple Carmona, the time was now. The Bolivarian Circles stepped up their mobilization in the shantytowns—sending more people to Miraflores and Fort Tiuna, as well as the bases in Maracay.

5 | Dominoes

Back in Fort Tiuna, General Vásquez Velasco and all the generals who supported him were about to go on national TV with their list of demands—Globovisión, Venezuela's twenty-four-hour news channel, had agreed to air the announcement. But just as the general was entering the room where Globovisión and two other international stations had gathered, General Antonio Navarro stopped him in the hallway. Navarro had been sent by Carmona, who had gotten wind of Vásquez Velasco's discontent.

"If you talk now, Carmona will fall," Navarro warned.

"I'm not here to prop up Carmona," Vásquez Velasco replied.

"I ask you not to commit this error," Navarro insisted.

"I'm not a politician," Vásquez Velasco said. "The purpose of this announcement is to clarify to the public that the army cannot support someone that illegally attacks the [country's] institutions."

Vásquez Velasco's aide cut in: "*Mi Commandante,* the press is waiting for you." Without another word, Vásquez Velasco left Navarro there in the wings.

Less than forty-eight hours earlier, the general's press conference had been pivotal in toppling Chávez, now his words would be pivotal in toppling Carmona. He was, once again, surrounded by an impressive number of high-ranking officials.

On April 11, 2002, there was an institutional announcement from the army in relation to the loss of life on that day caused by the failure of the president of the republic and his government to negotiate, whereupon a peaceful march—representing every stratum of civil society—was repressed by the security forces that pertain to the national government and attacked by snipers and unknown gunmen around the palace of Miraflores.

[The president] ordered the army to take tanks into the street without the consent of the commander of the army. This could not be tolerated as it would have caused thousands of deaths. This institutional announcement was based on articles 350 and 328 of the Bolivarian Constitution of Venezuela.

It was a pronouncement against the actions of the government. It was in line with the rules of the constitution and in support of the democratic institutions. It was not a military coup d'état on the part of the army.

In my position as the commander of the army, accompanied by the army high command, by this body of army generals, and by all of the active-duty commanders of Fort Tiuna, we are sending this message of calm to the people of Venezuela and informing them that the army is taking the necessary steps to quickly correct the errors and omissions in this transition process. In this sense, we demand that the following rules be carried out:

1. Establishment of a transitional government that is based on the 1999 constitution, consistent with the laws of the republic, and respectful of human rights.

2. Elimination of the decrees [of the transitional government] on April 12, 2002.

3. Restoration of the National Assembly.

4. Coordination of the social forces of the nation in order to set up a transitional government that is representative and marked by pluralism.

5. Insistence on peace and calm, and that all the actions of the government be conducted with the maximum respect for human rights.

6. Confirmation of the [posts of] members of the army high command and their corresponding subordinates.

7. [The army] pledges to support the authorities and institutions, as well as continue its unconditional adherence to the values and fundamentals of [a military] organization: obedience, discipline, and subordination.

8. Respect for our regional and local authorities (governors and mayors) who were legally and popularly elected.

9. Continuity of the benefits of all of the social programs that are currently running.

10. We demand the construction of a society without exclusions, where all grievances and protests can be conducted in a peaceful manner without weapons, and with the full practice of liberty inside a state of law that corresponds to a democratic society.

11. Respect and official recognition of the Supreme Court.

12. We guarantee the safety and respectful treatment of Lt. Colonel Hugo Chávez and his family. We ask that Lt. Colonel Chávez's request to leave the country be fulfilled immediately and that live television images be shown of him.

We the members of the national armed forces guarantee the security of all the people of Venezuela.

General Efraín Vásquez Velasco
Head of the Venezuelan Army

The people of Venezuela—wherever they sat watching their TVs—now knew that Carmona had lost control of the military. He was on his own. And the *chavistas,* in particular, knew that without Vásquez Velasco and the army, Carmona's presidency was like a sandcastle on the beach: It was only a matter of time before the tide swept it away.

———

While Vásquez Velasco gave his speech, Colonel Morao, the head of the honor guard, made his move to retake Miraflores. By now over a thousand people had gathered outside the palace gates, and the colonel decided to use this fact to his advantage. Under the pretense that they needed to reinforce the palace in the event the crowd became violent, he sent his men to key positions throughout the building and grounds. Using the tunnels that ran between the palace and the barracks of the Casa Militar, he amassed an overwhelming force inside Miraflores. When everyone was in position, he struck.

It was a simple business and no one put up a fight. The remaining Carmona staffers suddenly realized that the soldiers who were supposed to be protecting them were now arresting them.

But Colonel Morao only caught small fish—Carmona, most of the military leaders who were supporting him, and Isaac Pérez Recao had seen the writing on the wall and were long gone. In fact, just minutes before the assault, Vice Admiral Molina got a call from Colonel Gustavo Diaz, who tipped him off to Morao's plan. Molina immediately told Carmona they had to flee. As a result, Morao's best catch was Daniel Romero, the now defunct attorney general who had so gleefully dissolved the separate powers of government the day before. He and about fifteen other staffers were taken to a basement room filled with old school desks. Romero—shirt untucked and tie removed—sat sulking on the floor.

Back outside, the honor guard were basking in their victory. Seven or eight soldiers climbed up to the roof of the palace and began waving a heavy Venezuelan flag at the *chavista* crowd below. The crowd roared.

It was the type of victory that Baduel dreamed of—quick, efficient, and without bloodshed—a victory worthy of Sun Tzu. Things were coming together. But one piece of the puzzle still eluded Baduel and the *chavistas*: Chávez. Where was Hugo Chávez?

6 | The Prisoner President

At that moment Hugo Chávez was busy writing a note saying that he had not resigned. That was when he heard the helicopter—they were coming for him.

A little over twenty-four hours earlier, just after being placed under arrest by Vásquez Velasco and the other generals, Chávez had been taken to a holding cell in Fort Tiuna while they prepared to move him. Where? He didn't know. No one would tell him.

From his cell he could see a television. A marquee at the bottom of the screen pronounced in bold letters: CHÁVEZ RESIGNS. Chávez could hear the commentator saying something about how the former president, the former lieutenant colonel, the former coup conspirator now had his hands covered with blood. The commentator was talking about him, Hugo Chávez. *What a lie*, he thought, *what a manipulation! They have already tried and condemned me.*

He knew time was short. He was certain he would be dead soon—there was no one to guarantee his life now and no reason for his captors to keep him alive. He felt a desperate need to talk to someone he cared about, so he pleaded with the military attorney who was now in charge of him, Colonel Julio Rodríguez Salas. "Look, somehow I need to speak with my family, at the very least with my parents," Chávez said. The colonel acquiesced and gave Chávez his cell phone. Now Chávez had a new problem. He didn't know anyone's phone number—they were all programmed into his own cell phone, which had been taken away. To help him, the colonel called Miraflores to get the numbers that he needed—his parents, his wife, and his daughter. But Chávez still had trouble getting through. Neither his wife, mother, nor father answered, and he had copied his daughter's number wrong. When a strange voice picked up the phone, Chávez said, "It's the prisoner president, who am I speaking with?" Thinking it was a prank call, they hung up on him. Chávez might have found it comical if he hadn't been so sure of his looming death.

Finally he got through to his daughter, María Gabriela, his *pipiolita*. She was hiding out in a beach house with some friends. "*Dios te bendiga*,"

Chávez said; it was the standard Venezuelan greeting from a parent, may God bless you. "How are you?" he asked, then added matter-of-factly. "I'm in jail again."

María said that she was fine and tried to assure her father that God would look after him. Then she asked if there was anything she could do to help.

"First, just take care of yourself. Second, *mija*, call the world, whoever you want, I don't know who, a journalist, call Fidel if you can . . . tell the world. Or if something happens to me, if I don't ever get to talk to you again, tell them that I never resigned the power the people gave me. Tell them that I am a prisoner president."

A few minutes later he got through to his wife, Marisabel. She had arrived in her hometown of Barquisimeto and was also hiding with some friends. The kids were with her, sleeping. "We are fine," she said, "don't worry about us . . . it is us that are worried about you."

Now Chávez felt like he was really saying good-bye. "Take care of yourself Marisabel, take care of the kids, try to stay calm, I'm OK, but I don't have any kind of guarantees anymore. I don't know what is going to happen." Finally, he hung up.

Chávez spent the rest of the day there in Fort Tiuna, watching TV, but growing more and more depressed.

When Military Police Captain Otto Gebauer came to get Chávez, his face was swollen and he could see tears on his cheeks. Gebauer felt instantly sorry for him. This was not the fiery Chávez he was used to seeing on TV. With some effort, Chávez stood, and Gebauer saluted him and explained that he was there to protect him.

Initially the plan was to take him to the Ramo Verde military stockade, but then the plan changed: The navy was taking over his custody and they were going to fly him somewhere else. Not even his guards knew where. Captain Gebauer, along with a colonel and two other captains—who were brothers—would escort him.

By now night had fallen, and as the helicopter flew out over Caracas, they could see the lights of the city: the skyscrapers, and the thousands of white lights that dotted the shantytowns.

Soon they reached the coast. It was a clear night and Chávez could see the black-green Caribbean stretching out below him. The flight was only about forty minutes, but to Chávez it seemed an eternity. He was so sure they were going to kill him. Absolutely positive. And he relived his entire life—all forty-seven years—in that forty-minute flight. He thought of his mother, his father, Marisabel, Rosinés, his friends, all his kids, Rosa Virginia, María Gabriela, Hugo Rafael, Raulito, and his granddaughter, Gabriela.

This is my last flight, he said to himself. They are taking me to my death. So he did his best to prepare himself, gripping the crucifix that he had brought from Miraflores in his hands.

Fear is the mother of all gods.

Finally, they landed in a grassy field near the water.

"Where are we?" Captain Gebauer shouted to the pilot.

"Turiamo Station," the pilot shouted back—it was a small naval base nestled in a secluded bay about sixty miles west of Caracas on the Caribbean coast.

Out in the tall grass Chávez began giving away all the things he had brought in his small suitcase. He was sure he would soon be dead, and suspected that one of these soldiers would likely do the deed. Giving away his things was the only thing he could think of to make them think twice. He had a couple of books, which he gave to the brothers, and then he asked each man his shoe size. *And you, Captain*, he said to Gebauer.

Forty three [centimeters], he replied.

These will serve you then, Chávez said, *I am going to give you these American boots.* He held out the army boots that he had worn to Fort Tiuna before changing into his running shoes.

Gebauer, unaware of Chávez's panic, asked to what he owed the honor. Chávez said, *For the way you have treated me and because I am not going to need them . . . I am not going to put on a uniform again.*

Gebauer thanked him profusely, then the men stood and talked for a while. Chávez, trying to find common ground, spoke mostly about his time in the army. At one point Gebauer noticed Chávez looking out at the horizon. *Once again under arrest*, he muttered. Qué desgracia!

⁂

That had been last night. Now, as each hour passed, Chávez became more and more confident that he might live. He had been getting bits and pieces of news from some of the men. Many were good *chavistas*. The nurse who was sent to check his pulse and vital signs had been especially kind to him. She was young, with a five-year-old daughter, and she said that she had always wanted to meet him, although, she admitted, she had never imagined it would be like this. "My mother adores you," she said. Her sentiment, albeit small, touched Chávez, and after she had left him, he went into the bathroom and wept. It was a cathartic weeping—it helped release his feelings of frustration and despair—and when he emerged he felt better. The nurse's words, in the end, had given him a spiritual boost. He was beginning to hope; beginning to think that he might not be executed after all. Remembering Castro's words, Chávez was even beginning to think he might return to power someday. Maybe within a few months or a few years, he'd come back.

Then this morning, to Chávez's surprise, a young corporal had come into his room and locked the door. He sat down opposite Chávez and leaned in close. "Tell me one thing," he said, "is it true that you resigned?"

"No," Chávez said, "I didn't resign and I'm not going to resign."

The corporal then stood up and saluted him. "Then you are my president." The corporal was from the plains, near Chávez's hometown, and wanted to help him. "People need to know," he said, "because everyone is saying that you resigned; that you resigned and left the country."

"Well," Chávez said, "I am leaving."

"Then write me something [saying that you didn't resign]; write it then leave it in the trash can. I'll come back later and get it." Chávez nodded. OK, he would do it.

He was almost done with the note when he heard the helicopter. They were coming for him.

He quickly got to his feet as the men from the chopper came into the room. He guessed they were going to move him, but where? There were five of them and one had a video camera and was filming everything. Was that to protect him, or was it so they could capture his death on tape—proof for their masters that the deed had been done? What did they have planned for him? If he was going to survive, Chávez knew he had to get information, had to figure out what their orders were. So he turned on the charm . . . after all, his life might just depend on it.

"The boys have taken marvelous care of me since I arrived!" he said with a big smile. "They are tremendous soldiers, good people who have given me all that I need, including good conversation. I just finished jogging for a little bit and I was . . ." As he spoke, he shook the men's hands, patted them on the shoulder. He was trying to keep up the smile as best he could, to play the role of the president, the commander in chief, but it seemed forced, not quite right. All the soldiers were in uniform except Chávez, who was wearing shorts and a white T-shirt. Even in dress, Chávez seemed out of place.

The head of the new officers, a colonel, tried to say something—"Well, I'm very glad . . ."—but Chávez kept talking.

"I was saying to the captain that just left, Sosa, that until now I haven't been able to talk to a lawyer," Chavez said. "I put my trust in God and I hope that a ray of good judgment reaches those who are making decisions." Chávez was gesticulating energetically as he spoke (as usual) and here he saluted the colonel as if to say, I hope *you* exercise good judgment. Don't do anything you might regret. "I haven't talked with my *mamá*," he continued, "nor with my wife. I am incommunicado. I asked for a lawyer; they told me no." His fingers touched the colonel's chest . . . a supplicating gesture that belied his tough tone. *I need help.* "Well, the only certain thing is that I . . ." Chávez paused, not knowing what to say. He was visibly very nervous; a powerful man, now powerless. And now these men. Where did they intend to take him? Chávez looked at the colonel sternly. "The moment has arrived where I need someone to tell me where I am going; if not, I am not leaving here."

"Yes," the colonel began, "look, first I have been commissioned to take over your custody in every regard—your security—and the intention is to take you to Orchila for your, uh, possible subsequent trip out of the country." There was a pause. Chávez nodded, but it was plain he didn't like what the colonel was telling him. Orchila was another naval base, an island in the Caribbean about 150 miles off the coast, a place where the top naval brass liked to vacation. It was true that there was an airstrip there, so it was possible to take a flight to Cuba. But could he trust these men? Was it a trick? Maybe they would get him on the chopper, kill him, then throw his body into the ocean?

"Those are the orders that they gave me," the colonel added.

Chávez brought the tips of his hands together, thinking. "Now Colonel," Chávez said very slowly. "*Fíjate una cosa,*" consider this, he said,

"I am incommunicado. I have this fear. I . . . if I go to Cuba, or wherever I decide, because I can't be forced to go; Cuba could be a possibility, [one] that I have been considering since the night before last, but I haven't had the chance to talk to anyone. The thirst for power has taken control of them, and they thought, 'We made it! Chávez is done!' But there are a lot of people that still don't know . . . they don't know anything about me and . . ." Chávez paused, uncertain again. He changed direction and pointed to the table where he had a copy of the constitution. "That constitution, 82 percent of it, they have trampled on, and I, myself, so that you know, *I* proposed that night, *I* decided [to turn myself in]. General Raúl Baduel said to me, 'Don't give up,' and all of the high command betrayed me. Disloyal cowards!" Chávez shouted, shaking his fist.

Suddenly, the words were coming fast as Chávez's fears and frustrations began to pour out: "I ordered Plan Avila in the morning—I have the authority to do it—when I was informed by the intelligence community in the military and the DISIP that an insurrection was under way and that General Medina, Venezuela's [military] attaché to Washington, was here and that he had brought weapons! I found out about all that and I ordered—given all the evidence—'Plan Avila, General Rosendo!' But General Rosendo didn't want to." Chávez paused and looked the colonel straight in the eye, letting his words sink in. "He disappeared on me. 'Lucas [Rincón], Plan Avila!'"

Chávez retold his conversation with General Rincón:

"'Uh, Mr. President, I don't know,' [he told me.] 'Let's think about it,' or some such thing.

"What is there to think about? Plan Avila!

"'*Bueno*, I am going to Fort Tiuna.'

"'OK, fine go to Fort Tiuna then.' So once there [I called him].

"'No, it's that it's not convenient.'

"So I grabbed a radio I had and I began to go through the network and I got hold of García Carneiro, commander of the brigade. I said to him, 'García Carneiro, what is going on?'

"'*Coño, Mi Commandante,* I don't know. They are looking for me so they can arrest me.'

"'Who, *chico*?'

"'The generals.'

"'Why are they going to arrest you? What is going on?'

"'Well, it's that there is a military uprising.'

"So I told him, OK, then, look, I am in charge. Send the tanks here. We are going to activate Plan Avila.' They shut down the highway, the important roads, they tried to stop them, but the tanks went out nevertheless."

The colonel tried to be patient as Chávez spoke. It was not his place to cut Chávez off, nor did he want to upset him; he didn't want to do anything that might make Chávez hesitate about getting on the chopper.

"If they had followed orders," Chávez lamented. "Look, history will show who was responsible; if the high command had followed the order that I gave to implement Plan Avila on the morning of that day, given that I had all [the information] and they did, too, that they saw this insurrection . . . what happened is that some of them were already tied up with General Vásquez Velasco—traitor! That one, he hid. I ordered him to call Miraflores, and he hid. I ordered him to call, but the captain, [his] aide, he told me, '*Mi Comandante*, the general, I don't know, he has put himself in his room and he won't respond.' He is a coward! And he is the one that you have as your boss."

"*Mira*," the colonel interjected, trying to calm him down, "I am a soldier. First, let me fulfill my mission to give you the protection that you, like any Venezuelan citizen, deserves. In order to do that I have been accompanied by a group of officers that you know so that we can take you to Orchila."

Chávez clasped his hands in front of his waist. "*Te entiendo*, I understand, *chamo,* forgive the commentary. But consider this. At this level I could refuse to go, OK? Why? Because according to the constitution I am the president of this country." He placed his hand on the colonel's shoulder and was now speaking in an intense whisper to emphasize his point. More, Chávez was testing his limits, seeing how much he could influence these men.

"So just let me sit here. I'll eat my lunch. After lunch I am going to meditate a little to help me make a decision." The colonel nodded—letting the defunct president finish his lunch seemed a reasonable request. "But if I am under arrest, then fine," Chávez went on, "then I will stay under arrest here. I am not obligated to go. The night before last, yes, in order to prevent what I knew would happen . . . this." Chávez then told the colonel how a tank commander in Maracaibo—ten hours from Caracas—had said he would help Chávez, but that Chávez told him to stay put.

Again the colonel reiterated that his mission was only to transport Chávez to the Orchila Naval Base. "Please permit me to fulfill my mission," he said. Then he went on to say that Chávez would be safe, even saying that he would protect Chávez's life with his own if necessary.

"*Yo te creo*," Chávez said. I believe you. And again he put his hand on the colonel's shoulder. "I believe you."

Chávez would go with them. What else could he do?

Chávez, of course, had told the colonel that he needed extra time to finish his lunch so that he could finish his note. But in the end they didn't leave him alone again, so the letter went unfinished, hidden in the trash. Chávez soon forgot about it. He didn't really think it was likely that the corporal would be able to come and get it anyway. And even if he did, who would he give it to? Turiamo was a very isolated base. It didn't even have telephones or fax machines.

After lunch Chávez changed into blue jeans and an olive drab T-shirt. Then the nurse gave him some medicine—some pills for his cholesterol, medicine for his upset stomach (acid reflux), and drops for his eyes. The rumble of the waiting helicopter could be heard outside.

People were coming in and out of the room now—the flight crew, other nurses, gawkers who wanted to catch a final glimpse of the famous Hugo Chávez before he left Venezuela forever. He made sure he greeted all of them. When one officer came to the door, Chávez greeted him with a wave and a shout. "*Epa!* What's up?" Then halfheartedly Chávez said, "I haven't resigned." He said it with a smile and without conviction, as if it had become a joke and he knew that no one was taking him seriously anymore.

Soon the colonel and his aide returned. They discussed the trip and when Chávez might leave Orchila for Cuba. Chávez nodded and asked a few questions. He was still trying to woo them and complimented the colonel's aide. "I should make this one *my* assistant," he said pointing to the man and laughing. "He knows how to get things done, *boom, boom,*

boom." Chávez began to gather up his medication, then, oddly aware of how he was kissing up to them, he said, "I'm developing 'prisoner's syndrome,'" and went on to explain how captives often develop close relationships with their captors.

Finally, he put on a red windbreaker and began shaking hands as they prepared to go. "*Muchas gracias, muchas gracias por todo.* I hope that we can meet again someday under better conditions, and not this uncertainty that we are living through."

Outside the room, four soldiers stood waiting in a sort of receiving line to say good-bye. He shook their hands—clasping their outstretched hands in both of his. "*Muchas gracias, hasta luego.* May God watch over you."

Then he was out in the sunshine and quickly into the helicopter. Soon they were airborne. Despite the roar of the engine and the open doors, Chávez continued talking to the other men, chatting them up.

7 | Walking

Back in Caracas, Vásquez Velasco and the other generals were moving forward with their plans to find a constitutional solution. But the first two people in line of succession—Vice President Diosdado Cabello and the head of the National Assembly, Willian Lara—could still not be found. So Vásquez Velasco turned to the chief justice of the Supreme Court, Dr. Iván Rincón, another loyal *chavista* who was, according to the constitution, next in line of succession. Vásquez Velasco told him his plans and the chief justice agreed to help establish a transitional government that adhered to the constitution. Vásquez Velasco sent a car to get him and bring him to his office.

But just then, José Vicente Rangel, Chávez's minister of defense, called. *I just heard your announcement on TV,* he said and congratulated him on making the decision. Vásquez Velasco told Rangel that Chief Justice Rincón was going to oversee the transition. But Rangel said he was in touch with Diosdado Cabello, the vice president in hiding, and that they were trying to get him back to Caracas. Rangel insisted that Cabello, not Dr. Rincón, should lead the transition.

How do I know you're telling the truth, Vásquez Velasco asked.

Call back in an hour and you'll see that it's true, Rangel said.

Vásquez Velasco then called Chief Justice Rincón again and told him the news.

Look, Efraín, the chief justice said, *let me consult with the other justices because I am ready to oversee the transition, but if the vice president shows up, the constitution authorizes him to assume the presidency, at least for thirty days until new elections are held.*

<hr />

After fleeing Miraflores, Pedro Carmona had gone to Fort Tiuna. He was still trying to salvage the interim government, but his list of supporters was growing smaller by the minute. He again sent emissaries to Vásquez Velasco to try to appease him, but the general turned a deaf ear.

<hr />

Meanwhile, in the Caracas suburb of Altamira a large group of National Assembly deputies and political leaders had gathered. Upon hearing Vásquez Velasco's declaration, they began working on how to repeal Carmona's decrees and set up a "proper" transitional government. The most popular plan was put forth by Luis Miquilena (Dr. Frankenstein). He proposed they select fifteen deputies representing all of the political parties and that this group be allowed to name a new government in an open session of the Assembly. But there was some opposition to the plan. Julio Borges, a member of the Primero Justicia party, objected most vociferously, turning on the old communist, whom he suspected of making a power grab.

"How is it possible that in the middle of this crisis *you* are making this proposal?" Borges asked. Then he thought for a moment, produced his cell phone, and handed it to Miquilena. "Here is my phone. I want to hear you call—in my presence—all of the deputies that you personally control."

<hr />

While Miraflores and the country's military bases were swarming with activity, the news blackout meant that most Venezuelans remained largely oblivious of what was going on. Dr. Alicia Valdez and her sister, Florangel, had no idea all this was happening (despite the fact that Florangel had worked in Miraflores up until the coup). The raven-haired accountant and her sister were on their way to Alicia's daughter's house to drop off some things when something happened that they would never forget.

Out in the streets they found that things were very quiet. Most people were staying indoors. They were on the main highway heading in the direction of El Silencio when they saw a group of people marching in the opposing lane. Alicia and Florangel had not heard any news about a march, so they slowed down to get a better look. They could see that there were several hundred people stretched out over the highway; they were carrying flags and blowing whistles, but since these were things used by both *chavistas* and *escuálidos*, they still weren't sure who they were supporting.

As they grew closer, Alicia began to see red T-shirts and berets: They were *chavistas* demonstrating against the new government. All these people were going down to protest; to demand that Chávez be released and restored to power.

Florangel and Alicia decided then and there to join them. They stopped and loaded up their car with people. They had people riding on the hood and sitting on the trunk. Alicia soon learned that some of them had been walking from as far away as La Minas de Baruta, La Tahona, and farther— eight very unflat miles away! Alicia's emotions welled up in her.

As they got closer to El Silencio, they saw more and more people, all converging on Miraflores. Many were poor people, and Alicia knew that this was because Chávez was the only person who took them into account. He was the only one that said they had rights. The only one who tried to better their situation so that they were equal with everyone else.

Mohamad "Mike" Merhi was on his way to the cemetery to bury his son, Jesús, when he, too, began to see groups of Chávez supporters walking along the highway.

The last two days had been a nightmare for him and his family. He had found Jésus's body at the morgue yesterday morning and had to identify the naked corpse himself. As was the custom in Venezuela, they had held an all-night wake for him and were just now taking him to be buried. He was driving with his wife, his brother Ali, and his sister-in-law. Along the way they had seen some shops being looted and had to make a detour because they heard that the Pan-American Highway was closed. As they got closer to El Centro, the number of people walking along the highway grew—first a cluster of a dozen, then fifty, then a hundred. Eventually they had to slow down until they were crawling along among the marchers. It was obvious by their dress that they were *chavistas* heading to Miraflores. Mike rolled up the windows, and his sister-in-law became very nervous. A couple of times the marchers shouted at them and beat on the roof of the car. Mike knew that since they were dressed formally for the funeral, they must look like quintessential *escuálidos* in the eyes of the *chavistas*. He was making his way through them—breaking out of one pack, then slowing down as he entered another—but his sister-in-law was growing more and more hysterical. She was convinced that at any moment the *chavistas* were going to drag them from the car and beat them. Every time the car came to a stop, she became frantic, insisting that they turn around. Mike knew she was having a panic attack. He tried to calm her down and even took off his tie so they would not appear so bourgeois, but it was no use. She was out of control—shouting and weeping—and insisted that they take her home. Mike finally relented and turned the car around. By the time he dropped her off and got back on the highway it was completely shut down, *trancado*. The *chavistas* had blocked the road. There was no way for him to get to the cemetery.

He would miss his son's funeral.

⸎

By four o'clock *chavista* hard-liner Guillermo García Ponce could see streams of protestors from his apartment making their way toward Miraflores. He decided it was time to join them.

When he arrived outside the palace, the cheering crowd rushed up around him. It took a minute to calm them down—he had to shout to be heard—then he told them what they needed to do.

"We must go to the TV stations to set the record straight about President Chávez's 'resignation,'" he told them. "Making the TV stations tell the truth is more important than being here."

Spurred by García Ponce's words, protestors and angry mobs led by Bolivarian Circles began to congregate around the newspapers and TV stations. Globovisión and RCTV were hardest hit. By eight o'clock the attack was in full swing. The protestors threw rocks through the windows and fired their pistols into the buildings. Terrified, the journalists turned their cameras on the militant *chavistas* and televised their pleas for help. They beseeched the police, the National Guard, the army . . . anybody to intervene. But with the country's government in such disarray, no one was able or willing to help them. They had to simply hold on.

Despite the blackout, Generals Baduel and García Montoya had, by now, got their message to the international media. Stations in France, Mexico, Argentina, Colombia, and Cuba had aired their press conferences and reports. CNN alone contacted the generals five times throughout the day and gave regular updates on events. CNN also broadcast a message from Chávez's wife, Marisabel Chávez, who stated quite emphatically that her husband had not resigned.

While most of the country's journalists were safe at home or inside their respective offices, a few were still trying to cover the news. One of them was Gabriel Osorio, the photographer who had rushed to help the fatally wounded Jhonnie Palencia—"the Book Man"—on April 11. Although his colleagues said he was crazy, Gabriel decided to go to Miraflores anyway. *If your photos aren't good enough, you're not close enough.* As a precaution, Gabriel hid his press card (which said he worked for the anti-Chávez paper *El Nacional*) in his sock. Then he took off his shirt and wrapped it around his head to disguise himself. As he got closer to the palace he made sure to chant, "Viva Chávez!" louder and louder. Once there, he milled around for a while, discretely taking pictures, pretending as if they were for himself.

Then he noticed a woman in the crowd. He did a double take because he recognized the copper highlights in her hair and the slight Asian curve of her eyes. He was sure she was also a reporter from his paper, but she, too, was acting like a *chavista.* "Are you a journalist?" he asked her. She seemed startled by the question. "Why?" she asked suspiciously. He smiled and told her who he was. She relaxed. Her name was Lamking González Lum, a petite young woman who had a Venezuelan father and a Chinese mother. Even though she was still in her twenties, Lamking had a reputation as being a very tough reporter, taking risks that other reporters wouldn't take. It fit her personality: She was full of energy, always active, working, going to the gym, doing Tae-Bo. Indefatigable.

They agreed that they had to get inside the palace—that's where the real story was happening—so they conspired to impersonate international journalists to get past the guards. Gabriel at first tried to be Mexican, but he sounded ridiculous, so he tried acting like he was from Spain. Slowly he and Lamking pushed their way to the palace gate. "We are interwational journawists!" Gabriel said with his best Spanish lisp.

The captain of the guard came up. "Where are you from?" he asked.

"*Hombre,* I've come fwom Spain to see what has become of Comman-der Chávez," Gabriel said. He squeezed his hands and stiffened his shoul-ders, making any gesticulation he could think of to make him look like a foreigner.

"*Soy Mexicana,*" chimed Lamking.

"Let me see your IDs," the guard said.

Uh-oh. Gabriel and Lamking exchanged a glance. Reluctantly Gabriel fished his sweaty ID out of his sock. He reached his arm through the gate so that no one else in the crowd would see it. Lamking did the same.

"Ah, they are from *El Nacional!*" the captain exclaimed loud enough for everyone to hear.

This bit of news was quickly repeated all around them. "They are from *El Nacional.*" Three or four times they heard it, with increasing incredulity. "They are from *El Nacional!*"

"Let's burn them alive," someone said.

"Yeah, let's teach them a lesson."

Gabriel's arms and legs went slack with fear.

"*Medios golpistas!*" someone shouted. The media coupsters!

They were up against the fence, with a hectare of *chavistas* behind them. Gabriel knew there was only one place to go for safety—into Miraflores. Luckily, the guard was beginning to realize that if he didn't let them in, they would be beaten, and that was a mess he didn't want to deal with. He slowly (very slowly) opened the gate.

Once inside, Gabriel took a few pictures, but he had to conserve film. Unlike 99.9 percent of the photographers on the planet, Gabriel was still using film. He hadn't gone digital.

Soon, more and more high-level *chavistas* began to arrive. He saw Nicolas Maduro, Freddie Bernal, and Cilia Flores. One was in pajamas; another was in a sweat suit, but with dress shoes; another had clothes that must have been borrowed from someone much bigger. They looked ridiculous, but he tried not to laugh because he knew this was because they had been in hiding. They had fled the palace on April 11, and most had not been home since, so they were wearing whatever clothes they could find; whatever people had lent them in whatever neighborhood they had sought refuge.

When Gabriel called the paper to tell them where he was, his boss was shocked. The paper, which wasn't far from Miraflores, had an angry mob of *chavistas* around it. His boss was both afraid and angry, cursing the damn *chavistas*. He told Gabriel and Lamking they should get out of Miraflores immediately, but Gabriel said he wanted to stay. The conversation disturbed Gabriel because his boss made it clear that they were on their own. The paper wasn't going to do anything to help them.

The crowd in the street was steadily growing. From as far away as the neighborhood of 23 de Enero he could hear the *ding-ding-ding-ding-ding* of the *cacerolazo*. Gabriel was impressed. Two days ago it had been *cacerolazos* to get Chávez out. Now they were to get him back. Some people even had signs that read, "Where are the networks?" and Gabriel had to agree. The media should definitely be here.

—∞∞—

Dr. Espidel and his son Joan were one block away on the the Llaguno Overpass when members of the honor guard began passing through the crowd, saying that they were going to bring Chávez back. The crowd became very excited. Then Espidel's wife, Sabrina, called to say that Carmona had been on TV and retracted his previous declarations, saying he had acted too quickly in dissolving Venezuela's democratic institutions.

Soon they began to hear all sorts of rumors: Just twenty minutes later, his wife called again to say that Carmona was going to resign.

All this news was by word of mouth so he and Joan walked back to Miraflores hoping to learn more. People there were crying for joy, hoping it was true that Chávez would come back. One man spray-painted "Fuera Carmona," *Get out Carmona,* on the wall of the palace.

Then the minister of education, Aristóbulo Istúriz, arrived. "Don't worry," Espidel remembered him saying, "we will bring Chávez home." Soon after that, Espidel's wife called once again saying that VTV—the government TV station—was finally back on the air. Espidel began to breathe easy. He was beginning to believe that Chávez would really return, and as each hour passed and as more good news started to come in, and as more and more people arrived to join the multitude, they all became happier and happier. It became like a big fiesta. By nightfall, Urdaneta Avenue was filled with several blocks of supporters.

People were chanting, "*Chávez, amigo, el pueblo esta contigo!*"—Chávez, our friend, the people are with you—over and over again.

───※───

Around eight o'clock, Vásquez Velasco called José Vicente Rangel to check on the status of Diosdado Cabello. Rangel confirmed that he was on his way to Caracas. It was a fact.

The general then called Chief Justice Iván Rincón for a third time to tell him about the vice president. *If he appears, then he must assume the presidency,* Rincón reiterated. Vásquez Velasco consulted one last time with his advising generals and they acknowledged that according to the constitution Diosdado Cabello was the legal leader of the transition.

For a brief moment, the crisis seemed to calm. The *chavistas* and Vásquez Velasco were now in accord. Technically, everyone else—the National Assembly deputies, Miquilena, most of the opposition, and General Baduel—were also on board; they were all ready and willing to follow the constitution "to the letter." Only Carmona, his clique, and some of the media owners were out of step.

But the moment of harmony was short-lived, as each group was actually (once again) interpreting the constitution as it saw fit.

According to Vásquez Velasco, the high command, many National Assembly members, and the moderate *escuálidos*, Hugo Chávez was not the president. He had expressed his intent to resign because of the crimes committed in El Silencio and was about to be deported to Cuba. Even if he hadn't abandoned his post, he would have to be tried for human rights violations. According to their reading of the constitution, since the president had abandoned his post, it meant—according to article 233—that elections had to be held within thirty days. Vice President Diosdado Cabello would be interim president until then, but only until then.

However, according to José Vicente Rangel, General Baduel, and the other *chavistas*, Chávez had never resigned (or if he had, it had been under duress); therefore, he was still the president. Yet, curiously, they still swore in Diosdado Cabello—a way to ensure that power stayed in their camp (and not with the more pluralistic National Assembly) and also an inadvertent acknowledgment that Chávez was out of the picture. The ceremony took place in Miraflores at ten o'clock and the president of the National Assembly, Willian Lara (also just emerged from hiding), swore him in. As a result, for a short time Venezuela actually had two presidents.

Regardless, the *chavistas* recognized that Cabello's presidency was a temporary formality until Chávez was back in command. They knew that without Chávez they were nothing—there was no party, no movement, no revolution without Chávez.

When one of the generals working with Baduel, Julio García Montoya, called Vásquez Velasco demanding to know where Chávez was being held, the army commander didn't want to help him, likely knowing the consequences of Chávez's restoration—not only for his personal career, but also because restoring Chávez (given his complete control of the courts) meant that he would never stand trial for the crimes in El Silencio.

8 | Phoenix

Back in Maracay, General Baduel had gone out to address the growing crowd outside the gates of the base. He updated them on events: Although they still did not know where Chávez was or even if he was alive, they had by now taken control of Miraflores and brought many of the highest-ranking *chavistas* home. Diosdado Cabello had not yet been sworn in as president, but it was now clearly inevitable.

As Baduel spoke to the people, he was approached by a corporal and his wife who said they had an important note for him. So important, in fact, that the blushing woman confessed she had hidden it in her underwear so that it would arrive safely.

Baduel read the note:

> Turiamo, April 13, 2002 at 14:45
>
> To the people of Venezuela
> (and whoever it concerns).
>
> I, Hugo Chávez Frías, Venezuelan,
> President of the Bolivarian Republic
> of Venezuela, do declare:
>
> I have not resigned the
> legitimate power that the
> people gave me.
>
> Forever!
>
> Hugo Chávez F.

Well, that cleared up a few a few things for Baduel: Chávez was certainly still alive and, better yet, still in Venezuela.

Baduel decided then and there to read the note out loud to the crowd. They roared with glee. Soon copies of Chávez's note were rolling out of fax machines all over the country.

The Turiamo Naval Base was only twenty-two miles from Maracay, and Baduel hoped that they might be able to launch an immediate rescue, but they soon learned that Chávez had been moved to Orchila Island, which put him out of reach of ground forces, so Baduel began looking for boats, then helicopters, to mount a rescue.

9 | Minutes from Cuba

One hundred miles away on Orchila Island, the source of all this tumult was sitting quietly on the beach. Beside him sat none other than Catholic cardinal Ignacio Velasco.

It was a beautiful night and the waves lapped quietly on the shore as the two men sat looking at the ocean and the stars, unaware of all the important things that were happening back on the mainland. It had been Chávez's idea to go down to the beach, now that he was certain that he was about to leave Venezuela for good, unsure when, if ever, he would return, so he had invited the cardinal to walk with him by the water.

The cardinal had flown to the island several hours earlier as part of a delegation from the interim government that was trying to get Chávez to sign his resignation. After he signed, the plan was that the cardinal would accompany him all the way to Havana. The cardinal, however, was becoming skeptical of the whole thing and was beginning to think he might have been sent on a fool's errand. He had agreed to come to ensure Chávez's safety, but he was becoming more aware of the political machinery that was pushing and pulling him. Before they even left Caracas had the feeling that no one was really in control of the country.

Also in the delegation were José Godoy, the director of the human rights department at the Ministry of Defense, Admiral Shieto, and Colonel Julio Rodríguez Salas—the same military attorney who had lent Chávez his cell phone in Fort Tiuna yesterday morning so he could call his wife and daughter.

When the delegation arrived, they found Chávez in the presidential residence with about twenty marines.

Despite his incredible fatigue, his acid-filled stomach, and his exhaustion, Chávez did his best to work with the delegation. But the extended crisis was taking its toll on him, and one of the soldiers remembered how beaten and downtrodden he looked. Chávez had, by now, accepted the fact that he would go to Cuba. Once there, he hoped that with Castro's help he would one day return, but he knew that it was going to take time. In the meantime it was Cuba, and exile.

Colonel Salas could see that Chávez was ready and willing to get it all over with. In the colonel's eyes, Chávez was crumbling—a defeated man who was at the point of complete collapse. Colonel Salas presented him with the decree that he would need to sign before he could get on the plane. In the decree was the removal of Vice President Diosdado Cabello, who was now—unbeknownst to these men—the (second) president of Venezuela.

Chávez, likely remembering Castro's words, said he didn't want to resign.

"All right, then," Colonel Salas said, "that is your decision. Then I will go back [to Caracas] now."

But Chávez didn't want that either. He told Salas to wait, and that he would sign if they changed the wording to "abandoned his position" instead of "resigned." That would make it easier to come back, Chávez thought, even though, in fact, it wouldn't—according to the constitution, resigning and abandoning his post were the same.

Colonel Salas called the Ministry of Defense about the change. The ministry gave the go-ahead, so they rewrote the decree with the change. When Salas presented it to Chávez again, he said he didn't want to sign a decree, only a letter. By now the colonel was getting frustrated. He explained to Chávez that legally it would be the same thing. Chávez reluctantly capitulated.

Finally, with all the changes agreed upon, one of the officers went to type up the decree. By now it was well after one in the morning and the plane that would take Chávez to Cuba was ready. The only thing left to do was wait for the decree to be retyped.

It was all about to end. In a matter of minutes Chávez would leave Venezuela and who knew when he would return, if ever? It was then that Chávez turned to the cardinal and asked him if he would go down to the shore with him and pray. The cardinal agreed and, taking Chávez's hand, they walked down to the water's edge and sat and looked at the ocean and the stars.

At the water's edge Chávez said he was very sorry about everything that had happened and he asked for the cardinal's forgiveness. "Many times God sends signs," Chávez said. "And regrettably it appears that sometimes He decides to send them even with a drop of blood."

They sat there for a long time and spoke about many things. Now and then the cardinal would lead a short prayer.

It was just about two in the morning when the men heard something. It was very faint at first . . . very distant . . . a low thumping sound. They turned their heads toward the sound. Soon it was unmistakable. Choppers. Three army Super Pumas coming in low over the water. Chávez and Cardinal Velasco got to their feet, unsure of what this meant. Were they here to rescue Chávez, or were they here to keep him from leaving for Cuba?

Out on the tarmac, the arrival of the helicopters terrified the civilian pilots who had brought Cardinal Velasco and the delegation and, without a word, they took off, leaving their passengers stranded on the island.

But the helicopters had been sent by Baduel. It was a rescue. Hugo Chávez—who had been sure he was heading for Cuba just moments before—was about to go home.

Back in the residence, Colonel Salas also heard the helicopters and figured they had come to renegotiate the terms of the resignation, but when he called the Ministry of Defense to get instructions, he found himself talking to *Chávez's* minister of defense—José Vicente Rangel—who demanded to speak with Chávez.

───────

Unsure of what they would encounter in Orchila, General Baduel had prepared the rescue team for anything. There were twenty elite commandos on board, locked and loaded for a firefight; a military lawyer; a constitutional lawyer; and a doctor—the generals had heard rumors that Chávez had been mistreated. In fact, the initial plan was to fly Chávez directly to the military hospital in Maracay. But soon a very amazed Hugo Chávez called the generals and told them that he was in perfect health and that he wanted to fly straight to Miraflores.

<hr />

It was after three in the morning when the first helicopter buzzed Miraflores. The photographer Gabriel Osorio was still on the patio trying to conserve his remaining film when he saw its searchlight sweep the side of the palace. By orders of the honor guard, all lights had been extinguished—all the lights in the palace, even the lights that were on the tops of the video cameras had to be shut off. No flash photography either. The whole palace had been plunged into black. And it was a deeper black than on a typical night because of the smoke from the arson fires that hung in the air.

Soon another helicopter joined the first—its loud *thump-thump-thump* rattling Gabriel's chest.

Then there was another, and another.

The four choppers shifted in the air above the palace, patrolling, checking. Through the gaps in the trees he saw them circling about. For about fifteen minutes they circled, the whole time the crowd was growing more and more excited. They knew he was coming. This is what they had been waiting for all day, what they had been screaming for, what they had walked miles and miles to be a part of.

Then Gabriel suddenly realized there was a fifth helicopter. It was very close, but he couldn't see it because it was flying without any lights. He knew this must be Chávez's copter. It was there, only forty meters away, but he couldn't see it.

Gabriel waited. Where *was* he? There was the rumbling of the copter, and Gabriel could hear many people moving, but he couldn't see anything. Pitch black. Then he heard someone shout, "He's here, he's here!" He heard people laughing, cheering. But he still couldn't see anything. Then . . . finally . . . a photographer dared to snap a picture. Light flooded the scene.

There he was. At least thirty people were crowded around him, journalists and soldiers. His face was swollen and tired, but he was smiling. Grinning wide. Then he was consumed in darkness again. Another flash came, then all the photographers started breaking the rules. It created a strobe effect, like a Hollywood premier, and Hugo Chávez's arrival became a series of still photographs in the darkness.

An incredible roar washed over them as all the people in the street caught sight of him. He held his fist up high, still grinning. As if on cue, an army band struck up "La Diana," the Venezuelan version of *reveille*. A new dawn.

It seemed like one of life's perfect moments—there was an undeniable synchronicity between every person there, a connection between the relief of Chávez's aides, the pride of the honor guard, and the jubilation of the crowd as it pressed through the palace gates. To Gabriel it seemed as if everyone was crying, even him. He couldn't help it. What's more, at that moment, Gabriel became a *chavista*. Up until now he had thought of himself as pretty neutral. If anything, he was a bit anti-Chávez because of the way the president treated the media. Not now. This moment was too powerful. It was impossible not to be swept up in the emotion of it.

The crowd began singing: "*Lle-gó, llególlególlegó, llegó llegó!*"—He's arrived, He's arrived! They sang it over and over again to the same tune the opposition had sung, "*Se va, se va!*"—"He's going, he's going!"—just two days before.

⁂

Hugo Chávez made his way slowly through the crowd, taking his time and talking to people, touching them. As he tried to take in the scene, he noticed with quiet astonishment that the note he had left in the wastebasket at the Turiamo Naval Base was everywhere, it seemed to be in everyone's hands. He felt a wave of gratitude for the soldier who had retrieved it and sent it out.

Once inside the palace, the staff quickly prepared for a press conference, but this time they didn't do it in the ordinary way—with Chávez sitting by himself at his desk. No, this time they all sat together, Chávez, Willian Lara, and the rest of his aides . . . Diosdado Cabello stood close by. They were brothers and sisters in arms and this was their victory lap.

"'Render unto God the things which are God's, unto Caesar the things which are Caesar's, and to the people the things that belong to the people,'" Chávez said. "It is with those words that I want to begin . . . full of I don't know how many sentiments that are passing through my chest, through my soul, through my mind. I have to confess to you that at this moment I am like a multicolored sea. . . . I have to confess to you that I am still stupefied, I am still assimilating everything that has happened."

Everyone in the hall was so excited, so happy, and so relieved. The speech was moving, good-natured, and remarkably conciliatory. Chávez spoke with great affection about Cardinal Velasco and how he had come to Orchila Island to guarantee his safety and he told everyone how they had gone down to the beach to pray; how the two men had asked for God's guidance and how they had discussed man's purpose. Man's purpose, they had agreed, was to do the will of God. And what was the will of God? To fight for peace and the well-being of everyone. Something that Chávez said he would work for; that he would accept the differences of others and communicate and cooperate.

It seemed as if Chávez had learned a profound lesson, and that he would take the country in a new direction. Perhaps he had been scared straight. Echoing the letter that General Rosendo had sent him on April 11, Chávez said he was going to set up a federal government council—a commission of national leaders from all the sectors of Venezuelan society, of both the opposition and the government—that would advise the administration. It was an olive branch to the opposition. "Those who are not in agreement with our policies, with our decisions, can say so, but within the law, honestly, in order to find the best consensus possible, because the ultimate goal has to be the same for everyone—regardless of our differences—the fatherland."

He also (finally) announced that the board of directors of PDVSA that he had named—the action that had precipitated the whole crisis—would be replaced.

He ended the speech with these words:

I return spiritually charged with a great love. . . . If two days ago I loved you, then today, after these historic events, after this unprecedented demonstration to the world of how a people and its soldiers can stop a counterrevolution and make a counter-counterrevolution without firing a shot, without spilling blood, and put everything back in its proper place. Well, then, after all that, after this journey, after these memorable, historic, events . . . events that will never be erased . . . if yesterday I loved you, then today I love you much much more. Love pays for itself with love.

I wish all of Venezuela a good day; a good day to everyone!

In the palace courtyard, Gabriel Osorio and Lamking González Lum were still hanging around. They were the only journalists left and wanted to stay as long as they could. Gabriel knew he was living through something special and even though the first rays of dawn were hitting the Avila, he didn't want to go home. The *chavista* politicians seemed to feel the same way. Groups of them were hanging around, sharing stories about what had happened—their time in hiding, what they had seen, what they had done. Many were already telling stories about things that had happened only an hour before. Shaking their heads in disbelief, repeating, "*Un milagro.*" A miracle.

Chávez was there in the courtyard, too, and many people wanted Gabriel to take their picture with him, to capture this moment for all time. Gabriel didn't have the heart to tell them that he had run out of film long ago, so he went ahead and turned on the flash and took their picture anyway. Giving them a thumbs up after each pose. Someday he'd go digital.

Little by little the *chavistas* began to disappear into the passageways of the palace until there were just a few guards standing in the shadows, as well as Gabriel, Lamking, and Hugo Chávez. Lamking approached the president and extended her hand. Chávez gave her a big smile, then kissed her on the cheek. They spoke for a few moments. Chávez thanked her but said he had to go because the others were waiting for him. He turned to go, but then he stopped, remembering that Gabriel was there, too. He extended his hand.

"*Mi hermano,*" Chávez said. "My brother, you don't know how important it is that you are here, documenting all this. I thank you, and the country thanks you, too." Then he embraced Gabriel—a strong, emotional embrace.

Gabriel felt an incredible pride, a feeling of great importance. He flushed red and tried to dismiss the compliment, but couldn't. Into Chávez's ear Gabriel simply said, "Welcome home."

"Thank you," Chávez said, holding Gabriel at the shoulders and looking him straight in the eye. "Thank you."

Gabriel now understood what it meant to be a *chavista*, because at that moment he would have done anything for Chávez. Anything. If Hugo Chávez had asked him to take up a rifle and fight, Gabriel would have done it. Indeed, it didn't feel like he just met the president. No, he had met an ordinary man. A man who had recently been near death, who had wept and was still sweating out his fear, still trembling. Somehow that, *that* was much more powerful than meeting the president.

Then Chávez moved away, disappearing through an archway.

PART FIVE
AFTERMATH

1 | Rewriting the Coup

Following April 11, Baralt Avenue was closed off as a crime scene and remained closed while Carmona was in power. But following Chávez's return on April 14, work crews under orders from Freddy Bernal (the leader of the Bolivarian Circles and mayor of this Caracas district) began to repair the damaged street. With great speed and efficiency, traffic lights were repaired, kiosks were replaced, walls were painted, chips in the cement were patched, and the big Santa Marías (the metal garage doors that protected storefronts) were replaced free of charge. Workers pulled bullets from walls and searched the gutters for bullet casings. Within five days all physical evidence from the scene had been collected and destroyed. The street was reopened on April 20.

Thus began the Chávez administration's multi-million-dollar campaign to rewrite the history of the coup. What had happened in El Silencio—the fact that the government had repressed a peaceful march with gunfire—was a public relations nightmare for the regime. The government's first strategy was to block any investigation of the violence. Police detectives and prosecutors who opened investigations were summarily transferred and replaced by more malleable *chavistas*.

Next, the government tried to claim as many of the victims as their own so that they could say that it had been a clash between two equally belligerent groups, "a confrontation between brothers." They claimed that the opposition marchers had been armed, too, and had fired first, even though there was no evidence of this. The government would also say that many people killed or wounded in the opposition crowd had actually been shot by friendly fire from their own people.

In another tactic to increase the body count on their side, the government made national broadcasts asking that anyone who had been wounded or had family members wounded or killed fighting *for the government* should step forward. All such persons were offered an array of rewards, including money, jobs, free medical care (often in Cuba), and educational grants for their children. Many came forward, including people who had not been injured and had absolutely no involvement with the events but simply fabricated a story in order to collect money from the government.

No such compensation was offered to the victims from the opposition. Indeed, those who denounced the government were threatened and harassed. Chávez publicly stated that he would go after anyone who tried to bring a case against the government because all such accusations must be lies.

The government would even take bodies from the morgue—people who had been killed both before and after April 11—and say they had been killed by opposition snipers on the 11th. For example, the government insisted that José Alexi González, a man killed late on April 13 in a neighborhood near El Silencio, be included in the death count for April 11. By increasing the body count on its side, the government was able to sell the idea that the violence had been initiated by the opposition, and that the pro-Chávez gunmen had been acting in self-defense. And by repeating these claims again and again, Chávez was able to paint himself as the victim of a "classic coup" scenario, wherein he had done nothing to precipitate events.

The opposition would also try to spin the events in their favor—both to counteract Chávez's disinformation and to advance their own agenda. Spearheaded by the anti-Chávez media, they also scrambled to claim victims. For example, Jorge Tortoza—because he was a journalist—was claimed as a martyr by both sides. While it is true that he was killed while working in the opposition crowd, he was actually a Chávez supporter and was claimed by the government, too. Tortoza's own brother, Edgar, would initially denounce the government for killing his brother, but later, after he was offered a nice job in Miraflores representing the government victims, he would change his tune.

—⟨∞⟩—

On the first day that he was able to get out of bed, fifteen days after being shot in the leg, Andrés Trujillo went to the Justice Department (*la Fiscalia*) to file his case. He was on crutches. He took a number and sat down to wait. His number was 84 and they were currently attending number 23. It was nine in the morning and they told him that they would probably get to his number by three in the afternoon. After an hour, Andrés's pain became unbearable, and he asked if an exception could be made. Shortly, a woman came to attend him. He explained that he had been shot, but when he said that it was on April 11, the woman froze. "Were you shot above or below the overpass?" the woman asked. Andrés simply replied that he had been shot and needed a prosecutor to pursue his case. "There is no prosecutor for that case," the woman said. Andrés waited while the woman made some phone calls. She was on the phone for a half hour. "Where do I send him?" she said into the phone.

When she hung up, she gave him a piece of paper and told him to go to the seventh floor: Prosecutor 27 would see him. The elevator was broken so he started hopping up the stairs. When he arrived at the right office and explained that he had been injured on April 11, the prosecutor said that she was not assigned to the case. Andrés explained that he had been told she *was* assigned to the case by the people downstairs and showed her the slip of paper. "I have nothing to do with that," she said. He needed to go to the fourteenth floor. He picked up his crutches and went back to the stairwell.

When he got to the fourteenth floor, there was another gunshot victim from April 11 waiting there who was clearly a *chavista*. They sat together, uneasily, eyeing each other suspiciously. Here again Andrés was told that the Justice Department had not opened a case concerning April 11. When Andrés protested, the prosecutor's assistant said that she would call the attorney general's office to find out what to do. She spent an hour on the phone trying to get a definitive answer. "There is no prosecutor for that case," she announced and explained to both Andrés and the other victim that all they could do was go to the old Justice Department Building and give their testimony, and when someone was eventually assigned to the case, they would be contacted.

Although the pain in his leg was excruciating, Andrés and the other man made their way to the other building, but outside a large progovernment rally was blocking their way. The closer Andres got to the rally, the more panic he felt. All the memories of April 11 were coming back. He had to turn around and go the long way. By the time he reached the building, the family of the other victim had arrived and were making a lot of accusations Andrés thought were absurd. He suspected they were just looking for money. "Pedro Carmona shot him," they said. Finally the assistant prosecutor began to take Andrés's testimony. When he was done she made four copies that Andrés had to sign as his official statement. He asked if he could keep a copy and she said no. When he read over the testimony, he realized that where he had said he'd seen the police shooting upward, the prosecutor had written that they had been shooting at the buildings. He told her that statement was not correct, so she changed it. When he read it over again, it now said, "upward at the Llaguno Overpass." Andrés clarified that upward meant into the air. He remembered the prosecutor saying that she couldn't write that. Andrés had had enough. "This is *my* testimony. You are going to put what I tell you to put because that is what I saw, not what you say. If not, I am not going to sign it." The prosecutor reluctantly acquiesced.

There were four pages of testimony, and she directed Andrés to sign just the first page and last page.

But Andrés was leery. "I am going to sign all of them," he said, "because I don't know if you are going to change the middle pages and because, if right in front of me you changed my testimony, when I go through that door I don't know if you are going to change the rest of the pages." He took the pages, signed them, and marked each one "1 of 4," "2 of 4," and so on.

To this day he has not been contacted by the government.

A few weeks later, Andrés was reading the paper and recognized a photo of Jesús Mohamad Capote, Mohamad "Mike" Merhi's son, the boy who had been shot next to him on Baralt Avenue. Shortly thereafter, Andrés mentioned Jesús in an interview with the newspaper *El Nacional*. Mike Merhi saw the article and contacted Andrés. They arranged to meet, and Andrés was finally able to tell Mike how his son had died.

On April 14, Antonio Návas—the Chávez supporter shot in the jaw in front of Miraflores—was still in a great deal of pain. In fact, he would be in and out of hospitals for the next year as they tried to correct the damage to his face. Despite the pain, he went to the Defender of the People that day to file his case, but it wasn't until six months later that the CIPCP (the federal investigative police) finally contacted him and invited him to Miraflores to do a reenactment. Once at the palace, government representatives offered him some "special assistance." Antonio, of course, had heard about the compensation the government was offering the victims, but he had never wanted to go to the palace and demand compensation. He wasn't the type of guy to say, "Hey, I took a bullet for you." Still, he decided to hear them out. He met Captain Meléndez, who was leading ASOVIC (National Association for the Victims of the Coup d'État of April 11, 12, 13, and 14), an organization for government victims funded by the government. It helped the government victims with their medical treatment and with jobs. Since being injured, Antonio had lost his job as a bodyguard and had no money. Captain Meléndez told him that the government could offer him different types of compensation for defending Miraflores that day. Antonio chose free tuition at a private school for his kids. They also gave him a job working as a mechanic in the Miraflores motor pool.

Antonio remains very grateful to the Chávez administration. In 2004, when he was still suffering from complications from his injury, Miraflores approved a credit to pay for the operation. Antonio feels that if it had been another president or another time, he would not have received such help. And the president had helped many people, he knew, like the programs he has with Cuba where kids and the disabled can get free medical care. He considers it a very beautiful thing.

The marathon runner Douglas Romero as well as Carolina Campos and her Aunt Mílvida (who were both hit by the same bullet on Baralt Avenue) also received compensation from the government and currently work in the Miraflores compound. They also became part of ASOVIC and, like many of the other government victims who work at the compound, they give interviews to visiting journalists about their experiences (such as the ones they gave me).

Despite the conflict of interest presented by this situation (could these victims really give unbiased testimony given that their livelihood now depended on the government?), most of them gave surprisingly impartial accounts. At first, they did not want to meet one on one, and they coached each other on the "right" answers. But by returning to Miraflores several times, I gained their trust and many of them eventually opened up, providing information that deviated from the spin the regime had put on events. It quickly became clear to me which of these people had really been there on April 11 and which had not—in part because of the poor testimony they provided, but also by the way the true victims treated them.

Mike Merhi eventually became the most outspoken advocate for the victims from the opposition. At the urging of his friend Gustavo Tovar, he formed VIVE, a nonprofit group seeking justice for human rights violations and the counterpart to the government-backed ASOVIC. Mike has appeared on TV dozens of times; he has gone before the Inter-American Commission on Human Rights and the International Court in The Hague; organized a class-action suit with the families of other victims; and toured Europe, the United States, and parts of the Middle East trying to educate people about what he sees going on in Venezuela.

Since April 11, he has been beaten twice by Chávez supporters and in October 2002 he went on a hunger strike in a prominent Caracas park to protest the government's impunity. The protest gained national and international press. In a tactic that has become common when the Chávez regime wants to disrupt opposition protests, a group of Bolivarian Circle members came out to do a counterprotest against Mike. Then the National Guard, ostensibly to quell imminent violence, filled the area with tear gas, forcing everyone to disperse. One overzealous National Guardsman was filmed walking up to Mike's small igloo tent and shooting a tear gas canister straight into it. Fortunately, Mike had already fled.

In the course of Mike's independent investigations into April 11, he has watched all the available news footage over and over again and sorted through thousands upon thousands of photographs. By analyzing the evidence, he and the VIVE lawyers have identified sixty gunmen, four of whom are National Guardsmen. Of the sixty, he has matched the photo and an ID number to thirty-two of them, including the Guardsmen.

He is convinced that what happened on Baralt Avenue was a premeditated ambush designed to kill marchers and teach the opposition a lesson. Why did the National Guard block all the routes to the palace except Baralt Avenue? Why did they block only the side streets on Baralt, so that the march was funneled toward the Llaguno Overpass? Why did they let the Bolivarian Circles—who they knew were armed—stop the march here? Why didn't Chávez bring in more National Guard troops to repel the march with tear gas, as they did on the New Republic Viaduct?

Among the huge mounds of evidence Mike has collected, he has found pictures of Jesús after he was shot. He is lying in the street while a paramedic tries to help him. In the photo he can see Jésus's black Nike T-shirt and the cheap whistle he had around his neck as well as the braided surfer's necklace he always wore. There is a blood stain on his forehead and blood in his right ear. He is still alive. His eyes are slit open, and his arms are up around his head as if he has just run a long race and is trying to catch his breath.

It was not until three days after the violence, on Sunday afternoon, April 14, that the blond architect Malvina Pesate learned that she had been shot. She was still in the hospital when she overheard her family talking about a bullet. Her jaw was wired shut and she had to gesticulate with her hands. What? What are you talking about?

"Ah, well, we didn't tell you," her mother said. "You weren't hit with a rock . . . what happened was you were hit in the face with a bullet."

Malvina's eyes widened. "But don't worry," they said. "The wound is clean; there's nothing in there. You are going to be fine."

Two days later she was resting better in her brother's house, even though she was still taking a lot of medication and was perpetually dizzy. Then, in the early afternoon, she heard an eruption of screams and cries of amazement coming from the living room. She got up to investigate and found her whole family glued to the TV. When they saw Malvina come in, they all turned to her with frightened looks on their faces. "*Que pasa?*" she mumbled.

"It's that you're on TV," they said. Someone helped her sit, and she saw that the ultra-*chavista* deputy, Juan Barreto, was testifying before the National Assembly. He was showing an amateur video of Malvina being shot and was saying that the bullet had hit her from behind. She had *not* been shot by the Bolivarian Circles, he said, but by her own people. He also said that, regrettably, Malvina was dead.

They replayed the video several times, and it was simply incredible to watch: Malvina had her back to the camera, facing up Baralt Avenue, and the photographer Jorge Tortoza had just collapsed in the middle of the street in front of her. Malvina rose up on her tiptoes and put one hand to her forehead, shading her eyes to look for Gorka. Then she suddenly dropped like a puppet whose strings have been cut: She sort of cringed as she fell backward, both her hands coming up to her face. Very clearly you could see the hair at the base of her neck fly up as the bullet came out the back of her neck.

Not five minutes passed before the phone rang. It was Julio Borges, a National Assembly deputy from Primero Justicia—Malvina's party. Borges knew that Malvina was alive and wanted to know what the forensic report had said, namely, that the entrance wound in her cheek was small (a little under five millimeters) and the exit wound in the back of her neck was larger (almost two centimeters). Later, just after two in the afternoon, Malvina's brother-in-law turned on the TV again just as Borges was taking the podium in the National Assembly. Borges said that he was very sorry to inform Deputy Barreto, but Malvina was alive and well and that she had *not* been shot from behind—no, the bullet had come from the Chávez side of the skirmish. Malvina liked that Borges had stood up for her and she felt a sense of vindication against Barreto and the *chavistas* for trying to twist the truth in their favor.

Malvina would remember that was the day when she became famous. Now all the reporters in the country seemed to be scrambling to talk to her. There was all this controversy about the entrance wound, the exit wound. Her brother told her that the hospital was full of reporters looking for her. She and Gorka began to be invited to TV interviews and talk shows.

In the end, Malvina's recovery was almost complete; the only long-term effect was that the bullet had cut three nerves in her face leaving the inside of her mouth on the left side without feeling. Today, one has to look very closely to see the tiny scar on her cheek.

Eventually, Malvina and Gorka joined Mike Merhi's group, VIVE. She and Gorka kept going to every march. Malvina thinks it is sad that no one in the government will investigate what happened to her and the other victims from the opposition. They have to go to the international courts to find justice because there is no one representing them in their own country.

In August 2004, just before Chávez's presidential referendum, Malvina and Gorka were married. Their courtship had lasted nineteen years. Spurred on by the wake-up call of Malvina's brush with death, Gorka finally popped the question. When the engagement was announced, most of their friends responded the same way: kissing and congratulating Malvina, then turning to Gorka and saying, "*Coño!* It's about time!"

However, Malvina's long-standing condition that Gorka propose to her on top of one of the massive *tepui* plateaus in the jungle was not fulfilled. Malvina always insisted that Gorka still owed her that helicopter ride.

Tragically, in 2006, Gorka had a heart attack and died. He was fifty-nine years old.

The film that Luis Fernández had taken of the gunmen on the Llaguno Overpass remained very controversial. As the most vivid evidence of the pro-Chávez gunmen, it was a huge liability for Chávez, and his government tried to discredit it any way it could. First, it went after Luis directly.

Just before President Chávez was returned to power, on the night of April 13, Luis got a death threat. A group called M-28, with ties to Central University (Universidad Central de Venezuela) and the government called him while he was sleeping. They said they were going to kill him and his family.

Luis immediately called a friend who worked at the university to see if the group was real. It was. In fact, one of the gunmen on the Llaguno Overpass, Fausto Castillo, was a member of this group. Luis called Venevisión. That was when he found out that Chávez had returned. Luis fled to his aunt's house with his family—his mother, two sisters, and his niece. While he was there, the DISIP—now once again under Chávez's control—came and searched his apartment. His neighbors came out of their homes and did a *cacerolazo* with their pots and pans until the officers left.

Luis continued in hiding for a few more days while he tried to get help from the Organization of American States. The death threats continued. The calls rarely had caller ID and could not be traced. When Luis went to the phone company to ask about this, they explained that only certain government offices—particularly the DISIP—had these phone lines. Soon the threats became so intense and specific—the callers were identifying his sisters and his niece by name—that Luis decided that he and his family had to go into hiding. For two months they lived in the Gran Sabana, deep in Venezuela's interior.

When he and his family returned to Caracas, the death threats continued, but they became oddly routine. However, the pressure and fear were always there in the back of his mind. He found he couldn't work in pro-Chávez neighborhoods, he was heckled and spit on. Then, one day in December 2002, he was covering a PDVSA protest and trying to interview a National Guardsman when he was beaten by other soldiers and shot in the leg with polyurethane shot from a shotgun.

Publicly, President Chávez and his spokespeople declared that Luis's April 11 video was a fraud, a work of special effects artists fabricated in a laboratory. Venevisión, Chávez said, had contacts in Hollywood who had made the video in a studio.

Yet, seemingly unaware of the contradiction, the government also praised the gunmen as brave defenders of the revolution. "The truth is that these four [*sic*] compatriots with their short-range weapons had the courage to stand up to snipers and terrorists dressed as policemen firing with their military weapons upon thousands of defenseless compatriots. To them [I wish all] the honor they deserve and the acknowledgment of our people," Chávez said.

Some of the gunmen were given medals, and a monument was erected on the Llaguno Overpass in their honor. One gunman, Richard Peñalver, was widely lauded as a hero and eventually ran for mayor in the Caracas municipality of Libertador. Another gunman, Rafael Cabrices—the man who had confessed and pleaded for God's forgiveness when he was arrested on April 12—became the leader of one of the large armed militia units that Chávez openly funded.

The documentary film *The Revolution Will Not Be Televised,* made by the Irish filmmakers Kim Bartley and Donnacha O'Briain caught in Miraflores on April 11, also tried to discredit Luis's video. The film posited two rather contradictory claims about the Llaguno Overpass shootings. First, that the gunmen were obviously ducking and hiding to avoid incoming gunfire, so were shooting in self-defense. Second, that Baralt Avenue was in fact empty because the march had not come this way at all. To "prove" this, the film juxtaposes Luis Fernández's footage with a shot from an amateur film taken very late in the afternoon, when the fight was almost over, which showed a mostly deserted Baralt Avenue. "What the networks didn't show was this shot in which it is clearly shown that the street below was empty," the documentary's voice-over says. "The opposition march had not taken this route. They used the images of the people shooting to say that the *chavistas* had shot at the demonstrators and with that manipulation Chávez was blamed for the deaths." The only problem for the filmmakers was that even at this late hour the street wasn't quite empty—so the filmmakers put a black bar at the top of the frame to hide the Metropolitan Police trucks that were still there. This was only one of the many manipulations in *The Revolution Will Not Be Televised.* Phil Gunson, a writer for the *Economist,* wrote that "a close analysis of the film reveals something worse than political naiveté. Constructing a false picture of a classic military coup devised by an allegedly corrupt and racist oligarchy, [Bartley and O'Briain] omit key facts, invent others, twist the sequence of events to support their case, and replace inconvenient images with others dredged from archives." A blow-by-blow of the film's manipulations was done in another documentary called *X-ray of a Lie* (Radiografía de una Mentira) by Wolfgang Schalk and Thaelman Urgelles.

The next step in Luis Fernández's long ordeal was the trial of the Llaguno Overpass shooters in April 2003. Despite the overwhelming evidence against the gunmen, only four of the dozens who were identified were tried and they received only minor weapons charges and were set free. Here the Chávez administration was finally reaping the dividends from its ideological restructuring of the justice system. The case for the defense rested on two arguments: First, that the gunmen were firing in self-defense, and second, that the victims were out of range. The first argument played into the government's position that the skirmish on April

11 was an equal match between armed extremists that had resulted in deaths on both sides. The second key to the defense's case was that the bullets fired from the bridge could not have produced the wounds suffered because from that distance (between two hundred and three hundred yards) the bullets, mostly 9-mm handgun rounds, would lose stability and force at about two hundred yards. While one hundred to two hundred yards is technically considered the "effective range" of most handguns, their "terminal range" is far beyond that. Put enough rounds into the air at a target as far away as eight hundred to one thousand yards and you will eventually hit it and do damage. This, however, does not paint the whole picture because there were many shooters *below* the bridge who sallied back and forth, often within thirty-five to forty feet of the opposition crowd, which the government refused to acknowledge.

Yet despite the acquittal, the government's smear campaign, and the complicity of the Irish filmmakers, the same month that the gunmen were set free Luis Fernández and his cameraman, Julio Rodríguez, won the King of Spain's Award for Journalism for their footage. It was a prize decided by judges from nine different countries and considered the highest honor in journalism in the Spanish-speaking world. But even with this official validation, the government did not back off. In fact, it renewed its campaign with extra vigor: the death threats became particularly nasty and the pro-government press did everything imaginable to discredit him.

Luis has gone to the Justice Department and the Office of the Defender of the People many times, but they have been either unwilling or unable to help him. To this day he receives death threats, but has become more accustomed to them, or at least resigned.

The only people who were ever punished in connection with April 11 were the Metropolitan Police. They became the scapegoat for the Chávez government and were blamed for the violence in El Silencio. According to the government, they were helping the march reach Miraflores. As Guillermo García Ponce wrote in his book *The Coup d'État of April 11*, "The lightly armored vehicles of the Metropolitan Police, called the whale and the rhinoceros, were sent as the vanguard to attack the people congregated near

Miraflores. Their mission was to disperse the multitude and in this way open a passage for the assault against the Palace. They served as the 'point of the lance.' It was a macabre and premeditated plan." If this had been the plan, it would have been easy for the Metropolitan Police to execute it. They had the men and the firepower to overpower the pro-Chávez gunmen and the National Guard if they had wanted to. The truth of the matter is that the armored trucks were moved up Baralt Avenue to create a buffer between the two groups; after that, they proceeded no farther. Once this was done, the number of casualties suffered by the marchers dropped off dramatically.

Eight Metropolitan Police officers were detained for "conspiring with the opposition." I met with these officers, who were being held at police headquarters. They seemed to have been picked completely at random and most of them said they hadn't even been in El Silencio on April 11. They were eventually moved to a proper prison, where they sit today. Even though it has been more than seven years since they were arrested, they have never been tried.

In addition to these eight officers, three police commissioners—Henry Vivas, Iván Simonovis, and Lázaro Forero—were also arrested on trumped-up charges. They have now been in jail for four years without a court ruling.

Why did Chávez feel the need to go after the Metropolitan Police? Chávez had been very paranoid about the organization long before the coup because, outside the army, they were the largest armed group in the country, and he feared they might start a coup d'état. After April 11, he cleverly used the claims that the police had fired first at the Bolivarian Circles as an excuse to commandeer most of their weapons and gear—riot shields, rifles, MP5 submachine guns, rubber bullets, and tear gas—everything save their .38-caliber sidearms. While this often left the police outgunned by criminals, it also meant they no longer posed a threat to Chávez. When Mayor Alfredo Peña was replaced by Chávez loyalist Juan Barreto in 2004, the Metropolitan Police were completely politicized—party loyalty being more important than expertise and experience. Many people cite the changes to the Metropolitan Police as a major factor in the soaring homicide rate in Caracas. Since Chávez took office, Venezuela's homicide rate has increased by 67 percent, with Caracas being the most violent city. (It should be noted that while Peña was mayor, the homicide rate actually fell.)

On January 22, 2008, Chávez (using the power to rule by decree given to him by the Chávez-dominated National Assembly) officially made the Metropolitan Police part of Venezuela's executive branch by incorporating them into the Ministry of Interior and Justice.

As with his own coup attempt ten years earlier, fate favored Hugo Chávez, and the coup invigorated his presidency. Upon his return all the masks were off—he knew exactly who was with him and who was against him. He subsequently purged the government and the military of all those who had shown disloyalty, helping him tremendously in consolidating his power. Aided by Carmona's blunders, Chávez artfully painted himself as the victim of a right-wing conspiracy led by wealthy businessmen and fascist generals who were willing to set up a dictatorship in order to plunder Venezuela's oil wealth. Even though Carmona's clique represented only a small faction of the opposition, Chávez made him into the poster boy for the entire movement. The lack of reporting by the media on April 13, along with the accusation of U.S. complicity in the coup, further bolstered Chávez's image as an underdog fighting against the establishment. Even though this misrepresented the facts in many ways, it was a scenario so familiar in Latin American history—from the fall of Salvador Allende in Chile to the ousting of Jacabo Arbenz in Guatemala—that it was easily digested by the international news media and helped win Chávez new support overseas.

What's more, the religious parallels of a fallen leader who miraculously returns from the (political) grave after a short exile were not lost on Chávez and he was quick to use them to bolster his aura as a messiah figure. Chávez's dismal approval ratings quickly rebounded. In fact, the coup was so beneficial to Chávez that rumors would circulate that it was an *autogolpe* ("auto-coup"), that Chávez had intentionally orchestrated the whole thing.

While it is true that Chávez was ready for a limited coup led by Admiral Héctor Ramírez Pérez, he was not prepared for the spiraling chain of chaos that occurred on April 11. An anarchic concatenation of events precipitated by the march, the violence, and the dissension of his three top Generals—Rincón, Rosendo, and Vásquez Velasco. What's more, the video taken of Chávez in captivity at the Turiamo Naval Base dispels any credibility to the auto-coup theory, as it clearly shows a man aware of his vulnerability, a man who understands that he is a liability to any incoming regime, a man likely to be disposed of in the most belligerent way.

The one arena in which Chávez lost ground after April 11 was the Supreme Court. Although Chávez had appointed all of the justices, the court split when Luis Miquilena—Chávez's political mentor—officially defected on the evening of April 11. This left ten *chavista* justices and ten *miquilenista* justices with one justice sitting on the fence. On August 14, 2002, the high court declared that there was insufficient evidence to prosecute many of the accused, including General Vásquez Velasco and Admiral Héctor Ramírez Pérez. The court also said that the events of April 11–14 were not a coup but a "power vacuum" precipitated by the executive branch. "Once the announcement was made by [General Lucas Rincón] that the president and the military high command had resigned, the whole country had the obligation and the right to believe . . . that there was a crisis in the executive branch given the absence of a president." The ruling put into serious question the president's claim that he was a victim of a well-planned conspiracy.

Chávez did not restore his control over the Supreme Court until December 2004, when he packed the court with twelve more justices. Overturning the court's previous rulings was one of the reformed court's first actions. It was a blatant case of double jeopardy, but with the president's uncontested control of the courts, no one could stop him. As a consequence, many of the generals fled the country or went into hiding.

General Manuel Rosendo was among those who were eventually forced to flee.

A month after the coup, between May 2 and May 15, 2002, the National Assembly interviewed twenty-two witnesses as a preliminary truth commission to investigate the coup. Interim President Carmona, Defense Minister Rangel, Bolivarian Circle leader Freddy Bernal, and Vice President Diosdado Cabello were among the star witnesses.

The proceedings were a political circus and shed little light on what had really happened. Day after day the witnesses vociferously proclaimed their unwavering allegiance to Venezuela, democracy, and the constitution without actually answering any questions. Frustrated by the complete absence of any illuminating information, the National Assembly deputies began to rail at the witnesses in vicious cross-examination—pro-Chávez deputies attacked anti-Chávez witnesses and vice versa. For the people of Venezuela watching the proceedings, it did little to bolster their faith in their political leadership.

When General Rosendo took the stand on May 10, everyone expected more of the same—political dodging and doublespeak. But to everyone's surprise—particularly in the opposition—Rosendo gave a detailed and nonpartisan account of everything that had happened. "I was under oath," he later said, "and in front of a commission out to find the truth. I had to tell the truth." He gave the tribunal an amazing chronological report of the inner workings of the Chávez regime. Rosendo told about his conflicts with Defense Minister Rangel and the report he had received from his personal assistant that Rangel and Bernal had ordered the Bolivarian Circles to attack the march; he confirmed that Chávez had initially agreed to resign (something that Chávez now vehemently denied); and he even submitted the letters he had written to the president warning him that if he tried to implement Plan Avila, the military would likely revolt.

Four days after giving his testimony Rosendo received a dishonorable discharge from the military for revealing information that compromised the nation. He was also dismissed as an adviser to the truth commission. It was a hard blow for Rosendo. He tried to appeal the discharge but was not allowed. "They violated all my rights," he told me. "It says a lot about a government that is itself full of outrages and abuses, that they would dishonorably discharge an officer after thirty-two years of irreproachable service for telling the truth under oath in front of a commission that is seeking the truth."

Unfortunately, these preliminary interviews were all that became of the truth commission. The predominantly pro-Chávez National Assembly never investigated any further, in part because the hearings were hurting Chávez and his party. So the truth commission was suspended, never to be restarted, suggesting, very bluntly, that Chávez and his allies in the National Assembly preferred that the truth not be known.

Meanwhile, Rosendo quickly became persona non grata in the eyes of the Chávez regime. As time passed, he was increasingly labeled the principal traitor by the administration. In the fall of 2002, the DISIP came to arrest him, but the general's neighbors encircled his house and wouldn't let them through. The government eventually abandoned its case against him . . . at least for a while.

By 2003 Rosendo was a member of the opposition and was active in the *firmazo*—the two signature drives that launched the presidential recall referendum against Chavez in 2004. But when Chávez packed the Supreme Court and overturned the generals' amnesty, Rosendo was forced into hiding, where he remains to this day.

<hr>

Many of the coup's minor characters were also persecuted by the government, even people who had only the most tenuous connection to events. General Rosendo's personal assistant, Captain O'Bryan, was prosecuted because he testified that he had heard Defense Minister Rangel give orders to Freddy Bernal that the Bolivarian Circles should attack the march. O'Bryan refused to retract his testimony and was court-martialed.

Otto Gebauer, the military policeman who received Chávez's army boots as a gift for taking good care of him, was charged with "insubordination and for participating in the illegal arrest of the president." He is currently serving a twelve-year prison term. Chávez suspected that the men who flew him to Turiamo had been sent to assassinate him. However, public opinion in the opposition is that Gebauer is serving time merely because he was one of the few people to see Chávez cry.

Local mayor Henrique Capriles, the man who helped stop the mob from sacking the Cuban embassy on April 12, was prosecuted for leading the siege. The charge was bogus, but by incarcerating Capriles, Chávez could more easily consolidate his control over the Caracas municipalities.

Another noteworthy casualty of April 11 was the *cacerolazo*—the casserole strike—which was later outlawed by the government.

Interim President Pedro Carmona remained under house arrest in Caracas after the coup until, one night, he fled to the Colombian embassy and requested asylum. He now lives in exile in Bogotá where he teaches classes at a local university and is working on his Ph.D. in economics. He shuns reporters and tries to keep a low profile. He remains adamant that General Rincón's announcement of Chávez's resignation constituted a power vacuum necessitating a new government. As for the collapse of the transitional government, he feels that the military leaders were responsible, especially Vásquez Velasco. After all, the military called him on the morning of April 12 and requested that he help them create a transitional government. He hadn't gone looking for the job. And it was their vacillating and indecision that made a proper transition impossible.

Chávez continues to try to extradite Carmona back to Venezuela to stand trial. With typical Chávez flair, the president often refers to Carmona as *Pedro el Breve,* or "Peter the Brief."

The millionaire Rambo Isaac Pérez Recao boarded the family's private helicopter on April 13 and flew to Aruba. Shortly thereafter he moved to his family's $2.4-million home in Key Biscayne, outside of Miami.

For all his meddling, Isaac Pérez Recao's true goal was never to use Carmona as a puppet and rule Venezuela, but merely to place his friends in control of the DISIP and the Casa Militar so that he could conduct his martial arts training and war games with impunity.

Opposition leader and head of the Venezuelan Workers Union (CTV), Carlos Ortega, was not lucky enough to get away. He continued the fight against Chávez and was one of the principal organizers of the three-month national strike that started in December 2002 that devastated the economy and nearly toppled Chávez again. After the strike, he and the other strike leaders were indicted for civil rebellion and treason by *chavista* judge Danilo Anderson (a man who was an environmental lawyer by training and had lamely prosecuted the Llaguno Overpass gunmen). Ortega went into hiding for more than a year before he was arrested at a casino. He was tried, convicted, and was serving a sixteen-year sentence when he and three convicted military officers escaped from the Ramo Verde military prison near Caracas in August 2006. It is believed the jailbreak was assisted by opposition sympathizers in the military. By September 2007 he had been granted political asylum in Peru.

—∞∞∞—

While the generals who showed disloyalty to Chávez were summarily discharged, jailed, or persecuted, those who remained loyal were rewarded.

1. Defense Minister José Vicente Rangel was made vice president of Venezuela until his retirement in 2007.

2. Vice Admiral Carrero Cubero was promoted to the head of CUFAN (General Rosendo's old job), and later became the ambassador to Germany. Recall that he had been with Rosendo in Miraflores on April 11 and had also tendered his resignation because he had overheard Rangel order the Bolivarian Circles to attack. However, he decided not to resign; he stayed quiet and didn't testify before the National Assembly.

3. General Carneiro, the man who tried to implement Plan Avila but was stopped by General Vásquez Velasco, was later promoted to minister of defense, then made the head of the army (Vásquez Velasco's old job), and later became the minister for People Participation and Social Development.

4. General Gutiérrez, who was in command of the brigade of National Guard troops who helped repel the march around Miraflores, was made head of the entire National Guard.

5. General Rincón, even though he refused to implement Plan Avila (just like General Rosendo) and announced Chávez's resignation to the public, remained one of the president's most trusted advisers. For a time he was slightly demoted from inspector general of the armed forces to minister of the interior and justice (where he did not control troops), but after re-proving his loyalty was promoted to minister of defense. He is currently the Venezuelan ambassador to

Portugal. Just after Hugo Chávez's helicopter arrived back in Miraflores in the early hours of April 14, a reporter shouted to Rincón, asking him why he had announced the resignation in the first place. "Tactics," Rincón shouted back to her, "tactics."

⌖

General Raúl Baduel, the Taoist leader of Maracay's elite paratroopers who led the mission to rescue Chávez on April 13, was eventually made the minister of defense.

Yet even though Baduel was one of the four original members of Chávez's revolutionary movement, he, too, would eventually denounce his friend and defect to the opposition. In December 2007, there was a nationwide referendum on a package of sixty-nine constitutional amendments. The reforms were heavily backed by Chávez as they would have greatly increased his power, ending term limits and allowing him to be reelected indefinitely. They would have also given the executive complete control over the Central Bank. Baduel, who had recently retired, fought the changes, saying that the government was "attempting to usurp the constitutional powers of the Venezuelan people." "Don't let them cheat you," he told the public. He even wrote an op-ed for the *New York Times* titled, "Why I Parted Ways with Chávez." He wrote, "Venezuelan society faces a broad array of problems that have not been addressed in the eight years Mr. Chávez has been in office, even though the present Constitution offers ample room for any decent, honest government to do so." In addition to criticizing Chávez, Baduel laid blame on the entire electorate for the country's ills: "Venezuelans, from every social stratum, are responsible for the institutional decay that we are witnessing. The elite never understood—and still fail to understand—the need to include, in every sense, the millions who have been kept at the margins of the decision-making process because of their poverty. At the same time, President Chávez led the poor to believe that they are finally being included in a governmental model that will reduce poverty and inequality. In reality, the very opposite is true."

⌖

Guillermo García Ponce, the communist hard-liner who helped organize the resistance to Carmona, remained loyal to Chávez. He continued in his job as a member of the Tactical Command for the Revolution and in 2003 became the editor of the new newspaper *VEA*, which is the mouthpiece of the Bolivarian Revolution.

⸻

The photographer Gabriel Osorio, who had become a *chavista* on the night Chávez returned to Miraflores, was working at the Supreme Court on the day it ruled that there had been no coup, only a power vacuum. The decision sparked joyous celebrations from the opposition and violent protests from the *chavistas*. As Gabriel was leaving the court he was surrounded by a group of *chavistas*, some with T-shirts wrapped over their faces, others with sticks and stones in their hands. They demanded to know whom he worked for. He told them the truth (which he quickly regretted) and showed them his ID card.

The leader of the group shouted, "We have a CIA agent here! The CIA is conspiring against the revolution!" Gabriel couldn't believe it, how did being a photographer for *El Nacional* make him a CIA agent? But they were on him. All at once. They went after his face and head. He did his best to fight back, but despite being over six feet tall and weighing over two hundred pounds they were too much for him. While he fended off a few of them, others pushed him to the ground from behind. Once on the pavement they kicked him relentlessly. His back, his face, his groin. He curled up as best he could to protect himself, fetal position, with his hands around his head. He had to concentrate to keep his eyes open because they reflexively closed each time he was struck. It was hard to breath, too . . . his lungs seemed to be contracting from fear. Then one of them began stomping on him with both feet—jumping up and down on top of him. This was the coup de grâce. After that they left him alone.

As they ran off he recognized his camera bag strapped across the back of one of them. They had taken it as a souvenir.

After that Gabriel became an odd sort of "hero" for the opposition. The beating was widely publicized and he became another poster boy for the outrages of the Chávez regime. People even asked for his autograph. For

Gabriel it laid bare how polarized Venezuela had become and the absurdity of both sides. One side, in a fury of paranoia and resentment, had beaten, kicked, and bludgeoned him—they were ready to kill him. The other side kissed and hugged him, wrote eulogies about him, and called him their hero. Venezuela had become a strange fantasyland. In the end Gabriel was repulsed by both sides. He did not want to be a *chavista* or an *escuálido*.

Despite the fact that he had resigned as the finance minister in Miraflores on April 11, General Francisco Usón kept working throughout the crisis in order to keep the government solvent. However, on the Wednesday following the coup, April 17, he was "refired" by Vice President Diosdado Cabello. Usón took it as a snub that Chávez did not contact him personally. It was the end of their friendship. Usón suspected that even though he had helped Chávez as best he could that night in Fort Tiuna, the president considered his resignation a betrayal.

Usón at first had high hopes that Chávez was going to learn from his mistakes and take the country in a new direction. The president's declaration in the early hours of April 14 when he arrived back at the palace promised as much—a new start and plans to heal the fissures between the government and the opposition. Usón saw it as Chávez's golden opportunity, but within days he realized it was just more rhetoric.

Like Rosendo, Usón eventually became an outspoken but moderate member of the opposition. He was also active in the *firmazo* signature drive to remove Chávez.

But in March 2004, eight soldiers were placed in a cell and tortured with a flamethrower at the Fort Mara military base for signing the *firmazo* (in the military under Chávez, not supporting the president was unacceptable). Two of the soldiers died from burns and a third, who was pursuing a case against the government, subsequently drowned in the presence of his commanding officer in a suspicious training accident. In an interview General Usón merely explained how a flamethrower worked. Even though he was retired, Usón was arrested on charges of "insult and injury" against the military and on October 13 a military court sentenced him to five and a half years in prison. He was released in January 2008.

No one was ever charged in the killing or wounding of the soldiers.

When I spoke with General Usón in December 2003, he described Chávez as a scorpion—that by his nature he was militant and aggressive and could never change. Usón told me the fable of the frog and the scorpion: The scorpion says to the frog, "Let's cross the river. Let me ride on your back, and when we get to other side I can protect you." So the frog lets the scorpion onto his back, and when they are halfway across the river, the scorpion stings the frog. "What have you done?" cries the frog. "Now I am going to die and you will die with me." To this the scorpion simply shrugs and says, "It's my nature."

2 | U.S. Involvement

Was the United States involved in the April 11 coup? Had the White House been pushing for regime change? Had U.S. officials been plotting with the dissident generals to oust Chávez? Was this, as García Ponce and many in Miraflores believed, a black operation of the U.S. Central Intelligence Agency?

Many believed that it was, and many more were convinced in December 2004, when Eva Grolinger, a New York attorney with close ties to Chávez, posted documents on the pro-Chávez Web site www.venezuelafoia.info showing that the CIA knew of a coup plot before April 11. The CIA senior intelligence executive brief dated April 6, 2002, stated: "Disgruntled senior [Venezuelan] officers and a group of radical junior officers are stepping up efforts to organize a coup against President Chávez, possibly as early as this month." The fact that the CIA had predicted the coup gained wide media attention and was confirmed by the *New York Times*. While the documents did not show direct U.S. involvement, Chávez immediately charged the United States with backing the coup. He also claimed that the U.S. failed to notify him of the threat, an allegation the State Department says is not true.

Given America's record of sponsoring coups in Latin America, the charge of U.S. involvement was not the least bit shocking to many. But the facts make this extremely unlikely. If the United States had been involved, how does one explain that the primary leader of the "rebellion," General Vásquez Velasco, was the same man who both arrested Chávez on April 11 and, two days later, paved the way for his return by acquiescing to his vice president, Diosdado Cabello—hardly the actions of someone being manipulated by the United States and out to purge the country of *chavismo*. And if the U.S. State Department was conspiring against Chávez, would they install a young, inexperienced ambassador a few weeks before a coup?

Although history may prove me wrong, at the time of this writing, I have found no conclusive evidence that the United States was directly involved in the coup. Still, even if the United States was not *directly* involved in the events of April 11–13, the next question becomes whether it was *indirectly* involved. The answer is yes . . . and no.

The rise of Hugo Chávez posed a very difficult problem for the United States, especially for the U.S. officials in the embassy and the *tres letras*—CIA, FBI, DEA. Chávez was something new for many of them. Here was a host government that was not merely resistant to dialogue but was openly hostile to the United States.

To its credit, the U.S. embassy made many attempts to foster better relations with Chávez, pushing new initiatives in bilateral investment, counternarcotics, and taxation treaties. But the Chávez regime continually rebuffed their overtures. Given this closed door, many U.S. officials—people who were employed to gather information about what was going on in Venezuela—turned to the next best source: the opposition. The opposition, after all, was predominantly pro-American and probusiness and, accordingly, a lot easier to talk to. Another plus: Many Venezuelan military officers had worked with U.S. counterparts in the past, and many had even been to the United States for training and were sympathetic to the U.S. point of view.

What's more, Chávez's intractability and anti-U.S. rhetoric were having a personal impact on U.S. officials. Despite their best efforts to remain professional, Chávez was getting under their skin and the culture within the embassy was becoming increasingly anti-Chávez, further fueling a bias in favor of the opposition.

Interesting enough, the embassy itself was aware of its problematic proximity to the opposition. Long before April 11, the embassy was already trying to protect its image, fully aware of how it might look if it was in contact with rebellious officers who happened to take power. In November 2001, then U.S. Ambassador Donna Hrinak told the embassy's military attaché to cease and desist in all meetings with dissident military officers. In other words, a full four months before the coup, the rumor mill was so full of coup conspiracies and the number of dissident officers had become so large and U.S.–Venezuelan relations had become so poor that the ambassador did not want to take any chances of the United States getting intermingled in a potential revolt. As for why embassy officials were meeting with opposition leaders in the first place, one State Department official responded matter-of-factly, "Of course, we were in contact with them. That's our job. That's what an embassy does. It collects information on what is going on in the country so that our government can make good decisions. Venezuela is a very divided country. It would be irresponsible of us to only be in touch with the government."

A closer look at the interaction between the U.S. government and Venezuelan officials before the coup illustrates how each side was reading (and misreading) the other. In November 2001, Pedro Carmona went to Washington, D.C., as part of a delegation that was trying to get the United States to give Venezuela the same preferential trade status it gave other Andean countries. The delegation met with many senior officials, including John Maisto (former U.S. ambassador to Venezuela and then national security aide for Latin America), Spencer Abraham (energy secretary), and Otto Reich (the devoutly anti-Castro Cuban-American who was then the head of the State Department's Western Hemisphere affairs division and had also been ambassador to Venezuela). Ultimately Carmona's delegation was rebuffed by the Americans and they were told that a special trade agreement with the United States was impossible. Carmona later commented that the U.S. officials "were very angry at Chávez, really tired of him." Although there is no evidence of any nefarious plotting, there was still a message conveyed: Venezuela (and its trade) would be better off without Chávez.

Leading up to the coup, still more events helped to embolden the opposition. During U.S. congressional hearings on February 5 and 6, 2002, the then-secretary of state, Colin Powell, and CIA director George Tenet expressed concern about Venezuela and questioned Chávez's commitment to democracy. Even though the remarks were a small part of a general overview of global security, many Chávez supporters, including Guillermo García Ponce, viewed the statements as a green light from the United States to the opposition—a coded message aimed directly at the disgruntled military leaders—that now was the time to strike. Although there is no evidence of this, these statements, combined with the mounting economic and political opposition to Chávez in Venezuela, further encouraged the opposition and those who wanted to oust Chávez.

On February 8, 2002, the Inter-American Commission on Human Rights (part of the Organization of American States), issued a report that criticized the Chávez administration's crackdown on freedom of expression and urged "greater tolerance."

Meanwhile, events in Venezuela were also giving the opposition more reasons to be bold. A week after the report on freedom of expression, the Chávez administration implemented major changes in fiscal policy—cutting public expenditures by almost 22 percent and depreciating the bolivar by 20 percent. The move caused more public protests as well as an uproar from the banking industry.

The cumulative effect of all of this pressure certainly encouraged the opposition's belief that removing Chávez, perhaps by any means necessary, was welcomed by the United States. The opposition's confidence in U.S. solidarity was best articulated by Admiral Molina immediately after the coup. Under house arrest for working with Carmona (Molina was the short-lived head of the Casa Militar), Molina said in an interview, "We felt we were acting with U.S. support. [Both the United States and the opposition] agree that we can't permit a communist government here. The U.S. has not let us down yet. This fight is still going on because the [Chávez] government is illegal."

To their credit, U.S. officials did go to Chávez to discuss the coup rumors just days before April 11. But, according to newly arrived Ambassador Shapiro, Chávez dismissed them "as if it were no big thing." Chávez's reaction suggests what was likely the truth: The president had far better intelligence than the United States.

In the final analysis, I think we give too much credit to the U.S. government if we believe it masterminded Chávez's short ouster. Rather, both the opposition and the Chávez regime, each for its own reasons, "read into" the U.S.'s actions (or inactions) much more than they should have.

The current U.S. foreign policy supports the conclusion that the United States was not involved: The all-consuming focus on the war on terror has meant a complete lack of U.S. policy toward Venezuela. Accounts from the U.S. embassy in Venezuela show that—despite all the warnings—it, too, was caught off guard when the coup occurred. In fact, there had been so many coup rumors for so long that the embassy had become numb to them. The most interesting example of its lack of preparedness came on April 11 itself, when U.S. ambassador Charles Shapiro; the deputy in charge of mission, Fred Cook; and Political Officer Janelle Hironimus attended a luncheon hosted by opposition billionaire and media magnate Gustavo Cisneros and a group of media and church leaders (including Cardinal Velasco, Archbishop Porras, Caracas mayor Alfredo Peña, and, curiously, Luis Miquilena). The luncheon was held at Cisnero's estate in the Country Club neighborhood of Caracas and was an official welcoming of Shapiro as the new U.S. ambassador. In other words, in the midst of the largest civic protest in the history of Venezuela, the embassy leadership did not find it at all inappropriate to lunch with the principal leaders of the opposition. Upon returning to the embassy, one of the diplomats lamented that the posh luncheon they had been looking forward to for weeks had been ruined by the incessant ringing of cell phones among the opposition leaders, and that many people had left when the march started heading for Miraflores.

Of course, while there is little evidence of U.S. meddling, Washington's initial reaction to the coup was not neutral. The White House was unmistakably pleased with Chávez's apparent resignation, stating that he had brought the crisis on himself through his "undemocratic actions." While the U.S. State Department later pressured Carmona to "undissolve" the National Assembly, bring in an OAS delegation, and hold speedy elections, the White House response is what endured. When Chávez was restored, the Bush administration had to backpedal, scrambling to justify why it had shown initial support for an undemocratic regime change. What little goodwill that still remained between the Bush administration and the Chávez administration evaporated.

3 | Conclusions

While it might be satisfying to think of the crisis of April 11 as a well-orchestrated conspiracy led by a few shadowy figures, the evidence suggests that it was a complex and confusing event that was influenced by dozens of self-serving actors. This was not a coup in the classic sense. There was no armed struggle or military assault against the government. Yes, there *was* a march against the government intended to precipitate some kind of change, though not necessarily a coup. Then things turned violent and Generals Rosendo, Rincón, and Vásquez Velasco all refused to use the military to follow Chávez's orders. What happened next was unprecedented and took almost everyone by surprise, including Chávez. On the night of April 11, Chávez's actions were very telling: He and his administration had no reply to the military's "disowning." Much of his cabinet fled, and most of his military high command resigned. Chávez did not try to appeal to the Venezuelan people or the international community for support. He did not try to fight or undermine the generals who refused to recognize him. He did not go to Televen TV (or any other station) to address the nation. Instead, he turned himself over to the army without a fight. It is clear that he, too, was shocked by what had happened.

However, the events can still be described as a coup because Carmona's dissolution of the democratic powers was a blatant power grab. His actions represented a coup within a popular uprising. Yet the fact that the Carmona regime imploded so quickly also supports the idea that there was no premeditated plan. Just like Chávez, the opposition was also caught off guard, which led to improvisation and a series of mistakes. If they had truly been prepared, the new regime would have surely survived longer than forty-eight hours—especially in light of Chávez's low popularity.

The people who did act with the most discipline during the crisis were the Chávez hard-liners. After Chávez's arrest, loyalists like Guillermo García Ponce worked tirelessly to organize their political machine, deploy the Bolivarian Circles, and disseminate their message to every possible media outlet. They were also quick to exploit the blunders of the new regime. Although Chávez would have likely returned to power even without General Baduel's countercoup, the mobilization helped consolidate popular support against Carmona. Their hard work certainly accelerated Carmona's collapse and ensured that Hugo Chávez—and not a different interim government—took control.

Even though they have been made out to be the covillains in the crisis, the Venezuelan military, in my estimation, should be lauded for its behavior during these three days. By following the letter of the constitution instead of implementing Plan Avila as ordered by President Chávez, many deaths were avoided. The only acts of violence perpetrated by the military during these three days were committed by the National Guard troops who were implementing Chávez's orders around Miraflores on April 11.

The countercoup led separately, but in equal parts, by Generals Vásquez Velasco and Baduel was conducted with cell phones instead of tanks.

Although Vásquez Velasco and the military certainly stumbled by initially supporting Carmona, they eventually found their feet again and followed the constitution. It is worth considering that if this had been a true coup d'état, Vásquez Velasco would never have allowed Carmona (a man he had never met) to lead the transition. Instead, he would have picked a close confidant who would have done his bidding, allowing him to stay in a position of power indefinitely. He could have also killed Chávez while in his custody. Of course, Vásquez Velasco did nothing of the sort. In the end he forced Carmona's resignation and handed power back over to Chávez's party, resulting in the end of his own military career.

For Venezuela, April 11 marked an unfortunate resurgence of political violence. One need only go to the Web sites of nonprofit organizations like Amnesty International, Reporters without Borders, and Human Rights Watch to find long lists of human rights violations perpetrated under the Chávez regime—everything from death threats to journalists (like Luis Fernández), to political persecutions (like that of General Usón), to the untimely deaths of Chávez's opponents (like the deaths of three protestors at a December 2002 rally at the hands of a man who confessed that he had been sent by the government). One cannot fail to notice how the number of incidents increased in the wake of April 11. Indeed, despite the fact that Chávez's ouster on April 11 was caused by violence, the president seems to have only embraced violence and the threat of violence as an effective political tool.

On September 18, 2008, when Human Rights Watch issued a report of more rights violations, Chávez had its authors expelled. Daniel Wilkinson (an American) and Jose Miguiel Vivanco (a Chilean) were arrested by security agents at their hotel in Caracas that very night. The men had their cell phones confiscated when they tried to contact their respective embassies, were driven straight to the airport, and put on a plane to Brazil. As the men were being taken to the airport, the government ran a *cadena* to explain the expulsion. The Venezuelan foreign ministry said that the two men were working for the U.S. government in a "campaign of aggression against Venezuela." Speaking of his expulsion, Daniel Wilkinson perspicaciously observed what many Venezuelans had realized a long time ago, that "the Chávez government is more than willing to violate the country's constitution in pursuit of its own political agenda."

Despite having survived a decade in power—and his pledges to remain there until 2050—Hugo Chávez's future is anything but certain. Today, the most powerful opposition to Chávez is not the conservative right, but the left. The electoral defeat of the Chávez-backed constitutional amendments in December 2007, considered by many to be a major turning point in public sentiment towards Chávez, was largely credited to a group of well-organized college students who rallied both the right and the left. Another powerful foe from the left is the man who ran against Chávez in the 2006 elections, Teodoro Petkoff. Petkoff, you will recall, was one of the communist guerrilla leaders who tunneled out of the San Carlos military prison with Guillermo García Ponce back in 1967. Petkoff eventually made a transition from the Cuban-style socialism of the FALN to the more moderate social democracy espoused by the party he founded— MAS. "Chávez has created a society controlled by fear," Petkoff has said. "A fear of crime, a fear of the police, a fear of property being seized, a fear of corruption."

However, what eventually tips the scales against Chávez may not be the opposition at all, but the economy. As a petro-state, it is a widely accepted axiom that no Venezuelan leader can ever be ousted during an oil boom, and Chávez (from 2003 to 2008) has enjoyed the greatest oil boom in history, a boom that has given him the windfall profits necessary to keep his political machine going. But with the world financial crisis deepening, that axiom no longer applies. With half of the government's revenue coming from oil, the dizzying drop in oil prices (from $147 to below $40) means a corresponding cut in government expenditures. The very social programs that have fueled Chávez's popularity will have to be cut, and that will surely pull down his approval ratings. Corruption will also be harder to conceal. The fact that Chávez has not been able to diversify the economy away from its dependence on oil during his ten years in office will likely cause widespread resentment if the global slowdown lingers. Still, as April 11 proved beyond a doubt, Hugo Chávez is not only blessed with amazing luck, he knows how to survive.

Epilogue

At the age of eighteen, I went to Venezuela as a high school exchange student. It was a critical time for Venezuela. It was the year of the Caracazo—the moment that violently marked the end of the boom years and the beginning of the economic free fall of the 1990s—and I saw many horrific images of violence firsthand. The experience inspired me to study international relations and economics in college. The economics of it was particularly intriguing to me because I had seen how—quite literally overnight—the middle class had been ripped out of Venezuelan society. Savings accounts sucked away, pensions lost, salaries cut by over 60 percent. I remember very clearly how my host father, a professor of law at the state university, walked to work for three months because he could not afford a fifty-dollar battery for his car.

Almost every year since then I have returned to Venezuela to visit my friends and host family. These frequent trips—usually for just a few weeks—gave me a year-by-year snapshot of Venezuela's socioeconomic decline throughout the 1990s. Seeing this steady disintegration, the fleecing of oil money by politicians, the surge in crime that had directly scarred everyone I knew, and the rampant poverty convinced me that a radical change was necessary. Like marathon runner Douglas Romero, Hugo Chávez's call for a revolution seemed completely appropriate to me. In fact, it seemed that nothing less could turn the country around.

So when I returned to Venezuela in September 2002, six months after April 11, I was a devout *chavista*. I had, of course, heard a lot about the coup—how a small clique of business leaders had ousted Chávez. I was particularly appalled that many Venezuelans that I respected applauded the coup and they told me how mortified they had been when Chávez made his miraculous return. I wondered how they could support the ouster of a democratically elected president, especially one who echoed many of my own feelings about many international issues—globalization, the failure of neoliberalism, the war on terror.

My initial goal in 2002 was to write a book that captured the essence of modern Venezuela. Yet, I admit that for the first three months I was unproductive. Uncertain of how to proceed, I began traveling and conducting interviews, hoping that a direction would emerge.

In December 2002 the three-month national strike began, and many people felt that the country was on the brink of outright civil war. The security situation was so poor that I was forced, very begrudgingly, to return to the United States until things settled down; it wasn't until March 2003 that I was allowed to return. It was during that first weekend back that I met and interviewed Mike Merhi in Caracas. The next day, through a different contact, I met and interviewed Malvina Pesate. It was then that I knew what the book would be about: a book that would show the coup—the most tumultuous event of Chávez's rule—through the eyes of the everyday Venezuelans who were there.

Very serendipitously my network of contacts began to expand as each person I spoke to gave me several new names. The fact that I had attended high school in Venezuela almost fifteen years earlier was now paying big dividends as my old friends had split into the pro- and anti-Chávez camps; conveniently, many were now in positions of influence.

The timing was also important. Chávez had not yet packed the Supreme Court, so many important generals, like Rosendo, Usón, and Vásquez Velasco, had not yet been persecuted and were still available to be interviewed.

With so many personal accounts, complemented by books, newspaper articles, and dozens of hours of raw footage, I realized I could give an unprecedented panoramic view of the crisis. That I could really bring the characters and action to life in slow, vivid—and sometimes painful—detail and create a narrative that read like fiction.

From the outset, it was my aim to draw the characters as realistically as possible; to make them human. It was very important to me that English-speaking readers see them as I see them, as real people with ordinary—even mundane—lives free of the standard clichés and stereotypes about Latin Americans. This book was written to tell their stories, the too-often overlooked stories of the people in the street. While most accounts of the coup focus on the politicians and generals, it is important to remember all the other lives that were touched—and often shattered—by the coup, and to remember that what happened on those three sunny days in April still dominates all of their lives. Whether it is the wounds they suffered, the dead nerves, the cauterized scars, or the loss of sons, daughters, husbands, wives, mothers, and fathers, it is completely unforgettable to them. And even if they wanted to forget, they could not. The images of April 11 still play regularly on TV, are on the lips of journalists and writers, and are heard over dinner, beer, and whiskey all over Venezuela. And whether you are *chavista* or *escuálido*, the memories of April 11 almost certainly spark outrage and bitterness as neither side feels that justice has been served. I hope that sharing their stories reminds us of the human cost of political conflict—so that each time we see a headline like "19 Dead and Hundreds Wounded" we know that there is this much complexity and pain behind it. As the African proverb goes, "When two elephants fight, the grass gets trampled."

APPENDIX: THE SNIPER RIDDLE

Were there snipers in El Silencio on April 11? It is a crucial question because the presence of snipers suggests a higher level of premeditation; it suggests that there was indeed a conspiracy at work and that whoever was controlling the snipers planned on violence. The accepted wisdom is that there were snipers. Although none were caught in photographs or on video, there were many eyewitness accounts. But were these snipers working with the opposition to incite mayhem as the government claims? Or were they used by the government to first repress the march and then, later, to actually kill pro-Chávez supporters to give the violence the semblance of a balanced confrontation?

The Chávez government's cover-up and destruction of evidence makes finding solid answers to these questions very difficult. In addition, there is little reliable ballistic evidence and, most importantly, no suspects.

There were three centers of violence near the palace on April 11, and the presence of snipers was alleged in each location.

The first zone was on Baralt Avenue from the National Building to the Llaguno Overpass. Here I do not believe there were snipers; rather, I believe that the confusion of the situation, the low visibility, and the echoes in the streets gave people that impression. Imagine for a moment standing in a thick crowd and suddenly seeing people collapse from bullet wounds, this would likely make you think there were snipers. However, the forensics and photographic evidence suggest that those who were shot in this zone were hit by other people on the street (or the overpass) with handguns. Malvina Pesate, Jorge Tortoza, and Jesús Arellano were all shot at street level. All the Chávez supporters injured or killed around the overpass appear to have been shot by police or friendly fire and/or ricochets.

The second zone was on Eighth Street, where Carlos Ciordia, Nade Makagonov, and Gabriel Osorio all testified to seeing snipers. It is likely that in this zone there were National Guardsmen and members of the honor guard working as snipers in order to turn back the march. It is important to remember that for them, Plan Avila was in effect—these soldiers had been given orders to use deadly force to hold back the march and maintain the security perimeter around the palace.

The third zone, in front of Miraflores, presents the biggest riddle. The government insists that three people were killed here—Luis Alberto Caro, Luis Alfonso Ruíz, and Nelson Zambrano—while several others, including Antonio Návas, were wounded. What is strange is that there was no confrontation in this location, it was hundreds of yards from the other centers of violence on Eighth Street and Baralt Avenue and full of Chávez supporters exclusively. How would snipers out to kill *chavistas* work their way into the heart of the pro-Chávez rally?

What is more likely is that these people were shot in the other zones, then carried to the hospital tents in front of the palace and the government later insisted they were shot here to strengthen its story—that there were "coupsters" instigating violence to spark a coup. Unfortunately, due to the lack of a proper investigation I don't think we will ever know for certain, but given my research, I believe the following:

1. There was possibly one gunman mingling in the pro-Chávez crowd who shot Antonio Návas and Nelson Zambrano and, perhaps, Luis Caro. Whom he or she was aligned with is unclear.
2. The other gunshot victims were likely carried to Miraflores from other centers of conflict in the area.
3. *If* there were snipers in the buildings around the palace, it is more likely that they were acting on orders from the government than from the opposition because all of the surrounding buildings had been seized by the Casa Militar as soon as the government realized the march was on its way. As macabre as it sounds, the government's widespread rhetoric about "spilling blood for the revolution" shows that they were aware of the political capital that could be gained by

having martyrs for the cause and that deaths on their side would bolster their position.

Whatever the truth is, it is clear that the government has shown little interest in tracking down those responsible. No National Guard troops were brought before a court-martial in relation to the violence, even those caught on videotape firing at the march on Eighth Street. And if, as the government claims, the snipers were conspiring with the opposition, why hasn't the government, with the attorney general's office, all its prosecutors, and most of the federal judges at its disposal, attempted to find and prosecute them? Chávez will still mention the snipers when he talks about the coup and blames the Carmona administration for not arresting them, but there is a huge gap between his rhetoric and his interest in bringing them to justice. Several times Chávez has referred to opposition snipers firing from room 411 of the Ausonia Hotel, but I have visited this room, which faces northwest, and there is no angle from which to shoot onto Urdaneta Avenue, where the victims were allegedly hit.

The three people who were arrested by the Casa Militar in the Hotel Ausonia as suspected snipers were quickly released because there was no evidence that they were snipers. While they were found to have guns and some drugs, they failed the forensic test that shows if someone has recently fired a gun. The returning head of the Casa Militar, General José Vietri Vietri, who is a loyal *chavista,* described them as a drunk, a transient, and a hotdog salesman.

For more details on my conclusions about the coup and the snipers, please go to www.brianandrewnelson.com.

ACKNOWLEDGMENTS

Writing about a subject like this, one that incorporates so many different perspectives, meant that I became more of a caretaker of other people's stories than a storyteller myself, so my first acknowledgment is to those who have entrusted me with their personal stories. I have done my best to convey their views as honestly as possible, editing only when necessary to maintain clarity. Many of these people—both pro- and anti-Chávez—have become good friends and have advised and supported me throughout the evolution of this book. Gustavo Tovar, although only a minor character in this book, was very helpful and introduced me to many of the important actors in the coup. Guillermo García Ponce pointed me toward the long history of the socialist movement in Venezuela, a movement that is so crucial to an understanding of Hugo Chávez.

My sincere thanks to all the Venezuelans who were not directly part of this book, yet who saw the importance of the project and enthusiastically supported me during my two years of research: my host family, the Alvarez family, the Rios family, and the Velasco family. Also Hender, Simón, Steve Hege, and José Orozco. A very special thanks to those who helped with the rather tedious process of transcribing hundreds of hours of interviews— Adriana Velasco, Karen and Zimry Rios, Luis Nava, and Alvarito. And to the incredibly resourceful and clever Jaime, who drove me around Caracas week after week and always made sure I had spare batteries for my tape recorder.

Many thanks to all the people who helped get me to Venezuela in the first place, especially Bob Houston, Aurelie Sheehan, Eric Goodman,

Jason Brown, Carla Jablonski, and Karna Walter. Without them, this project would never have begun.

When I began my research, I was, for a time, overwhelmed by the size and complexity of the coup. There was so much conflicting information and so many characters that it seemed an impossible task to make it into a cohesive story. So I was forced to do a great deal of research not just on the coup and Venezuela, but on how to handle this type of cross between narrative nonfiction and investigative reporting. I am indebted to many authors whose work helped light the way—authors ranging from Michael Shaara to Sebastian Junger. The books of Mark Bowden were especially helpful, as he is very skillful in weaving together many different perspectives.

I wrote much of this book after returning from Venezuela, while I was teaching at Miami University, so I must thank all the students and faculty who helped with the manuscript and took a special interest in it—especially Steve Helba, Jen Schuett, Nick Warndorff, Philip Nelson, Jeanne Hey, Ramón Layera, and Herbert Waltzer. I am also indebted to the other Miami faculty members who helped me survive during my time in Oxford, Ohio: Barbara Heuberger, Mary Jane Berman, and John Skillings.

Others who gave advice and feedback as the book developed—James Bowie, Ted Genoways, Zimry Rios, Lisa Sutter, my sisters Diane and Erika, my father, Donald, and my mother, Lois, who, thank God, is a retired technical editor. Also thanks to those who helped me acquire the necessary photographs: Angel Echeverria, Jorge Aguirre (who was murdered while covering an opposition rally in April 2006), Monica Pupu, Luis Bisbal, and Gabriela.

My wife's unwavering belief in me was, without a doubt, the single most important factor in helping me see this project through.

My agent, Jill Marsal, is a treasure. She is persistent and stubborn (in the best possible way) and she worked hard to make sure that this book was made. I am very lucky to have her and indebted to the two men who helped me find her: Ben Reynolds and Madison Smartt Bell. At Nation Books, I thank my editor, Ruth Baldwin, for seeing the importance of the voices of "everyday" Venezuelans and making a strong manuscript into a beautiful book.

Last, I want to express my gratitude to the people who asked not to be named, people who wanted the truth about the coup to be known but knew that to speak out publicly could mean persecution by the government. In fact, several of the people who deserve the most acknowledgment and were pivotal in inspiring me and arranging interviews asked not to be named.

GLOSSARY

ASOVIC—National Association for the Victims of the Coup d'État of April 11, 12, 13, and 14 (Asociacion Nacional de Victimas del Golpe de Estado 11, 12, 13, 14 de Abril). A government-funded group that supports the victims who agree to specific terms and that demonstrate their loyalty to the Chávez regime. It is the government counterpart to VIVE.

Bolívar, Simón—A principal leader of South America's wars of independence from Spain. Bolívar was Venezuelan, born to aristocratic parents, and a brilliant strategist. He is often referred to as the Great Liberator. He founded Grand Colombia, the short-lived nation that split into present-day Ecuador, Colombia, Panama, and Venezuela. Tragically, Bolívar died in exile.

Bolivarian Circles—*Circulos Bolivarianos.* Community groups made up of people who are loyal to Hugo Chávez and support his Bolivarian Revolution. Most Circles are benign and devote their time to community service and spreading information about the revolution. Other Circles are modeled after the Dignity Battalions—the local militias used by General Omar Torríjos and Manuel Noriega in Panama—and receive military and insurgency training, sometimes in Cuba.

cadena—Literally, "chain." A special broadcast by the government that links or "chains" all of the nation's TV and radio stations together so that the government's announcement is the only thing that can be seen or heard.

cacerolazo—Literally, "casserole strike." It is a form of protest in which people take pots and pans out into the street or to their windows and bang them together, usually at a predetermined time. When enough people participate, it is an amazing thing to hear.

Caracazo—The civil uprising of February 1989, when tens of thousands of citizens rioted in response to the implementation of austerity measures by newly elected President Carlos Andrés Pérez. The official death toll will never be known, but between eight hundred and three thousand people lost their lives when President Pérez implemented Plan Avila and the military was called into the streets to quell the riots.

Casa Militar—Literally, "Military House." The detachment of military personnel in charge of the president's security, situated in the White Palace across from Miraflores. The presidential honor guard is part of the Casa Militar.

chamo—Kid; a casual term for a friend or close acquaintance. Usage is similar to *man* or *dude* in English. Feminine: *chama*.

chavismo—The ideology of Hugo Chávez and his Bolivarian Revolution.

chavista—A supporter of President Chávez.

CIPCP—Cuerpo de Investigaciones Penales Científicas y Criminalísticas, a federal investigation agency similar to the U.S. Federal Bureau of Investigation.

coño—An expression of surprise or anger; usage is similar to *damn* in English.

CTV—Confederación Trabajodores de Venezuela. Venezuela's powerful national labor union, headed by opposition leader Carlos Ortega at the time of the coup.

CUFAN—Unified Command of the National Armed Forces (Comando Unificado de las Fuerzas Armadas Nacionales). The organization that controls and coordinates the separate branches of the Venezuelan armed forces. General Manuel Rosendo was the head of CUFAN at the time of the coup.

DISIP—Direction of Intelligence and Prevention Services (Dirección de Servicios de Inteligencia y Prevención).The police force that reports only to the executive; often referred to as the secret police or the political police.

ELN—National Liberation Army (El Ejército de Liberación Nacional). A Columbian guerrilla group that adheres to the Cuban model of socialism.

Enabling Law (*ley habilitante*)—A special right given to the president by the National Assembly that allows him or her to make laws by decree (without further approval from the assembly). In November 2001, the day before the right would have expired, President Chávez pass forty-nine laws that made extensive changes in Venezuelan society. The laws included the very controversial land reform law. It should be noted that a second Enabling Law was enacted in 2007, allowing Chávez to again pass laws by decree. He has since exercised the right many times.

escuálido—Literally, "weak," "pale," or "thin." A term used by Chávez to describe the opposition, meaning to imply that the opposition is a small minority of lazy brats. The term was quickly and proudly embraced by the opposition to describe themselves.

FALN—National Liberation Armed Forces (Fuerzas Armadas de Liberacion Nacional). A leftist guerrilla group that was active in Venezuela in the 1960s and 1970s. Guillermo García Ponce was once a high-ranking member of this group.

FARC—Revolutionary Armed Forces of Colombia (Fuerzas Armadas Revolucionario de Colombia). The largest and most powerful of Colombia's guerrilla groups. The FARC controls large parts of Colombian territory. Leaders of the FARC and President Hugo Chávez formed an alliance while Chávez was in the army in the 1970s and 1980s. When Chávez came to office in 1999, the FARC dramatically increased its operations in Venezuela.

Fedecámaras—Venezuela's very large business guild that includes over three hundred separate chambers of commerce and other associations that represent businesses in production, commerce, and services. Interim President Pedro Carmona was the president of Fedecámaras at the time of the coup.

Fort Tiuna—A huge military base on the west side of Caracas.

gaita—The traditional Christmas music of Venezuela that comes from the Maracaibo region. The *gaita* band has a quartet of male singers, a *quatro,* a *foro* (bass instrument), and hand drums.

MAS—Movement to Socialism (Movimiento al Socialismo). The anti-Soviet communist party, which split from the pro-Soviet PCV in 1971 in response to the Soviet invasion of Czechoslovakia. It is more mainstream than the PCV and has more members. Teodoro Petkoff was a prominent leader of this party for many years.

miquilenistas—A supporter of Luis Miquilena, the political leader who helped launch Chávez as a political candidate.

MVR—Movement of the Fifth Republic (Movimiento de la Quinta Republica), President Chávez's political party. Originally named Movement of the Bolivarian Republic (MBR). There had been four Venezuelan republics since independence from Spain in 1811.

National Assembly—The Venezuelan legislature or parliament, a single house with 165 seats. Members are called deputies, the equivalent of a congressperson or member of parliament.

officialismo—Literally, "officialism." The official doctrine of the Chávez regime.

officialista—A supporter of President Chávez.

PDVSA—Petroleos de Venezuela S.A. Venezuela's state-owned oil company, which provides the government with over 80 percent of its foreign revenue.

PCV—Venezuelan Communist Party (Partido Communista de Venezuela). The pro-Soviet communist party (as opposed to MAS) with close ties to Fidel Castro. During the 1960s the party was outlawed and became the guerrilla group FALN (National Liberation Armed Forces). Guillermo García Ponce was an important leader of the both the PCV and the FALN.

Plan Avila—The military operation in which the Venezuelan armed forces take control of the country. The plan was last implemented in 1989 during the Caracazo and resulted in hundreds (perhaps thousands) of civilian deaths. The new constitution of 1999 made the plan illegal if it was used to control civilians (as opposed to a foreign power).

PPT—Fatherland for All (Patria Para Todos). One of the left-wing parties allied with President Chávez.

Primero Justicia—Justice First. A left-center political party in Venezuela that formed—like Chávez's MVR—in response to the inadequacies of the two traditional parties. Malvina Pesate and Gorka Lacasa were members of this party.

VIVE—Venezuelan Victims of Political Violence (Víctimas Venezolanas de la Violencia Política). The nonprofit human rights group started by Mike Merhi. It represents the opposition victims of the coup as well as others who have suffered human rights abuses under the Chávez regime. Malvina Pesate, Andrés Trujillo, and Catalina Palencia would join this group. It is the opposition counterpart to ASOVIC.

ENDNOTES

Introduction

1 **capture key military bases:** Cristina Marcano and Alberto Barrera Tyszka, *Hugo Chávez: The Definitive Biography of Venezuela's Controversial President* (New York: Random House, 2007), 64–72.

2 **"Comrades, regrettably, *for now*":** Hugo Chávez, "Por Ahora Speech," http://www.angelfire.com/nb/17m/Chavez/porahora.html. My translation.

2 **catapulted into the political spotlight:** Richard Gott, *In the Shadow of the Liberator: Hugo Chávez and the Transformation of Venezuela* (London: Verso, 2000), 66–72.

2 **world's fifth largest oil producer:** U.S. Department of Energy, *International Energy Annual 2003* (Washington, DC: DOE, 2004), http://www.eia.doe .gov/iea/pet.html (accessed March 4, 2006). I have omitted Canada (sometimes listed second) from the ranking of producers because most of its proven reserves are made up of oil sands.

2 **GDP per capita was the highest:** Venezuelan GDP per capita peaked in 1977 at $9,801. When Chávez was elected in 1998 it was $7,695. Allen Heston et al., Penn World Tables 6.1, http://datacentre.chass.utoronto.ca/pwt/ (accessed July 28. 2008). Amounts are in constant U.S. dollars.

PART 1

9 **"A Confrontation between Brothers":** Taken from the Web site of the office of the Venezuelan attorney general, Fiscalia, www.fiscalia.gov.ve/croquis .html (accessed May 16, 2003).

Chapter 1

11 **was very excited:** Unless otherwise noted, all information for this chapter comes from my interviews with Malvina Pesate on April 30, 2003, and June 19, 2003, and my interview with Malvina Pesate and Gorka Lacasa on January 28,

2004, or from our e-mail follow-up. All of these interviews took place in Caracas, Venezuela.

14   **"Eddy Ramírez, General Director":** Transcript of television show of Hugo Chávez, *Aló Presidente,* VTV, April 7, 2002, http://www.globovision.com/programas/yoprometo/200204/yoprometo080402.shtml (accessed May 5, 2004).

15   **Carlos Ortega's turn to speak:** Ana Marisol Angarita, "CTV convocó a paro nacional de 24 horas," *Últimas Noticias* (April 7, 2002), 15. There was some disagreement on who spoke first, Carmona or Ortega. Malvina Pesate says Ortega. La Fuente and Meza also say it was Ortega. See also Sandra La Fuente and Alfredo Meza, *El acertijo de abril: Relato periodistico de la breve caída de Hugo Chávez* (Caracas, Venezuela: Editorial Debate, 2003). But Pedro Carmona says he was the last to speak in his biography, *Mi testimonio ante la historia* (Caracas: Editorial Actum, 2005), 82.

15   **over 1.2 million workers:** Kurt-Peter Shütt, *On the Situation of Unions in Venezuela, Friedrich-Elbert-Stiftung* (February 2008), 3, http://library.fes.de/pdf-files/iez/05241.pdf (accessed August 14, 2008).

15   **"And I say that this march":** La Fuente and Meza, *El acertijo,* 50. After the coup there was speculation that sending the march to Miraflores was part of a plot by the opposition leadership to spark a coup. However, it should be noted that the opposition leadership was divided about this, and different speakers told the crowd different things. For example, Pedro Carmona told the marchers to go to Bolívar Avenue but no further, and once they had arrived at O'Leary Plaza, he tried to convince the marchers to disperse but was ignored. Caracas mayor Alfredo Peña did not speak at the Chuao rally, but he warned Carmona not to let the marchers go to Miraflores because he was sure the *chavistas* would react violently. On Peña's orders, the Metropolitan Police set up a cordon on Bolívar Avenue to enforce Carmona's limit, and the police even teargassed the marchers, but the marchers just took an alternate route to the palace. See Carmona, *Mi testimonio,* 82–83.

There was further speculation that the march was planned to coincide with a military attack on the palace, which is unlikely for several reasons. First, the opposition leadership in the CTV and the Fedecámeras had decided to hold a march only forty-eight hours earlier, on April 9, hardly time enough to coordinate the march with a military strike (Carmona, *Mi testimonio,* 49). Second, it begs the question, how would the coup organizers attack the palace if it was surrounded by a million marchers? In the end, of course, there was no military strike, and it was clear that none was planned for April 11.

Chapter 2

16   **to travel the five miles:** According to Google Earth, it is 4.7 miles from PDVSA headquarters to Miraflores in a straight line. I am rounding up to 5 miles to compensate for the nondirect route the marchers took.

16 **"The call is to Miraflores!":** *72 Horas de Crisis,* Globovisión documentary, April 11, 2003; Elianta Quintero, *11 de Abril: Crimen sin castigo,* Venevisión, April 11, 2003.

16 **Alicia Valdez, fifty-two:** All information in this section about Alicia Valdez comes from my interview with her, June 17, 2003, Caracas, Venezuela.

Chapter 3

19 **On the eleventh floor:** Unless otherwise noted, all information in this chapter, including the direct quotations, is from my interview with General Francisco Usón (Ret.), December 2, 2003, Caracas, Venezuela.

20 **The president began the meeting:** Several people I interviewed gave me information on this meeting: General Francisco Usón; General Manuel Rosendo; General Vásquez Velasco; and Guillermo García Ponce. The meeting is also discussed in La Fuente and Meza, *El acertijo,* 50–52 (essentially Usón's account). I have tried to use information from all sources for completeness, while narrating from Usón's point of view.

My interview with General Manuel Rosendo (ret.), January 29, 2004, Caracas Venezuela; General Efraín Vásquez Velasco (ret.), February 29, 2004, Caracas, Venezuela; Guillermo García Ponce, February 23, 2005, Caracas, Venezuela.

20 **While Rosendo was discussing Plan Avila:** There is a slight difference in versions between Usón and Rosendo. In our interview, Usón said that Rosendo was talking about Plan Avila when the Tactical Command entered the meeting. But according to my interview with Rosendo, he was talking about the plan to use military personnel to work as scabs at PDVSA to short-circuit the strike.

21 **The Tactical Command steered the meeting:** Efraín Vásquez Velasco, "La conspiracion de Miraflores del 7 de Abril de 2002," unpublished article.

21 **They also spoke of launching:** La Fuente and Meza, *El acertijo,* 51.

21 **200 billion bolivares:** Exact figures for the bonus differ. In "La conspiración," Vásquez Velasco said it was ten billion bolivares, or about two thousand per person. La Fuente and Meza, *El acertijo,* 51: 200 billion total and 1.5 million per person. This conversation about the loyalty bonus was also verified by Attorney General Isaías Rodríguez in his interview with journalist Nathaly Salas Guaithero on Globovisión on May 13, 2002. The conversions into dollars are based on the 2002 exchange rate of 1,160.44 bolivares per dollar.

21 **constituted half of all government revenue:** U.S. Department of Energy, *Venezuela: Country Overview* (Washington, DC: DOE, 2003), http://www.eia.doe.gov/emeu/cabs/venez.html (accessed January 20, 2004).

Chapter 4

23   **He was convinced:** Hugo Chávez, *Aló Presidente,* VTV, April 28, 2002.

23   **Chávez knew how coups worked:** See Richard Gott, *In the Shadow of the Liberator: Hugo Chávez and the Transformation of Venezuela* (London: Verso, 2000), 45, and Gabriel García Márquez, "The Two Faces of Hugo Chávez," *NACLA Report on the Americas* (May/June 2000), 21.

24   **And that coup, Chávez:** Gott, *In the Shadow,* 69–70.

24   **one group, led by Admiral Héctor Ramírez Pérez:** According to a confidential source, Marisabel Chávez learned that a group in the military was planning to overthrow Chávez. She called José Vicente Rangel to inform him. Rangel referred the First Lady to General Lucas Rincón. When Rincón appeared to be unimpressed by the information, Marisabel contacted Chávez directly, thinking that Rincón must be involved, telling Chávez that Rincón wanted to kill him. Chávez, according to my source, said she was crazy to think that but explained that there was information about a conspiracy led by Admiral Ramírez Pérez. Chávez, however, was on top of the situation because General Vásquez Velasco was feeding him information. When my source, a friend of the general's, questioned Vásquez Velasco about the authenticity of this account, he confirmed that it was true. Vásquez Velasco also confirmed the story of the conspiracy in my interview with him.

24   **More pressing than Admiral Ramírez Pérez:** Hugo Chávez, from an amateur videotape that was taken of him in custody and telecast by several of the Venezuelan networks.

24   **For weeks they had been talking:** Patricia Poleo, "La verdadera historia de un gobierno que duró sólo horas por estar sustentado en los intereses particulares y no en los del colectivo," *El Nuevo País,* one of a series of articles printed from April 16 to April 30, 2002.

25   **He ordered Plan Avila:** According to Vásquez Velasco, General Eugenio Gutiérrez's testimony, the timing of Shark Radio, and the time that Carneiro actually took out the tanks, the conversation in which Chávez gave Carneiro the order to implement Plan Avila took place in the early evening (around 6:00 p.m.). However, by Chávez's own account (*Aló Presidente,* VTV, April 28, 2002), he began requesting the plan around noon. It appears that Chávez was trying to implement the plan for most of the afternoon. My interview with General Vásquez Velasco; General Eugenio Antonio Gutiérrez Ramos, "Comisión especial política que investiga los hechos ocurridos los días 11, 12, 13, y 14 de abril de 2002," Asamblea Nacional de la República Bolivariana de Venezuela, Caracas, May 14, 2002.

Chapter 5

26   **"The president can be found":** Lucas Rincón, national broadcast, VTV, April 11, 2002. My translation.

Chapter 6

Malvina Pésate and Gorka Lacasa interviews.

27 **over 3.1 million people:** William A. McGeveran, *The World Almanac and Book of Facts 2003* (New York: WRC Media, 2003), 853.

29 **turned off at the Pedrera corner:** In Caracas each intersection is given a name distinct from the names of the streets that make up the intersection. The intersection of Baralt Avenue and University Avenue is called Pedrera, for example.

Chapter 7

29 **Mike Merhi was walking west:** All information in this chapter is from my interview with Mohamad "Mike" Merhi, April 28, 2003, Caracas, Venezuela.

Chapter 8

Malvina Pesate and Gorka Lacasa interviews.

Chapter 9

Unless otherwise noted, all information in this chapter is from my interview with Rafael Fuenmayor, June 20, 2003, Caracas, Venezuela.

Chapter 10

Malvina Pesáte and Gorka Lacasa interviews.

Chapter 11

Mohamad Merhi interview.

37 **Mike agreed:** Nitu Pérez Osuna, "Decisión del tribunal 40 de Control," *Yo Prometo*, Globovisión, Caracas, July 16, 2002.

38 **Mike and Gustavo moved up:** There is some confusion about when Gustavo Tovar and Mike Merhi left Jesús. According to Mike, it was before the firing started, but according to Gustavo it was after. Gustavo's viewpoint comes from my interview with him, March 4, 2004, Caracas, Venezuela.

38 **"Ahh, not so hard":** Malvina Pesáte and Gorka Lacasa interviews.

Chapter 12

Unless otherwise noted, all information in this chapter is from my interview with Andrés Trujillo, December 4, 2003, Caracas, Venezuela.

40 **Chávez's exercised the Enabling Law:** Not only was Chávez's exercising of the Enabling Law controversial, but so was the emergency powers provision that gave him the right to exercise that law. This provision passed the assembly with a simple majority when, according to the constitution, it was a *ley orgánica*, a fundamental law that required a two-thirds majority. Accordingly, many point out that Chávez never had the right to make laws by decree in the first place.

41   **"All those who intend to strike"**: Jorge Calmet, "Chávez en aprietos," *La Prensa* (December 9, 2001), http://www-ni.laprensa.com.ni/archivo/2001/diciembre/09/elmundo/elmundo-20011209-01.html (accessed April 25, 2004). My translation.

41   **But people went on strike anyway**: Carmona, *Mi testimonio,* 69.

Chapter 13

44   **About forty yards up**: All information in this section on Douglas Romero is from my interview with him, November 22, 2004, Caracas, Venezuela.

46   **freelance journalist Francisco Toro**: Francisco Toro's perspective comes from his unpublished account of the coup, "Venezuela's 2002 Coup Revisited: The Evidence Two Years On," and our e-mail correspondence and phone conversations December 6, 14, 15, 2007.

Chapter 14

48   **the general was furious**: Unless otherwise noted, all information on Rosendo's perspective comes from my interview with General Manuel Rosendo (ret.), January 29, 2004, Caracas, Venezuela, and his congressional testimony before the truth commission, "Comisión especial política que investiga los hechos ocurridos los días 11, 12, 13, y 14 de abril de 2002," Asamblea Nacional de la República Bolivariana de Venezuela, Caracas, May 10, 2002.

48   **"I am the commander"**: Some articles and books refer to Rosendo's position as the head of the joint chiefs. While this is the closest equivalent in the U.S. military, it is not quite the right title for Rosendo because he was actually above the joint chiefs, answering only to the inspector general and the president.

50   **Rosendo had expected the attorney general**: Officially, the attorney general (*el fiscal general*) is an elected position in Venezuela. However, President Chávez had been able to name Isaías Rodríguez to the position because of the national crisis. Supposedly, a real election was to be held "shortly" but never was.

50   **Rosendo had been sending the president personal letters**: Reading Rosendo's letters to Chávez gives the strong impression that they were meant by Rosendo to be exculpatory letters. Rosendo was documenting all his correspondence with Chávez, fully aware of the growing tension between them and likely aware that there could be legal action against Rosendo.

50   **"Take advantage of the 6th"**: From the testimony of Manuel Rosendo before the National Assembly. My translation.

51   **"Rosendo, we are going to direct"**: This conversation has appeared in the written record several times, usually from Rosendo's point of view. My quotation here is from my interview with Rosendo. There is a slightly different wording in La Fuente and Meza, *El acertijo,* 40.

52   **in accordance with article 329:** From the testimony of Manuel Rosendo before the National Assembly.

52   **"Freddy, the march has already started":** Ibid. My translation. Both Freddy Bernal and José Vicente Rangel denied that this conversation took place, and Rangel insisted he had nothing to do with the Bolivarian Circles. Captain O'Bryan was later court-martialed for refusing to retract his statement.

53   **the International Court of Justice:** Coincidently, April 11, 2002, was the day that the Rome Statute of the International Criminal Court was ratified. It established the broadest rules in history for prosecuting perpetrators of war crimes and crimes against humanity.

53   **"Did you get my letter?":** This dialogue is from Rosendo's perspective from my interview with Rosendo.

53   **had already spoken to Ortega:** In his testimony before the National Assembly, General Lucas Rincón said he also talked to Carmona that afternoon; however, Carmona said he never spoke to Rincón (Carmona, *Mi testimonio*, 85). According to Rincón, Carmona told him that he could not turn the march back and that the time for dialogue had passed.

53   **Ortega seemed open to dialogue:** Information on the exchanges between Ortega and Rincón comes from David Adams and Phil Gunson, "The Unmaking of a Coup," *St. Petersburg (FL) Times* (April 22, 2002).

53   **Rosendo's aide had Ortega:** The dialogue between Rosendo and Ortega is reconstructed from my interview with Rosendo, Rosendo's National Assembly testimony, and my interview with Rosendo's attorney, Gustavo Perilli Mendoza, February 3, 2004, Caracas, Venezuela.

54   **Chávez had wanted the crisis:** In his annual address before the National Assembly on January 15, 2004, Chávez himself admitted that he had intentionally provoked the crisis with PDVSA. It was, he said, part of a divide-and-conquer strategy he called Plan Colina. "Sometimes it is necessary to provoke a crisis," he said. However, I am a little dubious. Perhaps Chávez wanted to shake up PDVSA, but this intentional provocation should not be extended to the greater crisis of April 11, which included a street massacre, a fracturing of his party (with defections like Miquilena's), and a military disowning. If Plan Colina did exist, it concerned only PDVSA, and Chávez was, in his speech, trying to take credit for the way that the coup (miraculously) helped his presidency as if it had all been his grand design.

    For a further discussion of Chávez's strategy of intentionally antagonizing his opponents, see Javier Corrales, "Hugo Boss," *Foreign Policy* (January/February 2006), 35.

54   **Soon Ortega and Rincón were talking:** Information on the exchange between Ortega and Rincón comes from Adams and Gunson, "Unmaking of a Coup." I suspect that Adams and Gunson have this wrong and that Ortega was really talking to Rosendo here.

Chapter 15

55   **On South Eighth Street:** All information on Carlos Ciordia's perspective comes from my interview with Carlos Ciordia, December 3, 2003, Caracas, Venezuela.

58   **down University Avenue toward:** Technically, they went down West Fourth Avenue, which is really just a short forty-meter extension of University Avenue.

Chapter 16

61   **A block west of Carlos Ciordia:** This chapter on Juan Querales is based on three sources: (1) Edgar López et al., "Esta semana comenzarán allanamientos en busca de responsables de la masacre del 11," *El Nacional* (May 18, 2002); (2) information from the National Association for the Victims of the Coup d'État of April 11, 12, 13, and 14 (ASOVIC) and my interview with Mohamad "Mike" Merhi; and (3) a short phone interview I had with Yamileth Querales (Juan's sister), January 31, 2005.

Chapter 17

62   **later died in prison:** Gott, *In the Shadow,* 36, 37.

62   **"I dreamed of being":** Hugo Chávez, *Chávez, Venezuela and the New Latin America* (New York: Ocean Press, 2005), 14.

63   **"He inspired me":** Ibid., 69.

63   **Chávez became part:** Scott Wilson, "Clash of Visions Pushed Venezuela toward Coup," *Washington Post* (April 21, 2002), A01.

63   **When he became a statesman:** Moisés Naím, "Hugo Chávez and the Limits of Democracy," *New York Times* (March 5, 2003), A23.

64   **they parted ways:** Gott, *In the Shadow,* 60–64.

64   **"We made suggestions":** Ibid., 62. The translation is Gott's.

66   **"It's now 10:40":** Elianta Quintero, *11 de Abril: Crimen sin castigo,* Venevisión, April 11, 2003. My translation.

66   **"ugly" and "a little uncouth":** Marc Lifsher, "Chavez Combines Old, New to Keep Grip on Venezuela," *Wall Street Journal* (June 12, 2003).

66   **A devout Catholic, Chávez:** Gabriel García Márquez, "The Two Faces of Hugo Chávez," *NACLA Report on the Americas* (May/June 2000), 19.

66   **"Beautiful Jesus":** Hugo Chávez, *Aló Presidente,* VTV, April 28, 2002. My translation.

67   **feel Bolívar's presence:** Lifsher, "Chavez Combines Old, New."

67   **his vow to overthrow Spanish power:** Márquez, "Two Faces," 21.

68   **"The press is the artillery":** Guillermo García Ponce, *El golpe del 11 de abril* (Caracas, Venezuela: Instituto Municipal de Publicaciones de la Alcaldía de Caracas, 2002), 19.

69   **"'99 was the year":** Hugo Chávez, special broadcast, VTV, April 11, 2002. My translation.

Chapter 18

69   **After Finance Minister General Usón:** Unless otherwise noted, all information in this chapter comes from my interview with General Francisco Usón.

71   **left him like a sieve:** None of the people killed on the official lists died of wounds like this, so either this man survived, was not counted, or was killed and the cause of death was changed to support the government's position; that is, his wounds were described so as to make it sound as if he had been killed by the Metropolitan Police or snipers.

72   **"Pass me that walkie-talkie":** Chávez, special broadcast, VTV, April 11, 2002. My translation.

Chapter 19

73   **437 special broadcasts:** Quintero, *11 de abril.*

73   **block independent news coverage:** Abdel Güerere, "The Media: Civil Defense for Democracy," *Business Venezuela* (June 2002), 68.

74   **Chávez was trying to block:** Government officials had also prohibited planes and helicopters from flying over Caracas that day because they did not want the private media transmitting images of the enormousness of the march: Carmona, *Mi testimonio,* 85.

74   **The acrimonious battle:** The information, including the quotations, in the next seven paragraphs, is from International Press Institute, *World Press Freedom Review 2003* (Vienna: IPI, 2004), http://www.freemedia.at/cms/ipi/freedom_detail.html?country=/KW0001/KW0002/KW0032/&year=2003 (accessed November 22, 2008). Translations by International Press Institute. Like so many other sectors of the population, many of the media sources that Chávez was singling out for attack had once been pro-Chávez. Both Globovisión and Venevisión, for example, had contributed generously to his campaign.

75   **a bomb was thrown:** The year 2002 saw almost twenty acts of violence against journalists apart from April 11, including the simultaneous attacks on twenty-one TV and radio stations throughout the country on December 9. Attacks on the media included the kidnapping of journalists, beatings, and shootings. It should be noted that according to the Human Rights Watch report of 2003, Human Rights Watch, *Venezuela: Caught in the Crossfire* (New York: HRI, 2003), the Venezuelan courts had not punished a single person for any of these attacks, nor granted remunerations to the victims in any way.

76   **"Well, I am going to make":** Chávez, special broadcast, April 11, 2002. My translation.

77   **Jesse Chacón:** In 2003, Chávez named Jesse Chacón the minister of information and communication. The ministry's primary responsibility is the management of VTV. In a very tasteless appointment ceremony, the president spoke effusively of the glory with which Chacón would finally "take" the station.

78   **was completely abandoned:** There are differing accounts of why VTV was abandoned. Journalists who worked there and at RCTV told U.S. embassy personnel that they had received calls from someone in Miraflores informing them that the president was going to resign and recommending that they evacuate. Yet Chávez's advisers in Miraflores said that the failure of VTV was part of the military's conspiracy (even though it wasn't). What is clear is that the station was not taken by the military. Footage by a CMT news crew that arrived shortly after the evacuation shows that the station was completely abandoned.

78   **People who tuned in:** Francisco Toro, *Venezuela's 2002 Coup Revisited: The Evidence Two Years On*, http://caracaschronicles.blogspot.com/2004/04/untold-story-of-venezuelas-2002-april.html (accessed September 20, 2007).

Chapter 20

78   **Meanwhile, Luis Fernández:** Unless otherwise noted, all information in this chapter comes from my interview with Luis Alfonso Fernández, December 9, 2003, Caracas, Venezuela, and the video he took on April 11.

79   **one of the government spokespersons:** Luis Fernández is pretty sure this speaker was MVR Deputy Iris Varela.

79   **Gustavo Cisneros:** Ernesto Carmona, "Quién es Gustavo Cisneros?" http://www.geocities.com/expresionverazucv/cisneros.html (accessed February 16, 2004).

80   **So they think they can:** Chávez, special broadcast, VTV, April 11, 2002. My translation.

81   **Richard Peñalver:** López et al., "Esta semana comenzarán."

82   **Rafael Cabrices:** Solbella Pérez Rodríguez, "Busquen a los culpables," *Tal Cual* (April 17, 2002), http://www.venezuelanuestra.org/esp_Just_34.htm (accessed March 13, 2003).

83   **not captured on Luis's video:** An amateur video taken from a different angle showed more gunmen on the west side of the overpass. This footage appeared on many television programs, including *72 Horas de Crisis,* Globovisión, April 11, 2003.

Chapter 21

87   **Dr. Alberto Espidel was standing:** Unless otherwise noted, all information in this chapter comes from my interview with Dr. Angel Alberto Espidel, July 23, 2003, Caracas, Venezuela.

91   **Sometime before five o'clock:** Espidel said this was at 4:00 p.m., but I have judged it to be almost 5:00 p.m. by calibrating the events with footage of Chávez's special broadcast.

91   **"Some of Peña's police":** This portion of Chávez's broadcast is heard on Luis Fernández's footage.

Chapter 22

All information on Rafael Fuenmayor's perspective comes from my interview with him, June 20, 2003, Caracas, Venezuela.

94 **when an officer is fired upon:** On April 11 there was no specific order or instructions to shoot at the gunmen, according to Carlos Rodríguez of the Metropolitan Police.

Chapter 23

96 **It was just about five o'clock:** Unless otherwise noted, all information in this section about Antonio Návas comes from my interview with Antonio José Návas, February 27, 2003, Caracas, Venezuela.

97 **carried him to the hospital tents:** Antonio Návas (or at least a young man matching his clothes and his wound) is on the Luis Fernández tape being carried into the hospital tent at just about 5:00 p.m.

97 **standing with his arms crossed:** The specifics of Nelson Zambrano's having his arms crossed, the witness who thought he had fainted, and the tenth vertebra come from La Fuente and Meza, *El acertijo,* 100–101. Also note that La Fuente and Meza say the bullet was a 9 mm, whereas another article says it was a FAL round: López et al., "Esta semana comenzarán."

97 **Crelia de Caro:** The section about Crelia and Luis Alberto Caro is based on three sources: (1) La Fuente and Meza, *El acertijo,* 74–76, 84–85, 98, and 106; (2) Nelson Estanga, "Ultimo adios," on the ASOVIC Web site, http://www.asovic.org/ultimo_adios.htm; and (3) Néstor Francia, *Puente Llaguno* (Caracas: Monfort, 2002), 63–65.

Chapter 24

Malvina Pesáte and Gorka Lacasa interviews.

99 **Malvina's brother took him aside:** Gorka Lacasa and Malvina Pesáte argued about whether Malvina was in the room when Israel told him she had been shot. Gorka insists that Malvina was right next to them and conscious, but Malvina insists she has no recollection of Israel's statement and was unaware that she had been injured by a bullet until the following Sunday.

100 **this freak is still going:** I am translating Gorka's word *anormal* (abnormal) as "freak."

Chapter 25

101 **Vargas Hospital:** This section about Vargas Hospital is based on my personal observations of the hospital and my interview with Dr. Ricardo Serbenescu, December 14, 2003, Caracas, Venezuela.

102 **Dr. Pablo Rausseo was in charge:** The information in this section is from my interview with Dr. Pablo Rausseo, December 20, 2004, Caracas, Venezuela.

104 **Dr. Ricardo Serbenescu was working:** Unless otherwise noted, the information in the rest of this chapter is from my interviews with Dr. Ricardo Serbenescu and Dr. Pablo Rausseo.

105   **Red Cross asking for help:** This is not the International Red Cross, but Cruz Roja, a private emergency-care company in Venezuela.

105   **Josefina Rengifo:** Josefina's age has been reported variously as nineteen, twenty-one, and twenty-nine. See Maye Primera Garcés, "Tiros al aire en la Asamblea," *Tal Cual* (April 18, 2002), http://www.talcualdigital.com/ediciones/2002/04/18/p6s1.htm.

105   **embedded in his cell phone:** This story is based on my interview with Dr. Pablo Rausseo, and on La Fuente and Meza, *El acertijo*, 106–107.

Chapter 26

106   **Andrés Trujillo, who had been shot:** Unless otherwise noted, all information in this chapter comes from my interviews, with Andrés Trujillo and Douglas Romero.

107   **he was dead:** This young man did not appear on any of the official lists of fatalities.

Chapter 27

111   **Carlos Ciordia:** Unless otherwise noted, this section is based on my interview with Carlos Ciordia.

111   **Elías Santana:** At the time of the coup Elías Santana was a writer for *El Nacional* newspaper and coordinator of the civic group Queremos Elegir (We Want to Choose).

112   **Mike Merhi:** The rest of this chapter is based on my interview with Mohamad "Mike" Merhi.

113   **Mike would leave seventeen messages:** Mike said twenty-four messages, but his phone bill showed only seventeen to Jesús's cell phone number.

Chapter 28

113   **Jhonnie Palencia:** Palencia's name has been spelled many different ways in the Venezuelan press, usually *Johnny*. The spelling used here (*Jhonnie*) is how his mother and sister told me to spell it.

113   **One of the marchers:** The biographical details on Palencia come from my interview with his mother, Catalina Palencia, December 6, 2005, Ocumare del Tuy, Venezuela, and López et al., "Esta semana comenzarán."

114   **The party was so confident of Chávez's:** La Fuente and Meza, *El acertijo*, 56.

115   **a bullet caught him:** There is some speculation on how Jhonnie Palencia was shot that would create his particular entrance and exit wounds. One theory is that the bullet ricocheted off the street and caught him under the chin. The way I describe it is the most probable because the round was reportedly recovered from the wall behind him indicating a horizontal trajectory: "Palencia Hit While Throwing Rock," *El Universal* (December 29, 2002).

115   **Gabriel Osorio:** The perspective of Gabriel Osorio comes from my phone interview with him, July 10, 2008, Caracas, Venezuela, and from La Fuente and Meza, *El acertijo*, 105–108.

115 **All night he lay there:** The time of Jhonnie's death is estimated from the last phone call he answered. According to his mother, it was at 6:00 p.m. According to the woman who made the call, Faisa Codesido, the last conversation he had was at 5:30: La Fuente and Meza, *El acertijo*, 106. According to Mrs. Palencia, calls that attempted to reach him at 7:00 p.m. were not answered.

Chapter 29
Luis Fernández interview.

PART 2
Chapter 1

121 **At 5:25 p.m.:** Sandra La Fuente and Alfredo Meza, *El acertijo de abril: Relato periodistico de la breve caida de Hugo Chávez* (Caracas, Venezuela: Editorial Debate, 2003), 21.

121 **Chávez got back on the radio:** Ibid., 21, 22.

121 **Shark One [President Chávez]: OK:** The exchange between Chávez and Carneiro comes from their recorded Shark Network conversation, confirmed as authentic by General Carneiro himself during his congressional testimony, Comision especial política que investiga los hechos ocurridos los días 11, 12, 13, y 14 de abril de 2002, Asamblea Nacional de la República Bolivariana de Venezuela, Caracas, May 22, 2002, http://www.globovision.com/documentos/discursos.transcripciones/200205/carneiro/index.shtml. My translation.

123 **Then he called General Rosendo:** The exchange between Carneiro and Rosendo, including the direct quotations, is based on my interview with General Manuel Rosendo (ret.), January 29, 2004, Caracas, Venezuela. Note that this was Rosendo's version of what General Carneiro said.

123 **"Do you think I am going":** La Fuente and Meza, *El acertijo,* 22. My translation.

123 **Trying to conceal his alarm:** The sentiments of General González Cárdenas come from La Fuente and Meza, *El acertijo,* 23, 24.

123 **Chávez had also ordered Rincón:** From the videotape of Hugo Chávez in custody.

124 **Vásquez Velasco was not to be found:** Unless otherwise noted, the information in the rest of this chapter is based on my interview with General Efraín Vásquez Velasco (ret.), February 29, 2004, Caracas, Venezuela.

124 **Under Venezuela's old constitution:** La Fuente and Meza, *El acertijo,* 28.

124 **Chávez's new constitution:** The new constitution of 1999 also allowed military personnel to vote for the very first time. During the recall referendum to remove Chávez in 2004, the president would gain many votes by forcing everyone in the military to vote in his favor.

125 **the infant democracy:** Up to this time, no democratically elected Venezuelan head of state had ever lasted long enough to pass the reins of power to another democratically elected head of state.

126   **Briones Montoto:** On June 27, 2006, the Venezuelan government erected a
memorial in honor of Montoto, now considered a fallen comrade, not a foreign invader, and held a reenactment of the failed invasion. See Ricardo
Verlezza, "Homenaje a cubano caido en la invasion cubana comunista en
1967 a Venezuela," *Aporrea y Diario la Voz* (July 20, 2006).

126   **break all political ties with Castro:** Richard Haggerty, *Venezuela: A Country
Study* (Washington, DC: Library of Congress, 1990), 20, and Alberto Gar-
rido, "El eje revolucionario Chávez-Castro," *El Universal* (June 27, 2004).

126   **FARC training camps began to appear:** Linda Robinson, "Terror Close to
Home," *US News and World Report* (October 6, 2003), http://www.usnews.com/
usnews/news/articles/031006/6venezuela.htm (accessed November 29, 2008).

126   **Plan Bolívar:** While Plan Bolívar was a progressive civilian-military program
that used Venezuelan and Cuban soldiers to provide health care, food, and
school tutoring, and to build homes in poor areas, it was also plagued with corruption. In fact, the corruption in Plan Bolívar was what caused the resignation
of the former head of the army, General Victor Cruz, and paved the way for
Vásquez Velasco to ascend to the post: Silene Ramirez, "Venezuela Army Head
Replaced amid Graft Allegations," Reuters release (December 22, 2001).

126   **Venezuelan intelligence services:** Robinson, "Terror Close to Home," and
La Fuente and Meza, *El acertijo,* 29.

127   **many Venezuelan officers were furious:** Information about the level of discontent in the military comes from my interview with Gustavo Adolfo Perilli Mendoza, February 3, 2004, Caracas, Venezuela, and from La Fuente
and Meza, *El acertijo,* 28, 29.

127   **then he would rule Venezuela:** Chávez's words are based on General
Vásquez Velasco's recollections in my interview.

127   **"I am the *jefe*":** My interview with General Efraín Vásquez Velasco. It was
because of this meeting that Chávez and Vásquez Velasco began designing
Plan Shark, which created the Shark Radio Network for communication
with the more loyal officers should there be a crisis or a coup attempt.

128   **kept the announcement about PDVSA:** President Chávez's decision not to
announce the resignation of the new PDVSA board is confirmed by La
Fuente and Meza, *El acertijo,* 58.

129   **Rangel had more faith:** In his congressional testimony, Rosendo claimed that
at about this moment Rangel referred to the National Guard troops as "ese pa-
pelote de guevon," which roughly translates as "those lame excuses for dick-
heads." General Manuel Rosendo, Comisión especial política que investiga los
hechos ocurridos los días 11, 12, 13, y 14 de abril de 2002," Asamblea Nacional de la República Bolivariana de Venezuela, Caracas, May 10, 2002.

129   **Carneiro had gotten wind of:** Marta Harnecker, *Militares junto al pueblo*
(Caracas: Vadell Hermanos, 2003), 42, 43.

129   **"Look, there is no military coup":** The dialogue between Generals Carneiro
and Vásquez Velasco is General Vásquez Velasco's recollection, from my interview with him.

130   *Mi general,* **they are attacking the march:** The dialogue between Vásquez Velasco and the other generals is General Vásquez Velasco's recollection, from my interview with him.

130   **"*Shark Six*: Copy":** General Jorge García Carneiro, Comision especial política que investiga los hechos ocurridos los días 11, 12, 13, y 14 de abril de 2002, Asamblea Nacional de la República Bolivariana de Venezuela, Caracas, May 22, 2002. My translation.

131   **a nationwide military lockdown:** Of course, the lockdown of troops by General Vásquez Velasco had the added consequence of not allowing any troops to defend Chávez in the palace.

131   **The generals were all in agreement:** From the testimony of General Néstor González González, Comisión especial política que investiga los hechos ocurridos los días 11, 12, 13, y 14 de abril de 2002," Asamblea Nacional de la República Bolivariana de Venezuela, Caracas, May 14, 2002.

131   **each one voiced his support:** La Fuente and Meza, *El acertijo,* 26.

132   **Carneiro agreed to go:** The story of Carneiro going to Rincón's office and then to Miraflores is in both La Fuente and Meza, *El acertijo,* 26, and the interview with Carneiro in Harnecker, *Militares junto,* 43–44.

133   **The military high command:** Efraín Vásquez Velasco, "Posición institucional del ejército y reafirmación de los derechos humanos." Unpublished manuscript.

133   **Vásquez Velasco's announcement was followed:** This succession of news conferences (Vásquez Velasco, the air force, then the navy) comes from General Lucas Rincón, Comisión especial política que investiga los hechos ocurridos los días 11, 12, 13, y 14 de abril de 2002," Asamblea Nacional de la República Bolivariana de Venezuela, Caracas, May 4, 2002.

Chapter 2

      Unless otherwise noted, all information in this chapter comes from my interview with Luis Miquilena, January 26, 2004, Caracas, Venezuela.

136   **Chávez's response to the first:** The information in this paragraph is from Pedro Carmona, *Mi testimonio ante la historia* (Caracas, Venezuela: Editorial Actum, 2005), 29–38.

136   **"I solemnly declare":** "Miquilena: No quiero mi nombre vinculado a un gobierno manchado de sangre," *El Nacional* (April 12, 2002). My translation.

137   **an institutional solution:** *72 horas de crisis,* Globovisión, 2003. My translation.

Chapter 3

137   **While these events were unfolding:** Unless otherwise noted, all information in this chapter comes from my interview with General Francisco Usón (ret.), December 12, 2003, Caracas, Venezuela, and our e-mail correspondence of April 10–15, 2005.

138   **had bivouacked his entire army:** Gott, *In the Shadow,* 40.

139   **for only thirty-eight days:** La Fuente and Meza, *El acertijo,* 41.

Chapter 4

140   **It wasn't until Mike:** All information in this chapter comes from my interview with Mohamad "Mike" Merhi, April 28, 2003, Caracas, Venezuela.

Chapter 5

141   **By nine o'clock things:** Unless otherwise noted, all information in this chapter comes from my interview with Dr. Ricardo Serbenescu, December 14, 2003, Caracas, Venezuela.

141   **Sixteen dead:** La Fuente and Meza, *El acertijo,* 138.

Chapter 6

142   **Dr. Espidel—who:** All information in this chapter comes from my interview with Dr. Angel Alberto Espidel, July 23, 2003, Caracas, Venezuela.

Chapter 7

144   **When General Francisco Usón walked:** Unless otherwise noted, all information in this chapter comes from my interview with General Francisco Usón.

144   **a cup of coffee:** La Fuente and Meza, *El acertijo,* 42, and my interview and e-mail correspondence with Usón.

145   **"You acted badly, *Presidente"*:** Dialogue between Chávez, Usón, and Rangel from my interview and e-mail correspondence with General Usón and from La Fuente and Meza, *El acertijo,* 42, 43.

145   **"I think it would be well":** Usón gave two slightly different quotes: "I think, for the good of the country, you should also resign," and "I think it would be well if you resigned, too." I have chosen the latter because it has the suggestion of "good for the country." My interview with General Usón.

Chapter 8

146   **In the corridors of Miraflores:** Unless otherwise noted, all information in this chapter comes from my interview with Guillermo García Ponce, February 23, 2005, Caracas, Venezuela; Guillermo García Ponce, *El golpe del 11 de abril,* 2nd ed. (Caracas, Venezuela: Instituto Municipal de Publicaciones de la Alcaldía de Caracas, 2002); and Guillermo García Ponce, *La fuga del cuartel San Carlos,* 4th ed. (Caracas, Venezuela: Cortagraf, 1991).

147   **when the Carúpano coup attempt failed:** Haggerty, *Venezuela,* 20.

147   **They sabotaged oil pipelines:** "The Saga of the Anzoategui," *Time* (February 22, 1963), http://www.time.com/time/magazine/article/0,9171,828017,00 .html?iid=chix-sphere (accessed September 17, 2008), and "With Impunity and Immunity," *Time* (July 5, 1963), http://www.time.com/time/magazine/ article/0,9171,875028,00.html (accessed September 22, 2008).

148   **To cover up the murders:** Ironically, this modus operandi of executing enemies of the state by saying they resisted arrest, even though they had been ar-

rested days earlier, resurfaced after April 11 and was often used by the DISIP as they hunted down the military officers who had opposed Chávez.

148   **By the time the tunnel:** García Ponce, *La fuga*, 236.

149   **the FALN never gained:** Haggerty, *Venezuela*, 26.

149   **money and arms to the FALN:** In my interview with García Ponce, he emphasized that the Cuban assistance had been critical. He also made an indirect reference to the Breshnev-Castro dispute and the pulling of funds for the FALN in his book *La fuga*, 103: "Various factors contributed to this [deteriorating] political picture, but the principal cause was grave sectarian errors that caused the distancing of important allies." My translation.

149   **the PCV split:** "Rival Communist Conferences in Venezuela," Associated Press (Munich: March 15, 1971).

149   **5.1 percent of the vote:** Haggerty, *Venezuela*, 31.

150   **Given the communists' long history:** García Ponce, *El golpe*, 25–27.

150   **"It's an uprising":** Ibid., 28.

150   **To García Ponce:** Ibid., 28.

150   **the journalists from Channel 8:** Ibid., 29.

150   **at 3:15:** I believe that García Ponce's timing is incorrect. There weren't any wounded outside Miraflores at this time.

151   **They had thought:** Hugo Chávez, *Understanding the Venezuelan Revolution: Hugo Chávez Talks to Marta Harnecker* (New York: Monthly Review Press, 2005), 179.

152   **"The CIA is behind":** Kim Bartley and Donnacha O'Briain, *The Revolution Will Not Be Televised* (Galway, Ireland: Irish Film Board, 2003).

152   **Chávez asked to be left alone:** Garcia Ponce, *El golpe*, 32–33.

Chapter 9

General Manuel Rosendo interview.

153   *desconocimiento:* The word Rosendo used was *desconocimiento* which does not have an exact translation in English. It means to "know no longer" or "not to recognize."

153   **"I have also come":** My interview with General Manuel Rosendo. Vice Admiral Bernabé Carrero Cubero offered his resignation at the same meeting, according to Rosendo.

153   **"You know, I had been collecting":** Ibid.

153   **"I cannot guarantee":** Rosendo's version of Chávez's dialogue is from Quintero, *11 de abril.*

154   **The president is willing:** The specifics of the terms are from La Fuente and Meza, *El acertijo*, 43.

154   **Tell the president:** My interview with General Manuel Rosendo. In my interview with him, Vásquez Velasco insisted that he had not requested Chávez's resignation. Rather, he had refused to go to his house as Rosendo and Hurtado had asked him to do. Vásquez Velasco had also made it clear to

Rosendo and Hurtado that the rest of the military was firmly behind him and that Chávez should call him by phone immediately.

154   **Ministry of Defense:** The Ministry of Defense and the Office of the Inspector General were, at that time, in the same building.

155   **"One response is":** In my interview with him, Rosendo told me that he related the first option to Chávez but failed to tell him the second option. This omission is confirmed by La Fuente and Meza, *El acertijo,* 44.

155   **Rosendo then called:** Dialogue between Generals Rosendo and Vásquez Velasco confirmed by both men in my interviews with them.

Chapter 10

157   **"it looks like we got rid of *el loco*":** Confidential source.

157   **People of Venezuela:** Taynem Hernandez and Elvia Gomez, "Lucas Rincón confirmó la renuncia presidencial," *El Universal* (April 12, 2002), 1–2. My translation.

Chapter 11

158   **That night Andrés Trujillo's:** All information in this chapter comes from my interviews with Andrés Trujillo, December 4, 2003, Caracas, Venezuela, and Antonio José Návas, February 27, 2003, Caracas, Venezuela.

Chapter 12

159   **The top floor of the TV station:** Carmona, *Mi testimonio,* 29–38.

159   **In attendance:** Pedro Carmona said that this reunion was an ad hoc meeting, that it consisted of all the opposition members who happened to be at the station to be interviewed, and not anything that was planned with much anticipation. Ibid., 89.

160   **Trained as an economist:** Ibid., 29–38.

160   **a house in the Floresta neighborhood:** Information on the Floresta meeting and the details of the junta come from David Adams and Phil Gunson, "The Unmaking of a Coup," *St. Petersburg (FL) Times* (April, 22, 2002).

161   **Poleo received a call:** There are differing accounts of where Ortega was when he received this phone call. Journalist Patricia Poleo says he was still at Venevisión, whereas Adams and Gunson say he was at his home. Patricia Poleo, "La verdadera historia de un gobierno que duró sólo horas por estar sustentado en los intereses particulares y o en los del colectivo," *El Nuevo País,* a series of articles printed on April 16–19, 22–26, 29, 30, 2002, and Adams and Gunson, "The Unmaking of a Coup."

161   **"I'm not going to whitewash":** The dialogue during the Venevisión meeting comes from Poleo, "La verdadera historia de un gobierno."

163   **statistics showed that in 2002:** There are a lot of conflicting statistics for the percentage of Venezuelans living in poverty, generally ranging from 60 to 80 percent. Here I use the most historically reliable source: Catholic

University Andrés Bello, *Statistics for 2002* (Caracas, Venezuela: El Paraíso, 2003).

163   **Chávez's approval rating:** Adam Easton, "Chávez: More Than Empty Promises?" *BBC News*, April 16, 2002, http://news.bbc.co.uk/2/hi/americas/1932132.stm (accessed January 17, 2006).

163   **68 percent of the population:** Library of Congress Country Studies, 2003–2005 Country Studies US, http://countrystudies.us/venezuela/ (accessed June 20, 2006). Note that Venezuela does not request ethnic information in its national census; data are estimates from 1990.

164   **are given a handsome check:** For more on the nuances of Venezuelan culture and the impact of being a petrostate, see Brian Nelson, "Los Maracuchos: Life in Venezuela's Oil Boomtown," *Southern Humanities Review* (Spring 2008).

164   **the president's mother:** Simon Romero, "Expanding Power Puts Family of Venezuelan President Under Increasing Scrutiny," *New York Times* (February 18, 2007).

164   **Isaac Pérez Recao:** David Adams, "Alleged Coup Leaders Land in South Florida," *St. Petersburg (FL) Times* (April 24, 2002). Interestingly, Isaac Pérez Recao's uncle was Juan Pablo Pérez Alfonso, a former Venezuelan government minister and one of the founding fathers of the Organization of Petroleum Exporting Countries (OPEC). A great patriot, Juan Pablo Pérez had warned the nation about the pitfalls of oil wealth, referring to it not as black gold, but as "the devil's excrement." Prophetically, Pérez felt that oil could be more of a curse than a blessing for a developing nation like Venezuela because it inspired complacency and corruption.

164   **They owned big bingo clubs:** Testimony of Patricia Poleo, "Comisión especial política que investiga los hechos ocurridos los días 11, 12, 13, y 14 de abril de 2002," Asamblea Nacional de la República Bolivariana de Venezuela, Caracas, May 10, 2002.

164   **The family owned:** "Venezuela Hunts Escaped Coup Leader," *USA Today* (August 15, 2006).

164   **"a yuppie with guns":** Adams and Gunson, "The Unmaking of a Coup."

165   **The family's immense wealth:** Eligio Rojas, "Pérez Recao: 'Jamás Vendí Armas a la Fuerza Armada,'" *El Mundo* (May 16, 2002).

165   **financing a group of dissident military officers:** La Fuente and Meza, *El acertijo,* 68.

165   **he was bankrolling:** Ibid., 65.

165   **He had financed:** From the testimony of Patricia Poleo, "Comisión especial política que investiga los hechos ocurridos los días 11, 12, 13, y 14 de abril de 2002," Asamblea Nacional de la República Bolivariana de Venezuela, Caracas, May 10, 2002.

165   **During the Vargas floods:** My interview with General Efraín Vásquez Velasco.

165   **felt that these three years:** Poleo, "La verdadera historia."

Chapter 13

166 **García Ponce suspected a trap:** García Ponce, *El golpe,* 31.

166 **Some are in agreement:** Baltazar Porras, *Memorias de un obispo,* unpublished manuscript, 8.

167 **The plan was:** Cenovia Casas, "El 11: A fue un machetazo en el alma del pueblo," *El National* (April 20, 2002). This article is an interview with Archbishop Baltasar Porras.

167 **What I am asking:** The phone conversation is reported in Porras, *Memorias de un obispo,* 8.

167 **Before long Rosendo:** My interview with General Manuel Rosendo.

167 **he didn't trust *these* generals:** Ibid.

167 **the man whose advice he most valued:** Castro says he called at 12:38, but there is a one-hour time difference between Havana and Caracas, making the time 1:38 a.m. in Caracas. Fidel Castro and Ignacio Ramonet, "Castro Helps Chávez Avert Coup," *The Nation* (January 21, 2008), 22–23.

167 **"What forces do you have":** All direct quotations in this dialogue are taken from the *Nation* article and were translated by Ignacio Ramonet.

168 **if Chávez left the country:** Fidel Castro actually gave a more detailed account of his conversation with Chávez than I have put here. I have parsed his account down because much of what he said is incorrect and misleading. Principally, Castro's account is very self-aggrandizing and places the Cuban leader at the center of the decision making. According to him, he was the one who persuaded Chávez not to fight against a military attack they both felt was imminent. However, by the time of this conversation, Chávez had given up this option hours before. In fact, by this time, Chávez had already indicated to Rosendo and Hurtado that he would resign. Also according to Castro, he was the one who recommended that Chávez leave the country, when it was the rebelling generals who proposed this option, also hours before Castro's call.

Castro's account also shows symptoms of rewriting history, as it depicts April 11's events as a "classic coup" scenario focusing on a (suspected) violent uprising of generals instead of a "disowning." For example, Castro's account says that Chávez was cut off from the loyalist troops under General Baduel, when, in fact, Baduel had spoken to Chávez an hour before the Castro phone call, and Chávez had told the general—in no uncertain terms—that he should not get involved. See "Baduel: Epicentro de la reacción militar," *Ultimas Noticias* (June 2002), 48.

While Castro's counsel certainly affirmed Chávez's course of action—particularly his decision to go to Cuba—most of the major decisions had already been made. Castro's most important contribution appears to have been that he told Chávez not to resign even though by this time he was only minutes away from doing so. The tone of Castro's account is also interesting, because Castro paints himself as the strong father figure dispensing his sagacity to a frightened and inexperienced Chávez.

168   **Soon thereafter, Colonel Silvino Bustillos:** The reconstruction of this scene is based on my interview with Rosendo and La Fuente and Meza, *El acertijo*. The dialogue is from La Fuente and Meza, 46.

169   **One of the first things that struck:** Unless otherwise noted, all information in this section comes from my interview with General Francisco Usón.

169   **the chair of the commander of the army:** Carmona's sitting in the army commander's chair appears many times in the written record and was affirmed in my interview with General Francisco Usón. Carmona, however, insists that it is untrue: Carmona, *Mi testimonio*, 93.

169   **"For [minister of] defense":** Poleo, "La verdadera historia." My translation.

Chapter 14

171   **Chávez had told Rincón:** From the testimony of General Lucas Rincón, "Comisión especial política que investiga los hechos ocurridos los días 11, 12, 13, y 14 de abril de 2002," Asamblea Nacional de la República Bolivariana de Venezuela, Caracas, May 4, 2002.

171   **He gave the president fifteen minutes:** García Ponce, *El golpe,* 34. While some have claimed that Fuenmayor was conspiring against Chávez and may have had plans for a coup, this seems quite unlikely because he spent most of April 11 playing tennis at the posh Tamanaco Hotel in Caracas: Porras, *Memorias de un obispo,* 10.

171   **"President, you have made":** My interview with Manuel Rosendo. My translation.

172   **the kind of unsolicited commentary:** Much later, when Chávez had been restored to power and had purged the military of all those who had shown disloyalty, including Rosendo, the general would joke about how he had told Chávez it was best to leave: "How could Chávez accuse me of disloyalty when I said things like that?" My interview with General Manuel Rosendo.

172   **"All right," his mother said:** Christina Marcano and Alberto Barrera Tyszka, *Hugo Chávez: The Definitive Biography of Venezuela's Controversial President* (New York: Random House, 2007), 175.

172   **reminding him that:** La Fuente and Meza, *El acertijo,* 59.

172   **but not García Ponce:** García Ponce, *El golpe,* 34.

172   **"Politically, for the record":** Bartley and O'Briain, *Revolution Will Not.* My translation.

172   **"The president will say":** García Ponce, *El golpe,* 34–35. My translation.

173   **to let him to go:** Bartley and O'Briain, *Revolution Will Not.*

173   **"I'll only be gone":** La Fuente and Meza, *El acertijo,* 59.

Chapter 15

173   **Many miles away:** The information in this chapter comes from my interview with Catalina Palencia, December 3, 2003, Ocumare del Tuy, Venezuela.

Chapter 16

175   **"Once again under arrest"**: La Fuente and Meza, *El acertijo*, 60. My translation.

175   **The president greeted the archbishop**: Casas, "El 11."

175   **"OK, Mr. President"**: My interview with General Manuel Rosendo.

175   **With one cleric on each side**: Porras, *Memorias de un obispo*, 13. My translation.

176   **General Vásquez Velasco was surprised**: Except where noted, the account of this initial encounter between Chávez and Vásquez Velasco, including the direct quotations, comes from my interview with General Efraín Vásquez Velasco.

176   **The military leaders**: Unless otherwise noted, this scene is reconstructed from my interview with General Usón, who, in my opinion, was the least biased of the observers.

176   **The military leaders . . . We can't continue arguing**: While I have confirmed all of the dialogue in this section, I cannot be certain of the order in which it was spoken by each person.

176   **"You have changed the rules"**: Casas, "El 11."

177   **General Usón agreed**: Poleo, "La verdadera historia."

177   **Acting on the counsel**: The information in this paragraph comes from Roberto Giusti, "Si me dejan ir a Cuba, renuncio," *El Universal* (April 18, 2002).

178   **to take off his uniform**: La Fuente and Meza, *El acertijo*, 61.

178   **General González González ordered Chávez**: There is disagreement on exactly when Chávez changed out of his uniform. La Fuente and Meza, *El acertijo*, 60, say before the smaller meeting of the military leaders (as I have it). Archbishop Baltazar Porras says after that meeting: Porras, *Memorias de un obispo*, 15.

178   **"They fit nice"**: Porras, *Memorias de un obispo*, 15.

178   **Chávez still had his cell phone**: Ibid., 14.

178   **"*Bueno*, I am here"**: The dialogue in this scene is from Casas, "El 11." My translation.

179   **They talked of many things**: Porras, *Memorias de un obispo*, 14.

179   **Chávez seemed to be losing heart**: Casas, "El 11."

179   **Every now and then**: Porras, *Memorias de un obispo*, 14.

179   **Chávez's fortitude**: Chávez, *Understanding the Venezuelan Revolution*, 179–180. It is rumored that one of the generals told Vásquez Velasco he wanted a little private time with Chávez so that he could "take care of things once and for all." Vásquez Velasco purportedly said no; however, I have not been able to confirm this story.

180   **"There is no consensus"**: The following dialogue is quoted in La Fuente and Meza, *El acertijo*, 61–62. Much of this dialogue was reiterated by Bishop Porras in Casas, "El 11."

180   **He asked the archbishops to forgive**: Casas, "El 11."

PART 3

Chapter 1

183   **a million new unemployed:** Patricia Poleo, "La verdadera historia de un gobierno que duró sólo horas por estar sustentado en los intereses particulares y no en los del colectivo," *El Nuevo País* (April 16, 2002), http://www.simon-bolivar.org/bolivar/p_poleo.html (accessed December 1, 2008).

184   *El Universal's* **headline:** Mike Ceaser, "Venezuelan Media: 'It's Over!'" *BBC News,* April 12, 2002, http://news.bbc.co.uk/2/hi/americas/1926983.stm (accessed October 10, 2007). The translation is the BBC's.

184   **"history elevates or buries":** "Venezuela Press Condemns 'Autocrat' Chávez," *BBC News,* April 12, 2002, http://news.bbc.co.uk/2/hi/world/monitoring/media_reports/1926176.stm (accessed on December 1, 2008).

    The translation is the BBC's. Like many of the Venezuelan national papers, *El Nacional* had initially backed Chávez. When the newspaper reported on a particularly unfriendly reception Chávez had received in a poor neighborhood, Chávez had a violent crowd of his supporters surround the paper's headquarters. From then on, it had been war between Chávez and *El Nacional.*

185   **they discovered a large cache:** Solbella Pérez Rodríguez, "Busquen a los culpables," *Tal Cual* (April 17, 2002).

185   **found so many guns:** From the testimony of General Luis Camacho Kairuz, "Comisión especial política que investiga los hechos ocurridos los días 11, 12, 13, y 14 de abril de 2002," Asamblea Nacional de la República Bolivariana de Venezuela Caracas, May 13, 2002.

185   **it was assumed by many:** Sandra La Fuente and Alfredo Meza, *El acertijo de abril: Relato periodistico de la breve caida de Hugo Chávez* (Caracas, Venezuela: Editorial Debate, 2003).

185   **the minister had gone into hiding:** The information about Chacín's removal from hiding is from ibid., 131, and Kim Bartley and Donnacha O'Briain, *The Revolution Will Not Be Televised* (Galway, Ireland: Irish Film Board, 2003). The film shows footage of Chacín leaving the apartment building.

186   **Pérez Recao had named his friend:** La Fuente and Meza, *El acertijo,* 131. In 2005, General Poggioli was arrested and sentenced to two years and five months in prison for allegedly plotting an assassination attempt on Chávez.

186   **Outside the Cuban embassy:** The description of the crowd's activities comes from Bartley and O'Briain, *Revolution Will Not.*

186   **"Look here, señores":** Ibid. My translation.

186   **"Diosdado Cabello and your 'combo'":** The word *combo* is used here to refer to Vice President Cabello's advisers and other *chavistas,* as in "Quarter Pounder with Cheese Combo."

186   **he was hiding on a farm:** Bart Jones, *Hugo! The Hugo Chávez Story from Mud Hut to Perpetual Revolution* (Hanover, NH: Steerforth Press, 2007), 363.

186   **Sánchez called on municipal mayor:** Francisco Toro, "Venezuela's 2002
       Coup Revisited: The Evidence Two Years On," http://caracaschronicles
       .blogspot.com/2004/04/untold-story-of-venezuelas-2002-april.html (ac-
       cessed September 20, 2007), and Baltazar Porras, *Memorias de un obispo,* un-
       published manuscript, 18–19.

187   **a new board of directors was named:** Guillermo García Ponce, *El golpe del
       11 de abril,* 2nd ed. (Caracas, Venezuela: Instituto Municipal de Publica-
       ciones de la Alcaldía de Caracas, 2002), 42.

187   **Juan Barreto:** It should be noted that the U.S. rejection of political asylum
       was applied universally, at least initially. When Chávez was restored and
       began persecuting the opposition leadership, some of those leaders also went
       to the U.S. embassy seeking asylum and were also refused. Many opposition
       leaders did eventually flee to the United States, but they entered the country
       legally on valid visas. The exception was Robert Carmona-Borjas, the attor-
       ney who advised ex-PDVSA director General Guaicaipuro Lameda. On
       landing in Miami he declared he wanted political asylum. Since there was no
       political asylum for Venezuelans, Carmona-Borjas was promptly arrested.
       After a prolonged legal battle, he was eventually permitted to stay in the
       United States. He considers himself the first Venezuelan to receive U.S. po-
       litical asylum during the Chávez regime.

187   **One embassy staffer:** This embassy staffer asked not to be named. The
       staffer's story was verified by another embassy official who also asked not to
       be named.

188   **there is looting. Always:** The phenomenon of looting goes to the heart of
       the Venezuelan character and demonstrates why Venezuela is ranked the sec-
       ond most corrupt nation in Latin America. See Transparency.org, http://
       www.transparency.org/policy_research/surveys_indices/cpi/2003. Indeed,
       Venezuelan attitudes toward corruption are apparent even in language. The
       word "to take advantage of" in Venezuelan Spanish—*aprovechar*—does not
       have the negative connotation that it has in English or many other Spanish-
       speaking countries. On the contrary, in Venezuela it has the strong connota-
       tion of good luck and fortune. That is, if an opportunity is presented to
       "take advantage"—finding a cash register left open, for example—one
       should capitalize on this good luck and take the money.
           Venezuela's long history of corruption has only crystallized the *aprovechar*
       mentality in the national psyche as "normal" behavior. Recall that Venezuela
       has been in a steep economic decline since 1979, and the generally accepted
       reason for the nation's getting poorer is that corrupt politicians and busi-
       nesspeople steal the nation's wealth. Ironically, the general reaction to this
       fleecing is not to condemn it or fight against it, but to accept it and hope
       that someday you will get your chance to steal, too. Looting is an excellent
       example of the *aprovechar* mentality, of an opportunity for enrichment that
       should be taken. Of course, looting can also be a form of political expres-
       sion, as it was during the Caracazo in 1989 and after the death of Juan Vi-

cente Gómez in 1935. But often it is not, as in the case of the looting after the Vargas floods in 1999. What's more, once looting starts, the political aspects are quickly muddied by those who are simply out to take advantage of the chaos to enrich themselves. That is, greed often eclipses the political aspect. The thinking of the looters is basically, "OK, the police and the military are in a state of temporary disorder. Let's take advantage of the situation—'*vamos a provechar*'—by going into the streets and stealing everything we can carry." It suddenly becomes OK to loot the corner market where you buy your groceries every week, even if the owner is a friend of yours.

One can easily see how this notion feeds into Venezuela's rampant corruption. Those who attain positions of power and influence believe they have a right, even an obligation, to *aprovechar,* to enrich themselves through public (oil) funds.

Chapter 2

188   **"Good morning. I want to":** Unless otherwise noted, the section on the White House press briefing, including the direct quotations, is from United States, White House, "Press Briefing by Ari Fleischer," Washington, DC, April 12, 2002, http://www.whitehouse.gov/news/releases/2002/04/20020412-1.html (accessed September 10, 2005).

191   **"This is a coup d'état":** La Fuente and Meza, *El acertijo,* 131. My translation.

Chapter 3

191   **Twenty-two-year-old college intern:** Unless otherwise noted, Isabel Muñoz's perspective comes from my e-mail correspondence and phone conversations with her on June 12, 19, and 25, 2007.

194   **During the last three years:** Human Rights Watch report of 2003, Venezuela: Caught in the Crossfire (New York: HRI, 2003).

194   **block their news:** Abdel Güerere, "The Media: Civil Defense for Democracy," *Business Venezuela* (June 2002), 68.

195   **Ortega was from Coro:** The information on Ortega's trip to Coro comes from David Adams and Phil Gunson, "The Unmaking of a Coup," *St. Petersburg (FL) Times* (April 22, 2002).

196   **Cardinal Ignacio Velasco:** Ibid.

The presence of the cardinal would later fuel charges that the ultraconservative Catholic group Opus Dei was pulling some of the strings in Carmona's short-lived regime. Pepe Rodríguez, an Opus Dei member, was named foreign minister. However, as La Fuente and Meza explain, other Opus Dei figures like attorney Gustavo Linares Benzo tried to stop Carmona from liquidating the separate powers. Moments before Carmona's decrees, Linares Benzo and a small group of moderate members of the opposition urged Carmona to let the National Assembly convene to vote on an "abandonment of office" by President Chávez and Vice President

Cabello. If two-thirds of the assembly agreed, it would become constitutional to appoint an interim president, namely, Carmona. See La Fuente and Meza, *El acertijo,* 133–135.

196   **The mood in the hall was:** Details of the following scene come from my interview with Isabel Muñoz; Adams and Gunson, "Unmaking of a Coup"; and footage from Bartley and O'Briain, *Revolution Will Not.*

196   **in an Armani suit:** Poleo, "La verdadera historia."

197   **state governors would be replaced:** In a June 15, 2007, e-mail to me, Isabel Muñoz said (and others have concurred) that Romero called for the liquidation of the state governors. However, Carmona said that the governors and local mayors were going to serve out their terms: Pedro Carmona, e-mail to me, March 28, 2008.

197   **revert to the constitution of 1958:** Carmona's reasons for declaring a de facto government and for his dissolution of the democratic institutions were based on his belief that the entire Chávez regime was illegitimate. Carmona was thinking of the aggregate offenses of the regime, the whole list of violations and irregularities, including appointing officials to posts that required elections, repressing people's right to assembly, limiting freedom of expression, intimidating journalists, abusing the use of special broadcasts, politicizing the armed forces, promulgating "racist messages," and using the "state of emergency" for dictatorial ends (such as implementing the Enabling Law). Carmona's legal justification for the de facto period of government was article 350 of the Venezuelan constitution which reads: "The people of Venezuela, faithful to their republican tradition, their struggle for independence, peace and liberty, will disown any regime, legislation or authority that contradicts the values, principals and democratic guarantees or damages human rights." It should be noted that certain items in Carmona's justification did not occur until after April 11. See Pedro Carmona, *Mi testimonio ante la historia* (Caracas, Venezuela: Editorial Actum, 2005), 125–127.

While no one would condone dissolving the separate powers of a democracy, Carmona and many in the opposition felt that the checks and balances that the separation of powers was supposed to supply had already been compromised by Chávez. They felt that he had bent (and sometimes broken) the law to make all the separate powers (like the Supreme Court, Attorney General, and Defender of the People) beholden to him. Therefore, it is possible that Carmona's dissolution was actually aimed at restoring full democracy, if we assume—and this is a big assumption—that the separation of powers would have been reinstated under a new government with popularly elected officials.

197   **Carmona's plan:** Pedro Carmona, e-mail to me, March 28, 2008.

197   **"Democracia! Democracia!":** Adams and Gunson, "The Unmaking of a Coup."

198 **who was not cheering:** The following section is based on my interview with General Efraín Vásquez Velasco (ret.), February 29, 2004, Caracas, Venezuela, and on La Fuente and Meza, *El acertijo,* 152, 153.

Chapter 4

201 **When it came to the idea:** The description of García Ponce's activities following his leaving Miraflores on April 11 comes from García Ponce, *El golpe,* 47–48.

202 **For García Ponce it only confirmed:** Ibid., 12–13.

202 **Buses were also organized:** La Fuente and Meza, *El acertijo,* 148.

202 **"The constitutional president":** García Ponce, *El golpe,* 45–46. My translation.

Chapter 5

203 **At seven o'clock, National Guard troops:** This chapter is based on two articles: Cenovia Casas and Hernán Lugo Galacia, "Lara: Disolución de la Asamblea es un verdadero golpe de estado," *El Nacional* (April 13, 2002), and Elvia Gómez and Taynem Hernandez, "Allanada sede administrativa de la Asamblea Nacional," *El Universal* (April 13, 2002), 1–6.

203 **assembly members from virtually all:** Noticeably absent were the Primero Justicia and the La Causa R parties. These parties went along with the closure.

203 **Ernesto Alvarenga:** MVR congressman Ernesto Alvarenga left Chávez's party shortly after April 11 and caused a great deal of embarrassment to the government when he spoke openly of the corruption he had seen. While still very much on the left, he became part of a new "solidarity" party and a vocal opponent of *chavismo.* He received many death threats after his defection, and his office was bombed twice. On August 15, 2004, in the wake of Chávez's winning the presidential recall referendum, a large anti-Chávez rally was held in the Caracas municipality of Chuao, denouncing the results as fraudulent. Chávez supporters attacked the rally, and Alvarenga was shot in the shoulder, but not killed.

203 **"We have to rebuild":** Casas and Galacia, "Lara: Disolución."

203 **"How can a regime":** Gómez and Hernandez, "Allanada."

Chapter 6

204 **Sixteen-year-old Ión Guerra:** Comité de Familiares Victimas de los Sucessos de Febrero y Marzo de 1989 (COFAVIC)[a human rights NGO], "Las Víctimas," http://www.cofavic.org.ve/p-casos-victimas.htm.

205 **three of every one hundred accused murderers:** "Deadly Massage," *The Economist* (July 19, 2008), 47.

205 **Rommy and Yurmi Nieto Laya:** COFAVIC, "Las Víctimas," http://www.cofavic.org.ve/p-casos-victimas.htm.

PART 4

Chapter 1

209   **Chávez had given a stirring speech:** Gabriel García Márquez, "The Two Faces of Hugo Chávez," *NACLA Report on the Americas* (May/June 2000), 20. Marta Harnecker, *Militares junto al pueblo* (Caracas, Venezuela: Vadell Hermanos, 2003), 264–265.

209   **Chávez and his three friends:** Harnecker, *Militares junto,* 262–266.

210   **It was a historic spot:** Márquez, "Two Faces," 21.

210   **Felipe Acosta, was killed:** Ibid., 21.

210   **decision to promote Baduel:** It was not until the spring of 2000, after Chávez had been in office more than a year, that Baduel's link to Chávez was revealed. Nobel laureate Gabriel García Márquez was returning with Chávez on a flight from Cuba when the president told him the story. When Gabo published an article about it, even Baduel's mother was shocked. "I'm sorry, Mom, I couldn't tell you," Baduel replied. Harnecker, *Militares junto,* 315.

210   **Baduel was a:** David Adams and Phil Gunson, "The Unmaking of a Coup," *St. Petersburg (FL) Times* (April 22, 2002).

210   **the reason Baduel had refused to join Chávez:** Sandra La Fuente and Alfredo Meza, *El acertijo de abril: Relato periodistico de la breve caida de Hugo Chávez* (Caracas, Venezuela: Editorial Debate, 2003), 152.

210   **"The best soldier":** Harnecker, *Militares junto,* 293.

210   **"If any of you are not ready":** La Fuente and Meza, *El acertijo,* 151.

211   **virtually all the military leaders:** Eleazar Díaz Rangel, "Baduel: Epicentro de la reacción militar," *Ultimas Noticias* (June 2002), 48. General Montoya was technically Baduel's superior and was therefore the leader of the operation, but Baduel and his paratroopers became the enduring symbols of the counter-counterrevolution.

211   **When he returned:** La Fuente and Meza, *El acertijo,* 151.

211   **Vásquez Velasco's apparent complicity:** Díaz Rangel, "Baduel: Epicentro," 48.

211   **"The coup is imminent":** Baduel felt that he had become the victim of a smear campaign by the opposition media and the coupsters. They had tried various tactics to take him out of the game, including spreading rumors that he, *he*, was conspiring against Chávez. The press said he was hoarding arms and getting ready for something, when all he was doing was preparing for Plan Avila and Plan Soberania. Even Vásquez Velasco had paid him a visit on April 8, asking him directly if he was conspiring against the government and hinting that he might need to be replaced. Another general had also come to visit him, saying that as long as Baduel didn't intervene in whatever was about to happen, he would be rewarded with a promotion come July. Harnecker, *Militares junto,* 285–288.

211   **a man who posed:** La Fuente and Meza, *El acertijo,* 151.

211   **He and his oligarch friends:** Harnecker, *Militares junto,* 290.

212   **"My brother," Chávez had said:** Días Rangel, "Baduel: Epicentro," 48. My translation.

212   **They jotted down a manifesto:** The details of the manifesto come from ibid.

212   **more and more officers were calling Baduel:** From the testimony of General Julio García Montoya, "Comisión especial política que investiga los hechos ocurridos los días 11, 12, 13, y 14 de abril de 2002," Asamblea Nacional de la República Bolivariana de Venezuela, Caracas, May 13, 2002.

213   **Back in Caracas:** The recollection of the meeting between General Usón and General Vásquez Velasco, including the direct quotations, comes from my interview with General Francisco Usón (ret.), December 2, 2003, Caracas, Venezuela.

213   **Since the moment Carmona:** General Vásquez Velasco's thoughts on the Carmona government come from my interview with General Efraín Vásquez Velasco (ret.), February 29, 2004, Caracas, Venezuela.

213   **Vásquez Velasco had received another blow:** La Fuente and Meza, *El acertijo*, 153.

213   **Poggioli himself thought:** Ibid., 155.

214   **"The reestablishment of the constitution":** Ibid., 154. My translation.

214   **Some of the generals suggested:** Dhameliz Díaz, "El ex comandante del ejército Efraín Vásquez Velasco cuenta la historia, Part 1," *El Carabobeño* (2002).

Chapter 2

214   **fifty-six deaths:** La Fuente and Meza, *El acertijo*, 148.

215   **Metropolitan Police officer Mauricio Marín:** The story of this police officer comes from COFAVIC (Comité de Familiares Victimas de los Sucessos de Febrero y Marzo de 1989), "Las Víctimas," http://www.cofavic.org.ve/p-casos-victimas.htm.

215   **In the Caracas suburb:** This description of the violence comes from La Fuente and Meza, *El acertijo*, 149.

Chapter 3

216   **When freelance reporter:** Francisco Toro's story comes from "Venezuela's 2002 Coup Revisited: The Evidence Two Years On," http://caracaschronicles.blogspot.com/2004/04/untold-story-of-venezuelas-2002-april.html (accessed September 20, 2007); his and Megan Folsom's footage of events; and my e-mail and phone correspondence with Toro.

217   **He had come from:** Although actually Venezuelan, Francisco Toro hadn't lived in Venezuela since he was thirteen. He had grown up in the United States, in Vermont, in a small enclave of Venezuelans who had immigrated there in the 1970s.

218   **everyone was very friendly:** It is important to remember that these pro-Chávez protestors perceived Francisco Toro and Megan Folsom as international

journalists. If the protestors had perceived Folsom and Toro as part of the anti-Chávez national media, their reaction would have been very different.

Chapter 4

219   **supported by the United States:** U.S. Department of State, *Review of U.S. Policy Toward Venezuela November 2001–April 2002*, Report No. 02-OIG-003 (Washington, DC: Office of the Inspector General of the U.S. Department of State and the Broadcasting Board of Governors, July 2002), 1.

219   **Venezuela's interim government:** This short section on international reaction and the Rio group comes from "Latinoamérica condena ruptura e instan a realizar elecciones libres," Reuters release (April 13, 2002).

219   **When Carmona arrived:** Pedro Carmona, *Mi testimonio ante la historia* (Caracas, Venezuela: Editorial Actum, 2005), 113, 148.

219   **When a pro-Chávez journalist:** The recollection of the exchange between the journalist and Shapiro comes from my phone interview with Ambassador Charles Shapiro, April 11, 2008, Washington, DC.

220   **"put his cards on the table":** Hugo Chávez, "Press Conference for Spanish Journalists," VTV, April 24, 2002.

220   **asked the president to encourage:** U.S. Department of State, *Review of U.S. Policy,* 12.

220   **Like just about everyone else:** Ambassador Shapiro's and Ambassador Viturro de la Torre's concerns about the interim government come from my telephone interview with Ambassador Shapiro and from Carmona, *Mi testimonio,* 149–150.

220   **Shapiro then addressed:** Ibid., 42.

220   **Shapiro had actually got wind:** My telephone interview with Ambassador Charles Shapiro.

220   **Both the ambassadors reminded Carmona:** U.S. Department of State, *Review of U.S. Policy,* 77.

221   **Carmona did his best:** Carmona, *Mi testimonio,* 149–150.

221   **make a request for one:** Pedro Carmona, that very morning e-mail to me, March 28, 2008.

221   **Carmona felt that the two men:** Ibid.

221   **he also noticed:** Carmona, *Mi testimonio,* 149–150.

221   **Upon Shapiro's return:** The account in the text comes from two confidential sources in the embassy. In my April 28, 2008, telephone interview with him, Ambassador Charles Shapiro did not recall any feelings of relief because Carmona had replaced Chávez. Instead, he remembers trying to stay focused on weathering the immediate crisis.

221   **Around noon, Carmona met:** Patricia Poleo, "La verdadera historia de un gobierno que duró sólo horas por estar sustentado en los intereses particulares y no en los del colectivo," *El Nuevo País;* this article is part of a series of articles printed from April 16 to April 30, 2002.

221   **vice presidency to Manuel Cova:** Carmona, *Mi testimonio,* 148.

222 **"During the meeting, the new minister of defense, Admiral . . . people watch CNN":** Poleo, "La verdadera historia."

222 **At the same time that Carmona:** The following section is a composite from Morao's interview with Marta Harnecker, printed in Harnecker, *Militares junto,* 63, and Baduel's interview with Díaz Rangel, "Baduel: Epicentro," 48.

222 **By the time the meeting:** This section is based on Poleo, "La verdadera historia."

223 **By now Guillermo García Ponce:** This paragraph is based on Guillermo García Ponce, *El golpe del 11 de abril* (Caracas, Venezuela: Instituto Municipal del Publicaciones de la Alcaldia de Caracas, 2002), 52.

Chapter 5

223 **"If you talk now":** La Fuente and Meza, *El acertijo,* 154. My translation.

224 **"On April 11, 2002, there":** General Vásquez Velasco gave me a copy of this speech in my interview with him: Efraín Vásquez Velasco, "Exigencias del ejercito venezolano forjador de libertades que garantizan el cumplimiento de la constitución bolivariana de Venezuela de 1999 y afirmación de la continuidad de los poderes públicos del estado venezolano," delivered on April 13, 2002, at Fort Tiuna, Caracas, Venezuela. My translation. The speech is published in La Fuente and Meza, *El acertijo,* 184.

226 **While Vásquez Velasco gave his speech:** The honor guard's taking of the palace was captured by Kim Bartley and Donnacha O'Brien, *The Revolution Will Not Be Televised* (Galway, Ireland: Irish Film Board, 2003).

226 **just minutes before the assault:** Carmona, *Mi testimonio,* 154.

226 **the honor guard were basking:** Interim President Pedro Carmona blamed the retaking of the palace on Vásquez Velasco. In Carmona's opinion, Vásquez Velasco should have replaced the honor guard immediately (and should have kept General García Carneiro under arrest) but that he didn't do it because, Carmona felt, Vásquez Velasco didn't want to offend anyone or give them an excuse to rebel: Carmona, *Mi testimonio,* 154–155.

Chapter 6

227 **Chávez had been taken:** Hugo Chávez, "Entrevista Especial al Presidente Hugo Chávez Frías con Greg Palast," VTV, May 11, 2002.

227 **Colonel Julio Rodríguez Salas:** Chávez merely says that "a soldier" lent him a cell phone. The man was identified as Colonel Rodríguez Salas by La Fuente and Meza, *El acertijo,* 157.

227 **From his cell he could see:** Hugo Chávez, *Aló Presidente,* VTV, April 28, 2002, is the source of this section on Chávez's activities in the holding cell, except for the part about calling Fidel Castro, which is from Cristina Marcano and Alberto Barrera Tyszka, *Hugo Chávez: The Definitive Biography of Venezuela's Controversial President* (New York: Random House, 2007), 180.

228 **Military Police captain Otto Gebauer:** Patricia Clarembaux, "El hombre que vio llorar al presidente," *Tal Cual* (July 6, 2007). My translation.

228   **By now night had fallen:** Chávez, "Entrevista especial."

229   **suspected that one of these soldiers:** Chávez's conviction that these guards were going to kill him is from Miguel Bonasso, "Anatomía íntima de un golpe contado por Chávez," *Pagina 12, Buenos Aires (Argentina),* (June 12, 2003).

229   **asked each man his shoe size:** The anecdote about the boots is from Clarembaux, "El hombre."

229   **"Qué desgracia!":** The word *desgracia* can be translated as either misfortune or disgrace. So Chávez's words here can be interpreted as either "What a disgrace!" or "What bad luck!"

229   **getting bits and pieces of news:** Chávez, "Entrevista especial."

230   **"My mother adores you":** Bart Jones, *Hugo! The Hugo Chávez Story from Mud Hut to Perpetual Revolution* (Hanover, NH: Steerforth Press, 2007), 359.

230   **he might return to power:** Hugo Chávez, *Aló Presidente,* VTV, May 12, 2002.

230   **He quickly got to his feet:** All of the following dialogue and description at the Turiamo Naval Base come from my copy of the video taken by the military. Chávez's dialogue was very broken and disorganized, so I have edited it a little to make it readable, while still trying to maintain the disorganized cadence.

232   **that General Medina:** Medina insists that he was not involved in a conspiracy against Chávez. The general has said that he was aware of a growing conspiracy in the military and that the Chávez administration was also aware of it. Like General Vásquez Velasco, Medina believed that Chávez was letting the conspiracy "run its course" so that he could use it as an excuse to purge the military of his opponents. See La Fuente and Meza, *El acertijo,* 65.

234   **he could finish his note:** This anecdote about the letter comes from two separate tellings by Hugo Chávez: Chávez, "Entrevista especial," and Hugo Chávez, "Cadena nacional: Restitución de poderes," VTV, April 14, 2002.

Chapter 7

235   **Back in Caracas:** The information about planning the transition is from Díaz, "El ex comandante."

235   *I just heard your announcement on TV*: The dialogue between Vásquez Velasco and José Vicente Rangel and between Vásquez Velasco and Chief Justice Iván Rincón is from Vásquez Velasco's recollection in my interview with him.

236   **Meanwhile, in the Caracas suburb:** The following account, including the direct quotations, comes from La Fuente and Meza, *El acertijo,* 156. My translation.

237   **While Miraflores:** All information in this section about Alicia Valdez and Florangel Valdez comes from my interview with Alicia Valdez, June 17,

2003, Caracas, Venezuela, and my interview with Florangel Valdez, June 14, 2003, Caracas, Venezuela.

237   **Mohamad "Mike" Merhi:** This section about Mike Merhi is from my interview with him, April 28, 2003, Caracas, Venezuela.

238   **By four o'clock:** García Ponce, *El golpe,* 54–55. My translation.

239   **had, by now, got their message:** From the testimony of General Julio García Montoya, "Comisión especial política."

239   **While most of the country's journalists:** These recollections by Gabriel Osorio are from my phone interviews and e-mail correspondence with him, July 10 and July 21, 2008, Caracas, Venezuela.

242   **One man spray-painted:** Bartley and O'Brien, *Revolution Will Not.*

242   **the status of Diosdado Cabello:** The recollections of General Efraín Vásquez Velasco are from my interview with him.

    Note that Vásquez Velasco did not mention in our interview the time of his call to Rangel. However, in his congressional testimony, Diosdado Cabello said that between 7:30 and 8:00 p.m. he left for Caracas. From the testimony of Diosdado Cabello, "Comisión especial política que investiga los hechos ocurridos los días 11, 12, 13, y 14 de abril de 2002," Asamblea Nacional de la República Bolivariana de Venezuela, Caracas, May 15, 2002.

243   **When one of the generals:** From the testimony of General Julio García Montoya, "Comisión especial política."

Chapter 8

244   **he was approached by a corporal:** The anecdote about receiving the original note from Chávez is from Díaz Rangel, "Baduel: Epicentro," 48.

244   **"I, Hugo Chávez Frías":** La Fuente and Meza, *El acertijo,* 187.

Chapter 9

246   **Julio Rodríguez Salas:** Marianela Palacios, "Coronel Rodríguez Salas: Hugo Chávez sí renunció a la presidencia," *El Nacional* (April 19, 2002).

246   **When the delegation arrived:** Clarembaux, "El hombre."

246   **one of the soldiers remembered:** Ibid.

246   **Once there, he hoped:** Chávez, *Aló Presidente,* VTV, May 12, 2002.

246   **Chávez was crumbling:** In the interviews cited below Colonel Rodríguez Salas, who had known Chávez for thirteen years, felt it inappropriate to go into specifics about Chávez's condition and refused to confirm the rumors that Chávez was weeping: Palacios, "Coronel Rodríguez Salas."

247   **said he was very sorry:** Ibid.

247   **asked for the cardinal's forgiveness:** Chávez, "Cadena nacional—Restitutión."

247   **"Many times God sends signs":** Hugo Chávez, "Press Conference with International Media," VTV, April 15, 2002. My translation.

247   **just about two in the morning:** From the testimony of General Julio García Montoya, "Comisión especial política."

247   **Unsure of what they would encounter:** Ibid.

248   **It was after three:** Unless otherwise noted, Gabriel Osorio's account of
       Chávez's return to the palace is from my phone interviews and e-mail corre-
       spondence with Osorio.

249   **Hugo Chávez made his way:** Chávez, "Cadena nacional—Restitución."

250   **"'Render unto God'":** Ibid.

250   **spoke with great affection about Cardinal Velasco:** Chávez's affection for
       the cardinal would quickly dissipate when he learned how cozy he had been
       with Interim President Pedro Carmona. Indeed, there are some interesting
       theories—although not substantiated—that Cardinal Velasco had been the
       nexus between conspiring military leaders and the opposition leaders. How-
       ever, the true role of Cardinal Velasco would remain a mystery, as he died in
       June of 2003. Marcano and Tyszka, *Hugo Chávez*, 180.

250   **"Those who are not in agreement":** Chávez, "Cadena Nacional—Restitu-
       ción." My translation.

250   **"I return spiritually charged":** Ibid. My translation.

251   *"Mi hermano,"* **Chávez said:** The exchange between Gabriel Osorio and
       Hugo Chávez comes from my phone interview with Osorio and our e-mail
       correspondence.

PART 5

Chapter 1

255   **all physical evidence from the scene:** Solbella Pérez Rodríguez, "Las es-
       quinas de la massacre," *Tal Cual* (April 18, 2002).

255   **rewrite the history of the coup:** For more details of how the government
       blocked investigations of the violence, see Sandra La Fuente and Alfredo
       Meza, *El acertijo de abril: Relato periodistico de la breve caida de Hugo Chávez*
       (Caracas, Venezuela: Editorial Debate, 2003), 159–162.

258   **Antonio Návas:** This section comes from my interview with Antonio Návas,
       February 27, 2004, Caracas, Venezuela.

261   **Malvina Pesáte:** All information for this section on Malvina Pesáte comes
       from my interviews with Malvina Pesáte on April 30, 2003, and June 19,
       2003, and my interview with Malvina Pesáte and Gorka Lacasa on January
       28, 2004, Caracas, Venezuela, or from our e-mail follow-up.

263   **remained very controversial:** Unless otherwise noted, all information in this
       section comes from my interview with Luis Alfonso Fernández, December
       9, 2003, Caracas, Venezuela.

263   **Fausto Castillo:** Edgar López et al., "Esta semana comenzarán allanamien-
       tos en busca de responsables de la masacre del 11," *El Nacional* (May 18,
       2002).

264   **President Chávez and his spokespeople:** Chávez said on several occasions
       that the video was a fraud. See "President Chávez complacido por decisión
       en Caso Llaguno," *El Nacional* (September 19, 2003).

264   **"The truth is that these four"**: Hugo Chávez, *Aló Presidente*," VTV, June 2, 2002. My translation.

264   **Rafael Caprices**: Cabrices died of a heart attack in 2005 at the age of sixty.

265   **The documentary film *The Revolution***: Kim Bartley and Donnacha O'Briain, *The Revolution Will Not Be Televised* (Galway, Ireland: Irish Film Board, 2003). It appears that Bartley and O'Briain cut a deal with Chávez in order to get access to him to make this film. Even before the coup, Chávez was extremely leery of interviews and was worried about how he was being portrayed in the international media. Bartley and O'Briain tried repeatedly to get permission to do a documentary on Chávez but were always rebuked. Finally, they were given an audience with the president. The meeting did not go well, and it appeared that Chávez was going to say no. Then one of the filmmakers, knowing Chávez's spiritual identification with Simón Bolívar, invoked Daniel O'Leary, an Irish soldier who helped Bolívar in his wars of independence. The Irish filmmakers said that perhaps, like O'Leary, they could help Chávez. This agreement—although contrary to responsible documentary filmmaking—is immediately apparent from the film's unabashed pro-Chávez stance.

    The film was extremely influential in boosting Chávez's popularity after the coup. VTV (the government station) showed the film almost weekly after its release and the government had twenty thousand copies made in Cuba which were distributed through Venezuela's embassies worldwide. I myself have three copies of the film and have refused many more; all were given to me by government officials I interviewed who wanted me to have a better understanding of Chávez.

265   **"worse than political naiveté"**: Phil Gunson, "Did an Acclaimed Documentary About the 2002 Coup in Venezuela Tell the Whole Story?" *Columbia Journalism Review* (March 2004), http://www.cjr.org/issues/2004/3/gunson-docu.asp (accessed on September 9, 2008).

265   **blow-by-blow of the film's manipulations**: Wolfgang Schalk and Thaelman Urgelles, *X-ray of a Lie* (Radiografia de una mentira) (Caracas, Venezuela: El Gusano de Luz, 2004).

266   **imaginable to discredit him**: According to Fernández, VENPRESS, the state news service, claimed that the award was going to be revoked because it was a fraud. Although this wasn't true, the wide dissemination of the news greatly discredited the award and, Fernandez believes, incited more harassment. My interview with Fernández.

266   **"The lightly armored vehicles"**: Guillermo García Ponce, *El golpe del 11 de abril* (Caracas, Venezuela: Instituto Municipal del Publicaciones de la Alcaldia de Caracas, 2002), 14. My translation.

267   **arrested on trumped-up charges**: Simonovis did apparently have a connection to Isaac Pérez Recao, as they fled from Venezuela to Aruba together on April 13. But there is no evidence that Simonovis committed any criminal

act during the events of April 11–14. See La Fuente and Meza, *El acertijo,* 157.

267 **to commandeer most of their weapons:** "Venezuelan Army Partly Disarms Caracas Police," CBC News, January 14, 2003, http://www.cbc.ca/world/story/2003/01/14/venezuela_030114.html (accessed December 4, 2008).

267 **homicide rate has increased:** Simon Romero, "Chavez Keeps Lid on Boom in Murders," *Chicago Tribune* (December 3, 2006).

269 **"Once the announcement":** This excerpt from Supreme Court ruling can be found in Pedro Carmona, *Mi testimonio ante la historia* (Caracas, Venezuela: Editorial Actum, 2005), 95–96. My translation.

270 **"I was under oath":** From my interview with General Manuel Rosendo (ret.), January 29, 2004, Caracas, Venezuela.

270 **"They violated all":** Ibid.

271 **Rosendo was forced into hiding:** In our interview I asked General Rosendo if he thought Chávez was a religious man. "Chávez is not religious at all," he said. "Chávez is a communist. He shows allegiance to Christ when he wants to use [Christian] symbolism. The Venezuelan people are a Catholic people, and he takes advantage of that. Chávez talks to us with Christ in his hand but with the actions of the devil." Rosendo added, "If I speak like Christ, then I have to act according to the Christian doctrine: with love, understanding, faith, and so on, not with immoral deeds. The base of Christianity is justice, love, forgiveness, and these sorts of things, but here we have a high level of [political] persecution," which Rosendo feels goes against all that Chávez says. My translation.

271 **Otto Gebauer:** Patricia Clarembaux, "El hombre que vio llorar al presidente," *Tal Cual* (July 6, 2007).

271 **Chávez suspected that the men:** In an interview in June 2003, Chávez said that he was sure that two of the men on the helicopter that took him to Turiamo were mercenaries sent to kill him (Otto Gebauer was one of the four soldiers). Chávez even said that shortly after the arrival at Turiamo, an officer stopped the gunmen at the last minute. However, I don't find this story credible for two reasons. First, if there had been an order to kill Chávez, it could have been carried out easily at any number of points, with complete impunity. Second, in the videotape from Turiamo and in every other account that Chávez gave, he had nothing but praise for the way he was treated in captivity. See Miguel Bonasso, "Anatomía íntima de un golpe contado por Chávez," *Pagina 12 Buenos Aires (Argentina)* (June 12, 2003).

272 **He now lives in exile:** Pedro Carmona, e-mail to me, March 28, 2008.

272 **Isaac Pérez Recao:** David Adams, "Alleged Coup Leaders Land in South Florida," *St. Petersburg (FL) Times* (April 24, 2002).

272 **Carlos Ortega:** "Venezuela Hunts Escaped Coup Leader," *USA Today* (August 15, 2006).

273　**political asylum in Peru:** "Peru Grants Asylum to Venezuelan Dissenter," *El Universal* (September 3, 2007), http://english.eluniversal.com/2007/09/03/en_pol_art_peru-grants-asylum-t_03A980037.shtml (accessed December 14, 2008).

274　**"Tactics," Rincón shouted:** Because of the similarity, one has to wonder if General Rincón had ever read George Orwell's *Animal Farm*. When the animals question the contradictions and hypocrisies of Napoleon's government after he has banished his rival, Snowball, Napoleon's trusted henchpig, Squealor, says the following: "This, said Squealer, was something called tactics. He repeated a number of times, 'Tactics, comrades, tactics!' skipping round and whisking his tail with a merry laugh. The animals were not certain what the word meant, but Squealer spoke so persuasively, and the three dogs who happened to be with him growled so threateningly, that they accepted his explanation without further questions": George Orwell, *Animal Farm* (New York: Harcourt, Brace, 1946), 50.

274　**General Raúl Baduel:** "Venezuela Hunts," *USA Today*.

274　**"attempting to usurp":** Harris Whitbeck and Flor Santamaria, "Venezuelans Protest as Vote Nears," *CNN.com* (November 29, 2007), http://www.cnn.com/2007/WORLD/americas/11/29/venezuela.vote/index.html (accessed December 3, 2007).

274　**"Venezuelan society faces a broad array":** Raúl Baduel, "Why I Parted Ways with Chávez," *New York Times* (December 1, 2007).

276　**flamethrower at the Fort Mara:** "A Decade Under Chávez: Section V" *Human Rights Watch*, September 22, 2008, http://www.hrw.org/en/reports/2008/09/22/decade-under-ch-vez (accessed December 12, 2008).

Chapter 2

277　**showing that the CIA knew:** Ibid.

277　**"Disgruntled senior [Venezuelan] officers":** Juan Forero, "Documents Show C.I.A. Knew of a Coup Plot in Venezuela," *New York Times* (December 3, 2004), A12.

279　**dissident military officers:** Scott Wilson, "Chavez Regained Power While Plotters Bickered," *Washington Post*, April 18, 2002), A17.

279　**the ambassador did not want:** Incoming ambassador Charles Shapiro was also very worried about the one-sided contact the embassy officials had with the opposition and was trying to increase intelligence gathering on the pro-Chávez side. In early April 2002 Shapiro "instructed his reporting officers to broaden their contacts with, and reporting on, pro-government politicians." See U.S. Department of State, *Review of U.S. Policy Toward Venezuela November 2001–April 2002,* Report 02-OIG-003 (Washington, DC: July 2002), 14.

279　**"were very angry":** Wilson, "Chavez Regained Power," A17.

279　**During U.S. congressional hearings:** Powell made his statement before the Senate Foreign Relations Committee on February 5, 2002. Tenet's comments appear to have been made before a special Senate committee on intelligence (the Special Committee on Current and Projected National Security Threats to the United States) on February 6, 2002.

280 **Inter-American Commission on Human Rights:** Andres Canizalez et al., "Behind Venezuela's Two-Day Coup d'État," *Albion Monitor* (April 2002), http://www.albionmonitor.com/0204a/venezuelatimeline.html (accessed April 18, 2007).

280 **On February 8, 2002:** Ibid.

280 **was welcomed:** For an excellent article on the problematic stance the United States took on Chávez, see David Corn, "Our Gang in Venezuela?" *The Nation* (August 5, 2002), http://www.thenation.com/doc/20020805/corn (accessed April 20, 2007).

280 **"We felt we were acting":** Scott Wilson, "Clash of Visions Pushed Venezuela Toward Coup," *Washington Post* (April 21, 2002), A01.

280 **To their credit, U.S. officials:** In my telephone interviews with Ambassador Charles Shapiro, April 11 and 28, 2008, Washington, DC, he verified that he had discussed coup rumors with Chávez before April 11 and that Chávez had seemed unconcerned.

281 **a luncheon hosted by opposition billionaire:** Information about this luncheon was provided by one opposition leader who was there and who asked not to be named, and by Archbishop Baltazar Porras (in his unpublished manuscript, *Memorias de un obispo,* 6). The reaction of the diplomats upon their return to the embassy was provided by an embassy employee who asked not to be named.

281 **"undemocratic actions":** Forero, "Documents Show," A12.

Chapter 3

283 **National Guard troops who were implementing:** These National Guard troops who repelled the march were offered a "Chávez bonus" that morning if they would remain loyal to the president. Corroborated in my interview with General Manuel Rosendo. See testimony of General Eugenio Antonio Gutiérrez Ramos, "Comisión especial política que investiga los hechos ocurridos los días 11, 12, 13, y 14 de abril de 2002," Asamblea Nacional de la República Bolivariana de Venezuela, Caracas, May 14, 2002.

283 **deaths of three protestors:** Duncan Campbell, "The Mystery Assassin," *The Guardian*, 17 December 2002, http://www.guardian.co.uk/world/2002/dec/17/worlddispatch.venezuela (accessed December 11, 2008); and La Fuente and Meza, *El acertijo*, 166. I firmly believe that the assassin, Joao de Gouveia, was a mercenary hired by the government. He was caught on film with Bolivarian Circle leader Freddy Bernal just days before the shooting. (Similar to Luis Fernández's video of the Llaguno Overpass, the government also declared that this video was a forgery.) Captured at the scene of the crime, Joao de Gouveia admitted that he had been sent by the government. He later changed his story and was quietly sentenced to twenty-nine years in

prison. I also do not believe that he was the only gunman at the scene, as many witnesses said there were two others. But since Joao de Gouveia was the only one caught red handed, he was the only one prosecuted.

284   **"campaign of aggression"**: Simon Romero, "Venezuela Expels 2 After Human Rights Report," *New York Times,* September 20, 2008, http://www.nytimes .com/2008/09/20/world/americas/20venez.html?pagewanted=print (accessed December 12, 2008).

284   **"violate the country's constitution"**: Jose Miguel Vivanco and Daniel Wilkinson, "Hugo Chávez Versus Human Rights," *New York Review of Books*, November 6, 2008, http://www.nybooks.com/articles/22033 (accessed December 12, 2008).

284   **"until 2050"**: John Anderson, "Fidel's Heir," *The New Yorker*, 23 June 2008, 48.

284   **Chávez has created:** Peter Wilson, "Petkoff, Former Communist Guerrilla, Seeks to Unseat Chavez," *Bloomberg News*, April 21, 2006, http://www .bloomberg.com/apps/news?pid=email_us&refer=latin_america&sid=a2ltX VyAiq3A (accessed on December 12, 2008).

285   **half of the government's revenue:** James Painter, "Is Venezuela's Oil Boom Set to Bust?" *BBC World News*, October 28, 2008, http://news.bbc.co.uk/ go/pr/fr/-/2/hi/americas/7694757.stm (accessed December 11, 2008).

INDEX